THE MELODRAMA OF MOBILITY

THE
MELODRAMA

NANCY ABELMANN

UNIVERSITY OF
HAWAI'I PRESS
Honolulu

OF MOBILITY

Women, Talk,
and Class in
Contemporary
South Korea

Library of Congress Cataloging-in-Publication Data
Abelmann, Nancy.
  The melodrama of mobility : women, talk, and class in contemporary South Korea /
Nancy Abelmann.
      p. cm.
Includes bibliographical references and index.
  ISBN 0-8248-2596-9 (cloth : alk. paper)—ISBN 0-8248-2749-X (pbk. : alk. paper)
  1. Middle-aged women—Korea (South)—Social conditions. 2. Middle-aged women—
Korea (South)—Economic conditions. 3. Middle-aged women—Employment—Korea
(South) 4. Social mobility—Korea (South) 5. Social classes—Korea (South) 6. Korea
(South)—History—1948–1960. 7. Korea (South)—History—1960–1988. 8. Korea—Social
conditions—1945– I. Title.
  HQ1059.5.S68 A24 2003
  305.244—dc21
                              2003003579

University of Hawai'i Press books are printed
on acid-free paper and meet the guidelines for
permanence and durability of the Council on
Library Resources

Design and composition by B. Williams & Associates
Printed by The Maple-Vail Book Manufacturing Group

For Andy first and forever

And for Carmen, Simone, and Isaac

It was all according to the way you see things. Some people could look at a mud-puddle and see an ocean with ships. But nanny belonged to that other kind that loved to deal in scraps. Here nanny had taken the biggest thing that God ever made, the horizon—for no matter how far a person can go the horizon is still way beyond you—and pinched it in to such a little bit of a thing that she could tie it about her granddaughter's neck tight enough to choke her. She hated the old woman who had twisted her so in the name of love. . . . She had found a jewel down inside herself and she had wanted to walk where people could see her and gleam it around. But she had been set in the market-place to sell. Been set for still-bait. When God had made The Man, he made him out of stuff that sung all the time and glittered all over. Then after that some angels got jealous and chopped him into millions of pieces, but still he glittered and hummed. So they beat him down to nothing but sparks but each little spark had a shine and a song. So they covered each one over with mud. And the lonesomeness in the sparks make them hunt for one another, but the mud is deaf and dumb. Like all the other tumbling mud-balls, Janie had tried to show her shine.

—Zora Neale Hurston,
Their Eyes Were Watching God

CONTENTS

Acknowledgments xi

Preface xv

1 Introduction: The Melodrama of Mobility 1

2 The Eight Women 33

3 Key Words 59

4 Class Work: Education Stories 100

5 Social Mobility: "Facts" and "Fictions" 132

6 Personality Speaking 164

7 Gendering Displacement: Men, Masculinity, and the Nation 187

8 All in the Family: Class Distances and Divides 214

9 When It's All Said and Done . . . 240

10 Conclusion: Living Through Compressed Modernity 281

Coda 291

References 295

Index 313

ACKNOWLEDGMENTS

An embarrassing number of people helped me with this book. How absurd to reduce their generosity, work, and kindness to fleeting reference here.

More absurd, really, is that neither here nor in the body of the book do I name the eight women featured in it. To call their gift generosity does not even begin to do them justice. Earlier versions of the book included a number of passages that would have revealed the extent to which some of these women nurtured me so very far beyond the book project: one by one, for a variety of reasons, I cut those passages. I would like to single out the Education Mother and Mi-yŏn's Mother for tending to my heart, oh so lovingly.

The fieldwork culminating in this book, and the book itself, owe a tremendous amount to research assistants. Each and every one of them cared about the project, sharing their intelligence, skill, and insights so that I might do better, do less damage, in the tricky act of representation. And they have been cheerleaders during the many moments (and stretches) in which my confidence in the project and in myself flagged. Over the course of field research, I was aided by So-Jin Park and Jesook Song, both of whom continued to assist me in the writing process as well; also, both of them conducted follow-up interviews for this book in summer 2001. In addition, in the long process of writing, I have been foremost assisted by Hye-young Jo, Hyunhee Kim, and Soo-Jung Lee. The greatest honor and joy of my career has been the opportunity to mentor each of these five remarkable women in their doctoral studies. My field research was also facilitated by many more people: Cho Hae-joang, Cho Hŭi-mun, Cho Sŏng-ch'ŏn, Cho Ŭn, Chong Byung-ho, Chong Jin-kyung, Do-Hyun Han, Eun-shil Kim, Hyon-gyŏng Kim, Keun Lee, So-yŏn Lee, Oak Hwa-ja, O se-yŏng, Paek Uk-in, Pak Myŏng-gyu, Pak Pu-jin, Pak Sang-Ah, Pak Sang-kyu, Shin Hyo-ch'ŏl, Song In-ja, Yi Ji-yŏng, Yi So-yŏn, Yi So-yŏng, and Yoon Taek-lim. I am also grateful for conversations in the field with a number of helpful scholars: Kang

Myŏng-kyu, Byoung-Kwan Kim, Eunhee Yi Kim, Myung-hye Kim, So-young Kim, Pak Mi-hye, Pak Myŏng-jin, Song Bok, and Yi Chŏng-man. In the writing process I was also aided by Heather Foran, Kang Hye-sŭng, Susan Kelleher, Jin-hee Lee, and Yoonjeong Shim. In earlier articles culminating here, I was ably assisted by Carolee Berg, Rosa DeJorio, Ki-bom Lee, Sang Ryong Lee, and Judith Pintar. Thanks to Steve Holland for the many drafts of the kinship charts.

What can one say to thank friends, colleagues, and relatives who have read this book in full? I am silenced by the extraordinary generosity of my father, Walter Abelmann (yet again, and again), Nicole Constable, Roger Janelli, Hagen Koo, Kathryn LaTorre, Michael Robinson, Eun Hui Ryo, and Jesook Song. This book is the result of their feedback, (many, many) edits, and unfailing encouragement; the line by line contributions of Eun Hui and Jesook are particularly remarkable. I am also grateful to many kind people who read parts of this manuscript and related earlier articles: Rena Abelmann, Edward Bruner, Cho Hae-joang, Jung-Ah Choi, Ramona Curry, John Finch, Alma Gottlieb, Roy Richard Grinker, JaHyun Kim Haboush, Hiroshi Ishida, Hye-young Jo, Bill Kelleher, Laurel Kendall, Seung Kyung Kim, Shanshan Lan, Grace Lee, Keehyeung Lee, Soo-Jung Lee, F. K. Lehman, John Lie, Miho Matsugu, Kathleen McHugh, Laura Nelson, Theresa DeLeane O'Nell, HehRahn Park, Judith Pintar, Kendall Rafter, Linda-Anne Rebhun, Patricia Sandler, Ann Saphir, Ronald Toby, and Karen Winter-Nelson. I am also grateful to the editorial hands at *American Ethnologist* and *The Journal of Asian Studies*. Chapters 5 and 6 are drawn from articles published in *The Journal of Asian Studies* (Abelmann 1997b) and *American Ethnologist* (Abelmann 1997a), respectively.

This book has also received the generous support of external funding from the American Council of Learned Societies, the Korea Foundation, and the Social Science Research Council. At the University of Illinois at Urbana-Champaign this work has been generously supported by many research assistant grants from the Research Board and by the departments of anthropology and of East Asian languages and cultures, which allowed me ample time for field research and writing. I am grateful to the staffs of both departments, most particularly Karla Harmon and Jeanne Poole.

At the University of Hawai'i Press this book has been in wonderful hands. My editor, Patricia Crosby, came highly recommended, and it did not take me long to understand why: her every communication was delightful, making pleasant and even joyous what can be a rather torturous procedure. And as if this was not enough, there were Pat's lightning-speed turnaround on absolutely everything and, yet still, her patience with the clay-footed among us. I am also grateful to Cheri Dunn at the Press for her efficient management of the book, and to Barbara Roos, my indexer. And my copy editor, Karen Weller-Watson, is a veritable wonder.

And then there are great local colleagues—how could I manage without you? Thank you, Edward Bruner, Matti Bunzl, Clark Cunningham, Brenda Farnell, David Goodman, Alma Gottlieb, Bill Kelleher, Chin-Woo Kim, JaHyun Kim Haboush (alas, no longer local), Janet Keller, Alejandro Lugo, Martin Manalansan, Andrew Orta, Peggy Miller, Ronald Toby, and Arlene Torres.

And then there are friends who have contributed simply (and it is by no means a simple feat) by believing in and supporting me. Thank you, Ruth Abelmann, Carolyn Butterfield, Tina Choi, Nicole Constable, Ramona Curry, Bill Kelleher, Jeanie Taylor, Jack Lee, Kathleen McHugh, Keiko Sakamoto, Patricia Sandler, Cara Seiderman, and Karen Winter-Nelson. I am also grateful to the wonderful women in my reading group, who have long allowed me to participate whether or not I read the novel: Marilyn Booth, Frances Jacobson, Jo Kibbee, Sally McMahan, Bea Nettles, and Carol Spindel.

And Kelly Beaulin deserves a whole paragraph alone; it is because of the loving way that she has cared for Carmen, Simone, and Isaac since their births that I could hide away to write this book. Kelly is the first to say that hers has been the much more important work (and how could I disagree?), but she has nonetheless been unfailingly supportive of mine. And there have been other wonderful people who have allowed me to carve out time; thank you, Jill Kurtz, Grace Msangi, Patsy Schanz, Liz Stalzer, and Sarah Stalzer.

And, as if all this help, kindness, and generosity weren't enough, I have been blessed with the world's most supportive parents, siblings, and relatives. Rena and Walter Abelmann have taken no end of interest in all of this and, at the same time, always made me feel that none of this really matters when it comes to their love and support of me. Thanks also to Graham, Molly, Ruth, and Michael; Amanda, Arthur, and Kristen; Tobias, Charlie, and Emiliana; and Zack and Karen. And there is more wonderful family too: thank you, Emma, Carola, Maret, and Tim; Beverly, Gregory, Letty, and Mark; Dan and Nanette; and Susan and Kumar.

Books can be, I've decided, mean-spirited. They are unsympathetic to the rhythm of life, they are boundlessly covetous of time and energy, and they care little about other and others' needs. Alas, this one has asked way too much of my family! Every time my mother visits (thankfully, quite often) she tells me that I am the luckiest person she knows, what with Andy and those three children. And she's right. Andy Gewirth has lovingly put up with this sometimes mean-spirited book (and, more importantly, with me). However clichéd, I could not have finished it without him. And I am boundlessly grateful to the loveliest two five-year-olds and the most fetching ten-month-old in the whole world, Carmen, Simone, and Isaac. Here I can't resist a passage from a letter by my favorite novelist, William Maxwell: "The children have reached the age where it is like looking at flowers. Will they ever be so beautiful again as they are this second . . ."

PREFACE

Readers cannot help but pick up on the accents and the obsessions of a work, even a short work. What follows in this preface can thus be taken as hints for the reader.

The seeds of this project can be found in the field research that became *Echoes of the Past, Epics of Dissent: a South Korean Social Movement* (Abelmann 1996). Writing this ethnography of a 1980s tenant farmers' movement in the North Chŏlla Province (a region noted for its relative underdevelopment, its still-large agriculturist population, and its political activism), I became increasingly interested in the movement-seen—that is, in how it was viewed, contemplated, and participated in by nonlocals. The movement I examined in that work was one that had garnered the attention of many nonlocal people, from regional farmer activists to students in Seoul with antiestablishment convictions, to a host of professional political organizers who found considerable political significance in an actually quite small and remote land struggle. When two hundred of the farmers moved themselves to Seoul to occupy the headquarters of their landlord corporation, I was able to observe the encounter of these farmers and their activities with a broad swathe of Seoul residents, among them the urban relatives of the farmers.

Thus I found myself partially privy to the urban middle-class gaze at the farmers among whom I had been living, both in the countryside and during the "occupation" in Seoul. In short, I came to see them as "seen." Among these glimpses were several awkward encounters, such as when a man at a market in Seoul recognized me for having been among the demonstrators months earlier and then proceeded to liberally slander the farmers, or the also much later conversations with the brother of a close friend of mine who happened to be a manager at the landlord corporation in question. Across all of these encounters—encounters with the gaze at farmers as both a class and regional other—I was struck by visceral class prejudice or disdain for farmers' manners, looks, and ways of being. Important to note, however, is that in those late 1980s days, Seoul was still very much a city of adults with rural roots and home villages: a city of people who made at least occasional rural sojourns to visit family grave sites if not living relatives. The symbolic and historical proximity of farmers to the city made these palpable divides of class and circumstance all the more interesting to me, for they were distances traveled among siblings and cousins, and often within lifetimes.

I told myself that in my next project—always a welcome respite from the sometimes messy mire of the project at hand—I would somehow focus on class distinctions and distances. These interests found their home in a summer trip to Seoul to begin a project on cross-class encounters in middle schools and high schools. In the late 1980s I had become interested in the then burgeoning teachers' activism in South Korea, activism that amazed me because some of it seemed to go for the jugular of schools, as organs of class reproduction in Seoul. Most shocking to me was the moment in that struggle (a fleeting moment, as it turned out) when the teachers' union (Chŏng'yojo) proclaimed their members to be "laborers," thus eschewing the considerable cultural and symbolic capital accorded teachers. Also interesting was the intermittent insistence that teachers refuse parents' offerings, a longstanding practice in which parents make payments (referred to as ch'onji or pongt'u, meaning "envelopes") to teachers to enhance their children's favor; these envelopes revealed the on-the-ground workings of class privilege. It was in this context that I set out to locate a school in a residential area with class diversity. Quite frankly, this project did not take root, because my confidence in its ability to speak to my interests faltered; I wondered whether school ethnography would really offer a window on class relations. Furthermore, schools revealed themselves to me, in even a short research stint, as bureaucratic institutions that would call for considerable politicking on the part of the ethnographer. The politics of social-movement field research were just then still close enough in my own research history that I found myself wanting a project less governed by such management. I cannot quite recall the moment I began to think about women's stories of social mobility (their own and that of close kin), the ethnographic heart of this book, but they appealed to me in part because of their likely extra-institutional life. Along the course of the research culminating in this book, I came to realize I was at home in the one-on-one chatting that made for much of my activity. Field research negotiates a myriad of constraints—among them style, comfort, and timing.

But here I need to digress, because my focus on this project in fact digressed as I took up another, seemingly quite disparate project—one that would in turn redirect the project that finally took shape in this book. In spring 1992 I was teaching a small undergraduate seminar at the University of Illinois at Urbana-Champaign, on the Korean diaspora, focusing on émigré Koreans in China, Japan, the former Soviet Union, and the United States. I had decided to offer this course because in my teaching on South Korea—largely to first- and second-generation Korean Americans from Illinois—I had learned that my students were, not surprisingly, interested in the story closest to home, that of South Korean emigration and immigrant life. What would become known as the L.A. Riots or the L.A. Uprising (April 1992) splashed across the national media that spring; students' questions (many of them emotionally charged queries from the children of Chicago-land entrepreneurs, small-business owners very much like the ones whose stores had been firebombed in Los Angeles), and my inability to respond to them effectively, sent me to Los Angeles with sociologist John Lie. Intermittent field research over a year in post-riots Los Angeles culminated in *Blue Dreams: Korean Americans and the Los Angeles Riots* (Abelmann and Lie 1995). In the face of prevailing media representation of Korean Americans in the popular press, we sought to capture the diversity and complexity of the "Korean" response to the riots. I was particularly interested in the class geography of those responses.

I could have easily predicted class differences in the post-riots responses of Korean Americans, but there was something that surprised me: namely, that the class diversity was not merely a matter of fault lines between families, but within them (both nuclear and extended). For many families, the immigration spanned several decades, making for considerable diversity of economic standing and opportunity. I was, in short, learning about "poor cousins" or even "poor siblings" and their divergent immigrant fates. Later, during this book's research, one woman would aptly tell me that in "South Korea today," the proverb "Your belly aches when things go well for your cousin [i.e., from jealousy]" could well be refashioned as "Your belly aches when things go well for your sibling." I remember that soon thereafter I began to tell myself to look for class divides, for the universe of distinction, *within* the family—across siblings, cousins, and, perhaps most of all, across the divides of marriage. And so, in 1992 and 1993, as I shuttled between the L.A. Riots project and this book's research, and between Los Angeles and Seoul, I came to think of social mobility stories (ones that had through the Los Angeles story emerged as transnational stories, stories spanning countries) as the province of families and of other cohort groups, be they age-mates from school or from a farming village. The various cohorts in dialogue with which people live and render their lives are a constant in this book—dialogues (and cohorts) that can be real, metaphorical, or imagined.

Finally, this book has also taken shape alongside yet again another research project, which began in 1997 and continues to this day: research with Korean American students (and their parents) in public higher education in Illinois. This research follows the education and other histories of families. In many cases I have interviewed student-generation cousins flung across various nodes of public higher education in Illinois; in turn I have interviewed their sibling parents and, most recently, in summer 2000 in South Korea, the nonemigrated siblings and cousins of those parents. This work on Korean Americans has taken me foremost to the history of South Korean education, a remarkable story of expansion in which, for example, in 1955 only 5 percent of the college-aged (18 to 21 years old) were in college, while in 1988 that figure had risen to 28 percent (Jeong and Armer 1994, 539). Similarly, while in 1950 there were 55 institutions of higher education, by 1982 there were 236 (S. B. Kim 1983, 22). I have found myself exploring these numerical annals to learn about the ways in which dashed education hopes and unmet promises of education returns propelled South Koreans to emigrate (see chapter 2 in I. J. Yoon 1997). As I turned my focus in that project to emigration and education, the women's stories comprising this book also came into different focus. I found myself paying more attention during my discussions to the talk about relatives who left South Korea, and to the intricacies of education.

In the years in which I worked on the talks and articles that became the building blocks of this book, I often revisited my field notes, and perused again the notes compiled from those field notes, each time finding things anew. Anthropology, in recent decades, has chided itself for its ethnographic present (Fabian 1983): that is, the tendency of anthropologists to employ the present tense to speak about the historically specific and circumscribed moments of fieldwork that makes timeless others of the people met in their studies. While I embrace this critique (and do employ the past tense when referring to my field research in this book), there is truth to the ethnographic present; for it is the present of the ethnographer's eye perusing those notes, who edits, highlights, translates, and decides on those lines finding their way into ethnographic writing. Which convention is it, then, that best interrupts the oft-criticized timelessness or uniformity of ethnographic portrayal?

1

INTRODUCTION
The Melodrama
of Mobility

Although they necessarily fall at the beginnings of books, introductions strike me as foremost betwixt and between. With one arm they coax the readers, imploring them to read on, promising treasures in the pages that stretch ahead. With the other arm, they pull back, warning that the offerings are frail, that they falter here or there. Hubris makes her claims, just as humility softens, or even retracts, them. And ethnography, with its often resolutely local lens—focused, in the case of this book, on the talk of not even a dozen middle-aged South Korean women—similarly straddles diverse claims: at its brazen-most it argues that this-or-that corner of reality will render the world anew; more sheepishly, it often promises no more (or less) than the integrity and humanity of a small story.

To the reader, let me say: at its boldest, this introduction will proclaim that the lives of the South Korean women who figure prominently in this book tell a story that is nothing short of the history and sensibility of post–Korean War South Korea; in its more modest moments, this introduction will suggest that these lives introduce the "talk" of a particular generation of South Korean women. The reader wonders, "But what does the writer *really* think? Which is it, after all?" My answer: both, both, betwixt and between.

But in another vein, let me be perhaps even more bold: it is not just introductions that do more than one thing at once, at times even at cross-purposes, but all writing and speech—all words. And this is a book that examines many words, those comprising the stories of eight South Korean women, asking always about the various things they are doing, doing all at once. Boldly again, I will assert that the myriad social contests that rivet their words and stories reveal these women's times, in the historical sense.

Pulling in the reins a bit, I marvel at the complexity of their stories, and the struggles of their lives.

If introductions are, as I suggest, precarious, I take titles to be straightforward promises. They are promises about ideas that figure centrally in the book, and about places, often metaphorical ones, the writer visits. My title promises, then, that at the very least I will introduce the reader to "talk," "class" (and "mobility"), "women," and "melodrama." Much of this introduction is devoted to what I mean by these words and how I use them here. And the words, those five, vie for attention with other words, words that might just as easily have found their way into the title: "narrative," "family," "gender," and "identity" among them.

This Book in Short

This book draws upon women's social mobility stories, that is, their talk about the course of their lives and of the lives in their midst, most typically those of siblings, cousins, and in-laws (see Plath 1980, 8, on "consociates"; also see Stack and Burton 1993, on "kinscripts"). Unlike life histories, chronological accounts of people's lives, social mobility stories take up the particular problematic of social origins and destinations (see Ginsburg 1989, on "strategic life stories"). I appreciate origins and destinations not as fixed points but rather as narratives or stories. As such, social mobility stories engage the social imagination—a topic I turn to later in this chapter.

I met with these women intensively during two extended research stays in Seoul, South Korea (one in 1992 and 1993; the other in 1995 and 1996), and thereafter more briefly during shorter stays in 1998, 2000, and 2001. I met each of them at least eight times, some of them a dozen or more times. In shorter visits we sat together for a couple of hours, in longer ones, for the better part of a haif day. I tell in chapter 2 how I came to meet each woman—how they came to be what anthropologist John Langston Gwaltney calls "donors of personal documents" (1980, xxv)—stories that I use to begin my foray into the complexity of class and gender in South Korea. Although I assert that the women who figure in this book span South Korea's class spectrum, I also argue that class is not a structural variable to be considered in isolation of women's narratives like the ones readers find here. Hence, although I assert these women's class diversity, I resolutely refuse to classify them—by the terms of class or by any other single variable, for that matter.

I chose to speak with women of a single generation, appreciating that generation refers both to a stage in the life cycle and to a historical cohort. At the time of our first encounter in the early 1990s, the women were in their late fifties through, at the oldest, their early sixties. Why this generation? And why this historical cohort? In the context of life courses, these were mature women with much of their child-rearing behind them, but women who were nonetheless still in the middle of things, with at least some children yet to be educated and married. That is, in the more distant tones of social scientific language, they were still actively engaged in the social (and class) reproduction of their families, still worried about fashioning or fastening the lives of their children. This is not to say that at some magical age past their early sixties women—or men, for that matter—wake up one morning to have completed these tasks, but to suggest that there are ages when these concerns, and the activities they entail, govern life more fully, more tenaciously.

Historically—for life-span generations always span particular historical moments (see Elder 1974 and 1985; Halbwachs 1950)—these women came of age and matured over the period of South Korea's dizzyingly rapid post–Korean War social, political, economic, and cultural transformations, from the 1950s to the 1980s. The numbers that sketch the contours of these women's adult lives—be they rates of rural exodus, expansions of secondary and higher education, or the creation of industrial sector jobs—are mind boggling because they remind us that these women's lives ford such huge transformations so quickly. Indeed, it seems even problematic to speak of social or class "reproduction" over an era in which the grammar of social life would again and again be so transformed. At its boldest *and* humblest, then, this book aims to consider origins and destinations of lives in the context of mind-boggling transformation.

In broad strokes, I argue that in the social mobility stories of these women we can find the social, political, and cultural contests engendered by transformation; I will assert that transformation itself can be understood precisely in terms of such contests. This book, then, takes up the contests lodged in the talk about things big and little—a just world, a happy family, and so on; Gwaltney aptly refers to the personal narratives that made up his *Drylongso: A Self-Portrait of Black America* as "analyses of the heavens, nature and humanity" (1980, xxvi). A pillar of this book—the theoretical foundations of which I turn to later in this chapter—is my understanding (one shared by many in the human and social sciences today) that it is not that these women's stories "reflect" or "represent" these larger social, political, or cultural struggles, but rather that, to some extent, they comprise those transformations; that is, their stories writ large have played a part in fashioning the life and sensibility of South Korea's transformation. I want thus to appreciate that the life—the feeling—of transformation is made by people and through narrative, through the sorts of stories examined in this book.

This book thus asserts that these women's talk offers a window on the contests that are contemporary South Korea. To be sure, to assert that the social world is but talk and contests can appear far-fetched or far-flung. By no means, however, do I mean to assert that political economic histories or structures are irrelevant here. Furthermore, numbers do have their place in telling the story of contemporary South Korea, but it is important to remember that they tell a partial story (Clifford 1986). So too is the story told here partial—but, I like to think, critical.

Having briefly detailed my focus in this book, I now situate this research in the context of the 1990s. I turn to the 1990s to underscore its importance as the decade through and from which the women in this book spoke about their lives over the course of recent history. They spoke about their pasts (beginning as early as the late 1930s and 1940s) from the perch of the 1990s, a decade that was conflicted in its own right; we must remember that retrospective narratives, as I discuss in the following text, are fashioned in the present.

The 1990s: Betwixt and Between

My research began (1992–1993) during the election and early presidency of Kim Young Sam, South Korea's first democratically elected civilian politician. The next phase of my research (1995–1996) then continued throughout the very public arraignment of grave ills of the 1980s (of both the state and business, and foremost of collusion between them) and of the undemocratic practices of the Kim Young Sam regime (1993–1997) as well. My fieldwork finished up (1998, 2000, and 2001) under Kim Dae Jung's presidency (1998 to the present; the first democratically elected opposition-party president) and in the eye and early aftermath of the IMF (International Monetary Fund) Crisis (1997–2001), referring both to the debt crisis and to the IMF and International Bank for Reconstruction and Development bailout, which revealed again enormous contemporary and recent historical, political, and social ills.

Coming on the heels of the 1980s—a decade of enormous political oppression and popular struggle (one that I wrestled with in Abelmann 1996)—the 1990s was a decade of tremendous hope, much of which was dashed.

That the 1990s did not fulfill its promise of social and political reform is but another chapter in a history of volatile political relations throughout South Korea since 1948; South Koreans have been anything but quiescent (Koo 1999; H. Y. Cho 2000; J. J. Choi 1993). Again and again, we find the play of state repression and popular opposition, and the fleeting reality of social, political, and labor "victories." Turning back the clock, Koreans did not acquiesce easily to Japanese colonial rule (1910–1945) (Cumings 2002). In turn, the end of Japanese colonialism, in 1945, found an explosion of political activity in Korea, of all ideological variety—much of it very radical. Increasingly appreciated is that Koreans above all wanted to determine their own destinies, to create their own state (Cumings 1981; Cumings 1997); instead, external powers took over, leading to the partition of the peninsula, which remains divided to this day. South Korea's first regime, Syngman Rhee's presidency (1948–1960), was toppled by popular struggle in the 19 April 1960 student uprising. April 19 (referred to as 4-1-9) is but one in a chain of South Korean household dates—dates that commemorate either popular struggle or heavy-handed state crackdowns. The hope of 4-1-9 was answered in the fleeting democratic presidency of Chang Myŏn, only to be eviscerated by Park Chung Hee's military coup (5-1-6 for May 16) in 1961. Park's was a presidency (1961–1979) of double-digit economic growth, mounting autocracy, and tenacious labor struggle. Another link in the number chain is Park's 1972 so-called Yushin (restoration), which spared few collective or personal freedoms in the name of "national security" and "anticommunism." South Koreans were made into state subjects with the help of a very heavy hand (H. Y. Cho 2000; I. Kwon 1990).

Reminiscent of 4-1-9, another hopeful moment was witnessed by South Koreans, a "democracy spring" in 1980, in the transition from the longlived Park presidency to the Chun Doo Hwan regime (1980–1987) (see chapter 2 in Abelmann 1996, and Jager 1996a, for a discussion of the genealogical aesthetics in South Korea's recent narration of Korean history). Chun came to power, however, with the bloody suppression of the Kwangju Uprising (May 1980), quickly extinguishing the hopes for democracy. The memory of Kwangju was quietly nurtured throughout Chun's autocratic regime, which ended in widespread democracy and labor struggles, in summer 1987 (Lewis 2002). Although Roh Tae Woo's presidency (1987–1992) was one initiated by direct election and one that promised a great deal, Roh actually sustained many organs and practices of the repressive state (Cumings 1997, 390).

My point with this review is not to suggest the futility of the political opposition and struggles of the South Korean people. There have in fact been very real gains, and they have been hard won; South Koreans can and do celebrate a remarkable grassroots history that has spurred considerable social and political reform. Instead, I mean—en route to the 1990s—to underscore both the considerable participation of the South Korean people in social struggle, and the often bitter fruits of that activity. The women in this book were children at Liberation (1945), came of age under the Rhee regime, were of marital age in 1960, and raised children through the Park and Chun regimes. Into the Roh Tae Woo and Kim Young Sam regimes, most of them were tending to older or adult children—putting the finishing touches on these children's higher education; worrying about their employment and marriage; and, in some cases, caring for their children (i.e., these women's grandchildren).

Although the women in this book are not activists—none of them boast of particular political participation—they are women of their times, whose sympathies and frustrations have been fashioned amidst the political sweep outlined. That their personal accounts do not necessarily refer to the public watersheds of that history does not obviate the often quite political flavor of their stories. As mentioned, this book stakes a strong claim against any easy demarcation of the personal and the political, the individual and the social. I turn now to the 1990s.

"Collapse" is an important word for 1990s South Korea, one symbolic even long before the economic collapse of the market during the IMF Crisis (K. S. Chang 1999). Most literally, there were two important early 1990s architectural collapses: the Sŏngsu Grand Bridge over the Han River, and the Sampung Department Store in downtown Seoul (together killing hundreds) (K. S. Chang 1999, 47). On another front, the rate of South Korean traffic accidents reached an unprecedented (and globally impressive) high in the early 1990s (K. S. Chang 1999, 48). Be it the IMF Crisis, accident rates, or other disasters, many South Koreans understood these occurrences to be risks associated with their rapid-fire economic development—development at all costs. Furthermore, many appreciated them as risks associated with the character of that development: orchestrated by a strong state allied with a small circle of large and powerful capitalists or conglomerates (chaebŏl).

This sort of critical, if not cynical, understanding of prevailing state and business power took on a particular life in the 1990s precisely because this was the decade that, in the aftermath of widespread popular achievement in the late 1980s (culminating in democratic elections and considerable gains for labor), had promised political and economic democracy. What converged in the 1990s was unprecedented freedoms (of the press, etc.) to reveal and reflect upon both the ills (and numerous they were) of the 1980s (and earlier) and the persistence of many features of South Korean authoritarian governance. It was one thing for the public to learn daily of untoward aspects of their national past: that, for example, the collapse of the aforementioned bridge and department store spoke to shoddy contracting under President Chun's shady political leadership. But it was another matter entirely when in the mid-1990s South Koreans were daily learning of unlawful aspects of the Kim Young Sam regime, including his unlawful passing of a new labor law in 1997; the illicit acts of his son, Kim Hyun-Chul; and the Hanbo financial scandal (a case of enormous political patronage). While South Koreans might have appreciated to a point that the public airing of social and political ills itself spoke to considerable democratic reforms, it was certainly not enough to curb popular discontent. As South Korean sociologist Kyung-Sup Chang summarizes, South Koreans "could not but feel betrayed by these civilian politicians in whose political rehabilitation they had invested physical and emotional energy . . . public disgust with politicians grew stronger in the era of civilian democracy than in the era of military dictatorship" (1999, 35).

It is against this 1990s backdrop that the IMF Crisis, christened on the eve of Kim Dae Jung's presidency, would signal a final blow to public tolerance for state-corporate collusion. This collusion was named the culprit of the crisis, rendering "South Korea's capitalist economy totally devoid of cultural legitimacy" (Chang 1999, 40). A related important feature of the 1990s, which I take up in chapter 10, was the considerable class anxiety and realignment in this decade. Even before the IMF Crisis resulted in the downward mobility spiral (both in terms of circumstances and identifications) of many who had counted themselves among the middle class, there had been other economic and social shifts, of particular interest to this study, the retreat of interest and sympathy for manual laborers by many in the middle class and the increasing identification of some manual laborers with the middle class (see Koo 2001).

By Way of a Story

Small causes can have a determining effect on individual histories, just as moving the pointer of a railroad switch by a few inches can shunt a train

with one thousand passengers aboard to Madrid instead of Hamburg . . .
And a casual encounter, a bet at roulette, a lightning bolt . . .
—Primo Levi, *Moments of Reprieve*

As a result of that humiliating day in court Clarence Smith's sense of cause
and effect suffered a permanent distortion. His mind was filled with thoughts
that, taken one by one, were perfectly reasonable but in sequence did not
quite make sense.
—William Maxwell, *So Long, See You Tomorrow*

I turn now to the constructs in my title—talk, class (and mobility), women, and melodrama. I do so first by way of a story, one told to me by a woman I call the Education Mother in this book. I call her that because of her Herculean efforts to educate her only son, a story told in chapter 4. In previous publications that mention several of the women in this book, I have used surname pseudonyms (Mrs. so-and-so—problematic because Korean women never take their husbands' names); in one case, I referred to one woman as the mother of so-and-so, the much more typical way in which women in South Korea are spoken to and spoken of (most-often naming the oldest child) (see Abelmann 1997a, 1997b, 2002). After considerable deliberation over naming for this book, and following a creative suggestion by Hyunhee Kim, I decided to use diverse pseudonym styles. While some pseudonyms are descriptive, as with the Education Mother, others mimic the particular way in which a woman is known of and spoken to, or refer to the woman's vocation or avocation; and for one woman, I use the conventional surname pseudonym. This naming practice also echoes another aspect of this book, in which the women are not featured in parallel but rather appear variously in its course and arguments. Never do I seek to align them. For this group of women, such an approach would be folly given the complexity of their lives and narratives. This uneven practice also speaks to my encounters with them: never parallel. Foremost, however, I have opted for this naming convention in the hope that across this book's many conversations, the reader might be able to keep at least some of the voices distinct.

The story that follows is the Education Mother's account of the fate of her only sister. Enveloped in a rich web of interpretive asides and afterthoughts, the story was much more than a string of events.

At the time the story was told, the Education Mother's younger sister was peddling shellfish on the beaches of South Korea's southeastern coast.

Abandoned by her husband early in her marriage, and then part of a marginal economy, this sister inhabited an entirely different world than that of the Education Mother in Seoul, who defined her own "middle-class" identity in terms of the "leeway to live entirely off the interest of stock and real-estate investments" and the "time and money to join a health club and travel with international tours."

At the heart of this story is a melodramatic moment in which her sister's fate had turned suddenly—the sort of moment that could easily be accompanied by high-pitched string instrumentation or thunder and lightning in a melodramatic film or soap opera. It happened one day when her sister struck up a conversation with a stranger at a rural bus station. At the time evoked in the story, the Education Mother's sister and her husband were in transit. Her husband had recently quit his job as a policeman, and with his sizable severance pay in hand, they were off to the coast to open a business. Throughout the journey, the Education Mother's sister clutched the pocketbook that held these bills—the promise of their new lives. Chatting with the stranger (at the bus station), she somehow lost track of the pocketbook; the bus station thus became the couple's way station to poverty. The couple continued to the coast and began peddling wares, on the fringes of the formal economy, to feed their family. Shortly thereafter the husband took a mistress and eventually abandoned the Education Mother's sister entirely.

The Education Mother mused that by today's standards, the money she would have needed to stem her sister's fate is but a trifling amount (especially to a middle-class person). But in those days, the Education Mother's family was enveloped in their own struggles to survive in immediate post–Korean War Seoul. Moreover, it has always been harder in Korea to distribute resources against the patrilineal grain—to a woman's natal kin—although much more frequent than norms might govern (see Kendall 1985).

What I found most intriguing about this story was the Education Mother's reflections on her sister's fate—that is, the *way* in which she told the story. No sooner had she led me to the story's climax than she had attributed her sister's ill fate to her boyish personality (*sŏngkyŏk*), namely her sister's impertinence and impropriety. Snatching her sister's tragedy from the impersonal winds of fate, she delivered it to the workings of personal proclivity. For a moment I was baffled—for all her sister had done was to misplace her purse, or less still to have had it stolen; it struck me as unjust or even unkind to pin the blame for a turn of circumstance on personality. And yet I knew that this was a sister who the Education Mother loved dearly and whose misfortune she was deeply sad about. But my understanding of these seemingly personal attributions changed as the story of the downward mobility of the Education Mother's sister veered in a different direction.

As the Education Mother continued, she portrayed her sister's personality as not only the *source* of a particular—and in this case devastating—social fate but also the *product* of a particular family history and of particular social times. The Education Mother detailed her sister's relationship with their overly ambitious mother, a woman who had been permanently separated from her husband during the division of the country into what became North and South Korea (1945–1948). She explained that her sister's "mistaken" marriage to a policeman (in her words, "such a low-class profession") was the product of their mother's "ignorant ambition" that had fixed itself on the policeman's *yangban* (hereditary elite) origins. "*Yangban* only in name," the Education Mother continued, as his family coffers were empty and his father had long ago taken up residence with another woman.

While the Education Mother knew how to bear with her mother's domineering ways—to say "yes" while all the while quietly forging her own path —her younger sister grew up at once fighting against and, ironically, complying with her mother's "twisted and ignorant" ambition.

When I reviewed my notes from this rather extraordinary story, I could see that "personality" was not simply a catalogue of personal traits or proclivities but rather a discursive site where the workings of a particular family history and even of national histories were at play. When the Education Mother turned from the lost or stolen purse to her sister's personality, it was not to wrest this sad story from the larger course of South Korean social transformations but rather to place it squarely within them—from the national division to the structure of patriarchy, to the reconfiguration of status hierarchies.

This story captures the melodramatic dimensions of the profound personal dislocations that have accompanied South Korean rapid social transformation. The rapidity of post–Korean War development has made for many stories like this one, stories in which small turns of fate—like the "pointer of a railroad switch" or the "casual encounter" in Primo Levi's analogy—spiral into great tragedies or enormous social divides (1995, 76). In her ruminations over her sister's fate, the Education Mother was struggling with nothing less than social justice at its barest: whether people get what they deserve, whether "cause and effect" make sense, as Clarence Smith puzzled over in William Maxwell's narrative (1980, 112; see Kendall 1985, 92, on causality and Korean women). Writing about contemporary

South Korea, anthropologist Hae-joang Cho offered similarly: "People begin to feel that intentional acts only bring about unintended, disastrous consequences" (2000, 54).

Asking the reader to keep this melodramatic story in mind, I turn now to the book's central concepts and theoretical affinities. The reader who is less interested in the theoretical concerns of this book is invited here to meet the story of the Education Mother again on page 27 in this chapter and to thus proceed more quickly to chapter 2.

Talk

In this chapter's opening pages I briefly introduced "social mobility stories" to suggest what I take them to be, and the work that I take them to be doing. The brief melodramatic vignette just offered is a snippet from just such a story—a snippet in which a younger sister figures as a critical cohort member and interlocutor in the reckoning of the Education Mother's present. In this section, I draw on the words of several theorists of language and literature to reveal my intellectual sympathies with several understandings: that language or talk is an integral element in the constitution of social life; that talk is dialogic—its interlocutors are numerous and diverse, and it reaches here and there (its origins are often elusive, its extensions hard to follow, and so on) such that individual discourse reveals a dispersed, not centered, self; that conversation is integral to social change (the grand processes of industrialization, urbanization, and so on); that the imagination is constituted through narrative; and finally, that ethnographic dialogue is in no way exempt from any of these understandings. All of these sympathies inform my understanding of social mobility stories. I turn to theory neither to justify nor to rationalize, but in the simple hope that these borrowed words might help me to better articulate the understandings from which I proceed. In later chapters the reader will find other references, to a wider circle of writers who have helped me to see the world (and closer to the task at hand, these women's stories) in the ways that I do.

I divide this section into four subsections devoted respectively to the understanding that "private" language is necessarily public and is ideologically informed; that narrative is constitutive of social groups and social life; that personal narratives are inextricable from their familial contexts; and finally that narrative necessarily engages the imagination, thus challenging prevailing senses of the "real."

The Language of the Day

> At any given moment, languages of various epochs and periods of socio-ideological life cohabit with one another. Even languages of the day exist: one could say that today's and yesterday's socio-ideological and political "day" do not, in a certain sense, share the same language; every day represents another socio-ideological semantic "state of affairs," another vocabulary, another accentual system, with its own slogans, its own ways of assigning blame and praise . . . Thus at any given moment of its historical existence, language is heteroglot from top to bottom: it represents the co-existence of socio-ideological contradictions between the present and the past, between differing epochs of the past, between different socio-ideological groups in the present . . . and so forth.
>
> —Mikhail Bakhtin, *The Dialogic Imagination*

Mikhail Bakhtin found words to say, eloquently, that every day, even every moment, has its own language (1981, 291). He stressed this not to seal off each day, moment, and generation or family (these too are the provinces of languages, he offered) in its own social world, but quite to the contrary, to mark both their specificity and their seemingly endless reference to other moments, days, groups, and so on. In so doing, he underscored the dialogic nature of words and language, the infinite webs in which they are caught. Most foundationally, Bakhtin wrote away from what he described as the prevailing view in the 1930s: "A simple and unmediated relation of [the] speaker to his unitary and singular 'own' language" (1981, 269).

In Bakhtin there is thus a refusal to take "private" speech or discourse at face value, to see therein a private world. Instead, speech is forever suspended in its past, present, and future, in the lines of communication—real and metaphorical—that comprise it. Profoundly interrupted, then, are "individuals" or utterances as stable centers of anything at all. In Bakhtin we find foretold an array of theoretical moves that have colored much thinking in many circles in recent decades: the appreciation of the "Western" "individual" as a particular historical and theoretical artifact (e.g., Crapanzano 1992; S. Hall 1996b; Taylor 1989; Weiner 1999); the questioning of identities, groups, and classes as coherent and stable entities (e.g., S. Hall 1996a; Kondo 1990; H. C. White 1992); and the insistence that individuals are not centers of social reality.

In the speech of the women who figure in this book, we can find the tracings of a multitude of what Bakhtin calls socio-ideological systems, while at once appreciating that their discourse coheres, in this case as that of the women of a particular generation, and of particular times. This approach renders their speech at once the crossroads to all, and a humble way station. I suggest that such a perspective gives us a place from which to listen to talk, ethnographic and other; to ask, for example, what are the tracings of socio-ideological systems in the pocketbook story above? It is in books of this sort—that do indeed tarry close to "individuals"—that perhaps we need to work hardest to argue and to show that individual creativity is not the only point. This said, however, I am deeply interested in the gift that is good conversation and good storytelling. And I will not eschew the beauty of human words and stories, even as I mean to tell what British cultural theorist Carolyn Steedman calls "resolutely social stories" (1986, 6). In Bakhtin's idiom, I am interested in both the "taste" (1981, 293) and "accent" (1981, 290) of words as they give us a lively sense of places and people; and in the heterogenous worlds, real and imagined, that "heteroglot" words point to (see also Abu-Lughod 1993).

Indeed, this book proceeds from the understanding that in words there are tastes, accents, and various socio-ideological projects to be found. In the Education Mother's narrative, for example, she grapples with an important inequality at the heart of her own life. This book is interested precisely in the taste of social divides narrated in that story, and in the socio-ideological regimes that govern tellings like it: about women, personality, social stratification, and transformation.

Language Makes (and Unmakes) the Day

This book furthermore proceeds from the understanding that words are productive: that they contribute to the making of social identities and social worlds, class, and, most fundamentally, of rapid social transformation, like that of South Korea. Most basically, this book offers, then, a (women's) narrative perspective on the transformations that have configured postwar South Korea. Critical here is the aforementioned understanding that language does not represent a reality out there, but rather that it fashions the world (such that it looks, however, always already made). Margaret R. Somers summarizes this theoretical position in terms of a "shift from a focus on *representational* to *ontological* narrativity" (1994, 612; see also Ochberg 1994, 117). For Somers, social being is nothing other than the way in which events are made into episodes that comprise stories such as the pocketbook story (1994, 618). Somers is interested in the "social networks" (1994, 616), or "webs of interlocution" (1994, 618, borrowing from Charles Taylor), in which such episodes or stories reside. Thus, for my purposes here, the narration, traces, and networks of stories, in part make women's identities (see also Crapanzano 1992, 94; Rofel 1999, 14).

A narrative perspective fundamentally challenges prevailing thinking on human action and social organization. In theorizing the social world, for example, Somers is interested in "relational settings" rather than "societies": "A relational setting is traced over time not by looking for indicators of social development, but by empirically examining if and when relational interactions and institutions appear to have produced a decisively different outcome from previous ones" (Somers 1994, 626–627; see also Mann 1986; Tilly 1984; H. C. White 1992). In a similar vein Christina Toren argues powerfully against the often paired constructs, the "individual" and "society": "There is no society and there are no individuals—only the social relations in and through which we become who we are in play, in work, in eating together, in conversation, in war, in ritual, in love, in debate" (1996, 76). Harrison White's analysis of stories, ties, identities, and networks resonates here as he boldly asserts that all stories reveal human ties: "Anything about which you tell a story is a tie" (1992, 68). From human ties, he builds to "social spaces" (H. C. White 1992, 68–69) and to social networks, which only sometimes "map into physical space" (H. C. White 1992, 134). By extension White's "persons" are revealed as "a hybrid of ties . . . held together with stories" (1992, 212) or again as "a set of story lines" (1992, 215; see also Schiffrin 1996, 199).

From Bakhtin, Somers, and White, then, change or transformation—rather than veridically reported or represented in words, language, stories, or narratives of identity—takes shape through words and stories (see also Stack 1996). In a similar vein British literary critic and cultural theorist Raymond Williams coined the phrase "structure of feeling" (1973, 35) to describe in his discussion of the literary conventions surrounding Britain's urbanization a narrative perspective on change. Less interested in the "historical explanation and analysis" of change, Williams instead turned his attention to the "particular kind of *reaction to* the fact of change" (emphasis added) as constitutive of the life of that change (1973, 35; on "structure of feeling" see Gordon 1997, 198; see Good and Good 1988, 57, on the structures of feeling for nations).

This book also appreciates that as narratives are productive of the social universe, so are they thus inextricable from relations of power. Inequality lives in words and stories, where social struggles are waged. Carolyn Steedman refers to the fact that "personal interpretations of past time—the stories that people tell themselves in order to explain how they got to the place they currently inhabit—are often in deep and ambiguous conflict with the official interpretive devices of a culture" (1986, 6). Steedman looks, then, for tensions, ambiguity, and disruption in the stories she tells and draws from (1986, 22).

Finding Theory in Family Stories

I now return to the nature of social mobility stories, the primary method and texts of this research. This book takes family or cohort members as critical narrative interlocutors, the nearest yardsticks in social life. In my encounters with these women, I looked for those people, in and beyond the family (and in some cases for composite social types), in concert with whom they saw themselves and imagined themselves seen. And I found so many stories like the Education Mother's—of sisters, cousins, soap opera characters, and so on. I could not agree more with Daniel Bertaux that in times of dramatic social mobility, family stories "stimulate the sociological imagination" and are "loaded with sociological insights" (1995, 85–86). Bertaux thus joins many scholars who appreciate that theorizing is by no means the exclusive province of scholars, that life itself can relentlessly demand theory. As Charles Lemert puts it, "Social theory is the normal human accomplishment of social human creatures figuring out what other human creatures of the same sort are doing with, to, or around them" (1993, 2). To this, Gwaltney adds the vector of dispossession in his discussion of African America: "Principled survival in a familial and communal context, complicated by the iron inconsistencies of caste, is a *preeminently analytical process*" (emphasis added) (1980, xxx). Lemert's "theory" and Gwaltney's "analytical process" grapple, as does the Education Mother in the pocketbook story, with the justice and legitimacy of contemporary social stratification.

Beginning with those nearest to them, people think about whether social fates are deserved. Daniel Bertaux and Paul Thompson tell the story of a French family's youngest son, who ends up leaving a promising career to join his father in the family business, a bakery (1997). They describe the "local system" of the family and family business, which affected the course of that son's life (Bertaux and Thompson 1997, 18)—not unlike the local system of the family in the case of the Education Mother's sister. In this book, I turn again and again to the narration or creation of such local systems. In the story of that eldest son, Bertaux and Thompson find a lesson on causality: "Years of working with life histories and family case studies have made such complex tangles of causality and self-determination familiar to us, leaving us increasingly dissatisfied with the simpler notions of causality which underlie much empirical sociology" (1997, 18). I would argue that the pocketbook story—as told by the Education Mother—similarly challenges "simpler notions of causality." The "complex tangles of causality and self-determination" that Bertaux and Thompson write of—inextricable for them from intergenerational stories and sensibilities—take us also to the social (beyond the sociological) imagination in social life.

The Social Imagination

Those are the enviable people who live at enmity with unreality; and those are the pitiable who are knocked on the head by the thing done without knowing or caring.

—Virginia Woolf, *A Room of One's Own*

Happily, today's social and human sciences have wonderful interlocutors on the social imagination, teaching us that the storied life stretches far beyond the real (in the narrower sense of that construct). While many have stressed the ways in which the social imagination is stimulated by our ever more connected, mediated, and even wired social world, it is also clear that social transformation—even of a quite traditional variety—tirelessly offers other worlds, what Arjun Appadurai calls "possible worlds" (1991, 197). It is in the world of the imagination that Northrop Frye finds similarly the "motive for metaphor" (1964). Bertaux writes of people's "*champs des possibles*" (fields of possibility) (1995, 78), which articulate with "*champs mémoriel familial*" (family memory fields) (1995, 83). For Steedman, these fields of possibility and family memory are inextricable from desire: "There was no point in our childhood when we were not given to understand that the experiences mother described connected both with the world as it was, and the world *as she wanted it to be*" (emphasis added) (1986, 113). One element of the world, as Steedman's mother wanted it to be, took shape in a longed-for house—a "dream that dictated the pattern of our days" (see also Bertaux-Wiame and Thompson 1997, 174, and Cisneros [1981] 1991 on dream houses).

Allowing for this sort of imaginary has necessary implications for the consideration of the self or identity. The imaginary disrupts the present, decenters the self, and in so doing sketches a complex topography of identity or identifications. In this vein Stuart Hall writes of "displacement as a place of 'identity' . . . living with, living through difference" (1996b, 116). For his own part, Hall writes of living "in a lower-middle-class family that was trying to be a middle-class Jamaican family trying to be an upper-middle-class Jamaican family trying to be an English Victorian family" (1996b, 116; see also Bhabha 1994, 192). Richard Ochberg offers similarly that life is storied in the sense that we live it as one of many possible versions: our actions thus realize or negate particular life narratives (1994, 142–143; see also Peacock and Holland 1993; Schiffrin 1996, 169). Such understandings of narrative and identification suggest that we think about social mobility stories not as simple social maps but as complex narrative projects. Against a distinction between the imaginary and the real that "has dominated Western thought" (Crapanzano 1980, 7), we must take the imaginary *for real*.

In keeping with this sense of the real, it is critical to underscore the temporal characteristics of the women's narratives in this book. Many accounts are retrospective, though they take form in the ethnographic present and in the ethnographic encounter (see Briggs 1986; Kendall 1988; Tierney 1998). As such, the narratives are multiply dialogic, with pasts, presents, and futures. Furthermore, they are yet crafted again in the act of ethnographic writing; as Vincent Crapanzano notes, life histories are "doubly edited: during the encounter itself and during the literary (re)-encounter" (1980, 8). Ethnographic writing, then, momentarily fixes otherwise endless encounters (Crapanzano 1980, 140). In this vein, ethnographic writing spills, like all activity, unevenly over time—stepping forward and backward, as I have described in the preface, in projects that weave among other endeavors.

The narrative perspective on class and mobility that I have begun to sketch here speaks to long-standing debates on the very construct of class, debates that I turn to now.

Class

"Class" is intimidating because it is a construct that has been so powerfully articulated and struggled over, and because it refers to realities that are so palpable, sometimes painful, and always political. Here we can recall for a moment the easy way in which the Education Mother sketched the contours of being in the middle class—a veritable checklist. But in thinking about the class position of the policeman, the husband in her sister's story, we can also recall how such checklists dissolve. And most important in that story—and germane to my position here—is that it all keeps moving, unsettling the construct and moorings of class. Also intimidating are the well-worn capital-letter camps in which theorists have traditionally aligned themselves, Marxist and Weberian. Indeed, class takes us to the heart of modern social theory. In this book, I stand with those theorists who argue that the long-standing divisions of class thinking—Marxist/Weberian, structuralist/subjectivist, and so on—are better blurred (see, for example, Crompton 1993; Giddens 1973; Goldthorpe with Llewellyn and Payne 1980). And I adopt the perspective of those who demand a place for narrative at class's table. Finally, I follow those interested in challenging the prevailing notions of "group" and "society," opting instead for relations, social spaces, networks, and so on, as do Somers (1994), Toren (1996), and the other narrative theorists just named.

Pierre Bourdieu's was an epic career on class. He describes the presumption of the two long-standing positions on class: the one (structuralist) that "treats social phenomena [e.g., class] as things" and the other (subjectivist, constructivist) that "reduce[s] the social world to the representations that agents make of it" (Bourdieu 1990, 124). He argues that these positions were extreme. Taking the opposition to be an artificial one, one best transcended, Bourdieu asserts a "dialectical relation" between its poles (1990, 126). He argues that "Objective structures . . . are the basis of subjective representations" and, dialectically, "these representations . . . account above all for the daily individual and collective struggles which aim at transforming or preserving these structures" (1990, 125–126). In this vein, Loïc J. D. Wacquant observes, "Class identities, practices, and 'lived experience' are not 'afterthoughts' tacked on preexisting classes; they enter into the very making of these classes" (1991, 51).

Bourdieu considers that structures and representations both are necessary "moments" of research (1990, 127). I consider this book, and the research it draws on, to be spun of both these moments. Most simply, while narrative or observed behavior/interaction is not the whole truth, it is nonetheless truth making and thus a constituent in the dialectical relationship of which Bourdieu writes. It is in this sense that Bourdieu contests the theoretical slippage entailed in classical Marxism: namely, the notion that from structures, actions and interactions can be assumed; that from relations of production, we can expect classes (1990, 129; see also E. P. Thompson 1968). It is the case, rather, Bourdieu argues, that groups, among them social classes, must necessarily be made (1990, 129). He is nonetheless sympathetic to the historical belief in the "reality" of class precisely because Marxist "classes" have in large part corresponded to the reality of social structures and people have readily assumed they are there, in "reality." Bourdieu calls this the "theory effect" (1990, 129), an effect that "is all the more powerful the more adequate the theory is" (1990, 138; see also Bourdieu 1987, 4). Therein lies "the quasi-magical power to *name* and to make exist by the virtue of naming" (Bourdieu 1985, 729; see also 1985, 742).

Interested, then, in the making of social groups in space and through relations, Bourdieu writes of "spaces of difference" and "social spaces" (1987, 3). He describes the ways in which these social spaces are structured by the distribution of capital: economic; cultural or informational; social ("resources based on connections and group membership"); and symbolic ("the form the different types of capital take once they are perceived and recognized as legitimate") (Bourdieu 1987, 4). Bourdieu describes "the endless work of representation"(1987:10), which I consider to be more richly articulated by those who take up the work of narrative (Somers 1994; Steedman 1986; see also Kelleher 2000 and 2003). "Incontrovertible," Bourdieu states, is that "the *truth* of the social world *is* the stake of struggle" (emphasis added) (1987, 11). In turn, he returns dialectically to another incontrovertible truth: "That, depending on their position in social space, that is, in the distributions of the various species of capital, the agents involved in this struggle are very unevenly armed in the fight to impose their truth, and have very different, and even opposed aims" (Bourdieu 1987, 11; see also Ortner 1996, 20; Rapp 1982; Somers 1994, 630; Wacquant 1991, 58).

Resonant in this understanding of the endless and power-laden work of representation that is dialectically constitutive of class are the ideas reviewed in the preceding on narrative, the self, and identities. Somers brings this together nicely as she posits a narrative identity perspective on class against one based on "interests" or on "*one aspect* of their identity" (e.g., "work category"). To Somers' "sense of being," Steedman adds development: the sense in which class is developed over childhood and the life course, in an intergenerational crucible (Somers 1994, 624; Steedman 1986, 7). Steedman describes class consciousness as "not only . . . a structure of feeling that arises from the relationship of people to other people within particular modes of production, but . . . also an understanding of the world that can be conveyed to children" (1986, 123). Steedman's and others' consideration of the family as critical to the development of class is foundational to this book's consideration of mobility stories in their familial (and other peer-cohort) context (see also H. C. White 1992, 69). This addition to an ontological, narrative perspective on class is particularly critical in the examination of class mobility in times of extraordinary structural transition and reorganization—such as those of postwar South Korea. To wit, family lives and histories meander their way amidst such transformation. In a similar vein Sherry Ortner notes, "classes view each other as their own pasts and possible futures" (1991, 177; see also Gledhill 1987, 11).

Steedman's interest in class as learned in childhood echoes the life historical methods and perspectives of a collective of British scholars, including, most prominently, aforementioned Daniel Bertaux and Paul Thompson. Broadly, this British circle of scholars, keenly interested in work and class, has employed life stories quite differently from American counterparts, who have been more interested in the life course (infancy, childhood, adolescence, etc.) and in culture. Attentive to the family in the workings of class, Thompson, for example, describes mobility as "generated or impeded by subtle interactions between the chances and dangers created by changing economic and social structures and the particular transgenerational effects of family cultures" (1997, 56). His take on "intergenerational transmission" allows for "transmutation" as a possible strategy of transmission; he insists that while "straightforward imitation is simple enough to trace statistically," the life-story interview can reveal transmutations that are nonetheless deeply embedded in families (1997, 46). Bertaux similarly considers familial "transmissions" over the "longue dureé": "They operate little by little in everyday practices that often escape consciousness, and with slow motion effects that only become visible after periods measured in years and even decades" (1995, 73). Bertaux and Thompson write provocatively of families as "units of production of their members' energies . . . of 'anthroponomic production' " (1997, 19; Bertaux 1994; see E. Yi 1993, 467 for a discussion of mothers as the nurturers of children's ki [spirit, energy] in South Korea). In sum, class—and social mobility—is not a thing to be catalogued and charted but is, rather, a project that happens partly through narrative, in families, and transgenerationally. As narrative and the family are inextricable aspects of the consideration of class, so too is gender— a topic I turn to next.

Women

In and out of the field, I have been asked (mostly by men) why I did not interview men for this project. In fact, I did (briefly) interview the husbands of three of the women and the brother of another. My primary commitment, however, was to the women's realities; for the most part, the women were not interested in my following the genealogy of their stories to men (or other women) involved—"I've already told you what they would say" was their common refrain. This is not to say that men's social mobility stories would not have been interesting. Brief encounters suggest, however, that they would have been differently elaborated, spun closer to "central interpretive devices" (Steedman 1986, 6). This said, however, I do not want to think of women's stories as running entirely against the grain. Ortner describes the conundrum well when she writes, "It is unsatisfactory to assume that women wholly identify with the hegemony, but it is nonetheless difficult to come up with an alternative that does not fall into the opposite trap, casting women as enacting wholly different projects" (1996, 16). I will return in several chapters including the final one to the question of women's particularity.

This book takes as a premise that a focus on women and their narratives speaks to both their important contribution to class distinction and to the central socioeconomic roles they have played over the course of South Korea's era of rapid development. Although dominant narratives of South Korean "development" (see chapter 5) have both focused on and been articulated primarily by men, the development of people's selfhood has largely been the domain and interest of women—the guardians of the home, child rearing, and family narrative. Women's attributes and cultural expression have been particularly important to class in South Korea (see Kendall 1996; M. H. Kim 1995, 79, and 1993, 81; S. K. Kim 1997, 254; O. Moon 1990; E. Yi 1993) both because of the long-standing Korean elite tradition in which women's being and achievements have indexed the morality and propriety of families (and patrilineages) (see Deuchler 1977; Haboush 1991) and because of the economic and social roles assumed by women in the face of the twentieth-century dislocations and disasters that de-centered masculine selfhood and social life (see chapter 7; also see H. J. Cho 1988; Em 1995; Mun 1995). It can even be said that over the course of male-centered national development, the development of class culture and distinction has been largely ceded to women—an observation that has been made for many national settings and historical periods (see Armstrong 1987; Bertaux 1995; C. Hall 1992, 95; Rapp 1982; Scott 1988; Smith-Rosenberg 1986, 34).

This book, however, is not only interested in women as social subjects or entities, but in gender as inscribed throughout social life and narrative. This follows from the widespread feminist understanding that gender "does" rather than "is" and, as such, is forever at work (Moore 1999, 155, 157). I am interested in the ways in which public and private narratives are gendered (particularly in the articulation of social change), and in how gendered subjectivities and gender relations (i.e., between men and women) are produced in relation to these narratives. In other words, I want to think about gender difference as a sign or metaphor system for talking about social differentiation and power relationships generally and for considering gendered identities (Scott 1988; see also Rofel 1999, 20).

Gender is at the heart of every chapter in this book. One of the primary arguments of chapter 3 is that the words I call key words are all deeply enmeshed in systems of gendered relations and socio-ideological formations. Chapter 5 argues that women and gendered experience are inextricable from the workings of class formation in postwar South Korea. Chapter 6 asserts that gendered attributions are central to the profoundly social discourse on personality, like the discourse we met in the pocketbook story. Chapter 7 asserts that South Korean modernity operates through thoroughly gendered imaginaries, and chapter 8, in turn, considers how gender operates in class distinctions within the family. In short, this book is always both about women and about gender, as intricate socially and historically elaborated systems of meaning and attribution that are at the heart of social life.

I turn now to "melodrama" as I employ it in this book, hoping to convince the reader as to why I have featured it so prominently, beginning with the pocketbook story.

Melodrama

> She waited for her to laugh and say, "you sound like some movie." But her
> mother stood freeze-frame still, her head locked as if to catch the distant
> strains of violins, the rustle of women reaching into purses for Kleenex.
> Nancy Welch, "The Road from Prosperity"

There is hardly a page of my field notes without mention of a television soap opera (called tŭrama in Korean for "drama") or melodramatic film. It is not an exaggeration to say that the women in these pages considered their lives to be dramatic, not unlike those lives represented in dramas for television and film (see Abu-Lughod 2000 for a fascinating discussion of the ways in which this sort of identification produces a modern individualistic subjectivity for the case of women in Egypt; see also Abu-Lughod 1997). Indeed, mediated narratives are critical interlocutors for the women featured in this book. In chapter 7 I argue that films are critical sites in which to find the sensibility of social transformation that I have been discussing in this chapter. In that chapter, I take up particularly what I call melodramas of social transformation, popular films from South Korea's so-called Golden Cinema Age in the late 1950s and early 1960s (see McHugh and Abelmann n.d.). Also chapters 4 and 6 each take up a woman's extended engagement with a television soap opera. It is, however, in the broader sense of melodrama as a narrative convention and sensibility that I have brought this construct to this book's work and title.

I use "melodrama" here to refer to a complex of theatrical, literary, and cinematic conventions characterized by excess—of affect (the overdrawn, overmarked) and of plot (strange, almost unbelievable twists, coincidences, connections, and chance meetings). Thomas Elsaesser writes that the general use of "melodramatic" describes the "exaggerated rise-and-fall pattern in human actions and emotional responses, a from-the-sublime-to-the-ridiculous movement, a foreshortening of lived time in favor of intensity—all of which produces a graph of much greater fluctuation, a quicker swing from one extreme to the other than is considered natural, realistic or in conformity with literary standards of verisimilitude" ([1972] 1987, 52). Excess also characterizes melodrama's overdrawn characters—moral hero/ines and evil villain/esses (Brooks [1976] 1995, 11–12; Kaplan 1993, 10). "A particular form of dramatic *mise en scène*," including decor, color, and music, has also been critical to the enactment of excess (Elsaesser [1972] 1987, 51). Some have argued that this is particularly pronounced for cinema (see Mulvey 1989).

I argue here that a melodramatic sensibility has been pervasive in contemporary South Korea, as it has been in many times and places of rapid social transformation (see also J. An n.d.). Indeed, many theorists of melodrama assert that the genre rose with the social and class transformations of the rise of capitalism (Brooks [1976] 1995; Watt 1957). Peter Brooks, premier melodrama theorist, writes about melodrama as both a "mode of expression and representation" and a "means for interpreting and making sense of experience" ([1976] 1995, 205). In my use of "melodramatic sensibility" I follow his convention, referring not only to the properties of a particular field of texts (including personal narratives) but also to their dialogic context (that is, to the talk that so often surrounds them). I argue that the dialogues engaging melodramatic texts, narratives, or moments—dialogues that include comments like "You sound like some movie" from Nancy Welch (1996, 16)—similarly share, in Bakhtin's sense, particular tastes or accents. Broadly, I consider that melodramatic texts and narrative conventions are effective in South Korea because they dramatize issues central to rapidly changing societies and because they draw their audiences into dialogue. In this section I argue that we can learn something about the nature of this dialogue by listening in on some of the scholarly debate about melodrama.

Over the last twenty years, melodramatic novels, films, and television soap operas that were once considered of little cultural or scholarly value have been resuscitated in academic writing. That these works are now legitimate texts for inquiry in part reflects the increasing interest in popular culture generally, but it also reflects transformations in theoretical and historical perception that have opened these texts to new and exciting analyses. In the case of melodrama, scholars have taken up the very touchstones of its devaluation to proclaim its value. Of course, the transformation in appraisal is not singular—nor is the genre clearly defined. In fact, the scholarship on melodrama is not agreed on the features that constitute the genre itself. My own interest in these debates about melodrama is rather particular: I think they can teach us something about the efficacy and popularity of melodramatic texts themselves. In the interest of brevity, I present these as five debates on melodrama, recognizing that I am oversimplifying matters.

First, some scholars have questioned the use of "melodrama" for the non-West or for non-Western genres (Turim 1993, 155). Others, however, have asked whether it is imperialistic to suggest that melodrama has arrived in the non-West whole cloth from the West (Rofel 1994, 707). And again, some have suggested that it is imperialistic to abandon Western genre and theory in the examination of non-Western texts (Kaplan 1993, 26). Yet other scholars focus on non-Western melodramas' distinct features (Dissanayake 1993), or argue that the characterization is problematic because of the historically limited ways in which it has been formulated in the West (Rothman 1993, 269). These critiques of the cross-cultural use of melodrama suggest necessary cautions: that there is no reason to assume analogous histories of similar narrative or dramatic forms; that it is important to consider the limits of theory devoted to the particularities of Western genres; and that there is no need to assert universal or pan-historical arguments. Nonetheless, I argue here that "melodrama" can signal shared properties that are worth thinking about cross-culturally. Furthermore, for cross-cultural study, it is important to consider literary and genre developments in their particular historical crucibles. In the case of South Korean melodrama or melo-mul (melo[dramatic] things), we find a local vocabulary and popular sensibility—the contours of which all the women in this book would recognize—that conjures images of excess, tears, and drama in keeping with widespread Western characterization. Relevant here are Korea's premodern literary and dramatic traditions that are easily characterized as melodramatic. This said, however, Korea was likely influenced by its considerable contact with Western melodramatic genres over the twentieth century.

Second, not all observers agree on the relation between melodrama and realism. Melodramatic excess can seem unrealistic with every flourish, and it is precisely this "unrealism" that has led many in the past to trivialize melodrama (Elsaesser [1972] 1987, 47). From another vantage point, however, it can be argued that the excess dramatizes the real: namely that, while realistic genres are naturalized or ideologically unmarked, the drama of excess highlights the unreal and by extension the real (MacCabe 1976). In this vein Ien Ang notes that the constructedness of the text is itself highlighted by melodrama ([1982] 1985, 38; see also Abu-Lughod 1995, 9; Ang and Stratton 1995, 126; Dissanayake 1993, 2; L. Williams 1998, 53). In this sense, the efficacy of melodramatic unreality derives precisely from its transgressions of reality.

Distinct from the argument that melodrama works by transgressing reality is the position that melodrama can be effective on account of reflecting "reality"—the melodrama of "real" life. Ariel Dorfman makes such an argument for Latin American magical realism, suggesting that the North American academy has misunderstood the reality of its representations (1991). The matter of "reality," of course, turns again on the sense of the real and the imaginary (or possible), the here and now versus the desired, as I discussed in the preceding consideration of narrative and class (see Appadurai 1991; J. Bruner 1986). In this sense, the debates on melodrama negotiate between competing aesthetics in the apperception and narration of the social world: the realm of the possible versus the accommodation to the real.

Third, observers are not in agreement on how to understand melodrama's primary focus. Some argue that melodrama serves to collapse the social and political into the domestic. In this vein Elsaesser writes that in melodrama "the characters are . . . each others' sole referent, there is no outside world to be acted upon" ([1972] 1987, 55–56; see also Mulvey 1989). Christine Gledhill argues, however, that such assertions limit the "real" to the "set of socio-economic relations outside the domestic and personal sphere," thus ignoring the domestic with its "sexual relations . . . fantasy and desire" (1987, 13; see also Ma 1993, 33; McHugh 1999 and 2001). Gledhill refuses to relegate the domestic to a "surrogate level," finding there precisely " 'real' social conflicts" (1987, 13). Peter Brooks argues similarly that melodrama "evokes confrontations and choices that are of heightened importance because in them we put our lives—however trivial and constricted—on the line" ([1976] 1995, ix; see also McHugh 1999). These theorists thus challenge us to question the dichotomies (e.g., public (political): domestic; and personal: social) that obviate the sociopolitical workings of the home and of private lives—dichotomies that I challenged in the preceding consideration of women's talk and lives.

The matter of how to think about the domestic is critically gendered because of melodrama's overwhelming consumption by women whose lives have been, in many cases, centered in or relegated to the domestic. These discussions ask, does melodrama isolate and trivialize or, alternatively, elevate the domestic?

Fourth, observers have debated whether characters in melodrama are centers of ("realistic") psychological interiority, or alternatively, social composites or social projections. This discussion is critical because so much of melodrama is enlivened by good and evil characters. When characters are fashioned as "individual" psychologies, their social fates are somehow deserved and their good or evil is celebrated or condemned respectively. When, on the other hand, characters are considered social composites or projections, their good or evil operate differently. In this latter vein, Elsaesser argues that for Hollywood melodrama, evil "is firmly placed on a social and existential level, away from the arbitrary and finally obtuse logic of private motives and individualized psychology" ([1972] 1987, 64). Brooks notes similarly that melodramatic characters have "no psychology" or "interior depth," and Gledhill cautions that personalization is not necessarily "a mechanical reflection of the ideology of individualism" (Brooks [1976] 1995, 35; Gledhill 1987, 30). Also some commentators on Asian melodramatic genres in particular have noted similarly that characters' troubles are framed outside of the self, in "social codes" (Kaplan 1993, 24), or beyond human agency entirely (Yoshimoto 1993, 109).

Fifth, there are discussions as to the extent to which melodrama renders a moral order legible, one of Peter Brooks' central assertions about the genre ([1976] 1995). Melodrama's meta-drama of the affective makes for what Brooks calls the "moral occult"—"the domain of spiritual forces and imperatives that is not clearly visible within reality, but which they believe to be operative there, and which demands to be uncovered, registered, articulated" ([1976] 1995, 20–21). In another idiom, writers on North American soap opera have asked whether melodrama is "open" or "closed." Some have argued that the serialized and open-ended nature of that genre makes for open texts that invite audience involvement and reflect the pace and style of women's lives. It has been observed, however, that non-Western soap operas are typically not as open—that although serialized, they tend to complete the narrative, to close off the moral questions and plots (Allen 1995, 18). My own sense is that melodrama is most often open in that it fosters dialogue and as such lives on. Linda Williams (1998, 44) extends this sort of perspective by celebrating, not reviling, the emotional engagement engendered by melodrama, which she dubs a "mode" rather than a genre.

At issue then is whether to understand melodrama's engagement with moral concerns as fostering a particular moral universe or as merely dramatizing, rather than closing, moral debate. It seems that in his later writing, Brooks veers toward a more "open" approach to melodrama's moral universe, offering, for example, that the "moral occult" lays bare "large choices of ways of being" ([1976] 1995, vii).

I argue that in popular discussion of melodramatic texts, we find echoes of these five debates about melodrama. That is, melodrama in part engages its consumers because it inspires similar debates. Furthermore, these debates are critical in times of great social transformation, when the real often seems unreal; when the domestic is easily comprehended as social; when persons are easily taken as social composites; and when the moral universe is unsettled. It is thus the dramatic tension of these debates that sustains the piqued interest and attention accorded melodrama, or melo-mul —and narratives like the pocketbook story.

Back to, and Beyond, the Story

The pocketbook in the Education Mother's story certainly works as a melodramatic sign of excess. The Education Mother knew that a listener—in this case me—would be somewhat incredulous at the puissance of the pocketbook; it seems almost unreal that the turn of events in the aftermath of the stolen pocketbook would not have reversed themselves to this day. The reality of the story, however, comes not so much from the plausibility of a woman carrying or losing her entire life's savings but more from the realities that both enabled and resulted from the melodramatic moment. First is the misplaced ambition of her mother, who suffered the scars of national division (through her social widowhood) that not only burdened her with responsibilities she was "totally unprepared for" but "distorted" her personality (in the course of my interviews, I found frequent, if subtle, commentary on the effects of socially enforced celibacy on young widows).

Second, critical to this story, are the fluid and changing contours of class—and of the times. The Education Mother's mother—like so many people of her era—miscalculated: privileging her future son-in-law's *yangban* legacy over his meager prospects and low social standing as a policeman. Many of my conversations turned on women's praise or disdain for their parents' ability or inability to effectively "read" the changing times. The Education Mother faulted her mother for being out of synch with the new rules of the game, for the anachronistic decision that set her sister's course. Indeed, Koreans have been straddling multiple status systems for generations; the melodrama of the story of the Education Mother's sister is intimately tied to the personal strategies that people have mobilized amidst the sea changes of social transformation. Although with hindsight it was perhaps easy for the Education Mother to have dismissed her mother's ignorant marital choice for her sister, it has in fact not been so easy for people at one or another juncture to know what to do (strategically or ethically). The enormous changes in stratification systems have been neither uniform nor total: premodern status distinctions did not, for example, suddenly or completely lose their social significance or political sway. Rather, the ways in which people calibrate human worth and achievement have been continuously contested. Psychologist Jerome Bruner argues that stories are dramatic and worth telling precisely when justice is at stake: "Stories need *characters* in *action* with *intentions* or *goals* in *settings* using particular means"; the drama emerges, he continues, "when there is an ambivalence in the 'ratio' of these constituents . . . [when a character] is in an inappropriate setting, or an action does not warrant the goal to which it is leading the character" (1986, 20). South Korean recent history has made for precisely this sort of ambivalence in the "'ratio' of these constituents"; dramatic personal and family stories abound.

A third reality entailed in the melodramatic moment featured in the pocketbook story is patriarchy. Patriarchy first fashioned the ignorance of the Education Mother's mother (being unschooled), and it was also at work in a *yangban*'s son becoming a policeman, for he was also the son of an abandoned woman.

The melodramatic moment is also enlivened by the weighty realities of its aftermath. These include the stark downward mobility experienced by the Education Mother's sister and the further effects of patriarchy (the sister's desertion by her husband for another woman, and her unfordable economic distance from her natal family).

Echoing another melodramatic debate, the style or character of the Education Mother's sister was also at issue in the Education Mother's telling: her boyish personality, her "inability to keep quiet if she disagreed," and her "unwillingness to hide her feelings or engage in pleasantries" "destined" her for a difficult relationship with her mother and a difficult life course. The Education Mother explained that her own femininity, on the other hand, had been well-suited to the strictures and structures that women in Korea have had to negotiate. She explained that a "woman like my sister would have never survived the early years of my marriage," referring to the early difficulties the Education Mother herself experienced both with her husband and mother-in-law. She highlighted her sister's limitations in this way because her own marriage had become, in the final analysis, both a successful and prosperous one. The Education Mother offered not a defense of patriarchy but rather a commentary on the effects of personal proclivity under patriarchy. Her sister's personality—its origins and effects—are neither entirely interior nor personal; it is precisely this tension that makes for the Education Mother's reflexive, dialogic telling of this story—a telling that prompted me to begin with it here.

Finally, in keeping with yet other melodrama discussions, it is very difficult to identify the villain(esses) or hero(ines) in the Education Mother's story. Each flawed character is an intricate social product. The agent in the purse-snatching story is after all quite irrelevant or absent, and the sister's father-in-law is so remote from the story as to be rather inconsequential. The story is messy, and as such, it serves, I think, to open a moral debate.

It is one of this book's primary contentions that the episodes comprising women's social mobility stories work to open the debate on South Korea's contemporary scene. The taste or feel of that debate is what I argue makes for South Korea's present—or at least for some generational and gendered nodes of it.

From the purse strings of this melodramatic account, where do we go? Chapter 2 introduces both this book's women and the complexity of their class positions and identities. I do so through the stories of how I came to meet each of them. Here, I am attentive to the class contours of the social networks through which I found my way to them. As I have underscored in this introduction, it is impossible to think about women's class position or identities apart from their social relations. By way of these stories, I mean to complicate the class map of South Korean women of this generation.

Chapter 3 continues this chapter's foray into the taste of the stories of these women of a particular generation with an examination of a dozen or so key words—words that figured again and again in their talk. I argue that these key words are difficult to define and that they work so well precisely because they elide easy definition (as do melodramatic texts as I have already discussed). To wit, they allow women to capture the complexity of their lives and times. Largely emotionally charged terms that describe people, these key words do not pass final judgment easily. The reader will get a feeling for the subtlety of these women's talk and for the ways in which this talk often refers to larger matters than those seemingly at hand.

In chapter 4 I examine a critical venue for class work: education. I consider the ways in which two of these women have managed their children's education. Appreciating that education stories offer a revealing window on strategies for social reproduction or mobility, I take up both the Education Mother's narration of her successful struggle to propel her son to college and the Janitor's tale of having not managed to send either one of her two sons to college. I assert that these narratives also allow us to see the social world in flux, for education is a gamble about the future. As such, the education stories are fraught: walking precariously the precipice of imagined futures. This chapter also takes the reader into the IMF Crisis moment that inspired enormously conflicted ideas about education, employment, and mobility.

Chapter 5 begins at some distance from women's social mobility narratives with a general review of social mobility over South Korea's recent past: it attends to both "facts," numbers that speak to this mobility, and "fictions," widespread understandings that have affected popular senses of social mobility. I assert that we must consider both productive of social life. In particular, I take up the challenges of thinking about women and social mobility; I argue that many prevailing understandings of social mobility in South Korea have largely ignored women—as mothers, daughters, wives, and workers. I offer the social mobility stories of the Laundress to illustrate these points. Through her case I also explicate the particular ways in which women's mobility narratives selectively engage both facts and fictions.

Central to chapter 6 is an argument about South Korean women's narrations of personality, such as those of the Education Mother on her own and her sister's style. Echoing the discussion on melodrama in this chapter, I assert that the discourse on personality is anything but personal. "Personality" invites a consideration of agency and selfhood, and to both I bring a narrative perspective. I focus this discussion on the Moviegoer's thoughts about the personalities of key people in her family. I argue that for the Moviegoer, "personality" affords her nothing short of a commentary on social justice issues.

Chapter 7 veers away from the seemingly personal to public narratives about men: particularly their displacement. I argue that prevailing narratives about the loss of male subjectivity—on account primarily of colonialism, the Korean War, and economic restructuring—offer a critical context for thinking about gender generally. This chapter begins with three films from South Korea's 1950s–1960s Golden Cinema Age; dubbing them melodramas of social transformation, I consider the revealing ways in which they screen or stage patriarchy. I argue that these films capture a critical tension: between the exercise and displacement of male authority. I then take up the story of the men (and women) in the life of Mi-yŏn's Mother, the woman who figures most centrally in this book. I assert that both "female" and "male" refer richly to national narratives such that women's narratives must be seen in their broader narrative or socio-ideological context (as I have discussed, via Bakhtin, in this chapter). Public sensibilities on the displacement of men over the course of recent Korean history are such that Mi-yŏn's Mother is hard put to speak easily or uniformly against the men (or women) dear to her.

In this book it is chapter 8 that extends furthest beyond the nuclear family, as it considers the universe of class distinction within the extended family. I take up discussions of Hye-min's Grandmother on her husband's siblings, and of Mi-yŏn's Mother on her paternal kin. The chapter considers the visceral accounting of difference in the minutiae of lifestyle and personal affect. I argue that the day-to-day management of kin—and the rendering of difference within the family—is the template from which women come to reckon the workings and justice of the broader social world.

The most detailed life story of this book is to be found in chapter 9, that of Mi-yŏn's Mother. Adding many details to Mi-yŏn's Mother's story, this chapter also highlights the considerable inconsistencies, or even reversals, across her telling. It does so not to question their veracity but rather to appreciate the "truth" differently. Mi-yŏn's Mother's voice is a highly ambivalent one, wavering on many details of how she has—or should have—lived. I consider Mi-yŏn's Mother emblematic of the women of her generation: women whose times have not let them settle with life easily. The chapter is organized thematically: Mi-yŏn's Mother on her husband, her work, her education, her children's education, and her country.

Concluding this work, chapter 10 considers the book's contribution to the understanding of South Korea's compressed modernity. In so doing, it revisits issues of women and class for contemporary South Korea. I discuss the implications of this book's repeated assertions about the complexity or ambivalence of the talk of the South Korean women featured here. I also take up the question on which this chapter began: how much can be said on the basis of the ethnographic material presented here?

2

THE EIGHT WOMEN

This chapter introduces the eight women who figure in this book, as well as the paths that led me to them. Reflection on these paths begins this book's consideration of South Korean class maps. My stories toward these women are dispersed over space and time, critical coordinates for thinking about class. At the close of this chapter, I discuss these women in a shared social field in order to begin my foray into the complexity of class location and identities for women of this generation.

People Trails and Research Tales

That the stories of how I met the women in this book are my stories is, for purposes here, incidental, for I offer them to reveal the spaces, structures, and subjectivity of class—the complexity that I began to assert in chapter 1. As the reader will have already gathered, this is not ethnography with a geographical or institutional center, as I do not locate it in a neighborhood, city ward, organization, or village. The fieldwork culminating in this book was strewn across Seoul, and long forgotten are the bus numbers, subway stations, apartment numbers, and the like guiding me to these women. But the feel of the different nodes of Seoul and its vast transportation network lingers: the skeleton of a city, the traces of oh-so-much talking, intractable summer heat, and bone-chilling winters. The fact that in recent years the end points of all the subway lines have changed, that whole new lines have been added to the system, makes anachronisms of me and the daily travel culminating in this book.

A widely understood but less often written about truth of ethnography is that anthropologists meet many more people than those who make their way into their books. The editing happens at so many points, which is entirely reflective, I think, of social life generally. We begin a conversation with somebody that never takes off, we strike up a relationship that goes nowhere, the serendipity of timing ends a relationship that seemed to have been going somewhere, and so on. We feature one person in our writing and, in so doing, another person fades into the background, a matter of personal affinity. I personally like all the women in this book, but I must confess I did not have an affinity for every woman I spoke with—hence not all found their way here. In this book, then—as in my personal life—I edited along the path of talk and friendship. A piece of paper with a phone number disappears, a correspondence is forgotten, and so on. Also, of course, in research we turn to the cases, the details, and the talk that conform to points and proclivities of the writing self of the moment. This is not meant to be cynical, for the points and proclivities have not been mustered whole cloth from some other social reality.

As this project took shape, I told myself I wanted to talk with a range of women, classwise, not fully understanding then how vexed the matter was. If these tales convince the reader of that—the vexed question of class—they will have done their work.

By Way of the Countryside

The Laundress and Hye-min's Grandmother

I begin with one of the people trails that figured in this research: a trail beginning with a North Chŏlla Province village from my mid- to late-1980s fieldwork, and particularly with one of the men who had been active in the tenant farmers' movement that had then captured my interest. I turn to him because it was through his younger brother, Mr. Kang, that I came to meet both the Laundress and Hye-min's Grandmother. The forty-something farmer in question was known in the village for his demure diligence. Rare among farming men, he was a teetotaler. The local common-sense about his active participation in the grassroots farmers' movement in the late 1980s was that it was mostly a matter of his wife's resolve—that hers was the stronger will of the household. While he was the sort who blushed if any attention wafted his way and who hardly spoke a public word, his wife was brazen, abrupt, prone to say too much, and at times a bit irascible. Like most of the people in that village, they were petty farmers with modest tenant landholdings. Both husband and wife had some schooling; they could read and write, but haltingly. It was clear, however, that their children (barring personal limitations) would finish high school; times had changed and they were motivated to ensure this basic level of training for their children, living in a country that had achieved almost universal secondary education by the 1980s. By 2000, 68 percent of high school graduates entered a college of some sort (including those who failed the first time around) (Korea National Statistical Office 2000). When in the early 1990s, however, the couple's eldest daughter left for Seoul, it was to find work, not to ride the waves of the remarkable expansion of South Korea's postsecondary education.

During my summer 2000 visit, I learned that the family's second son was attending a two-year college in a nearby province. That same summer, I was surprised by the family's newly built inside kitchen—they had enclosed what had been an earthen floor kitchen area. Remarking as always on the husband's diligence, neighbors were quick to tell me that he had done all of the work himself. I was so happy to find the husband's elderly mother still alive (periodic countryside visits are tense that way: Who will have passed away? Which house will be vacated?). In the years that I have known the family, the husband's mother has been intermittently present, more so after the arrival of the youngest daughter, born with cerebral palsy. When this youngest daughter was a toddler and it was becoming clear that her development was delayed, I once traveled with her and her mother to a hospital in the nearest large city (a four-bus two-hour trip), where a specialist examined the girl. When the kind and capable young woman doctor began describing the sorts of mental and physical stimuli the family should provide the little girl, and the mother's eyes glazed over a bit, I remember thinking that the doctor had very little sense of the daily rhythms and realities of this child's life. Most days the little girl sat with her largely immobile grandmother in one of the two rooms in their farmhouse while her parents worked in the rice fields. Both the girl and the grandmother would teeter about—each dragging their legs behind them—no farther than the sliding door of the room opening onto the enclosed yard. Most of what the doctor mentioned simply would not have worked for this girl's life: missing were the hands, the things, and the know-how to make good of it. The girl's mother, though, would do what she could; she is a tireless person, the sort who pushes herself, and then again some.

This woman had been a favorite of the educated activists who were drawn to her village during the farmers' movement. Fearless, talkative, spry, and emotional, she had earned their attention. And she loved the company of educated people, whose lives and stories took her far from her small corner of the world. At a time (not so very long ago) when phones were rare commodities, kept under lock and key (literally), and phone calls to people outside of the village were rare, she took to quite often calling some of the key activists, long after the affairs of the movement required it. In the immediate years following the movement, when often I was in better touch with the city activists than were my countryside friends, my visits with her were occasions to chat about the latest goings on of the activists: that her favorite of all of them had divorced, that so-and-so had married and was with child, and so on. In his own, quiet way, her husband made clear that he too cared about this world of educated outsiders, so years later on another visit, I was not surprised to see that they had befriended a young college-educated couple (the husband hailing from the region; the wife a city girl) who had decided to become farmers, while the rest of South Korea was closing the door on years of just that sort of activism. The decision of such young people to settle in rural areas was based on their realization that the only way to effectively promote such activism was to become farmers themselves. My visit recalled the movement, which in turn brought to mind the educated sorts who had traveled to the village during those years, and in an instant the mother had phoned the young couple to ask them to come by, which they did.

I offer these details to say that among the hundreds of households touched by the movement and by the attention of outsiders, this family's was one of a handful that was somehow permanently transformed. Not surprisingly, in the light of these affinities, they had welcomed my company. And this digression brings me to Mr. Kang, the younger brother of the father I have described here. To be frank, I do not know many details of Mr. Kang's family background. I do know that he and the husband/father farmer share the same mother, that their surnames are different, and that there are other siblings, both in the countryside and in the city. When I came to know the couple I have just described, Mr. Kang had long been absent from that village, though, from the beginning, the farmer and his wife spoke to me (the American girl working on her dissertation) about that brother—the college-educated brother, "now working on his masters," and (on later visits) "now working on his Ph.D." (and by then I was the American professor). I am pretty sure that I first met him on one of his trips home, and on my later visits, the couple would always search for the piece of paper, tucked away somewhere, with the brother's latest whereabouts and phone number. I would then meet up with him in Seoul at oldfangled coffee shops, dark and dingy cafés that were becoming harder and harder to find in Seoul.

Mr. Kang was a high school Chinese teacher. He was a very quiet person, not unlike his brother, and our conversations were often a bit halting. He inquired about my studies; I about his. And we worried together about the little girl in the countryside who still was not walking, still was not talking. He remained unmarried long past the appropriate age; for that matter, so did I. Our faithful, if intermittent and awkward, meetings were entirely tethered to the village: to his older brother and sister-in-law. Somewhere along the course of things, I made an attempt at "arranging" a marriage for him by introducing him to the younger sister of a friend of mine (with the enthusiastic consent of her parents). Both parties were very short (a debit in South Korea's contemporary marriage market) and late to marry, and the prestigiously educated mother of the woman in question insisted (to my surprise) that Mr. Kang's humbler, rural origins did not matter. I was not confident, but it seemed worth a try, for I knew well that both families were worried about their respective "old Miss" (oldŭmisŭ) and "old Mr." (noch'ongkak)—ideas that still loomed large in the South Korean landscape of family and the normative life course. I was not there for the meeting, and as it turned out, nothing came of it.

Today Mr. Kang is married, with two young children (the "old Miss" I introduced him to remains single). For Mr. Kang the rural world of his brother speaks to his own childhood poverty and hardship. Indeed, the farmer and his wife's rural life has quickly become the experience of a vanishing minority. While 80 percent of the labor force were agricultural workers in the late 1950s, by the late 1980s only 20 percent of the labor force worked on a farm (Koo 2001, 33–34). For the most part, Mr. Kang assumes that the world of his childhood is distant and unfamiliar to most Seoulites in his midst. In summer 2000, now forty-something, Mr. Kang spoke with one of my thirty-something South Korean Ph.D. students whom I had employed to conduct a follow-up interview. In his initially halting answers to her questions about his early education and migration to Seoul, it was eminently clear that he did not assume that his childhood world—rural, poor, and of another era—would be familiar to her.

When I decided on the project coming to life in these pages, I thought to ask Mr. Kang for help. I hoped he would introduce me to women whose lives had straddled similarly diverse worlds, and he understood. Most of my urban connections had taken me to women of relative privilege; I turned to Mr. Kang for help with a different sort of lead. He first introduced me to one of his distant relatives in Seoul, a widowed elderly woman living alone with her daughter. A seller of petty wares, she was past the age of caring about the things that the middle-aged cling to tenaciously (e.g., success, status), and furthermore she wanted most of all to talk about Jesus and God. This project, and others that have followed it, have taught me how to talk comfortably about Christianity, for it is such an important part of the landscape of South Korea and of Korean America. At that time, though, in the early days of this project, I did not know what to do with Christianity. Frankly, I did not know how to think about that talk as doing anything other than getting in the way of other things I was interested in—a naïve position, to say the least. Mr. Kang kindly took me to her home, and I visited several times after that, but the talk dwindled. In the meeting with my student in 2000, Mr. Kang described that our talk (mine and that of his relative) had not been "natural," that it had not proceeded smoothly.

Meanwhile, Mr. Kang introduced me to the Laundress. Among Mr. Kang's fellow teachers of Chinese was the eldest son of the Laundress. The high school at which Mr. Kang and her son taught was one that the Laundress once described to me as being in the less prestigious rungs, where teachers could not garner the income lavished upon teachers in wealthy neighborhoods. My own conjecture was that the shared humble backgrounds of Mr. Kang and the Laundress's son—one from the countryside; one from the city—had secured their friendship. The first call I made to this friend's mother was a social one. The Laundress's residence was on the outer edge of Seoul, and to get there I traveled to then one of the furthest nodes of the subway system, a station known to be a factory center, and from there went by bus, past many manufacturing and assembly plants. Mr. Kang and I together made this trip—to the small laundry where the husband and wife labored alongside one another—on a very rainy night.

I met the Laundress's eldest son (Mr. Kang's colleague) that evening; we exchanged pleasantries and phone numbers. He spoke lovingly of his mother's suffering, a suffering that, he described, "knows no words." Her story, he explained, was worthy of a novel or television tŭrama (soap opera), something I often heard over the course of my research. In later meetings, his mother would say the same thing—that she ought to write a novel, that her life was the sort that should be chronicled, and so on. During that first very brief encounter, the Laundress let me know that this was the son she had "hoped to make a professor of." Over the years, when I would see this son as he passed through the tiny laundry either up into or descending from the raised room that was their abode, we would nod and he would again mutter something about his mother's suffering. As I think back to it, in the minds of Mr. Kang and his friend, it was this suffering that had "qualified" the Laundress for my project.

I hesitated to name her the Laundress in this work, but settled on it as she is the only one of the eight women included to have labored in small business and to have traded on a skill—needlework—for her entire adult life. I decided to be comfortable with this appellation because she likes her occupation in spite of what she described as its "lack of social recognition." Well aware of the popular image of a poor, bespectacled, and disheveled woman folded over her sewing, the Laundress had promised herself some fifteen years before we met that she would never wear glasses. Indeed, she still did not when we met, and she was proud that she could still thread her sewing machine's needle easily, though she admitted this was less from sight and more from body memory. But having made good on her promise, she said, "Words are powerful things."

I also have Mr. Kang and the Laundress's son to thank for introducing me to Hye-min's Grandmother. Here the connection stretches remarkably thin and circuitous: Mr. Kang had generously solicited his colleagues for their connections. It seems the Laundress's son must have then mentioned my project to one of his students' mothers, perhaps thinking she herself would have been appropriate. That mother was uninterested, though she thought she knew of the perfect person: the elder sister of a close friend. The Laundress's son then gave me the name of the friend, and when I called, she kindly explained that her older sister had (again) suffered and had "known the Korean War" (i.e., was old enough to have suffered from that as well). She asked on the phone if I went to church, and when I had to answer no, I wondered if I had failed some test. Shocked, she said, "Don't all Americans go to church?" but after some chitchat, she thought to tell me that she in fact did not go to church either. Later I would come to understand the situation better, for her sister, Hye-min's Grandmother, was an ardent churchgoer. That this younger sister had fallen from the church by marrying into a family of nonbelievers was noteworthy in her own family. As it turned out, this younger sister of Hye-min's Grandmother was the child of her father's second marriage—a divide that was in fact difficult in the family. But she was certain that her older sister was a woman I should meet, and so she encouraged me to contact her, explaining that it would be best for me to meet her after church on Sundays, for the other days she was busy taking care of Hye-min.

Although she was not the only grandmother I interviewed, I call her Hye-min's Grandmother because she was the only woman residing with her grandchild and actively involved in child care; she was also the only widow and the only woman whose children had all married. Furthermore, I was introduced to her that way. Hye-min was, in the eyes of her grandmother, a feisty little girl, and, above all, boyish—feisty and boyish just like all of the women in Hye-min's Grandmother's family, she would tell me again and again. Hye-min's Grandmother even spoke spryly at that time about the fact that Hye-min (still a preschooler) urinated standing up like a boy. That tidbit came to mind during my visit with her in summer 2000, when we posed for a photo in a pottery shop and café under construction. With élan and a chuckle, Hye-min's Grandmother posed herself next to a full-sized sculpture of a corseted buxom woman, quickly cupping her hand over one of the ceramic breasts spilling out of the corset.

Hye-min's Grandmother first met with me on a Sunday, after church, at a café, one of the first generation of the new-style coffee shops—Starbucks-like coffee shops located at street level. Older-style coffee shops like the ones where I met Mr. Kang were salonlike, with plush if ratty furniture, and always perched at the top of steep staircases, dark and hidden from the streetscape. At that very first meeting, and in meetings to come, Hye-min's Grandmother insisted that I not waste money on expensive beverages or food; she often wanted to lunch at the reasonably priced church cafeteria. After I thanked her profusely for having been willing to meet a perfect stranger, she offered that God had chosen her for this. We spoke then about the serendipity of our meeting, and we spoke of the two Chinese teachers on that serendipitous path, teachers who had both come from difficult backgrounds. "They are like dragons who have risen from tiny streams," she had explained, adding, "Don't tell them that, though—it would make them feel bad to be spoken of that way." Conversation had ambled easily, and remarkably within minutes, she was chatting about the soap opera of the day *Adŭl kwa ttal* (A son and a daughter), then a favorite of mine, which I discuss in chapter 4. We were off and running.

Before leaving Hye-min's Grandmother, and in the spirit of the education stories in chapter 4, I want to briefly enlarge the story of Hye-min's Grandmother's younger half sister—the phone intermediary for my connection with Hye-min's Grandmother. When I met Hye-min's Grandmother, in summer 2000, she caught me up on her siblings. Just a year earlier that half sister, who had admitted to me she was nonchurchgoing, had emigrated to Reno, Nevada, following her younger sister and leaving her husband behind in Seoul. Hers was an example of the then quite widespread education emigration: one or two parents leaving for the expressed purpose of educating their children. In her case, it was for her only son, who had in fact managed to enter a prestigious college in Seoul by the time the family's emigration papers came through. The son was now attending a community college in Nevada and finding it hard to adjust to the United States.

When at Hye-min's Grandmother's request I spoke with the half sister by phone, she used the word *"taptaphada"* (stifling, frustrating)—one of the key words I discuss in chapter 3—to describe how she and her son had been feeling as they maneuvered their way in the American education system. She hoped that soon he could enter a prestigious American engineering program. Meanwhile she planned to return to Seoul to gather the transcripts and other papers that he would need for his application. Her younger sister, who had emigrated decades before and lived in the same city was too busy with work to help out. As for the future, it was not certain whether her husband would follow, to perhaps join his brother-in-law and sister-in-law in business in Nevada.

After I met Hye-min's Grandmother, in summer 2000, she gave me many phone numbers in the United States; most memorable was that of a man who had "escaped to" the United States decades before, never paying her the one hundred or so dollars he had owed her. The United States is indeed part of her nexus, as it is for most of the women in this book.

The Janitor

I have another village, and another village contact, to thank for having met the Janitor. I settled on calling her the Janitor because she was forthright and proud about the hard labor that had allowed her to raise her seven children alone after being widowed in her early thirties. The Janitor is the least schooled of the women in this book. And the costs of illiteracy are ones she knew only too well. The reader will find that among the women of this book, the Janitor was the most outspoken and brazen regarding matters of inequality. Above all, she was confident that she was deserving of respect. During one of my visits, a woman was trying to dictate something to her over the phone, a message for the Janitor's eldest son. The Janitor matter-of-factly told the woman, "I am woman of no learning," and explained that she would not be able to write the message down. After she hung up the phone, she said to me, "Thank goodness, though, I did learn my Arabic numbers—those really help. I might be a janitor, but people think that I am really chic [*mŏtchaeng'i*]. I look really intelligent, but I tell them outright that I am a janitor [*ch'ŏngsobu*]. I tell them the truth. Why shouldn't I? I am not one to deceive others."

The Janitor is one of nine children: the third child, and the second of three daughters. During my 1980s fieldwork in the region, in a village a half an hour's walk down the then unpaved road from Mr. Kang's brother's house, the Janitor's eldest and widowed sister lived in a small, decrepit, and at the time thatched house, which was in those days a rapidly vanishing sight and today has almost entirely vanished. Thatched houses were an undisputed sign of poverty and underdevelopment, except the thatched houses commemorated in reconstructed or preserved "traditional" villages. Also in that village were three of her younger brothers. In a village of some fifty houses, these siblings were the proprietors of four of them. In the late 1990s the youngest brother's infant and toddling children were the joy of the village's main drag, a dusty path tracing the shore of a reservoir; remote countryside villages, which have so little to offer young people, are mostly drained of younger generations. I have vivid memories of the eldest sister—whose children were by then all grown—caring for these children while their father, the youngest brother and second to youngest of the nine siblings, ran the village mill (pang'akkan). By that time many villages no longer had an operating mill, and these decrepit, most often red buildings, left for rubble, seemed to cast sad shadows on the villages. Indeed, when some years later the youngest brother left for Seoul, this mill was deserted, never to be used again.

That youngest brother's life, now in Seoul, has been checkered. His two older brothers in the village, both constant interlocutors during my 1980s fieldwork, were among the tireless fighters in the movement, and they were both feisty, chatty, and known for their quick tempers. Although a village with generally small landholdings, and almost exclusively tenant plots, the brothers' holdings (tenant and nontenant) were among the largest, including the mill. The family had been newcomers to the village late in the colonial period, and the Janitor remembers moving there in her teens. As we will learn from the Janitor in more detail in chapter 4, hers was a family with greater status pretensions than most of the village families. When I lived in the village, the middle of the three resident brothers was building himself a new home at the "very end" of the main drag—the "house at the very end" is how the house and its family became known. The Janitor told me that she had told her brother to build an inside bathroom, but he did not. Had he done so, he would have been the first in the village, and at the helm of a trend. Today a number of homes, including those of some of the poorest farmers, do have inside bathrooms.

This middle brother's house, though, still remains among the two or three largest and most well-constructed. Far and away the most remarkable of the homes today is a newly constructed double-story home—the only double-story home I have seen in the entire region—with a stone wall façade (again, entirely anathema to rural architecture), where a pastor and his wife live. In this home's complex is also a newly constructed church; there had been no church when I lived there. The pastor and his wife, city people, have three children, and at present it is these children who bring joy to the main, dusty drag, which the church abuts; there are no other small children in the village. The villagers I met in summer 2000 told me that the church was not much of a success but that a handful of older women do attend. My dearest friend in the village had been going but stopped in order to instead travel half a day, to and fro, to a church of the globally infamous Reverend Moon of the Unification Church. She joined that church hoping to find a bride for her disabled only son because she had heard about the marriages with overseas brides that the Unification Church arranged for South Korean farmers (it has been hard for farmers to find women willing to settle into the rural farming life). By the time of that 2000 visit, my friend had spent her life savings on finding an overseas bride for her son.

The inside bathrooms, the showy church, the prospect of an overseas bride, the decrepit mill; these are among the changed vistas of the village I had come to know in the 1980s. I offer these details of yet another village, and of these four siblings of the Janitor, because I think they matter. Women of the generation featured in this book hail overwhelmingly from villages like these, villages that recent history has busily sculpted anew. It is because I found my way to the Janitor from this village that I can partly trace her back to it. In chapter 4 we learn from the Janitor and her children fascinating reflections on the education of these countryside brothers. For the other women in this book, I cannot offer these details, as my encounters with them begin decades away from all of that. One of the things that makes Seoul more and more changed is that fewer and fewer people sustain ties to villages like these, and the line drawn between those with and those without such village paths is an indelible one.

I think that I first met the Janitor not during one of her trips to her childhood village or her hometown (kohyang) but at the headquarters of the corporation the farmers were occupying as part of their tenant struggle in Seoul—the occupied floor of the building of their corporate landlord, which swelled during the day with such relatives. Though I remember nothing about the Janitor at that time, she remembered me there; I was a bit of a sight. How often did she visit? What had she thought about the land struggle in which two of her brothers and sisters-in-law were among the most outspoken and fearless? My first contact with her for this project was through her brothers in the countryside, who had phones in that village early on; they gave me her number.

I never met the Janitor alone for long; the mother of seven, with two or three living at home at any time, the house was seldom empty. I usually went at night because she worked during the day, cleaning buildings. Hers is an existence cherished by seven adult children, who—like Mr. Kang's friend the Chinese teacher—are convinced that their mother, widowed young, is a veritable wonder. And she is. The first time I visited her house, I met her eldest daughter, exactly my age, who made it only a few years into elementary school; this seemed remarkable to me—even in the context of the education landscape of the quite poor village from which her mother hailed.

The Moviegoer

Last among the women I met by way of the countryside is the Moviegoer, again, quite circuitously. I call her this both to capture her enduring love of film, and our shared interest in movies (and television soap operas) that ran the course of much of our talk together. Although film is but one part of her life, I am comfortable calling her this because it speaks to a passion that she is proud of (and that she has had to defend against her husband's sense of its frivolity), and because it is for her a passion that recalls the happiest moments of an otherwise difficult youth. At moments when the Moviegoer seemed overwhelmed by the heaviness of her own stories, she interrupted herself to ask me if I had seen such-and-such a movie. Or she would turn briskly to the narrative of a film she had seen or a novel she had read.

The Moviegoer is the mother of a college graduate who was my research assistant in the final stages of my late 1980s dissertation research. I met her daughter, however, not through Seoul or university connections but through the farmers' movement. She was one of the so-called outside activists who had devoted her time and attention to the cause. The days when I met her were interesting ones in her own activist trajectory. She and her boyfriend at the time (today her husband) had been among those to decide to settle in rural areas for political reasons—the sorts of Seoulites that Mr. Kang's brother and his wife had found so appealing. Far larger in those years were the numbers of college graduates or dropouts who became factory laborers as a part of their activism, many of them in fact ending up merging their own social fates with those of laborers because they forfeited their education. Just as I was meeting the Moviegoer's daughter, she and her boyfriend had decided to leave farming. He had decided that he was more drawn to labor activism, and she was uncertain as to what to do next. She helped me at precisely this impasse in her own life.

In my friendship with the Moviegoer's daughter since those years, I have followed the ways in which she and her husband, as members of a cohort of 1980s activists referred to now as the 3-8-6 generation (samp'al'yuk sedae) (in their thirties, 3; attended college in the 1980s, 8; and born in the 1960s, 6) made their way into, and now beyond, the 1990s. Their lives, and their hearts, have turned in ways that I would have thought unthinkable. The grips of youth and of social movements made it hard to imagine that the parties in question would ever be doing or caring about anything other than what they were doing or caring about at just that moment. Life's course, though, is the best teacher of all. I could no more have imagined the Moviegoer's daughter today than she could have perhaps imagined this book, one far removed from activist organizations and agendas. In the final chapter of my book on the farmers' movement, I wrote about the Moviegoer's daughter and her husband as beacons of the changing social aesthetics of the times (Abelmann 1996, 246–247). By my most recent visit to Seoul, the lives of the Moviegoer's Daughter and her husband had turned again. By summer 2000, the Moviegoer's daughter had entirely abandoned social activism, after a decade or so of work devoted to evening education for laboring adults. Her marriage in trouble, she had moved home with her elementary-school-aged daughter and had focused her energies on saving money to emigrate to the United States. Largest among her motivations was her daughter's education. She hoped to raise a creative child unfettered by the demands of South Korean schooling that keeps its eyes on the prize: the still-rigorous college entrance examinations. By summer 2001 she was undecided as to whether to emigrate or move to a South Korean farming village—this time not for political organizing but to be able to educate her daughter in a clean and more wholesome environment. The husband of the Moviegoer's daughter meanwhile had recently taken a job in the post-IMF social service bureaucracy to aid the unemployed, following a failed attempt at running for city district office, a not uncommon course for 1980s activists; on the side, he remained busy with labor organizing. Although he ended up following his wife to her home, the Moviegoer's daughter is ready to chart her own future, deathly tired of her husband's inability to adjust to changing times. When I asked about activist goings-on these days—she had always been so good at providing a synopsis of that ever complicated world—she confessed, entirely unabashedly, that she hardly even read the newspaper now, and that "all of that" was behind her.

My paths via the countryside to the Laundress, Hye-min's Grandmother, the Janitor, and the Moviegoer are each quite distinct. I began with Mr.

Kang, my intermediary to the Laundress, because his own trajectory straddling a poor rural childhood and a somewhat upwardly mobile present is part and parcel of the friendship with the Laundress's son that brought me to the Laundress. Later discussions with the Laundress will reveal in chapter 5 the critical context in which she thinks about her sons' achievements, those of the Chinese teacher among them. The rural past of the Laundress, however, is not one to which I had direct access. Nor did I have such access for Hye-min's Grandmother; there too my path was forged across critical imaginaries: first that of the Chinese teacher (the Laundress's son) about his student's mother, next that of this mother about her friend's older sister, and finally that of the friend about her half sister. These are precisely the sorts of circuitous networks in which people come to imagine or to place themselves. My path to the Janitor, on the other hand, was via one of the nodes of her own rural past: both that past and the rural present of some of her siblings are critical references in her own senses of self (see chapter 4). Finally, my path to the Moviegoer touched on the countryside differently again: not from her own rural past but instead through the rural activism of one of her daughters. Later discussions with the Moviegoer will show, however, that her daughters' activism is a critical context for her own class identity (see chapter 6).

By Other Routes

Mi-yŏn's Mother and the Education Mother

I met both Mi-yŏn's Mother and the Education Mother, the middle-class elder sister in the pocketbook story from chapter 1, in 1984. It was my first visit to South Korea for a summer of language study. By the time I asked them if they were willing to participate in this research, I had known them for almost a decade already. I had strong friendships with some of their children, had even "arranged" by establishing the contact for one of their children's marriages, and had spent time living in both of their households. Now, the millennium turned, it is nearly decades that we have known each other, and they doubtless feel that they have watched me grow up, from my mid twenties to my early forties. It is Mi-yŏn's Mother who will appear in this book in greatest detail. I call her Mi-yŏn's Mother because in my own head, and to others, I have so long referred to her as so-and-so's mother that it would seem entirely wrong to do otherwise. As previously mentioned, many women in South Korea are referred to, and in many cases only known as, the mother of so-and-so. Thus of all the pseudonyms in this work, hers is the one with the most natural social life, alongside Hye-min's

Grandmother. Mi-yŏn's Mother and the Education Mother—they have never met but know about each other—and their families are mainstays in my personal encounter with South Korea. Their kindnesses to me over the years are uncountable.

I rented a room in Mi-yŏn's Mother's house the summer of 1984. It was only at the tail end of our talks for this project that I learned they had just appropriated the second floor of their home as their own that summer; till then they had lived on the first floor and used the second floor as a so-called *hasukchip* (boardinghouse), a system by which students rent a room and are provided board more or less quasi-family-style (see chapter 9). I was the last person to rent a *hasuk* room on that second floor; thereafter, their upwardly mobile family *really* lived in a two-story home. Mi-yŏn's Mother, though, continued to have her hand in a boardinghouse, one down the street and managed by her maternal uncle. By the time I began this research, the family had moved to a gorgeous, capacious home in a ritzy, though old, Seoul neighborhood, famous for the residence of a recent president. The trappings of her home and garden—including a commissioned sculpture of Mary and child in the garden, purchased in honor of Mi-yŏn's engagement; paintings by renowned South Korean artists; antiques; and wallpaper trim from Switzerland—are those of the upper class. She once took the trouble to show me the antique trunk from Cheju Island in which she had been gathering dowry items for Mi-yŏn's then upcoming marriage. The trunk took on further symbolic meaning when she explained that she had taken the hint to gather items in an antique trunk from her travels in Norway. She was especially proud of a European tea and cake set that she had purchased in Russia, telling me, "I think it's Hungarian. Actually I'm not sure of the country, but I know it's from the country that makes the best china."

The house where I had lived with them in 1984 was later torn down to make room for a so-called one-room-system apartment building: namely, a building of studio apartments rented according to South Korea's *chŏnse* system, in which people rent by placing very sizable down payments that they later retrieve. In the IMF aftermath, Mi-yŏn's Mother ran into trouble when many of the renters looked to quickly liquidate their down payments. These days Mi-yŏn's Mother is thinking of yet another system to respond to a changing South Korea: a cross between the old *hasuk* and the one-room system—namely small apartments with centrally offered dinners, cafeteria style, for students who need to move close to their universities temporarily (e.g., to prepare for particular state examinations). The long and involved story of Mi-yŏn's Mother's property management is her mobility story. In that summer of 1984, the family's three children were in preschool and elementary school, and I witnessed a very interested mother, working arduously to fashion the early school careers of would-be successful children, discussed in detail in chapter 9.

The home where I rented the room was perched at the top of a steep side street that backed into lower-income housing. At the apex of that side street, at the corner where their house was located, unkempt children from families of modest means spilled out into the street. Mi-yŏn and her little brothers were impeccably well-dressed and would never have played in the street with those children, who must have seemed like street urchins to Mi-yŏn's Mother. That I played with them was, I could tell, a source of consternation for her. Had I been able to communicate in better Korean at that time, no doubt we would have explored the matter further—to what ends I am not sure. Eminently clear to me then, and more so with every passing year, was that Mi-yŏn's Mother was a thinker, and a woman of savvy, not just social savvy in the engineering of her children's future, though that too, but political savvy. She shared, for example, in my youthful—and in my case quite ignorant—interest in bootleg South Korean dissident music and books that were made quietly available behind the counters of certain left-leaning bookstores in the nearby campus town. I remember her passionate interest in one of the lyrics books I brought home, lyrics of dissident folksinger Kim Min-gi. Prominently displayed in the first floor of her home was a poster of Mt. Paektu, synecdoche of North Korea. Hers was my first encounter with Korea's so-called divided families, as her family hailed from the North.

Another crucial figure in that home was the bent-over grandmother, whom I had mistakenly understood to be her biological mother, who showered me with food and smiles. That I had known and been charmed by that now-departed remarkable lady—whose story, as Big Mother, the reader will learn in chapters 7, 8, and 9—made it easier, I think, for Mi-yŏn's Mother to tell me years later about her having lived with two mothers. Also crystal clear to me that short summer was the sort of man her husband was, and that was not a pretty story. There was nothing I would learn about him over the 1990s, during the research for this book, that would surprise me—perhaps this too made it easier for Mi-yŏn's Mother to talk about her husband, which she did at great lengths. Over the years, her husband tolerated my visits, although with some trepidation; I am, he knows, privy to much too much.

The first writing and presentation from this project featured Mi-yŏn's

Mother; indeed, much of my thinking about these women began with, or through, her stories. In that first piece (Abelmann 2002), some parts of which made their way to chapter 7 of this book, I portrayed a woman a number of my readers and listeners recognized as the prototypical women of a host of media labels, including: *pokpuin* (housewives who buy and sell real estate on speculation for investment purposes, and engage in money lending); *ch'ima param i ssen yŏja* (women who invest heavily and even illicitly in their children's education) (see Kendall 1996, 217; she translates *ch'ima param* as "skirt impulses" or "women's influence"); *kŭksŏng majŭn ŏmŏni* (mothers who go to extremes pushing their children to study); Madam Ttu (mercenary matchmaker) (see Kendall 1996, 135); *k'ŭn son* (women engaged in usury); and *yuhan Madam or nonŭn yŏja* (wealthy housewives who do nothing). (See chapters 4 and 5 in Nelson 2000 on the gendered discourses of overconsumption in South Korea.) In short, it appeared that Mi-yŏn's Mother was that economic sort of woman, living to amass upper-class trappings for her family, and to ensure her children's upper-crust education and marriages—at all costs. At the time, I was very upset that such was the image readers had taken from my writing, and listeners from my presentations. I felt entirely misunderstood, or more importantly, I felt that Mi-yŏn's Mother had been totally misunderstood, and as the author, I felt responsible for the miscommunication.

So, then, where do I stand on the matter of properly representing Mi-yŏn's Mother? Do I hope to do her justice in this book? Yes. Do I think that the "others" of all these women—the women they contrast themselves with, for better or for worse—are overdrawn in such a way that, look as we might, the "real" women corresponding to the stereotypes might be hard to find? Yes. Do I think that this representational economy, most narrowly of "types" of women, is spun entirely of media machinations? No. For my purposes here, the very fact that these women's lives and their talk speak to, and of, social portraits that have social lives, real and mediated (and of course that distinction does not really even work), convinces me of their salience, of their play in the social discourses of South Korean contemporary lives and times.

That first summer in Seoul, I also met the Education Mother's daughter, then a student in a health profession at the prestigious university where I was studying Korean language. If my memory serves me, she had gotten to know a Korean Japanese young man who was one of my classmates. The Education Mother's daughter is one of the loveliest people I know—kind, generous, expansive, passionately curious—and still today touched by a youthful spirit. Deeply interested in each other's worlds, we became fast friends, and over the years our lives have intertwined in interesting ways, including (as previously mentioned) her marriage. I came to know and cherish her family, and to stay with them for an extended period during the time of my late 1980s dissertation research.

My interviews with the Education Mother did not go as far as those with Mi-yŏn's Mother—it was harder to stay on course, to carve out time independent of the long established patterns of my visits, which had also included visits with her husband, mother, and sister. In the case of both the Education Mother and Mi-yŏn's Mother, I have in some cases met, and often heard about, the relatives who figure in these stories, such as the sister from the pocketbook story in chapter 1. However, I learned little of that story in all the years that I had visited her. I have followed several residential moves of the Education Mother—out of a house to an apartment, to a larger apartment, and now she is about to move to an even larger one outside of the city, for cleaner air and the company of her closest friends. And I have watched the marriages of both her daughter and son, and the contours of their respective moves and mobility.

Both Mi-yŏn's Mother and the Education Mother are privileged, and both of them have had a hand in fashioning their family's well-being far beyond the squarely middle-class earnings of their husbands. Each in her own way might be called *pokpuin* (wives who buy and sell real estate on speculation for investment purposes) by other women, for they have dabbled in property and other investments—Mi-yŏn's Mother more aggressively and with greater daily involvement. It is this dabbling, large and small, that distinguishes these women from the Janitor, the Laundress, and Hye-min's Grandmother (who have worked in the formal economy; also the Laundress and Hye-min's Grandmother were not home owners), and from the Moviegoer, the Twins' Mother, and Mrs. Pak, who are all home owners of different varieties but who have not contributed extra income to the family coffers.

Mrs. Pak and the Twins' Mother

I will briefly review how I met Mrs. Pak and the Twins' Mother, although the paths are less circuitous, more contemporary, and, as such, less revealing than those that led to the other women; also, these two women figure less prominently in this book. The woman I call Mrs. Pak is the mother of a former student of mine, a young woman who briefly studied abroad. Mrs. Pak herself spent several years abroad for her husband's graduate study, early in her marriage, leaving one of her children back in South Korea, a lifelong regret that she and I spoke about at some length.

For having children who studied abroad, Mrs. Pak joins a number of the other women. Hye-min's Grandmother's eldest son spent time in the United States for graduate study of art. In fact, the entire family thinks that Hye-min herself is the blessing (in the Christian sense) of that time abroad. Hye-min's mother is a neonatal nurse in South Korea and is convinced that Hye-min, who entered the world in a medical emergency in the United States, would not have made it in South Korea; indeed, the baby of her subsequent and similar birthing in Seoul did not survive. One of the Moviegoer's daughters, the sister of my close friend, studied abroad for a year; her stay was taxing for the family financially, and she eventually decided to return. The Education Mother's daughter followed her husband abroad and received some health-professional training while there. And one of Mi-yŏn's brothers spent a year abroad as part of his undergraduate training (discussed in chapter 4). As for time abroad themselves, much later in the life course than for Mrs. Pak, Mi-yŏn's Mother followed her husband to England because he was sent there for his job (see chapter 9). As for other sorts of immediate family ties beyond South Korea: one of the Janitor's daughters worked in Japan for a stint after high school; one of the Laundress's sons emigrated to New Zealand and has started a small business there, and one of her brothers runs a laundry in the United States; the Moviegoer has two sisters abroad—one who went alone decades ago through the American military, and the other, later in her life, to start a small business and in the hopes of reforming a wayward, alcoholic husband. (When the Moviegoer's daughter, my old friend, thinks to emigrate with her daughter, she counts on initial help from one of these aunts.) As previously mentioned in this chapter, Hye-min's Grandmother's two half sisters are both in the United States, and Mi-yŏn's Mother has numerous second cousins abroad. Finally, the Education Mother, Mi-yŏn's Mother, and Mrs. Pak have all traveled abroad for leisure.

This digression reveals, even for a small cohort of women, the considerable extent and variety of contact beyond South Korea, be it as the sister of an early emigrant via the American military (the Moviegoer), the young wife of a graduate student on a shoestring budget (Mrs. Pak), the mother of a young woman working (illegally) in the service industry in Japan (the Janitor), the mother of an immigrant starting with nothing (the Laundress), the wife of a high-level corporate official sent abroad (Mi-yŏn's Mother), or the mother of a child studying abroad (Hye-min's Grandmother and Mrs. Pak).

While the paths are various, taken together they speak to a truism: rare is the contemporary—or, for that matter, the twentieth-century—Korean life untouched by immigration.

I came to the Twins' Mother more predictably, via an anthropologist whom I had met many years earlier. After only a casual acquaintance more than a decade earlier, we ran into each other in a small paper-goods shop attached to a large upscale apartment complex south of the Han River (Kangnam), an upscale residential part of Seoul that rose from nothing in the blink of history's eye (see Lett 1998, 101–109, for an excellent discussion of the real and symbolic differences between the neighborhoods north and south of the river). We exchanged phone numbers, research stories, and later she introduced me to three women: one who found it too painful to even talk about her life (we agreed not to meet again, but later shared a most enjoyable lunch for fun); another, almost a generation younger, who does not figure in this book; and the Twins' Mother, who appears only intermittently, being a half generation or so younger than the other mothers. For some months, I was privy to this anthropologist's perspective on these three women, as her friends, old school chums, neighbors, and mothers of her children's classmates. So much of the fieldwork culminating here was otherwise very private. Seldom did I hear other people's thoughts on the women appearing in this book.

Although my paths to the Education Mother, Mi-yŏn's Mother, the Twins' Mother, and Mrs. Pak are again various, I found them via middle-class coordinates: property, in the case of Mi-yŏn's Mother; well-educated children, in the case of the Education Mother and Mrs. Pak; and elite networks, in the case of the Twins' Mother. In short, I made my way to these women via my own networks as an educated American coming into contact with particular social circles in Seoul. Here too, however, I offer this neither to assert their class homogeneity nor fixity; as later chapters reveal, their class locations and identifications are never simple matters.

Class Maps

I began this book with class in mind. Class, that is, not as fixed location or uniform identification but as the networks—paths—and stories discussed in chapter 1. Indeed, class was addressed variously by the women. Furthermore, it was crosscut by accounts of origins and destinations that always complicate the picture: the future promise of a child's education, childhood class capital that did not translate into education attainment; the meaning of home ownership; the status markers, and so on. Chapter 5 takes up these issues through an extended discussion of the Laundress. Referring to the women I have now led you to, I touch upon some of the coordinates of their senses and sensibility of class (Urciuoli 1993). Beginning with work and education, classical indicators in the consideration of class, I then turn to property and to other more subjective factors in class identification.

These eight women are a diverse group on several counts. The Laundress, the Janitor, and Hye-min's Grandmother have worked in the formal economy throughout most of their lives; Mi-yŏn's Mother and the Moviegoer worked in their early lives, and the Twins' Mother, Mrs. Pak, and the Education Mother have been housewives. Among them, the Twins' Mother, Mi-yŏn's Mother, and the Education Mother have lived most prosperously, and the Moviegoer and Mrs. Pak comfortably. Two of them enjoyed little formal schooling (the Janitor, who remains functionally illiterate, and the Laundress, who is a daily newspaper reader), one did not make it to high school (the Moviegoer), two finished high school (Hye-min's Grandmother and Mi-yŏn's Mother), and two attended postsecondary schooling (the Twins' Mother and Mrs. Pak).

The Janitor thought aloud to say that she is not, after all, in the "lower class," because she owns a house (on class and housing see Lett 1998, 109–117). But she is also certain that she is not really a member of the middle class, because she does not have the requisite assets. She was certain, however, that she and her family live better than the "very poor" or "the lowest of the lower class." The story of her house, though, is a saga in its own right: for several years of her ownership she and seven children shared its loft (a small space quite literally in the eves of the rooftop) while she rented out the rest of the house in order to make house payments. The three-room house was a decent building in an otherwise shantylike neighborhood perched on a hill (called *taltongne*, or "moon villages") that had in the late 1990s recently gone the way of so many such neighborhoods: demolished to make way for high-rise new apartments that the displaced residents, political rhetoric to the contrary, could seldom afford to buy (Thomas 1993).

Although home ownership itself seemed to promise the Janitor a certain standing, that too was ambiguous. In another of our meetings, she declared herself at "the bottom of the humble classes (*sŏminjŏk*)," going on to say that many who rent by *chŏnse* live in fact much better than she does. The Janitor also spoke about her place in the world by describing the ironies, for example, of the rural/urban divide. Speaking about one of her brothers, on the one hand, she stressed, "In that countryside, he is at the top of the heap but that means nothing in terms of the city." On the other hand, both of that brother's children—a half-generation younger than her own—have made their way to postsecondary schooling in that rural region; contrasted here is that none of her children have made it past high school (discussed in chapter 4). Adding yet something else to the picture, the Janitor asserted that her salary was far too modest and that she deserved to make at least 50 percent more monthly.

The reader will meet the coordinates of the Laundress's class identification and location in detail in chapter 4, but in thinking about the Janitor, it is also worthy to note that the Laundress is resentful that she has been unable to purchase a home. In contrast with the Janitor, however, all of her children proceeded to some postsecondary schooling, two of them becoming teachers. We can recall, though, that she was quick to point out her eldest son's employment at a lower-tier high school, and, thus, his lower wages.

Hye-min's Grandmother, for her part—today residing in her eldest son's apartment, squarely middle class but by no means extravagant—experienced enormous downward mobility over the course of her marriage, at one time living with her whole family in a single room at the church. But she was crystal clear on one point: that "laborer for laborer" (or petty shopkeeper for shopkeeper, as she and her husband managed a small and modest dry-goods shop), she and her husband were never the same as other workers. Their poverty—over much of their married life—was from having failed miserably at business, which they had begun with the families of her sisters. She considered that she and her husband were different from other petty shopkeepers because she came from property and education and he had managed to extricate himself from his poor and uneducated family (see chapter 8).

Hye-min's Grandmother explained in detail just what set her and her husband apart from other shopkeepers, always referring to this work as "labor." She and her husband knew how to use their heads more effectively; they were better equipped to judge, for example, when it made sense to put things on sale, when it made sense to buy customer loyalty with small giveaway items, and how and when to most efficiently sell perishable items. Furthermore, throughout it all, she and her husband went to church on Sundays. Hye-min's Grandmother was certain that closing shop on Sundays, in spite of their hard times, won them a more faithful clientele. Interestingly, at the height of their earlier business that had failed and bankrupted them, they had not been faithful to the church: something she in fact blames their bankruptcy on. In short, Hye-min's grandmother described a range of business calculations that spoke to her and her husband's cultural and education capital, quite distinct from their poverty. Her conviction in the capital of her fine breeding and education aside, however, she resolutely identified herself as being against material extravagance of any kind, refusing taxis, expensive clothes, and extravagant dining out. She celebrated thrift of all variety.

The Moviegoer joined Hye-min's Grandmother and the Laundress in asserting her distance from the rich, in spite of owning an apartment: their privilege, their politics, and their corruption. The daughter of an abandoned wife and a ne'er-do-well father, she began laboring earliest in life among the women here: during her teens, in the industrial sector. Although her husband has been quite successful as a technical laborer, she expressed keen awareness of his particular skills having become quite anachronistic. Her husband left his company to work stints in the Middle East. It was those stints abroad and his severance pay from the company that allowed him to purchase an apartment and educate his children. In recent years, however, he has met with great difficulty finding work, a sore point for the Moviegoer, one that speaks of the injustices of South Korean society in which, for her, the "diligent are never rewarded." The reader will learn more about the Moviegoer's husband in chapter 6. The Moviegoer's children have all graduated from college, although her daughters' economic situations are not yet secured, as we learned in the previous discussion of her once-activist daughter.

The Education Mother and Mi-yŏn's Mother are, as I have suggested, unequivocally privileged: they own large domiciles in upscale neighborhoods. They have been able to help their twenty- and thirty-something children purchase apartments, a dream deferred for most young people in Seoul; they continue to improve their homes; they travel abroad for recreation; they swim at expensive health clubs; and although neither of them is educated beyond high school, they consider themselves to be in-the-know. None of this is to say that they consider themselves any less the products of South Korea's rapid-fire modernity (see H. J. Cho 2002). Mi-yŏn's Mother, the child of northern refugees in the aftermath of the war, suffered considerable displacement in her youth, and her adult life reveals enormous inner turmoil over the ways of the world and a difficult marriage. Emotional suffering of her sort runs independent of material well-being, as it does everywhere.

That leaves the Twins' Mother and Mrs. Pak. The Twins' Mother, as I have described, lives in a large apartment in a good building in an upscale neighborhood. Although her law-school-graduate husband has used his education and his education connections to secure a prosperous life, her class story too is not uncomplicated. She understands her husband to have married her for her *yangban* pedigree, in spite of her family's modest economic means. Her family's story is that of the *yangban* family (or family with such pretensions) that tethers its sons to their land, with family prestige in mind, primarily interested in their Confucian and ritual learning, in ritual observance, and in the maintenance of the family homestead and ancestral graves. This portrait is, in turn, posed in contrast with the sort of family that knows to educate its sons, to send them away, precisely to allow them to sever their ties with the land (see Janelli 1993, 33, on lineage struggles over property vs. education). I discuss a version of this human and social drama when I take up the film *Pak Sŏbang* (Mr. Pak), one of the melodramas of social transformation, in chapter 7. It is on account of this sort of background that the Twins' Mother, with her two-year college education, is in fact more educated than her brothers, discounting learning in the Confucian classics. For her own education, she has distant relatives to thank—a couple who took a liking to her, and in deference to the genealogical standing of her family in the lineage, entirely supported her high school and junior college education. Although stories of this sort are in fact quite widespread, hers is the only one like it among the women in this book.

As for the Twins' father, in spite of his prestigious education credentials (a "brand" that the Twins' Mother regrets having been so blinded by), he hails from a poor and uneducated family in which he is the eldest son and the only child to have succeeded. The Twins' Mother reserved her greatest hardship tales for her trials as the eldest daughter-in-law (i.e., the wife of the eldest son, an often unenviable position), and sister-in-law to her husband's many younger siblings. She felt that she single-handedly cared and provided for her in-laws and had been required to be unfairly generous to her siblings-in-law. These are details of family history, structure, and organization that are in fact inextricable from the easier coordinates of her class story: her upper-middle-class apartment and her husband's education and employment.

Mrs. Pak, the woman who thinks of herself, as does the Moviegoer of herself, as a woman to never have bettered the family economy, often spoke of her family's modest means, in spite of owning an apartment, of having educated two of her children abroad, and of her husband's respectable job as a professor at a fine university. Her identifications are mediated threefold. First, because of her much more prosperous natal siblings, who have been nothing but selfish. Second, because of her conviction that her own education—the only four-year college graduate among the women in this book—and development, through paid employment, were thwarted by her family's conservative gender ideologies. And third, because her husband, similar to the Twins' Mother's husband, is also the eldest of many siblings in a family with few resources. Mrs. Pak, like the Twins' Mother, has born considerable responsibility for those parents- and siblings-in-law. Here too these are origin stories and accounts of the web of kinship relations and the kinship distribution of goods and services that bear upon her class identities and identifications (see chapter 8).

Beyond material or education matters, the eight women are divergent on other counts—counts that matter for class: among them marriage and religion. Their marital fates have been various: two were widowed early (Hye-min's Grandmother in her fifties, and the Janitor in her early thirties); two have experienced abusive marriages (the Laundress and Mi-yŏn's Mother); two spoke of difficult marriages (the Twins' Mother and the Moviegoer); while three referred easily to their loving relationships (the Education Mother, Mrs. Pak, and Hye-min's Grandmother). Although a number of the women in this book would say they are Christian, including the Laundress, the Moviegoer, and Mrs. Pak, and Mi-yŏn's Mother was nominally Catholic, Hye-min's Grandmother had by far the most active religious life. It is relevant here to note that South Korea's Christian population is estimated to be about 25 percent, with considerably higher concentrations among women and urban dwellers (Korea National Statistical Office 1995).

The paths I took to meet these women are classed in their own right: by the range of personal connections they draw upon—siblings in relatively humble farming villages, children studying abroad, moneymaking activities (e.g., running a boardinghouse)—to the trappings of widely shared ideas of suffering (e.g., the introductions secured through Mr. Kang), the politics and education affiliations of their children, and the friends and acquaintances of an anthropologist. But these connections did their work at particular moments fixed in time. However, the women are not fixed in time, and neither are the complex workings of their class identities.

Chapter 3 illuminates the complexity of key words shared across these women's talk. Being hard to pin down, these words do justice to the subtleties of their social lives and times. The key words in chapter 3 are also ones inflected by class. The reader will begin to get a feeling for the various ways of which relative privilege and deprivation are spoken. Although chapter 3 is based on the primarily dyadic conversations I had with the women, I juxtapose their narratives in order to imagine these women, if not speaking to or about one another, at least as participating in a shared social world—one tied together by the sorts of paths and networks I have sketched in this chapter.

3

KEY WORDS

An openly acquisitive society, which is concerned also with the transmission of wealth, is trying to judge itself at once by an inherited code and by the morality of improvement.
—Raymond Williams, *The Country and the City*

During my conversations with the eight South Korean women I introduced in chapter 1, a particular world of words emerged, demanding that I take note of them. Over time I began to underline these words in my field notes, to anticipate them in my conversations, and to use them myself as prompts in conversations. In the earlier days of this project, I imagined that I would write a book with some sort of a glossary to serve as a guide to the women's stories. Over the course of the research, however, it became clear to me that the hardest words to gloss were these very words. This chapter introduces the reader to a dozen or so words that mark the talk of a generation of women. They are all words that do not do well solo because they so often comprise the refrains of stories and reflections, and because they make best sense in concert with one another.

Let me recall Mikhail Bakhtin's comment on words: "Each day has its own slogan, its own vocabulary, its own emphases" (1981, 263). Bakhtin also described the "language of a day, of an epoch, a social group, a genre, school, and so forth" (1981, 273), asserting that a word has "tastes of the context and contexts in which it has lived its socially charged life" (1981, 293). The words the reader finds here are indeed charged mementos of a day and a generation, fleeting and in flux. Bakhtin used the word "heteroglossia" to capture the "contradiction-ridden, tension-filled unity of . . . embattled tendencies in the life of a language" (1981, 272). Bakhtin tells us that the day or the moment asserts itself in words that are then shadowed by new words, or new twists on old words. Thus, "languages of various epochs . . . at any given moment . . . cohabit with one another" (Bakhtin 1981, 291). Language, then, is a stratified, sedimented affair in the sense that "at any moment of its historical existence, language is heteroglot from top to bottom: it represents the co-existence of socio-ideological contradictions between the present and the past, between differing epochs of the past, between different socio-ideological groups in the present, between tendencies, schools, circles and so forth" (Bakhtin 1981, 291).

I call the words discussed in this chapter "key words" after Raymond Williams' *Key Words*. Williams reserved key words for just the sorts of words for which "'I see from my *Webster's*'" simply will not do "for words of a different kind . . . for those which involve ideas and values" or "deep conflicts of value and belief" (1976, 17, 23). He was furthermore interested in the ways in which clusters of words work together (22). Williams recommends that the reader make his own way among the key words "to change as we find it necessary to change . . . [to] go on making our own language and history" (25). To remind the reader of the open character of inquiry, Williams' book ends with six numbered blank pages (344–349).

It is through Williams' spirit of conflict and change that sense is made of the cluster of words presented in this chapter. I suggest that these words are indices of change, and of the necessary conflict that change engenders. The words are dated in two senses: for belonging to a particular historical moment, and for being already out-of-date in South Korea for which the word "change" seems somehow understated. Change in South Korea is not of the step-by-step variety; rather, it races, leaving behind perhaps only the likes of plodding ethnographers to dare to author some pages, just as so many blank ones unfurl ahead. During a recent brief sojourn to South Korea, I asked an anthropologist acquaintance of mine about the field-research project she had described to me in enraptured detail several years earlier. She responded hastily, "Oh that." South Korea is simply not a place for very long-lived interests or projects. Of the ethnographer of South Korea who resides outside of the country, South Korea makes an anachronism. Of my reader—and of her encounters with South Korea—I ask that she read on in the spirit of Raymond Williams' blank pages, all six and many more of them. I look forward, to the future ethnographer who travels with clusters of key words, these or others, into the Web that is just now taking South Korea by storm.

It was only days after I returned from South Korea in summer 2000 that I heard a speaker describe the so-called new technologies and the ways in which the technological frontier redresses the basic condition of "human heaviness and slowness" (Weber 2000). Ethnography of the variety that the reader will find in this work is of the human, heavy, and slow variety. Furthermore, I consider myself lucky to have been able to slow down my research. As a nonnative speaker of Korean, I could stall a conversation so as to dwell on some of the words that appear herein. In the later years of this project, I had begun the project described in the preface, with its English-language ethnography of Korean Americans; I was surprised to find myself breathless with its pace, as I had no good reason to place conversations on hold, to put them on pause, or to draw them out where it suited me.

The words here are of a different kind than the lofty entries of Williams' handy collection. While Williams' words stretch from "aesthetic" and "alienation" to "western" and "work," the words here are largely of personal style, character, and disposition—words that the women who figure in this book used to describe themselves, and their friends, relatives, and acquaintances, real or mediated. The boxes in this chapter—abbreviated summaries of some of the chapter's anecdotes—are intended to serve as handy references back to these women and to highlight some of the key words.

I think of the women clustered here talking with one another, not because they did, or are in any real sense interrelated, but because I traveled among them intermittently over the course of several years and so often heard words and stories that would have been equally at home around other kitchen tables, in other living rooms or domestic spaces. Most of the women, in turn, seemed to understand the unspoken dialogue through which I was listening to them, and would ask about my other interlocutors, women they would likely never meet. Indeed, some of my own talk during the many interview hours was of other women far flung in Seoul's social geography. I offered such accounts because they asked about one another. As Vincent Crapanzano writes, "Dialogues . . . are never dyadic. Each partner in a dialogue is simultaneously participating in . . . shadow dialogues with absent (though significant) interlocutors who change as the primary dialogue changes" (1992, 6).

The phrases introduced here are entirely inextricable from their gender and class inflections. These words are conflicted in that they engage values and beliefs about ways of being female and feminine in South Korea, and about the distribution of wealth and privilege. Thus, the conflicts over beliefs and values revealed through clusters of little words describing this trait or that way of being tell a big story of considerable personal and social ambivalence. It is the multiple valences of these words that make them so ripe for ambivalence; or, rather, the ambivalence itself makes for the multiple, competing valences of words, their heteroglossia, in Bakhtin's terms. And, consistent with all the stories, episodes, and anecdotes of this book, these ambivalences reveal a cluster of women whose personal narratives take up, and sometimes bristle against, the largest political economic stories and structures of the day. Although some of the women engage these larger matters head on, with their own commentary, for others the engagement is stitched into the conflicts over the seemingly prosaic words upon which this chapter hangs. Importantly, in the frequent absence of explicit commentary offering its own conclusions, the social conflicts or debates that are played through these words are, as Williams argues for key words generally, open-ended and in flux.

The conflicts seeded in words come to life because historical flux lodges there. Aptly, Bakhtin writes of the traces in words, and of their accents and social atmosphere, and it is none other than the accent and atmosphere of a social historical moment, and of a generation, that this book aims to capture. "The word, directed toward its object, enters a dialogically agitated and tension-filled environment of alien words, value judgments, and accents, weaves in and out of complex interrelationships . . . and all this may crucially shape discourse, may leave a trace . . ." (Bakhtin 1981, 276). Bakhtin thus describes the word "brush[ing] up against thousands of living dialogic threads" (1981, 276). I aim here to partially follow a few of those threads as they reveal the workings of gender and class in their South Korean social and ideological specificity.

I have come to think that sheer repetition of these words acted as my teacher in the field; even in repetition, they refused to be fixed or pinned down. In later chapters, which preserve more of the course of women's lives, the reader will see that it was the sheer repetition of stories—from one meeting to the next—that similarly insisted upon analysis (see Kendall 1988).

I turn now to several clusters of words and phrases that are themselves quite intertwined.

A Kind of Woman

Through the talk of the Laundress and the Moviegoer, a cluster of words are shown to be alike for being at once disparaging and praising of a set of often feminized traits. More specifically, together these women engage a set of feminine descriptors (e.g., "nice," "kind") that are variously evaluated (e.g., as enlightened or inferior). The listener then is challenged to wonder: How are they using these words? Or prompted to consider: How do these women mean to situate themselves with the use of a set of descriptors including even derogatory terms such as "inferior" or "stupid"? Their talk will demonstrate that it is the words' competing registers that allow these women to render themselves with great subtlety in times in which, as I have stressed, the jury is not out on ways of being or living.

The Laundress

Let me begin with the Laundress, whom I always spoke to over her sewing machine and under the glare of a light bulb covered by a makeshift hat fashioned from a tattered magazine cover. Some feet away, her husband labored at an ironing board. We can recall that the Laundress is proud of her trade, in spite of its "lack of social prestige."

An ill-fated marriage proved the Laundress's steady conversational companion—particularly when her husband left the room. That a woman's fate turns on the "choice" of a marriage partner is commonsensical for South Korean women of this generation. The narration of marriage often reflects on the nature and circumstances of that choice (see Kendall 1996), and here we may recall the Education Mother's sister in the pocketbook story in chapter 1. Although the Laundress had entertained marriage proposals, even ones from men she had liked, she had left the matter of the arrangement to her family, caring only that the man be Christian, as was her family. "I couldn't choose my own life," is how she put it. But the Laundress was adamant in not blaming anyone for the marriage: "What do you get from griping to others?" She lived by the motto, she said, "The filial daughter is the one who lives well [i.e., or does not let on otherwise]." Many women of the Laundress's generation were introduced to their spouses by relatives and go-betweens. Although there was by her time some margin of choice in the case of such marriages, they would have still been considered "arranged" (chungmae) marriages in contrast to "love" (yŏnae) marriages (see Kendall 1996). As for her marriage, hers has been an abusive one. In reflecting on her very lack of choice—on not having chosen—two key words emerged as discursive parentheses: "gentle" (ch'akhada) and "inferior" (monnada).

To begin somewhere on these words, let us dabble for a moment in the 1992 Urimal k'ŭn sajŏn, a large and authoritative Korean dictionary (Han'gŭl Hakhoe 1992). The reader might notice that for some of the Korean words (e.g., monnada) the translations vary contextually. Also verb and adjectival forms (in both English and Korean) vary according to sentence form and usage; this reflects the fact that the distinction between what we call adjectival and verb forms in English does not always hold for Korean. With these conventions of translation and presentation, I have aimed to preserve the Korean for those who can discern the difference, while also adhering to English grammar and form—often a difficult balancing act.

Ch'akhada registers as follows: "That the heart or mind (*maŭm*), or actions or behavior (*haengdong*) are proper (*parŭda*) and gentle (*ŏjilda*)." Listed are several phrases using the word, including "a gentle (*ch'akhan*) sort of nature (*maŭmssi*)" and "our baby is really gentle (*ch'akhada*), isn't she" (Han'gŭl Hakhoe 1992, 4010). *Monnada* is described this way: "a person who can't be smart or intelligent (*saram i ttokttokhaji mothada*)"; "ugly or unattractive (*motsaenggida*)"; and "inferior or mediocre (*yongnyŏlhada*)." The following demonstrate the word's use: "if a person is told to capture an ugly (*monnan*) guy, he should look for a poor guy (*monnan nom chaba tŭriramyŏn ŏpnŭn nom chabaganda*)"; "no matter how great [*challada*—the opposite of *monnada*, discussed in the following paragraph] a person is, if he has no money, if he's poor, he will only be treated like a stupid (*monnan*) guy (*amuri challattŏrado ton i ŏpko kunghamyŏn monnan nom taejŏp pakke mot patko*)"; and "if a stupid (*monnan*) guy has a lot of money he can be treated well (*monnan nom to ton man issŭmyŏn choŭn taejŏp ŭl patnŭnda*)" (Han'gŭl Hakhoe 1992, 1447).

The Laundress clarified for me regarding her marriage that "it wasn't a matter of being gentle (*ch'akhada*) but rather of being stupid (*monnada*)"; so that, collapsing the subtleties for a moment, it was not about being proper or gentle but instead a question of stupidity or inferiority. In saying so, she prevented a gendered understanding of her story: that of a gentle and proper daughter who had dutifully agreed to her parents' marriage arrangements, quite a common course for women of her generation. Instead she weighed in about her *monnam*, or ignorance. If we listen further about her *monnam*, however, stupidity or ignorance ring a little differently, spilling outside of this or that personal trait. She explained, "Had I been more enlightened (*kkaen*), I would have chosen my own husband"; *kkaeda* is described in the dictionary as "thought and wisdom awakening or opening up" (Han'gŭl Hakhoe 1992, 646). In this sense *monnada* leaves the province of a static trait (to be dumb, smart, etc.) and walks squarely with the march of Korean modern history, where the matter of being enlightened (*kkaem*) stands for those who have been able to ride with the tide and pace of social change. The enlightened person (*kkaen saram*) is the one who knows and befriends that which lies over the horizon; I learned to hear "*kkaeda*" in South

Korea as a word on the move, always socially situated. The stupid person (*monnan saram*), then, is the one who lingers behind the times.

To understand being inferior (*monnam*), however, as somehow contra enlightenment or the fate of being left behind, does not capture another, and quite different, sense in which the Laundress used the word in talking about herself. On one occasion she had been describing her tendency to quietly and calmly (*ch'abunhage*) suffer things (*tanghada*), elaborating that hers is a "basic personality" that yields or concedes (*yangbo hada*) to others. She continued, "Perhaps what makes me inferior (*monnan kŏt ŭn*) is that I don't even care if I lose." Here, *monnada* captured something beyond a trait or tendency to yield: namely, not caring about the consequences. Here too, the Laundress seemed to challenge an easy, feminized portrayal of her traits. Although quiet suffering and concession are (like *ch'akhada*—to be gentle, proper, or kind) feminized traits in a gendered Korean universe, by insisting on adding that she didn't even care, the Laundress again insisted on a larger story—larger or different from that of the "good girl" or "the image of a traditional Korean woman who doesn't fight back," something she once said of herself. For the Laundress, then, *monnada* extends beyond feminine virtue: it is about at once not caring and caring—about having given up, not merely given in. Let us listen to the Laundress's elaboration that followed her saying, "I don't care even if I lose"—to where *monnada* turned a very different corner. She continued, "I hate to fight." But what she said next turned things topsy-turvy, calling attention to the conflicts inherent in *monnada* and *ch'akhada*, and in the conversation between them. "But, if you win a fight, have you really won?" From here, meanings veered, in the course of but a few sentences, in two very different directions. First, she spoke about her sister, "the sort of woman who doesn't yield, who cannot endure things (*ch'amta*), the kind who ends up fighting"—a woman who "because of her personality" has never been able to marry (an unenviable fate in the Laundress's eyes). In this first sense, the Laundress speaks to and for the utility of those feminine traits encircling *ch'akhada*. This recalls the similar terms of the Education Mother for her sister, in chapter 1.

In a very different second sense, however, she continued, "In South Korea it is those people who live ardently (*yŏlsimhi salda*) who lose." And we need only finish the thought that it is those people who live diligently—as she has—who lose (as she has) with a hard or ill-fated life. The Laundress repeated this thought on several occasions, which I take as a commentary of sorts on social ethics. Here we can begin to understand the particular way in which *monnada* takes on life for her. She was talking, as she so often did,

about having stood by her husband. She described waivering in her thinking: sometimes contending she was great (taedanhada) for having done so,
other times musing that she was stupid (monnatta). Here we glimpse the
possibility that, as with her description of the diligent loser, there is virtue
and ethical value to being inferior or stupid (monnam). The great virtue or
stupidity (and I suggest that these are not opposite sides of the coin) of
staying with her husband is far from just a celebration of feminine docility,
although for the Laundress, it is in part that as well:

> As for being unable to leave my husband, sometimes I think I am great
> (taedanhada), and sometimes I can only think that I am stupid (mon-
> natta). But I felt strongly that I had to take care of the children I gave
> birth to, that I had to raise them upright. Were they to have fallen, they
> would have blocked the path of others and their downfall would have
> been more than just a private matter. A criminal is just such a fallen
> tree. A tree [i.e., a child] that grows upright will not hurt the precious
> children of others, for which there is no indemnity. Even the thought
> of my children falling like that . . . I simply had to raise them upright.
> I never told them this, but I thought to myself that were they to fall, to
> go astray, that they would be better off dead.

The greatness, then, of the Laundress's being inferior (monnam)—and I
realize the liberty I take with her sentences in this arrangement—is the ethic
of, as she put it, "living with (by) the circumstances that were given to me."
On another occasion, she contrasted her ways with those of women who
some think of as great, and who put on airs (challan yŏja) and ignore their
husbands. She described that the children of such women grow twisted,
veering off course: "Just look at the youth violence today that we never saw
before." She went on: "They see their mothers making more money than
their fathers and because they come to think that their fathers are worthless,
they don't listen to them." Her conclusion: "Regardless, a woman must elevate her husband in the eyes of her children." I asked, "How did you come to
think that way?" She answered, "My mother lived like that, and I took a look
at society for myself, and that's the way I saw it too." Indeed, in another conversation she had described her mother too as a gentle woman (ch'akhan
yŏja). Here again, her argument strays from feminine virtue or docility in its
own right to a savvy reading of child rearing. Furthermore, her remarks extend to the workings of the formal and informal economies, which afford
some women moneymaking opportunities outside of the formal wage struc-

ture, opportunities that came to be seen by many in South Korea as embroiled in a feminized (demonized) graft economy (see chapter 2). Importantly, although caught up in a predominately male nexus of graft, these activities came to be branded, in the name of their housewife managers, female. Such accusations took on public life in both the Roh Tae Woo and Kim Young Sam regimes when, during various cleanup operations, the illicit activities of wealthy capitalist and political families often fell on the wives, who (disproportionately to the reality of things) were made into demonized media scapegoats for the ills of South Korean society. Indeed, although male institutions and ideologies such as the military, the state, and Confucianism have fashioned South Korean capitalism, women's greed and excessive consumption have often been named as social and moral culprits (see Nelson 2000). As Laurel Kendall notes, "Korean women make matches, make marriages, make money, make rituals for the spirits; and all of these activities fall under the shadow of disapprobation: money lending and real estate dealings are sordid and avaricious, religious activities are superstitious and sometimes disreputable, celebrations and ceremonious exchanges have the potential to become an unwholesome extravagance, a source of intra-familial strife, and a target of reformist campaigns" (1996, 219). In this way, the Laundress's descriptions of feminine virtue take on quite particular and historically specific meaning. Closer to home, we can recall that the Laundress managed to successfully make a teacher of one of her sons, the son who was the contact in my circuitous path to her.

The Laundress
CH'AKHADA to be gentle, proper, or kind
    ch'akhan (gentle); ch'akhage (gently); ch'akham (being gentle)
MONNADA to be inferior or stupid
    monnan (stupid); monnage (stupidly); monnam (being stupid)
KKAEDA to be enlightened
    kkaen (enlightened); kkaem (being enlightened)
TAEDANHADA to be great
    taedanhan (great); taedanhage (greatly)

(Speaking about her ill-fated marriage, having dutifully followed her parents' wishes in marrying her husband, and having been unable to leave him)   (Continued on next page)

> (The Laundress—Continued)
>   "I couldn't choose my own life."
>   "It wasn't a matter of being gentle (ch'akham) but rather of be-
> ing stupid (monnam) . . . had I been more enlightened (kkaen), I
> would have chosen my own husband."
>
> (Speaking about her "basic personality")
>   "Perhaps what makes me inferior (monnan kŏt ŭn) is that I don't
> even care if I lose."
>   "But [on the other hand], if you win a fight, have you really
> won?"
>   "As for being unable to leave my husband, sometimes I think I
> am great (taedanhada), and sometimes I can only think that I am
> stupid (monnatta)."

From her talk of upright trees (her three sons), she turned to the mothers of policemen who killed student activists in the line of duty. It was 1996
when she spoke of these mothers; such conversations focusing on the
1980s, a decade of popular struggle culminating in considerable democrati-
zation and labor reforms, grow remote in the twenty-first century. She described those mothers as having been made mute while the mothers of the
slain students can proclaim the injustice of things. "Life is such," she went
on, "that you can't say anything until you die . . . even if you live quietly, you
can never know what will happen. That is how I have lived, and that is how I
will continue to live." "That" refers, I think, to a quiet ethic of living with
or within one's circumstances, and with the humble sense that one is never
entirely the master of these circumstances. The Laundress thus asserted
that because life is an open-ended proposition, it demands such reserve.

I hope these brief glimpses at the stories and musings of the Laundress
begin to reveal the workings of a pair of words—ch'akhada and monnada—
and the words that cluster around them, including tanghada, ch'amta, and
taedanhada. As I have argued, these words talk to one another in such a way
as to resist easy class or gender attribution. First, there is the Laundress's
seemingly simple statement of her stupidity—for her own hand in submit-
ting to an ill-fated marriage. In this sense, she referred to having been out
of synch with the times, a mark also of a lack of privilege—her childhood
poverty. Also beyond easy gender attribution was her sense of monnam as

not caring, as somehow defiant. But we cannot rest easy here either because she also, in a very gendered way, contrasted herself with her sister, who did not give in or give up and has remained single and childless (an unthinkable fate from the Laundress's perspective). And here, in an inextricably gendered and more confident sense, the Laundress spoke of her own *taedanham* for having been traditionally female (*ch'akhada*) and for the virtue of her hard and legitimate work—work that she explained is classed, because it is physical labor. In these ways, these various considerations of even the few words I have introduced through the Laundress's talk, we find deep-seated social struggle over the right, just, or good way to live amidst changing times. We have seen that gender, its norms, its transgressions, figured throughout the Laundress's talk, and that class is an inextricable reference in the story of her own traits and her response to the world.

The Moviegoer

I turn now to the play of these and other words in my conversations with the Moviegoer. Like the Laundress, the Moviegoer often referred to her own gentle (*ch'akhan*) ways, but in an important cacophony with being stupid (*pabo katta*) and being lacking (*mŏngch'ŏnghada*). I also turn to the dictionary on these words and then to their play with *ch'akhada* in the Moviegoer's talk.

"*Pabo katta*" is a phrase that in my own informal lexicon I have always equated with "being stupid," realizing, however, that the translation does not entirely work. In its noun form, "*pabo*" refers to "a foolish (*ŏrisŏkŭn*), *mŏngch'ŏnghan* (the word I take up next), or *monnan* (the word the Laundress referred to so frequently—inferior, stupid) person." The dictionary offers the following exemplary sentence: "That guy seems foolish (*pabo katta*), but he isn't." I was interested to find that sentence, because it answered to, to some extent, my own malaise with easy translation: that the seeming fool might be nobody's fool, somehow captures the spirit of the sense in which I often heard the word used. I argue in the following that in parallel with what I reviewed in the preceding for *monnada* (and indeed *monnada* appears in the definition of *pabo katta*), the matter of "whose fool" is a creative rhetorical device employed by a number of the women who figure in this book.

"*Mŏngch'ŏnghada*" (to be foolish or lacking) emerges readily in the same cluster of words; "*pabo katta*" and "*ŏrisŏkta*" (foolish) are offered as synonyms of the personal noun form of "*mŏngch'ŏnghada*," "*mŏngch'ŏng'i*": "[One who is] foolish, whose mind is cloudy, and who cannot intelligently manage his own affairs" (*Ŏrisŏkko chŏngsin i hŭrithayŏ samul ŭl ttokttokhage ch'ŏrihanŭn him i ŏmnŭn saram*) (Han'gŭl Hakhoe 1992, 1377).

Let us continue now, before burying ourselves further in the very indices that I hope to unsettle, to the Moviegoer's talk. The Moviegoer, who described herself as barely clutching the trappings of the middle class, nonetheless lives considerably better than those among her sisters who remained in South Korea (two sisters left for the United States). Over the years she "lent" her sisters money that was yet to be repaid, a bit of a sore point for her husband. An overarching context for the comments that follow, on the matter of her having been generous with her sisters, are the differences that the Moviegoer repeatedly sketched between her and her husband: that she had been uninterested in making money, in doing her part to advance her marital family (i.e., beyond wage employment, where she knew that many women have been active), while he, on the other hand, had harbored visions of grander things for the family. She often mused that theirs was a mismatch because she could do nothing but disappoint him, and he could do nothing but set her ill-at-ease. He could not, for example, begin to understand her pleasure in movies, nor could she his material fancies and fantasies. But their marriage seemed to be a largely harmonious arrangement, not like that of the Laundress and her husband.

The Moviegoer often spoke of herself as seen by members of her family (particularly her husband) and by society at large. Here we can recall the Moviegoer's self-consciousness as the mother of a student activist. Building from these thoughts on her husband, she foremost imagined herself viewed as a woman who had chosen not to make money, a woman content not to occupy herself with the family coffers. All of the women in this book referred, from time to time, to themselves as seen by others. I do not, however, want to culturally reify such manners of speech—to suggest that there is something uniquely Korean here; I am inclined to think that a certain quotient of self-consciousness is a pretty ubiquitous human matter. But I am struck that in times of radical transformation in which, as Bakhtin wrote, whole languages rise anew day to day, the meaning and frequency of seeing oneself seen can be particularly intensified. It is in this context that the women were keenly aware of social types to which they did or did not conform.

Speaking about having "lent" money to her sisters, the Moviegoer reflected, "My heart is weak (*maŭm i yakhada*)." She paused, and mused, "How should I put it?" It was then that she spoke of herself seen: "From my husband's perspective, it isn't that I'm kind (*ch'akhada*), but that I'm stupid (*pabo katta*)." On many such occasions, I was struck that in spite of her seeming deference to the voices of others, real and imagined, she reserved considerable dignity for her own ways, in this case for her generosity to her sisters who had lived hard and poor—for her having been *ch'akham*. Also, the Moviegoer often subverted a pat sense of herself as somehow lacking. For example, she followed another account of having been generous to her sisters, in which she had referred to herself as foolish (*mŏngch'ŏnghage*), with this comment: "But I'm not extravagant. What would I do with being extravagant?" Unspoken here is a contrast with the pretensions of wealthy people—the types who "make money from money"; the foolish (*mŏngch'ŏnghan*) people in her world are rather those who are kind, generous, and ethical. Indeed, she went on to criticize the reward structures of South Korea, in which the diligent suffer, and the investors are rewarded. Again and again, she distinguished those who have worked hard from those who have made money from speculation. It is in this way that nothing short of what Bakhtin calls a socio-ideological context works its way through utterances, in this case *ch'akhada* and *mŏngch'ŏnghada*. All the while noting that others have called her—or gathered her to be—lacking (*mŏngch'ŏngham*), we can sense that in part she thinks of herself as having been *ch'akham*: upstanding in a social or ethical sense, albeit not upwardly mobile.

Constant figures in the Moviegoer's talk were her female counterparts: "distinguished" (*challan*) women, posed in contrast with stupid (*monnan*) women. She mobilized these women as a vantage point—women from which to imagine herself. Through the course of many conversations with the Moviegoer and others, I came to think of "distinguished" (*challan*) women in an ironic or sarcastic tone, a description reserved for women who rather than being somehow superior were those who tended to *think of themselves* this way. Although the dictionary offers a flattering portrayal of a *challan* woman: "A person whose basic composition is intelligent and distinguished" (Han'gŭl Hakhoe 1992, 4389), the word is often combined with the suffix "*ch'e*" or "*ch'ŏk*," meaning "pretense" or "pretending." It seemed to me that although the word was usually spoken without the *ch'e* or *ch'ŏk*, that it nonetheless most often sounded ironically, wavering between pretense and reality. Importantly, while the women in this book always used "*monnada*" (to be inferior or stupid) to refer to themselves, they reserved "*challada*" for other women, most often for composite social portraits of women, but in some cases for friends or acquaintances. In this way, then, "*monnan*," easily understood as the "opposite" of "*challan*" ("*mot/n-*" and "*chal-*" are in fact negative and positive prefixes respectively), was employed, as we have seen, in a similarly ironic fashion.

The Moviegoer's distinguished (*challan*) counterparts seemed to hover as shadow figures in her life. She elaborated once on being foolish (mŏngch'ŏngham), explaining that she has lived without self-confidence, "unlike those snobbish (challan) women." Earlier during our meeting that same day, she had spoken of being a foolish (mŏngch'ŏnghan) woman for having thought only about raising her children (again, rather than extending the family's wealth). She retreated to a description of ways in which she was wanting, especially in not having the courage or the confidence to do (economic) things. It became clear, however, in echoing the Laundress, she was quite confident about having done just that by rearing her family without falling prey to material desires.

In this more confident vein, the Moviegoer complained in another conversation that women's work at home is devalued and that people think of housewives as ignorant: "My children too, they don't think I have done anything. Everyone treats women like me like fools (pabo)." She explained, however, that this has not always been the case in Korea: "It used to be that a woman who was frugal at home and raised her kids well was the ultimate, but these days that isn't the path that the world about me is taking."

The Moviegoer often wavered in her assessment of personal assets. Describing that she is a person who simply lives with the reality meted out to her (chuŏjin hyŏnsil) (again recalling the Laundress) and that she is not one to be jealous, she once concluded with an ironic air, "So maybe I am a foolish (mŏngch'ŏnghan) woman." What followed in our conversation that particular day was, at first hearing, an odd aside about top'i yuhak. The word refers to the practice in which students who have failed to remain competitive in South Korea escape (top'i) their fate by studying abroad (yuhak). This is typically depicted as the province of the children of wealthy families who use their means to buy an education overseas. Many of the women I spoke with were fascinated by top'i yuhak, intrigued as to the inside story—a story that they hoped I might be able to illuminate. I was asked, "Is the United States [i.e., that supposedly 'advanced' country] really a place where South Korea's weakest students could succeed in school?" For the Moviegoer's part, she raised this aside about rich kids abroad to say that she would not be one to escape reality (i.e., one's failure in South Korea); she declared skeptically, "How can they possibly go to a foreign country and do better than they did in their own country?" What had become clear was an ethic to being lacking (mŏngch'ŏngham): a humble accommodation to social reality. At one point the Moviegoer was straightforward, if ironic: "Why do those 'distinguished' (challan) women who work even bother to have children?" That the accommodation to reality is gendered, in this case in the commitment to child rearing—and for the Laundress in the matter of standing by her ill-fated marriage—is not irrelevant but is by no means entirely subsuming either.

In musing on having reared her children (i.e., and done nothing more), on what were then escalating media stories of rich kids "escaping" abroad, and on the ethics of humbly living within the terms of one's reality (within one's means), the Moviegoer was, in the name of being lacking (*mŏngch'ŏnghada*), mounting a pretty robust critique of that very world that she imagines would see "a woman like her" as just that, a foolish (*mŏngch'ŏnghan*) woman. Through the play of being snobbish (*challan ch'ŏk*), being gentle (*ch'akhada*), being foolish (*pabo katta*), and *mŏngch'ŏnghada*, the Moviegoer gazed reflexively at herself and at the goings-on of her times, not unlike the Laundress with her extended metaphor about upright and fallen trees. The Moviegoer's reflections, always sharp, sometimes piercing, were, however, somewhat muted in the telling—as if she knew that her own trenchant critiques were made to be set aside by a world with another plan. After the this-and-that of her thoughts on *top'i yuhak* (study abroad in order to escape), for example, she retreated: "But then again, it isn't only one or two things about this world that I can't make sense of."

The Moviegoer
CH'AKHADA to be gentle, proper, or kind
    ch'akhan (gentle); *ch'akha'm* (being gentle)
PABO KATTA to be stupid or foolish
    pabo kat'ŭn (foolish); *pabo kat'ŭm* (being foolish)
MŎNGCH'ŎNGHADA to be foolish or lacking
    mŏngch'ŏnghan (foolish); *mŏngch'ŏngham* (being foolish)
CHALLADA to be distinguished, to put on airs, or to be snobbish
    challan (distinguished); *challam* (being distinguished)

(Speaking about having been economically generous to her sisters)
    "From my husband's perspective, it isn't that I'm kind (*ch'akhada*), but that I'm stupid (*pabo katta*).
    "But I'm not extravagant. What would I do with being extravagant?"

(Speaking about herself generally)
    "I'm stupid (*mŏngch'ŏnghada*) . . . unlike those snobbish or 'distinguished' (*challan*) women."   (*Continued on next page*)

The Moviegoer's sense of her own *pabo kat'ŭm* (stupidity, foolishness) or *mŏngch'ŏngham* (foolishness, lacking) takes on a different light in the context of distinctions drawn in conversations with her husband, an old friend, and neighbors in her apartment building. As mentioned, the Moviegoer often borrowed her husband's gaze—citing his perspective on her—to tease out the ways in which she was somehow out of step with the times. Lest I seem to be suggesting that irony and wordplay are the exclusive province of women, I want to add here a comment offered by the Moviegoer's husband (who is featured in some detail in chapter 6), unemployed and at home during much of the period over which I chatted and watched movies with his wife. On this particular occasion, the Moviegoer's husband returned home to find his wife chatting with me and an old friend of the family from the days when the family had lived in a company dormitory (i.e., housing provided by the company where the husband had been working) in a regional city. The Moviegoer and her friend (a woman) had been busily reminiscing about films and about the yesteryear raconteurs (*pyŏnsa*) of silent films. The Moviegoer's husband teased that the friend was looking younger than ever, and then, glancing back and forth between his wife and the old friend, joked, "Isn't it stupid (*pabo katta*) to just endure it all (*ch'amnŭn kŏt ŭn*), staying with the same husband for your whole life?" How is it best to understand the husband's stage-entrance one-liner?

The Moviegoer's husband's use of *pabo katta* was, I think, a play on his wife's long-standing use of the phrase for her own ironic and even sometimes triumphant sense of herself as foolish (*mŏngch'ŏnghan*) or stupid (*pabo kat'ŭn*). If a well-worn flourish of the Moviegoer is that she is "stupid" in the eyes of her husband, what did it mean for her husband to joke that perhaps her greatest stupidity of all was to have stayed with him for so long? His use of the word teased that she had stood by him in hard times, and hers in turn played with his visions of grandeur, largely unrealized, that paint her as somehow lacking. Although neither entirely affectionate nor wholly bitter—matters conjugal do not lend themselves easily to a facile read between a

line or two—there was endearment in the air: both his comment and her re-
ception of it. It was as if he had known, and in a sense he could have, the lilt
of the kitchen-table banter that afternoon. The visitor, bearing money and
gifts for the Moviegoer's only son who had just gotten married, had just
taken a job selling insurance, a not uncommon job for middle-aged women
returning to work. Such saleswomen typically peddle door-to-door, particularly to the doors of their relatives and friends near and far, cutting an image not dissimilar to that of the Tupperware lady in the United States. While
the visitor was sharply dressed, in a skirt and blouse tailored close to her
petite figure, the Moviegoer, by contrast, was dressed in the hues of a country ajumŏni (a middle-aged woman; on the term, see H. J. Cho 2002, 177,
188–190), in an over-sized dark, floral blouse and long skirt that did not
quite match, and she moved almost sluggishly about her small kitchen and
eating area. Within minutes the visitor turned to me to tease the Moviegoer:
chuckling, she said: "If a woman like [The Moviegoer] were to develop
(palchŏn hada) this [pointing to herself] is what she would become . . . so
you should interview me too [i.e., a 'developed woman']."

After a quick review of the well-being and whereabouts of their children,
the visitor and the Moviegoer began bantering about the sort of woman they
each are:

> VISITOR: I am South Korea's standard (kijun) woman. I am exactly in
>   the middle—I am the middle of the middle. [The Moviegoer] is a
>   really special person: she is much more than meets the eye. We
>   [i.e., South Korean women] aren't like American women, the ones
>   in films; we don't kiss our husbands good-bye in the morning
>   because we know that regardless we'll be living together for the
>   rest of our lives.
> MOVIEGOER: I don't think of myself as special at all.
> VISITOR: [The Moviegoer] is the image of the sacrificing Korean
>   mother.
> MOVIEGOER: I'm just your average (p'yŏngbŏmhan) mother, just a
>   woman who knows nothing but housework.
> VISITOR: She's just joking . . . she is so smart, and thanks to [her
>   daughter] [a reference largely to the daughter's social activism],
>   she's a mother with a heightened consciousness.

I have asked the reader to listen in on this moment to get a feeling for the
playful way in which many women talk about and among themselves; the

key words I am following in this chapter come to life in such dialogues. And words such as these are apt tools for such play, for they are flexible, not easily pinned down, and rife with conflict. I have also asked because I think that the "*pabo katta*" of the Moviegoer's husband's one-liner rings differently in light of this conversation. Queried, I think, is who among the two women was "developed," and who among husband and wife has really been the one to "endure"; at stake, then, are basic values about living, the times, and even social divides. I think that this is the way in which the discourses of families, of clusters, of places, and of generations (recalling Bakhtin) work.

As all dialogues begin already in the middle, the ethnographer, through no choice of her own, necessarily begins exactly there and amidst the thousand dialogic threads of which Bahktin wrote. We can wonder about any pretense to understanding, but we nonetheless forge ahead, grasping at the conversational threads. The Moviegoer's husband had come in on the middle of a conversation, but in a larger sense I had too, and it was one in which the Moviegoer's husband was very much present. It is not, after all, surprising that the Moviegoer and her husband would each offer their own sense of *pabo kat'ŭm*, each with its own taste.

Let me carry the husband's words—particularly those about ch'amta (to endure things), namely that his wife had been a fool to put up with him—to other conversations that similarly help us appreciate his seemingly off-handed remark. "Ch'amta" had been the word of the day during an earlier visit, when two women from the building had dropped by; the Moviegoer had been visibly both bored and a bit perturbed by them. One of them—a woman who had seemed interested in my approval—waxed poetic about the wonderful ways of young people today. The Moviegoer interrupted her to quip that young women should not be having kids if they do not plan to care for them themselves (referring primarily to those women who rely on their mother or mother-in-law for child care). In passing, the visitors mentioned a television film from the evening before about a woman caring at home for her mother with Alzheimer's disease. They added in unison that it is exactly the sort of women who have lived enduring this and that (ch'amko ch'amko) who end up demented like that. By now the Moviegoer, who was just then in what turned out to be the final stages of caring for her own Alzheimer's-inflicted mother, was visibly agitated and remarked, "Well in that case *all* South Korean women [i.e., of my generation] are going to get it [i.e., Alzheimer's disease] . . . (But) these days people don't endure (ch'amta) anymore and that is why there is so much divorce today; we [i.e., our generation] endured (ch'amta) in order to keep our families together. . . . Daughters these days are just like sons: They only think about getting help from their mothers [i.e., natal]. All they can think about when they come home is taking stuff away with them." When the visitors had gone—they had stopped by only to settle on a date for getting their hair permed together—the Moviegoer complained to me about how very tiring those women were and that she could not believe how they had lit into her on this and that; she seemed to imply "with friends like that . . ." But she returned to the matter of *ch'amta* and spoke—as she had in meetings before—about the burden born by both herself and her husband over the course of their marriage: "I know that I wasn't really the right person for him; I was lacking. It wasn't as if I was particularly pretty, and I did nothing in the economic sphere. It wasn't just me who had to endure (*ch'amta*). Who knows about those 'distinguished,' intelligent (*challan, ttokttokhan*) women [here I think she was in part thinking back to her visitors, and more generally musing over the matter of how different their lives were or were not, as the case may be] . . . Of course, I endured more than he did; we're not talking about a matter of a moment here or there [i.e., but about something constant]."

I began this discussion of the Moviegoer by noting the prevailing sense in which she saw herself seen, perhaps not surprising for a moviegoer—and for all those who find the likes of themselves in film and television. I close with another word for our cluster, "*taptaphada*" (to be frustrated, or to feel suffocated or stifled), for she often mentioned that this is others' sense of her. Moreover, she feels it herself and about herself (two somewhat different senses of the word). Least metaphorically, "*taptaphada*" refers to feeling stifled or suffocated; describing people, it can also refer to their narrow views or their lack of versatility. The two senses of the word seem to combine interestingly when signifying what it is like for others to behold a frustrating (*taptaphan*) person or situation—namely that it is somehow suffocating to witness such stifled situations or persons. When the Moviegoer spoke of herself as a frustrating (*taptaphan*) person, she seemed to both refer to her sense of herself and to her sense of what it is like for others to behold her—foremost her stasis. She often used "*taptaphada*" to describe tradition-bound people in soap operas who seemed unable to get on with their lives. For herself, and media protagonists, she was foremost commenting on their inability to act or to act in synch with the times. About one of the soap operas that she really did not like but watched faithfully nonetheless, she said, "There is no content to that thing; it is nothing but frustrating (*taptapham*), just like daily life—how long are they going to let it go on?"

I began on the Moviegoer's own rhetorical use of "*pabo katta*," that some might consider her stupid for having been generous (lending money to her sisters, etc.), and for not having made any money herself. On the matter of her sisters, however, she left open the possibility that it was about her being a kind person (ch'akhan saram). She asserted that she might be a foolish person (mŏngch'ŏnghan saram) but that she was not extravagant; thus she offered that those who are stupid (pabo katta) and foolish (mŏngch'ŏnghada) are generous and not extravagant. It was snobbish or "distinguished" (challan) women whom she imagined (alongside her husband) looking on at her "foolish" ways. She was lacking (mŏngch'ŏnghada), "unlike them." But it was clear—as it was for the Laundress—that she was quite certain about the virtues of staying at home and raising children and of living within the reality one is dealt. It was here that she concerned herself with those who escape to study abroad—for she is not one to "escape reality." The discussion with her husband revealed the way in which pabo kat'ŭm had likely been bandied about in the household, suggesting that it also affectionately implied noble virtues, conjugal commitment, and fidelity. With the old family friend, we learned that an "average mother," not unlike a foolish (pabo kat'ŭn) or lacking (mŏngch'ŏnghan) person, can be quite a distinguished or intelligent one.

On "ch'amta" (to endure), the Moviegoer sang out the virtues of bearing with circumstances and criticized the youthful hubris that she thinks plagues South Korean women today—women like her visitors who had blamed South Korean women for enduring (ch'amnŭn kŏt). And she then spoke of her own marriage, a story about bearing with things. Her use of "taptaphada" reveals her own sense of the taste and style of her daily life, somehow constrained and a bit suffocating to behold. Made clear between the lines—in parallel with the Laundress—are several contests: about gender roles, marriage, greed, social mobility, and laudable human characteristics. The Moviegoer's is not a monolithic voice—she and others struggle over the same changing times.

The Twins' Mother

I turn here to the Twins' Mother, the acquaintance of the anthropologist who lived in a prosperous apartment complex, because of the robust way in which she discussed the effects of being distinguished (challada)—that strange space between greatness and its pretenses and pretentiousness that we met briefly in the Laundress's comments on women who ignore their husbands, and in the Moviegoer's sense of women unlike herself—women who would, she surmised, look down on her, women who work to make money. Interesting for my purposes here is the Twins' Mother's way of thinking about character and privilege. For her, many of the traits we have explored, from inferiority *(monnam)* to foolishness *(mŏngch'ŏngham)*, are the products of stress—stress from not having been able to study or to assert oneself in the company of others. Of her husband, the lawyer from a humble background, she described, "The 'distinguished' *(challan)* [twins' father] can only think, 'I am the greatest.' " She reserved *"challada,"* then, for those at the social and education pinnacle, like her husband. For the Twins' Mother (the boy-and-girl twins were in high school at the time), the matter of *challada* was somewhat different than for the Moviegoer or the Laundress; namely, it was neither reserved for women, nor for a vague category of people she did not necessarily know firsthand. Rather, the *challan* person in her midst was her husband: a graduate of Seoul National University's department of law. Her curse, she described, was having chosen to marry by "brand," namely a graduate of the most prestigious department of the most prestigious university in South Korea. For her, the marriage had been a way of escaping—hoping to leave behind the cultural trappings (often dubbed "Confucian") of her own impoverished *yangban* household.

Korea's premodern status system was a rigid hierarchy of fixed stations in accordance with Confucian ideology. The state bureaucracy was recruited through a state examination system that rewarded Confucian learning, and *yangban* was a status distinction reserved for the Confucian-scholar officeholders and their descendants. By the end of the Chosŏn dynasty, however, the system of status hierarchy had become quite fluid, and *yangban* status allegedly became increasingly available for purchase by merchants, who had been traditionally shunned according to Confucian ideology, or by others with economic resources. *Chokpo*, genealogies in which elite families recorded their pedigrees, actually became available for purchase in this period (Wagner 1974). To this day most families—and particularly those with *yangban* histories or pretensions—maintain their *chokpo*, although many of these have been fashioned in the contemporary era. Today, as the historical markers of status become remote and hard to locate, the claim to *yangban* origins seems almost ubiquitous. Also, for some users, *yangban* indexes an individual's or family's social acceptability more generally.

The Twins' Mother had wanted to walk away from *yangban* trappings: from, for example, the tables of ritual offerings piled high during the frequent *chesa* (ancestral services) of her father's lineage. She thinks of her marriage to her husband, and of her education before that (at a junior college—

she managed to become more educated than either of her brothers, who were raised to stay on the land in order to sustain their illustrious patrilineage), as the fruit of her own considerable ambition (*yoksim*). She sometimes meets with the wives of other men who similarly graduated in law from Seoul National University; they agree that were they to meet someone today about to venture into such a marriage (she went on humorously, but clearly serious about what she was saying), they would pack food, travel to the young woman's home, and camp out until they had convinced her otherwise.

The Twins' Mother spoke often of "stress" (*sŭt'ŭresŭ*): the stress of living with someone with a different level of education attainment. About her two-year college, her husband chided, "You call that a college?" and of her college alumni gatherings (it is quite typical for women and men to gather periodically with their same-year departmental classmates), he quipped, "What sort of an alumni group is that?" Being *challan*, she described, meant "getting no stress from anybody": "*Challan* people like him [her husband]— what stress could they possibly get from others?" She took it further, asserting that "*all personality* is made from complexes for not having been able to study." Given that her husband was afforded the best education possible, it was inconceivable to her that he could ever be the bearer of stress from anyone else's sense that he was not measuring up. "*Challan* people, then, are the ones who give stress to others, the stress of feeling inferior." She described that, regardless of what it is her husband says to her, his very manner of speech (*malt'u*) is stressful for her. She figured this was the same sort of stress that burdens the poor in their dealings with the rich. She explained, had she married a wealthier man, the stress would have come from his entire family. Education stress, however, in her case is "a matter just between the two of us [i.e., husband and wife]."

The stress the Twins' Mother described also had a life for her twins (her only children), in high school at the time. Her daughter, she explained, was an excellent student, taking after her husband, while her son was but a mediocre student just like she had been. Her son, for his part, lived with stress imposed on him by his sister. She described the typical dinnertime scene in their home: while father and daughter talked about matters that "make one's head hurt," she and her son did nothing but "enjoy and praise their food." And, the Twins' Mother continued, each evening she waited quietly for the inevitable moment when her husband would remark that the son took after her, followed by her daily refrain, "Yes, yes, you are absolutely right."

The stress from her husband's attitude made her *taptaphada*, she explained—like the Moviegoer—and impatient *(kŭphan)*. Interestingly, the story of education stress has deep roots in the Twins' Mother's life, whose own mother had suffered great stress from the enormous difference in education between her and her husband. The Twins' Mother described growing up hearing nothing but her father ordering her mother around. Before leaving the twins' father behind, however, I want to briefly complicate the picture. In spite of the Twins' Mother's blanket statements about her husband's status, his imperviousness to stress from others, and the seemingly straightforward workings of elite education capital, she also understood that things were not that simple. Some of his character and its real effects on others, particularly on her and on her son, she explained, were the result of his own frustration at never having passed the South Korean bar exam, which very few do, and at never fully realizing his elite-most education. Likewise, returning to her own father, she reflected that he too was a source of greater stress for others because of his own frustrations, not having been able to fully exercise his status. This book repeatedly asserts the ways in which class, or more broadly systems of social capital, are entirely inextricable from the workings of narrative, gender, family, and identity. The matter of not being able to fully execute or realize education capital is intimately tied to changing historical circumstances that continuously refashion the workings of class, culture, and education.

The Twins' Mother
CHALLADA to be distinguished, to put on airs, or to be snobbish

(Speaking about the difficulties of living with her overeducated husband)
   "The 'distinguished' *(challan)* [twins' father] can only think, 'I am the greatest.' "
   "*Challan* people, then, are the ones who give stress to others, the stress of feeling inferior."

Another Kind of Woman

If the women we have just heard from (the Laundress, the Moviegoer, and the Twins' Mother) all imagined themselves to be the brunt of some social criticism—for being ignorant, or out of synch with the times, or stifled/stifling in some way—Hye-min's Grandmother and the Janitor managed to employ the same cluster of words and yet present themselves as anything but all of that.

Hye-min's Grandmother

Hye-min's Grandmother is a woman convinced that in changing times it is folly to cling to old ways. She was not one to endure things (ch'amta), she had little patience for feminine reserve, and she celebrated a healthy impatience with the world, the very quality that allows a person to develop, to ride the times. We can recall Hye-min's Grandmother worked as a petty shopkeeper after her husband's company went bankrupt; she spoke with great confidence about the skills and cultural capital that set her apart from the other small shopkeepers in her midst. Hye-min's Grandmother struck me as being, above all, happy, spirited, and unfettered by convention; this is not to say that hers has been an easy life—it has not. But she had little patience for those who wallow in self-pity, are mired in the past, or caught up in airs. She declared that she had been living "right under God" and continued, laughing, to say that she would "receive a passport to heaven." She described that hers is a family of strong, capable, and even masculine women and was less sympathetic toward those lacking such attributes. About uneducated people, "the kind who can't make out even a single letter of English," Hye-min's Grandmother described, "there is something stifling (taptapham) about them." She seemed to be saying that she could not be bothered with whatever it was that held them back.

The constant female others in Hye-min's Grandmother's stories were the feminine, stifling (taptaphan) women in her late husband's family (discussed at some length in chapter 8); we can recall that the Moviegoer used "taptaphada" to refer both to herself and others, and that the Twins' Mother described her husband with the term. Hye-min's Grandmother set these country women—who had not been able to make it to the city—against the "wild" (in English) "masculine" sorts of her own family. She described those other women as gentle (ch'akhan) and submissive (sunhan), and as the type of women who silently endure (ch'amta)—the sorts of words through which both the Laundress and the Moviegoer partly imagined themselves seen. Hye-min's Grandmother explained that these are the kind of women who lose out, who are unable to develop (paljŏn hal su ga ŏpta)—exactly the observation that the Moviegoer's friend had made about the Moviegoer. In

Hye-min's Grandmother's view, the type of women (like herself) who succeed, who make it in the city, are women who can distinguish right from wrong (ttajida), who can judge people and the situation at hand, and who have the capacity to be rude (sanapta); with "ttajida," Hye-min's Grandmother put a very positive spin on a word that can have negative connotations—a move that she made with many words, foremost "kŭphada," describing the sort of woman who does not endure, who is impatient and headstrong. The dictionary describes a kŭphan temperament as exactly that of a person who is impatient (ch'ojohae hanŭn) and unable to bear with things (ch'amŭl su ga ŏpnŭn); the Laundress and the Moviegoer, for their part, were invested precisely in bearing with things, and in conforming to circumstances.

For the impatient (kŭphan) person, the dictionary lists a number of interesting aphorisms, all resolutely negative: "if you are impatient (kŭphamyŏn) you will end up wrapping the thread around the needle [i.e., rather than threading it]"; "if you are kŭphada you will [need to] hug the leg of the Buddha (kŭphamyŏn puch'ŏ tari annŭnda)" (i.e., "if you consistently work diligently, regardless of what happens you have nothing to be embarrassed about [i.e., you won't need to hug the Buddha's leg])"; "being impatient (kŭpham) is such that you go to the well, thinking you can ask for rice water tea (kŭphaginŭn umul e ka sŭngnyŭng ŭl tallagetta)" (i.e., if you are only thinking impatient (kŭphan) things on the spot, your plans will go awry) (i.e., because you have not gone through the proper steps, you will come up empty-handed) (Han'gŭl Hakhoe 1992, 580).

For Hye-min's Grandmother, however, "kŭphada" was valorized precisely against a feminized other—the sort of woman who has not managed to ride the waves of her world and times. This is not to say, however, that Hye-min's Grandmother espoused unbridled personal ambition. To the contrary, in the discussions of greed and generosity that follow, we see that she asserted a very clear moral position. So often Hye-min's Grandmother told me that all of the women in her family are impatient (kŭphada). People who are not, she said, simply do not get things done: "People who are not impatient (kŭphajianŭn) think, 'Oh, if not today, tomorrow; if not tomorrow, the next day,' and so on." And Hye-min's Grandmother prided herself on getting things done—on having worked her way out of the depths of poverty. Every time Hye-min's Grandmother brought up variants of the word kŭphada, it was to argue against letting the world pass you by: "Where the person with an impatient (kŭphan) personality will get a persimmon from a persimmon tree, the submissive (*sunhan*) person will just stand there [i.e., dumbly] until it falls." Being submissive (*sunham*) is another trait that is often feminized. Although Hye-min's Grandmother's claim on the world contrasts with some of the other women introduced thus far, they spoke in parallel terms: Hye-min's Grandmother asserted that women should grab the world by its horns, while the Laundress and the Moviegoer opted (at least in their speech) for meeting the world as it came to them.

Not surprisingly, so as to argue for a changed world, Hye-min's Grandmother confronted head-on the very meaning of being feminine; the Laundress and the Moviegoer, on the other hand, weighed in against some of these transformations. Hye-min's Grandmother spelled it out this way:

> Being a feminine woman isn't merely about being gentle (*yamjŏnham*). Being gentle (*yamjŏnham*) is in fact being stupid (*pabo kat'ŭm*): Just sitting there, motionless, without knowing anything, having no words . . . It used to be that being submissive (*sunham*) was about not speaking the truth, never contesting things: agreeing that 'this is an apple,' even if it wasn't. In times past, being feminine was about being obedient (*sunjong ham*) and being stupid (*pabo kat'ŭm*): the woman who says nothing but "Yes, yes, that is exactly the way it is."

In many places in my notes I found women indicating that "these days" the traditional feminine virtues are nothing but foolish (*mŏngch'ŏnghan*). Hye-min's Grandmother spoke interestingly about the changes that have, she thinks, necessitated new ways of being generally, and particularly of being feminine: "My mother was an obedient (*sunjong hanŭn*) woman, but when all the men died, there was no one to put her down anymore and she became very strong." Here she suggested, albeit obliquely, that the matter of being obedient (*sunjong ham*), clustered as we have seen with *sunhada*, *ch'akhada*, and *ch'amta*, is about gender and other relations, about being "put down," as her mother had been, until in her case the men died off. The women in her family, her mother and her three sisters, were all widowed early; they did not have the luxury of being anything but headstrong (*kŭphan*) is how I think she would have put it.

Hye-min's Grandmother set her own terms: she was content to turn words on their head for a world transformed—a topsy-turvy world demanded no less. Foremost, she wrested personality from her understanding of its traditional coordinates: hers are the feminine virtues of a new world—intelligence and a healthy impatience with that world.

> *Hye-min's Grandmother*
> YAMJŎNHADA to be gentle or modest
>   *yamjŏnhan* (modest); *yamjŏnham* (being modest)
> PABO KATTA to be stupid or foolish
>   *pabo katʼŭn* (foolish); *pabo katʼŭm* (being foolish)
> SUNHADA to be submissive or obedient
>   *sunhan* (submissive); *sunham* (being submissive)
> SUNJONGHADA to be gentle or obedient
>   *sunjong hannŭn* (obedient); *sunjong ham* (being obedient)
>
> (Asserting the need for new ideas—for a new day—on what it means to be "feminine" in South Korea)
>   "Being a feminine woman isn't merely about being gentle (*yamjŏnham*). Being gentle (*yamjŏnham*) is in fact being stupid (*pabo katʼŭm*) . . . It used to be that being submissive (*sunham*) was about not speaking the truth . . . being feminine was about being obedient (*sunjong ham*) . . . : the woman who says nothing but 'Yes, yes, that is exactly the way it is.' "

The Janitor

As with Hye-min's Grandmother, the matter of having an impatient or headstrong (*kŭphan*) temperament was a constant refrain in my meetings with the Janitor. She described that hers was "a temperament like my father's." Being *kŭpham*, the Janitor continued, means that she has no ability to bear with things (*chʼamta*) and that she consequently gets in fights all the time. Speaking about when people do things she does not like, she explained, "I should just let things go (*chʼamta*), but I can't. I can't just be quiet. That is why I say that my temperament is a bad one." She attributed her "bad" temperament to the combination of being smart and entirely unschooled, though we can recall her conviction that her illiteracy was nothing to be ashamed of. And all of this, she said, made her frustrated (*taptaphage*), in the sense, I think, that the world was not to her liking but that she had little ability to control it. While the Moviegoer spoke of herself seen, or perhaps misunderstood, as suffocating (*taptaphan*), the Janitor's sense of herself as *taptapham* refers to an impatience that made her get angry and spurred her to action. Like Hye-min's Grandmother, she also described herself as one who knows right from wrong (*ttajida*) and acts on it.

The Janitor knew what was right and what to do. The problem though, she once stated, was that the world was not fair. Then she launched into a lengthy discussion of her unfair wages, in spite of government designations that ensured a higher wage for janitors. An impatient or headstrong (kŭphan) character is what you need to survive, she once offered, in order to have a capacity for life (saenghwalryŏk): "People with a kŭphan character (sŏngjil) know how to pick themselves up, to solve situations." She had just then been contrasting herself with her one brother whose character was more middle-of-the-road (pot'ong ida) than the rest of the siblings (i.e., he isn't impatient), describing how he had been unable to get out of a bad marriage: "I tell him that he is stupid (monnatta) to be suffering under a wife like that; my other brothers would have thrown her out a long time ago." To recall from chapter 2, the Janitor is the sister of the several brothers I met in the countryside during my 1980s field research. She continued that a person without "character" of this sort becomes incapable of doing anything (munŭnghage toeda—a phrase discussed in the following paragraph). An impatient (kŭphan) personality, then, is a necessary one, a survival template, especially for the uneducated. But, she declared, the kŭphan person is "a tiring sort to live with." She continued that she was in fact tiring and difficult to be with, as was her late husband. Describing one of her impatient (kŭphan) brothers, she said, "Why, he once got so mad at his wife that he burned down one of the rooms in their house!"

The Janitor explained that munŭnghan (incapable) men are equally tiring

---

The Janitor
CH'AMTA to endure things
  ch'amnŭn (enduring); ch'amnŭn (being enduring)
KŬPHADA to be impatient or headstrong
  kŭphan (impatient); kŭpham (being impatient)

(Speaking about the virtues and difficulties of her own temperament)
  "I should just let things go (ch'amta), but I can't . . . That is why I say that my temperament is a bad one."
  "[A kŭphan character like mine] is a tiring sort to live with . . . Why he [a brother resembling her] once got so mad at his wife that he burned down one of the rooms in their house!"

---

and difficult to live with. She went on to say, "Thankfully, my husband wasn't one of those." "Munŭnghada" (to be incapable) figures very largely in chapter 7, where it describes the father of Mi-yŏn's Mother. "Munŭnghada" was more often applied to men, although its spirit is one we have seen here in the cluster of words that include "pabo katta," "mŏngch'ŏnghada," and "monnada." It speaks literally to a lack of ability or incompetence, with "mu" as a negative prefix, in this case meaning "lack," and "nŭng" the Chinese character for ability. Most narrowly, for men, it refers to those who are unable to support themselves and a family, and who have no life ability (saenghwalryŏk), was how the Janitor put it. In my experience with the word, I have been most struck by the ways in which people situate it socially and historically; it seems to refer to an inability to get on with life or to jump into life at a particular time and place, namely postliberation South Korea. The Janitor explained that "munŭnghan namja" describes "men who, even if they are educated, send their wives off to work while they do nothing . . . In a word, they are men who, even if they have no money, don't think to go out and work." Explaining incapable (munŭnghan) men to me further, she added:

> They are men who went to college but rather than settle on a job that isn't up to their education level, decide to not work at all. And they don't have any money to start a business with, so they just play, and then over time they become stupid (pabo katta). The problem is that there are lots of men like that—men who won't swallow their pride in order to do whatever it takes to educate their children. And then they turn to drinking—all because they won't go out and push a cart (riŏk'a) [i.e., become a street vendor]. And for the women who marry those sorts, life is nothing but suffering (kosaeng).

Although the Janitor did not limit her remarks on incapable (munŭnghan) men to those with yangban pretensions, she joined many of the women in suggesting that yangban pretensions have often mediated against a healthy adjustment to a changed world (see chapters 1 and 3 in Jager 2003, on the figure of the weak male as a national allegory in Korea; see also Robinson 1991; Schmid 2002). These sorts of reflections are part of larger cultural calculations about the ways in which personalities are made in child rearing—reflections that are often classed, in the ways suggested by Carolyn Steedman (1986) (see chapter 1). People consider, for example, what it is that makes for a munŭnghan man. Most often these are theories about the effects of adult ideas that were somehow extreme or out of synch with the times; importantly, it is often the anachronisms of older systems of social privilege (e.g., *yangban*) that are highlighted in such accounts. The Education Mother from the pocketbook story in chapter 1, for example, was convinced that behind incapable (*munŭnghan*) men, her brother and her brother-in-law among them, were parents—particularly mothers—who had raised their sons ever so preciously, leaving them to know no one but themselves and their own self-importance, and thus having few resources with which to survive socially, to weather life's storms. The Education Mother was convinced that her brother, for example, had been raised to be incapable (*munŭnghage*) in large part because of *yangban* trappings, accentuated by her mother's having been abandoned by her husband.

> The Janitor
> MUNŬNGHADA to be incapable
>   *munŭnghan* (incapable); *munŭngham* (incapability)
>
> (Talking about her brothers, and men in general)
>   "Incapable (*munŭnghan*) men are equally [in comparison with impatient (*kŭphan*) men] tiring and difficult to live with."
>   "Incapable (*munŭnghan*) men [are the sort] who, even if they are educated, send their wives off to work while they do nothing."
>   "They [incapable (*munŭnghan*) men] are men who went to college but rather than settle on a job that isn't up to their education level, decide not to work at all . . . for the women who marry those sorts, life is nothing but suffering (*kosaeng*)."

Thinking back to both Hye-min's Grandmother's and the Janitor's ambivalence about traditionally feminized attributes (in favor of traits that are more often disparaged), it is interesting to note that traits such as *munŭnghada* are gendered quite particularly in their negative attribution to men.

The Gender of Greed

Here I take up conversations that wrestle with gendered attributions of greed and, conversely, of generosity—*yoksim* (greed, ambition) and *pep'um* (generosity). These conversations tarry closest and most explicitly to a stratified world in which personal attributes correlate with material desires and instrumental behaviors.

Hye-min's Grandmother

Hye-min's Grandmother, the woman so convinced about the impatient (*kŭphan*), masculine character of the women of her family extending to Hye-min, was equally certain that knowing how to be generous (*pep'ulda*) was also a family trait, beginning particularly with her late mother. She often contrasted generosity (*pep'um*) with *yoksim* (greed, ambition) and even described *pep'um* as "having no *yoksim*." *Pep'ulda* is described in the dictionary as "giving others benefits, such as providing money or help (*nam ege ton ŭl chugŏna il ŭl towasŏ hyet'aek ŭl chuda*)" (Han'gŭl Hakhoe 1992, 1759). Several sentences elaborate that *chasŏn* (charity), *sŏng'ŭi* (faith or sincerity), and *ŭn-hye* (kindnesses) can be extended in the name of *pep'ulda* (Han'gŭl Hakhoe 1992, 1759). For "*yoksim*," the dictionary offers: "The heart that wants to do more, or possess more, than is reasonable for one's station in life (*punsu e chinach'ige hagoja hagŏna chinach'igo sip'ŏ hanŭn maŭm*)" (Han'gŭl Hakhoe 1992, 3128). The dictionary continues with several expressions, including "*yoksim* can kill (*yoksim i saram chuginda*)" to mean that "unbounded *yoksim* is such that people lose their ability to discern right from wrong, and can even end up doing dangerous things without hesitation (*yoksim i nŏmu chinach'imyŏn sari rŭl punbyŏl haji mothago wit'aeroun il kkaji kŏrikkim ŏpsi hage toenda*)" (Han'gŭl Hakhoe 1992, 3128).

During one of our conversations, as I jotted things down, Hye-min's Grandmother asked for the pen and then wrote, "I have a generous, loving heart and no greed (*pep'ulgo sarang hanŭn maŭm i itko yoksim i opta*)." She elaborated: "Blood can't be deceived—I have my mother's personality." To describe how her mother knew how to be generous (*pep'ul chul aratta*), she explained that lacking *yoksim*, her mother had used the money they earned (on a prosperous farm) to help people in need, and that there had been rumors of her mother's goodness far and wide.

It was not until our eighth meeting, and by then a friendship over some years, that Hye-min's Grandmother connected the word "*pep'ulda*" to religion. When Hye-min's Grandmother used "*pep'ulda*," she had been describing how her sister knew how to be generous (*pep'ul chul aratta*), and she said, "just as our mother had before her, just like Jesus." The reader will recall that Hye-min's Grandmother and I met most often after services, on the steps of the church. As an elder in her church, Hye-min's Grandmother traveled forty or so minutes (taking two buses) to church almost every day.

Although this commitment to church in part bespeaks her station in life as a widow who, by the late 1990s, had been entirely liberated from caring for grandchildren, it also speaks to her religious conviction.

The portrait that emerged in the earlier discussions of Hye-min's Grandmother—of a woman who is brisk, active, and humorous, and has little patience for the plodding or the tradition-bound in her midst—takes further and delicate shape as we listen to her thoughts on *yoksim*. She drew a distinction between indulging greed (*yoksim ŭl purinŭn kŏt*) and living diligently (*yŏlsimhi sanŭn kŏt*). Much of what she had to say aimed to strike a balance between the demands of modern living and those of the human heart.

> As for people who dress well, who make money so as to live well—what an embarrassing thing to have such *yoksim*. Furthermore having *yoksim* doesn't guarantee the good life anyway. To live diligently (*yŏlsimhi sanŭn kŏt*), though, is a whole other thing, entirely different from *yoksim*. *Yoksim* is bad because you are willing to hurt others for your own benefit, but living diligently (*yŏlsimhi sanŭn kŏt*) isn't about hurting others, it is just a matter of putting in six hours where other people would put in five. In the Bible, people with *yoksim* get punished, and those without *yoksim* reap rewards. If you live by the Bible, you can know heaven on earth.

The problem, then, is the excess and instrumentality of *yoksim*: setting it apart from diligence is needless acquisition and harm to others. But Hye-min's Grandmother is equally critical of those people (women in particular) who are somehow unable to live diligently (*yŏlsimhi salda*), as we saw in the discussions of being impatient (*kŭpham*) and being suffocating (*taptapham*). Hye-min's Grandmother both admires and counts herself among those capable of healthy and active living. The lines she draws are fine but important ones. In one discussion with me, she made a distinction between "good" and "bad" *yoksim*, arguing that although her own zeal for life was indeed *yoksim* in its own right, it was of the "good" variety.

> Bad *yoksim* is when people only know themselves, when they don't know how to be generous (*pep'ul chul*). Good *yoksim* is about living ardently, passionately—that is the sort that I have. Bad *yoksim* is like that of *pokpuin* (women who buy and sell real estate on speculation for investment purposes and who engage in money lending)—women who get rich with no effort, no work.

Hye-min's Grandmother
PEP'ULDA to be generous
    pep'unŭn (generous); pep'um (generosity)
YOKSIM greed, ambition
YŎLSIMHI SALDA to live diligently
    yŏlsimhi sanŭn (living diligently)

(Speaking about herself)
    "I have a generous, loving heart and no greed (pep'ulgo sarang hanŭn maŭm i itko yoksim i ŏpta)." She elaborated, "Blood can't be deceived—I have my mother's personality."

(Speaking about people generally)
    "As for people who dress well, who make money so as to live well—what an embarrassing thing to have such yoksim . . . To live diligently (yŏlsimhi sanŭn kŏt), though, is a whole other thing, entirely different from yoksim. Yoksim is bad because you are willing to hurt others for your own benefit, but living diligently (yŏlsimhi sanŭn kŏt) isn't about hurting others, it is just a matter of putting in six hours where other people would put in five."

The Laundress too spoke of the proper balance between being generous (pep'um) and having greed or ambition (yoksim), in much the same way as Hye-min's Grandmother—sketching a fine line. She considered the appropriate fashion in which a person must be generous (pep'urŏya): "Things are amiss if a person tries to make it look like they have more than they do." She described, on the other hand, that "it is only the generous heart that can be at peace." Money usurers, she went on, "wear their miserliness (kkakchaeng'i) in the lines of their faces and can never know calm, for they do not know how to be generous (pep'ul chul morŭda). A woman's face after forty is the one she has made."

Like the Moviegoer, Hye-min's Grandmother and the Laundress shared a sense of a particular sort of "other" woman who transgresses all sorts of propriety. But the matters on which these distinctions turn vary from woman to woman. While the Laundress reserved her sense of women's transgression foremost for the woman who sacrifices her husband's ego, and the Moviegoer for the woman who thinks she is above homemaking,

Hye-min's Grandmother's sense was for the greedy (and economically motivated) woman and, as we saw above, for a certain type of ignorant woman. Important, however, are the ways in which class and privilege are so often inflected in this sense of social others. Indeed, Hye-min's Grandmother's "bad *yoksim*" is reserved for women whose diligence is not the ethical solution to healthy living but instead the unethical province of accumulation and greed. For the Laundress and the Moviegoer, "other" women were those who were economically privileged—privileged to forgo domestic responsibilities. And for the Twins' Mother, "other" women—though not limited to women—were those burdened by the stress from lacking education, which was inextricable from her sense of a certain kind of status privilege.

Accounting for not having any *yoksim*, or at least any of the "bad" variety, Hye-min's Grandmother drew on her religious conviction, good fortune, middle-class trappings, and her sense of the shared characters of the women in her family—including an ability to be generous (*pep'ulda*). But if the excesses of class privilege are the province of bad *yoksim*, Hye-min's Grandmother is a stalwart champion of the middle classes, who have enough but not too much. She was in this vein also careful to explain, perhaps ironically, that her own middle-class privilege has worked to curb her *yoksim*:

> Why do I have no *yoksim*? How did I come to this? Because I believe in Jesus. I had my children. I sent them to college. I found them marriage partners, and I gave them the ability to support themselves. Through the Bible, I have learned that we come to and leave the world empty-handed. What, then, is the point of *yoksim*? What would it be for? We should live with kindness. It isn't as if I will live till one hundred. I too will die.

Here, the love of Jesus and of Bible teachings encircle another thought: that there are reasonable things to expect of the world, reasonable aims for which to live zealously. These can be summarized as the trappings of middle-class social reproduction, namely her children's college education, marriage, a living wage, and so on.

On the afternoon we gathered in June 2000, Hye-min's Grandmother updated me on the well-being of all of her children. We slowly turned every page of a pamphlet from her eldest son's recent, first art exhibit, talking all the while about his very successful art school for children and about his new apartment that was just then under construction, where she would continue to live with this son and his family. After lunch, we visited the hospital where her second son is a dental surgeon and professor; she was tickled by the warm greeting of the guard seated at the building's entrance, who referred to her as the "professor's mother." She was also proud to show me a painting by her eldest son, and a calligraphy scroll made by her sister, a calligraphy teacher, hanging in the waiting room of her son's dental clinic. And she reported on the successes of her daughter and son-in-law's recently opened franchise restaurant, albeit in the aftermath of losing his job, related to the IMF Crisis. That same afternoon, however, as we browsed together at some upscale shops, she complained about the absurdity of spending like that for clothing or material things, and delineated her own clear limits: never, for example, more than $150 for a new-style *hanbok*, a mid-calf-length easier-to-wear variant of the traditional Korean woman's dress that she had taken to always wearing since I had last seen her in 1998.

Mi-yŏn's Mother

Mi-yŏn's Mother's uses of *yoksim* were precariously balanced. On the one hand, she spoke often of lacking *yoksim* herself—of her own lack of desire to change her circumstances. Here, we may recall the earlier discussions of "feminine" traits (e.g., *ch'akhada*) and the matter of living in accordance with, or struggling against, one's circumstances (the Laundress and the Moviegoer, the former, and Hye-min's Grandmother and the Janitor, the latter). On the other hand, Mi-yŏn's Mother's *yoksim* refers to the perverse ambition of people whose characters are somehow twisted, most of all, her husband's, of whom we learn more in chapters 7 and 9. It is relevant to recall from the preceding chapter that Mi-yŏn's Mother's domicile and lifestyle stand out for their material trappings. This tension over *yoksim* recalls so many of the discussions we have had here in which traits can be both enviable and despicable, sometimes at once.

The first instance of *yoksim* referring to her own lacking was one Mi-yŏn's Mother spoke about in relation to a key matter in her life, one explored in some detail in chapters 8 and 9, namely the matter of her not having gone to college. An extremely sensitive issue for Mi-yŏn's Mother, she calculated that she could have gone had she had more *yoksim*. She had been working at a bank as a high school graduate, and the opportunity arose, through a colleague at work, for her to attend a newly established university, but it would have meant asking both to be transferred and for some flexibility with her work schedule. She wondered again and again how it was that she had not been able to bring herself to do so, to have made arrangements that would have changed the course of her life. In one of several attempts to understand what came to pass, she reflected, "I really didn't have much *yoksim* for life. I just thought about making a bit of money and living . . . I couldn't burden other people [i.e., at her place of work] so as to be able take the college courses." My talks with Mi-yŏn's Mother often oscillated between triumphant stories of her successes against many odds, and quiet, sad reflections on her many weaknesses, her lack of resolve and purpose among them.

The second, perverse sense of *yoksim* was mediated against a contented life that makes peace with its givens, its limitations. Talking about her brother's children who were about to be sent off to boarding schools in the United States because it had become clear that they would not fare well in South Korea's competitive college entrance system, she said, "If you can't get into college in South Korea, why not become a happy, cheerful (*palgŭn*) person. Why not discard that *yoksim* and live instead with a grateful heart (*kamsahanŭn maŭm*)." As reviewed in chapter 2, most of the women in this book, like most South Koreans, have one or more relatives abroad. Relations abroad, I have found, are critical touchstones for life reflection on paths both taken and not taken. (Chapter 8 takes up class distances and distinctions across extended families, including relatives residing abroad.)

We see, then, that recalling her own thwarted college dreams, Mi-yŏn's Mother found her *yoksim* wanting, and thus, to some extent, appraised *yoksim* positively. However, when reflecting on her brother's college dreams for his children—and on his willingness to send them abroad for study—she judged his *yoksim* excessive. Nonetheless, her zeal for her own children's education was considerable. In summarizing her thoughts this way, I do not mean to suggest that hers was a double standard, but, rather, I mean to walk for a moment the delicate lines according to which so many of the distinctions I have been following here are drawn. And as I noted in the beginning of this chapter, sedimented in these clusters of words are precisely the negotiations of these fine lines.

Mi-yŏn's Mother
YOKSIM greed, ambition

(Reflecting, as she often did, on not having made it to college)
"I really didn't have much *yoksim* for life. I just thought about
(Continued on next page)

(Mi-yŏn's Mother—Continued)
making a bit of money and living . . . I couldn't burden other people [her colleagues at work who had offered to help her] so as to be able take the college courses."

(On why she thinks her nieces and nephews should not be sent abroad for high school)

"If you can't get into college in South Korea, why not become a happy, cheerful (palgŭn) person. Why not discard that yoksim and live instead with a grateful heart (kamsahanŭn maŭm)."

Mrs. Pak

Mrs. Pak, the only four-year-college graduate among the women and who eschewed interest in material goods or acquisition, similarly treaded precariously around yoksim. In our second meeting, she drew the discussion of her entire family history to a close by depicting herself this way: "I always think, 'I am a woman who never made any money.' " This recalls the Laundress's and the Moviegoer's thoughts on the same matter. Mrs. Pak toured her genealogy for me, assessing each person's level of yoksim. For some relatives with yoksim, she explained, it was that they were enlightened (kkaen) people, that they knew, for example, the importance of getting educated. Her portrayal of her brother's abundant yoksim, however, was quite different. When her parents died, her brother had been unhappy about his inheritance (yusan); it fell short, Mrs. Pak described, of his yoksim. When he complained to her, she silenced him: "What are you saying? That your health isn't an inheritance (yusan)? That your learning isn't an inheritance? That your belief in Jesus isn't an inheritance? What are you talking about —inheritance (yusan)!" About herself, Mrs. Pak said again and again that she is a woman without yoksim. The source of her sense of her own dearth of yoksim is threefold: her religious conviction (echoing Hye-min's Grandmother's), her own acquiescence to circumstance (echoing Mi-yŏn's Mother's, the Moviegoer's, and the Laundress's), and finally her relatively privileged background (again echoing Hye-min's Grandmother's). She reflected on having made no money and on having wanted to get a job upon her college graduation but instead having submitted to her eldest paternal uncle's whim. That uncle had not wanted her to go far for a job: "Why do you need to make money?" he had chided. It was, she described, her obedience (sun-jong) that kept her from the labor market, then and thereafter. And in one of our final meetings, she spoke of failed attempts later on in her life to work, thwarted by her in-laws and her own parents. Here she joined the Laundress and Mi-yŏn's Mother (and the Moviegoer to a certain extent) in pondering her accommodation to circumstances.

In an interesting twist, however, Mrs. Pak historicized *yoksim* as an attribute of those people who have suffered—classwise and otherwise. She elaborated that it is the people with hard lives who have *yoksim*, who have that desire to amass wealth; here she echoed Mi-yŏn's Mother on the perversity of *yoksim*:

> When I think about it, I have never gone hungry. I had both a mother and a father, and I have never been kicked out of a classroom by a teacher [i.e., for not having been able to pay tuition]. So, it has never occurred to me to make money. I do, though, feel a bit apologetic to my husband for having made no money.

In a similar vein Mrs. Pak elaborated, "When I think about it, I am a woman who hasn't been able to make money my whole life long. And that is a really stressful thing for me . . . Unlike a number of my friends [she had earlier spoken of several who had lost a parent early in their lives], the idea that 'in order to live I need to make money' has always been distant from my consciousness." In this guise, her dearth of *yoksim* had as much to do with her proclivities as with her privilege.

Mrs. Pak also spoke positively of having no *yoksim* in terms of enlightenment and religious virtue:

> I have no interest in family property. I just want to eat from what we make. And so we are poor [her husband is a college professor]. I have no *yoksim* for my parents or my in-laws. This is probably because of my Christianity. I think my [Christian] mother told us not to live like that [i.e., with *yoksim*]; to do so would only be to deceive yourself. And I don't really have *yoksim* for my children either.

Shortly after these remarks, her thoughts turned to a *yuhaksaeng* (a student abroad) that her daughter had known while working on her masters in the United States. The particular *yuhaksaeng* in question had, shortly before our meeting, committed suicide, shaking up the South Korean community at that university, needless to say. Having just said, "And I don't really have *yoksim* for my children either," Mrs. Pak continued, "I can't stop thinking about that [now deceased] student at [that] university." Unspoken here, I think, was the presumed *yoksim* of the student's parents; as it turns out, the *yuhaksaeng*'s parents were poor farmers, and the local Korean community had easily assumed that the parents had sacrificed everything to send this son abroad. Such imaginings follow the course of well-trod class and gender tropes, in this case about "poor farmers," "study abroad," and a "precious son." It is interesting that just as Mi-yŏn's Mother and the Laundress wondered about *top'i yuhak* (study abroad in order to escape), so too did Mrs. Pak wonder about the thinking and ambition entailed in sending a child abroad—even as she had done so herself (as had Mi-yŏn's Mother).

Mrs. Pak
YOKSIM greed, ambition

(Reflecting on her dearth of *yoksim*)
  "When I think about it, I have never gone hungry. I had both a mother and a father, and I have never been kicked out of a classroom by a teacher [i.e., for not having been able to pay tuition]. So, it has never occurred to me to make money. I do, though, feel a bit apologetic to my husband for having made no money."
  "I have no interest in family property. I just want to eat from what we make. And so we are poor [her husband is a college professor]. I have no *yoksim* for my parents or my in-laws. This is probably because of my Christianity. I think my [Christian] mother told us not to live like that [i.e., with *yoksim*]; to do so would only be to deceive yourself. And I don't really have *yoksim* for my children either."

The Education Mother

I turn finally and briefly to the Education Mother, the middle-class elder sister in the pocketbook story from chapter 1, and, with Mi-yŏn's Mother, one of the two most prosperous women in this book. Her brief comments on her brother's and son's lack of *yoksim* extend Mrs. Pak's preceding discussion. While Mrs. Pak spoke primarily of the ways in which class and gender are coordinates of *yoksim*, for the Education Mother, it was the strange combination of status privilege and a woman's lacking education that made for a motherly ambition, which would, in turn, produce an unambitious son. The Education Mother thus went furthest in talking about the intergenerational effects of *yoksim*, particularly that of her mother for her brother, as discussed in chapter 1. The Education Mother explained that her mother's "ignorant" (she was largely uneducated) *yoksim* for her son, a trapping of both her *yangban* origins and of her ignorance, ruined him. She described it quenching his spirit (*ki*), making him entirely unable to thrive, most basically unable to even earn a living. Interestingly, the Education Mother described her own son's education, saying she had to nurture his *ki*—indicating he too had been lacking in the *yoksim* requisite for education achievement (see chapter 4).

In the Education Mother's stories, *yoksim* can be understood, as it was by Mi-yŏn's Mother and Mrs. Pak, to arise from twisted circumstances and to produce twisted results. Cases such as that of the Education Mother's brother are quite difficult to pin down. That is, the virtues and vices of *yoksim* are complicated. The matter of intergenerational transmission is complex, made ever more so by the particular contingencies of social status (in this case, a reference to the mother's *yangban* upbringing) and education (in this case, the mother's lack of schooling). Furthermore, status and education are gendered in important ways. Throughout this book, for example, are stories of the plight and problem of the uneducated wives or daughters of *yangban* men. Greed and generosity are spoken of in gendered terms and with a self-consciousness about a stratified world in which personal attributes and proclivities have made for material difference and distinction.

This chapter has introduced clusters of words that figure incessantly in these women's talk. The words and turns of phrase featured in this chapter are by no means employed always to the same ends, to offer the same commentary on the world, but I submit that taken together they offer the taste, in Bakhtin's sense, of the vocabulary of the women of a generation. The words' heteroglossia—the way they have pulled this way and that—indexes the push and pull, the radical transformation of their times. Herein we have glimpsed radical transformation, for example, of gender norms, and of status hierarchies. With these words, these women were debating ways of being, ideals and realities for the world, the changing world in which they found themselves. All of the women in this book, each in her own way—sometimes quite similar—sketched the limits of reasonable ways of being.

As I have been suggesting, the contingencies of contemporary South Korea have demanded such calculations; the very shape and sheer clip of transformation have made for the sort of talk that this book is attempting to listen in on, however partially and sporadically.

These women juggle the "inherited code" and the "morality of improvement," to echo Raymond Williams (1973, 115). In this chapter I hope to have begun to convince that the largest social contests can be seen in personal stories; later chapters argue that the largest of social stories have the taste of these personal accounts. The women's stories are presented at greater length in the chapters to come. But the vignettes here have provided a feel for their words and the talk of this book.

With chapter 4, I turn to a critical domain for the work and workings of class: education.

4

CLASS WORK
Education Stories

There is little that is more vulnerable or more volatile in the South Korean social imagination than education. That is, as education has so long captured the aspirations and dreams of South Koreans, even slight changes in its meanings are felt in seismic proportions—-ripe for a melodramatic sensibility, as discussed in chapter 1.

Perhaps the most sensitive of social registers in South Korea, education is shorthand, a Rorschach for, dare I say, almost everything else. The education stories that follow take us into the early through middle years of the 1990s, in which this project is anchored, and extend to the century's closing parentheses, conversations in 2000 and 2001. These stories reveal the considerable social confusion over class work, namely the work people do to ensure class reproduction or mobility (see also Janelli 1993, 37, and Kendall 1996, 229, on the competing claims of status; see Nelson 2000, 149–160, on mothers, education, and class work; on education and the middle class, see chapter 5 in Lett 1998).

In this chapter, I turn to the education stories of two of the women, the Education Mother and the Janitor, and to the story of Mi-yŏn's youngest brother. These education tales demonstrate the story of class work in South Korea today. The education musings of Mi-yŏn's brother are recent, post-millennial reflections. Importantly, they are thoughts expressed in the aftermath of South Korea's IMF Crisis. I argue that with the IMF Crisis, the rules of the game have changed. That social calculations are precarious and so forth is in one sense old hat: namely, South Koreans have long reflected upon, and negotiated their way through, changing rules, as we saw in the last chapter. Indeed, the thoughts of Mi-yŏn's brother that I heard in 2001, the official end of the IMF Crisis, echo elements in the accounts of the Janitor and her children in the early 1990s, prior to the IMF Crisis. But there have been important structural changes in the dynamics of the social game: the taste of twenty-first-century venture capitalism in South Korea, although waning at this moment in 2002, is very new; the shocking pace at which South Korea and South Koreans have become "wired" is also noteworthy, as are the neoliberal politics promulgated by President Kim Dae Jung. What has remained familiar amidst these changes is the feeling of the personal and social contests—about a just world, and about personal circumstances, calculations, and chances.

The Education Mother and Her Son Who Made It into College

I turn now to the Education Mother, whom we met through the pocketbook story in chapter 1, again in chapter 2, and briefly in chapter 3 for her discussions of ki (spirit, energy) and how her mother's child rearing and ambition had led to her eldest brother's never amounting to anything. The story that follows, about her only son, is not unrelated, for it too concerns a boy's ki, education course, and life horizons. In the pocketbook story, we saw how the Education Mother came to think of her sister's story: a story of personality and, at the same time, a transgenerational story about her mother, the times, and social transformation. Before turning to the education story of the Education Mother's only son, I return to the story of her brother and to some more details of her own family history. I begin by discussing conversations on a television soap opera (tŭrama) that was popular in 1993, particularly among the women of the generation featured here, because it ran through my first three meetings with the Education Mother. In fact, to wrest the Education Mother's story from its intersection with that of the soap opera would, I think, do it an injustice.

By Way of a Soap Opera: Adŭl kwa ttal (A son and a daughter)

Adŭl kwa ttal, the story of boy-and-girl twins, Kui-nam and Hu-nam, was foremost a dramatization of Korean gender prejudice. Interestingly, the soap opera revealed the costs of such discrimination for both the son and the daughter, who were each its victim. About the hardships experienced by these twins, one article noted: "People who have felt suffocated in life, people who haven't quite known what to say or how to voice their silence, find the words with which to express themselves. For many people like this, for our silenced masses, this soap opera offers two names, Kui-nam and Hu-nam, with which to think, to break their silence" (M. S. Kim 1993, 151). Set in the 1960s, the soap opera was popular for its nostalgic appreciation of

South Korea's both urban and rural yesteryear—a recent, but rapidly receding, past. On this nostalgia, the same article went on: "This soap opera, every Saturday and Sunday, takes us back to a remote time, some thirty years ago, that grows only more and more distant. It draws us to those times when we were poor but had time and space (yŏyurowŏttdon kŭ sijŏl)" (M. S. Kim 1993, 146). If Hu-nam (meaning literally "after, boy," indicating the hope that a boy follows) suffers from the extremes of her mother's disfavor on every front of daily life, Kui-nam (precious boy) suffers from familial expectations that exceed his capacity. Although Hu-nam turns her suffering to productive ends, becoming a high school teacher and the writer of the fictional novel on which the soap opera is based (as the story goes), Kui-nam ends up a low-level bank worker who eventually quits his job to try, yet again, to pass the law exam that he has already failed several times and has few real prospects of passing.

A number of the women in this book wondered about the "reality" of the extreme gender discrimination to which Hu-nam was subjected in this soap opera: "Could it have really been?" In so asking, they echoed a feature of melodrama that I reviewed in chapter 1, namely that it invites just such questions. The discrimination persisted to the soap opera's last gasp, when the mother asked Hu-nam to purchase an egg from a passing peddler and then offered it only to Kui-nam. The Education Mother, though, was among those who thought that the gender discrimination in Adŭl kwa ttal was more than believable, and furthermore not unlike that meted out by her own mother. Pak Jin-suk, the writer of the soap opera (whom I interviewed), reported that she was contacted daily by viewers convinced that she was telling their story, that they were Hu-nam or Kui-nam. Soap opera folklore of the day purported that some women had taken to calling their husbands Kui-nam or to referring to themselves as Hu-nam.

In the earliest moments of our conversation, the Education Mother explained that her mother, the yangban daughter, had raised the eldest of her two brothers, who came to nothing, exactly as Kui-nam had been raised, and that she herself had been raised exactly like Hu-nam. This eldest brother, three years younger than she, was really smart—"the smartest in the neighborhood, actually a bit of a genius." Also this brother, son of a mother with no brothers, was the first boy of his generation in his father's family, a position prone to coddling. She described that she too helped to raise her brother that way, "forever bolstering him higher and higher." Raising a boy "in the way of Kui-nam," she went on, "makes a man incapable (munŭng). They end up with no ability, only able to think about themselves, without even a thought for an elder sister." Her brother was the sort of person, she went on, who could be oblivious if the world around him was crumbling, as long as his affairs were in order. "It would have been one thing," she said, "if we had been rich, but we weren't, and still we raised him that way, even though we really couldn't afford to."

If others queried the reality of the soap opera's sexism, for her part the Education Mother thought that the soap opera was far too optimistic, that Hu-nam and Kui-nam had in fact weathered their upbringing with greater aplomb than they would have in reality. "Hu-nam would have never succeeded like that—a girl with her personality would have been sent home by her in-laws no sooner than she had arrived . . . and Kui-nam's personality is actually pretty good for having been raised like that." Her bottom line was that children raised "like that" cannot "develop" to the extent that Kui-nam and Hu-nam had managed to in the soap opera. More specifically, she speculated that Kui-nam would have been even more incapacitated, as was the case with her own brother, unable to do anything. And she thought that Hu-nam, like her, would have been unable to achieve the education she does in the soap opera. I had the impression that Hu-nam's successes were perhaps even a bit insulting to the Education Mother, for they seemed to mock her own education and employment course, one much less distinguished than that of Hu-nam.

The "reality" of what came of Hu-nam interested many people at the time. The women I spoke with discussed Hu-nam's personality for having been raised that way, her education success, and above all her upwardly mobile marriage. The Education Mother, who could relate to the quiet way in which Hu-nam bore her mother's discrimination, could not fathom her doing so well. This said, however, the Education Mother was herself quite satisfied with her own family work, economic and extra-economic, and was assured that it was her own housing investment that had secured her family's social position. Among the families of the men who worked at the same level (civil service) as her husband, she noted that hers was by far the most prosperous.

The writer of the soap opera, Pak Jin-suk, had interesting things to say about Hu-nam's personality, which revealed a tension similar to that in the Education Mother's reflections on her sister, a tension between personality as personal, and personality as social and historical. In our discussions, Pak reminded me that Hu-nam's two sisters in the soap opera were not victims of their mother's gender discrimination in the same way as was Hu-nam. I had noticed this, but I had assumed, with many of the women I spoke with, that it was her position as Kui-nam's twin that incurred her mother's wrath. Our sense was that Hu-nam posed a threat to Kui-nam's masculinity and promise because she was more talented and accomplished than he. Pak, however, in explaining the sisters different reaction to the mother's ways, believed otherwise:

> They had the personalities to handle it. When she said something, they talked back and so over time the problems dissipated. But Hu-nam doesn't talk—she is the sort who just remains quiet and the mother can't tell what she is thinking. Although a daughter just the same, one like Hu-nam is hard to handle. At one point the mother tells Hu-nam, "You think that you are better." Even a mother's love (mosŏng'ae) can't handle Hu-nam so easily.

Pak's explanation confuses matters, wresting Hu-nam's fate from the workings of Korean patriarchy alone.

As for Hu-nam's fairy-tale marriage to Sŏk-ho, Kui-nam's closest college friend, most of the women I spoke with agreed that it was unrealistic—that a girl who had been treated the way she had would have had neither the presence of mind nor the personal assets to attract and marry such a man. Not only was Sŏk-ho kind, tall, and handsome, but he was also from a prosperous family and had successfully passed the bar exam. Pak explained, however, that she had not intended to have Hu-nam marry Sŏk-ho: "I had intended to marry her to a regular guy—maybe a teacher at the school [where Hu-nam is also a teacher]—not a particularly distinguished man but one who was emotionally stable and who could make her life easy." Her marriage to Sŏk-ho was, it turns out, a marriage of popular demand and production convenience. First, there were problems plotting and casting a new character. Moreover, there was considerable viewer and producer pressure. South Korean soap opera writers (who compose the script as the program is televised) are subject to the ongoing input and pressures from producers, from ratings, and from viewers' phone calls and letters, in this case a barrage. Viewers wanted Hu-nam to marry up. Interestingly, even Hu-nam's mother—in perhaps the drama's most hideous scene of gender discrimination—told Hu-nam that she was in no position to be even thinking about such a marriage; perhaps this was writer Pak's way of ironically staging her own protest to the social and narrative unreality of Hu-nam's marriage to Sŏk-ho. Feminists of the day objected to the fairy tale of "social mobility through marriage" as the answer to gender oppression:

Because women identify their own lives with Hu-nam, they are enormously concerned about her future. They think, "Hu-nam's hard efforts will be rewarded and she'll live well," and they want the soap opera to end with Hu-nam's success, happiness, and marriage to a good man. That is exactly why I worry that this soap opera might end up making Hu-nam into yet another Cinderella . . . One woman in our discussion group [a media study group organized by Tto Hana ŭi Munhwa (Another Culture), a feminist organization] suggested, "What if immediately before succeeding, Hu-nam were to get sick and die? Wouldn't that scenario go further to expose the vices of patriarchy?" I think that this woman's words touch on the reality (hyŏnsilgam) of things. It is not that it is necessarily wrong for Hu-nam to marry Sŏk-ho, a certified lawyer, but for Hu-nam, who spent a really unhappy childhood constantly being put down, it would be better if her upward mobility didn't simply take place through marriage. (M. S. Kim 1993, 149)

Pak described the pressure she was under to write in this marriage: "There was a real psychology that wanted Hu-nam to do well precisely because she had suffered so much. People really wanted her to shine. I thought it would be far too naïve and routine to have such a marriage . . . But it is in our national character to want the likes of Hu-nam to marry somebody like Sŏk-ho." One fan, the mother of a daughter who was rejected by her lawyer boyfriend because of her humble origins, took such solace in this happy outcome that she implored the writer to make that part of the story even bigger so as to "educate the South Korean people." It is perhaps precisely the tension between viewers' desire for the unrealistic and their demands for the realistic that kept people tuned in, as I explored in the discussion of melodrama, in chapter 1.

About the mother in Adŭl kwa ttal, the Education Mother had plenty to say. From previously recorded discussions of the Education Mother's mother, you may recall that she blamed her mother's ignorance—an ignorance that came to life in twisted ambition for her children—on her yangban upbringing as the daughter of a yangban wife who had been left in the countryside while her husband lived with mistresses and thus didn't have the benefit of a father around, and on her mother having been left without a husband, at twenty-nine. During a more sympathetic moment, she said, "My mother is good; it isn't that she isn't good. All the women of her generation are like her, like frogs in a well (umul an kaeguri) [a very common expression]. It's that she was ignorant because she was uneducated." The Education Mother—echoing a number of the women in this book, including particularly Hye-min's Grandmother, Mi-yŏn's Mother, the Laundress, and Mrs. Pak—is a firm believer in women's education: "For the country to succeed, it is women who have to be smart." On another occasion she said, "It is more important for women to be well educated than [for] men because they are the ones responsible for education in the home (kajŏng kyoyuk)." The Education Mother thinks of her mother's ignorance, as demonstrated in the pocketbook story, as having wreaked havoc in her family: it sapped her children of their energy (ki rŭl chugida), and none of them developed as they might have. She explained: "We were all smart and pretty, and if things had gone on course, we would have all been smarter, but they didn't go that way." For herself, she thinks of her "original personality" as quite different from what it became under her mother: "It is much more active, but my mother really put me down, and raised me like a frog in a well [i.e., like her mother before her]." Dramatically, she offered, "If my mother had ordered me to die, I would have!"

The Education Mother is certain that everything in her life would have been different had her father not "died." She referred to his "death" until she revealed to me that he had in fact gone to North Korea; she does not know if he is still alive. For example, her brother's ki (spirit) would not have been killed, and the family's economic situation would have been better, which would have enhanced her own education course. As it was, in spite of having had property in Seoul, her mother was entirely unable to make anything of it, and with no income, and no ability to budget or invest, everything deteriorated. Also, as a yangban's daughter, her mother had absolutely no inclination to work. She said, "If it was me, I could have made something of it." And she went on to explain that had things been different, "I could have gone to a teacher's college, or maybe to the nursing high school in a nearby town." As it was, her mother only thought to marry her off. But the Education Mother struck an ambivalent note here, saying that in her era, at the end of the day, it was the educated girls who lost out: "Young men didn't want to marry young women with jobs—they weren't popular. They [the young men] worried that they [the young women] would be too smart and would just run away the moment they came upon any marital difficulty. But in fact it was the girls who ran away who lost out. It was different here than in the United States, so their mothers came to regret having educated them."

The Education Mother remains ambivalent today about women's education. She explained that "women are so busy gallivanting about that they don't give their children the love they need. You need to feed children to give them love." On an entirely different tack, however, she said, "Kids today don't know what it is to suffer *(kosaeng iran ke muŏsinji)* . . . They are just like the vegetables grown in greenhouses *(onsil esŏ charan hwach'o)* [a very common expression]—not nearly as strong or delicious as the vegetables raised in the elements. They are raised too comfortably." She was also ambivalent about education zeal more generally. While she lamented her and her siblings' suffering in the face of her mother's twisted ambition, she also said it is that suffering—and even that ambition—that "stimulated the development of this country." She went on: "The education zeal of my mother's generation and of my generation has been a great help to this country . . . The next generation won't be able to do what we have done." The reader will observe the workings of her own quite remarkable zeal in the story of her son that follows.

To return first, for a moment, to Adŭl kwa ttal, in the way that our conversations periodically did, there was something else that made the mother in the soap opera controversial. Beyond the question of how realistic was her treatment of her children is the issue of the way in which the soap opera portrayed her excesses: Was it sympathetic enough? Did it pay sufficient attention to what might have made for such behavior? Was she, in the final analysis, but another woman who had been demonized in a patriarchal drama? Writer Pak described how the famous actress Chŏng Hye-sŏn, who played the role, "fretted over whether to take the part, fearing that people would end up hating her." Pak insisted, though, that "people who could, would understand her [as the mother]," and she described how the script had done its part to foster such an understanding: "In the first episode, I showed how Hu-nam's mother had been put down by her own mother-in-law for not giving birth to a son . . . I really didn't intend to paint her in such a negative light." In this way, Hu-nam's mother was herself portrayed as the product of generations of gender discrimination. Pak thinks, nevertheless, that many viewers did not understand her point. Indeed, Kim Mi-suk, in Saem i kip'ŭn mul, a high-class woman's journal, opined that Pak didn't go far enough: "It is wrong to portray the mother as merely an evil person hampered by individual problems. It must be clearly exposed that she is the victim of patriarchy" (1993, 150). The article continued, claiming Hu-nam's mother "has given up even trying to talk with her husband, who only talks at her as if she were a dunce. In reality, however, she is the one who single-handedly supports the family economically. Given these circumstances, she cannot but focus her energies on her son. In reality this is how our mothers have been—simultaneously both patriarchy's victims and its relentless guardians" (M. S. Kim 1993, 147). Here Kim complains that we do not learn enough about the father in the soap opera, "truly the greatest defender of patriarchy" (1993, 151). Popular actor Paek Il-sŏp played the father in Adŭl kwa ttal, a bumbling, burly, warm, country fellow who is somehow removed from worldly concerns. In the discussions of 1960s melodramatic film in chapter 7, the reader will discover that elision of, or confusion over, men's patriarchy has long been a feature of South Korean media. Although there were times that the Education Mother was relentless in describing her own mother, at other times she went to considerable lengths to explain the circumstances of her mother's failings.

To return finally to the Education Mother's family, constant in her stories were the contrasts she drew between herself and her sister, the protagonist of the pocketbook story, and her eldest brother and a younger one. The Education Mother thinks that her own way of responding to her mother, quietly and without protest, prepared her for a woman's life in Korea—for dealing with the hardship of a heinous mother-in-law and so on. Her sister, on the other hand, had not been docile, and did fight back, but had nonetheless married according to her mother's twisted calculations. The Education Mother figures that her sister, as well as Hu-nam, would not have lasted a day in the marriage that she herself has put up with. She explained there was nothing to shatter her own ignorance (kkaeji mothaettda)—her mother did not let them read books or magazines, or go to the movies—but somehow her sister had managed to learn about the world (kkaeŏtta). She lamented that her own inborn talents and intelligence had never flourished: "Even today my husband complains that I don't know enough, that I don't read books, but that is how I was raised." In a sense, the Education Mother found in Hu-nam qualities of both herself and her sister: a quiet way of dealing with her mother, and the guts to break away.

It was above all the Education Mother's eldest brother—the son ruined by the doting mother—who seemed as a subject to most often invite the mention of Adŭl kwa ttal. The eldest brother figured most prominently in the Education Mother's stories because of the family's persistently awkward economic relations. Never managing to be gainfully employed, that brother was largely supported by his younger brother. Moreover, in the years during which I spoke with the Education Mother, the eldest son was living rent-free in her and her husband's former home. This was a sore spot for the Education Mother, and for her husband. Again and again she described that people like him, people who have never worked, have absolutely no idea what it takes to buy a home, and hence they have no ability to appreciate it. Chapter 8 is devoted to the complicated relations within families, and there we meet other stories like this one, in which economic distribution within families is a delicate matter.

The Education Mother had very interesting things to say about her youngest brother, about how it was that he somehow escaped his brother's fate. For starters, she noted he was not an eldest son, but there was more to the story than that. She thinks the mother somehow had less of an effect on the youngest brother than she did the other children: "My eldest brother listened to my mother and his ki (energy) died, but the youngest didn't listen. When my mother was angry he just left the house and came back when the storm was over; he would stay at the house of a younger uncle." The Education Mother thinks that he was also protected for not having done well at school, having thus escaped the clutches of his mother's ambition: "She sort of treated him like us, like a girl." She thinks of the older brother's natural talents and intelligence as having diminished over time, while her younger brother's "genius came out as he got older such that he came to resemble our father." True to this account, she blamed her mother for the youngest brother having flunked out of middle school: "My mother refused to buy us books; the eldest was the only one who mattered to her." Later, though, the youngest brother managed to pass the high school equivalency exam (kŏmjŏng'gosi) and eventually to attend college. Interestingly the older brother—well-read and knowledgeable in spite of his inability to work or sustain a public life—was instrumental in the younger brother's having been able to attend college because he tutored him diligently.

I close the discussions of the Education Mother's stories (told in concert with a soap opera narrative) with the story of the Education Mother's father, and the Korean War context of her stories. As mentioned previously, it was not for quite some time—after already having known the Education Mother for a decade—that I learned her father was a wŏlbukja, a person who went north in the immediate postliberation (1945) years or during the Korean War (1950–1953). It is widely understood that the families of wŏlbukja suffered over the ideologically charged (Cold War) post–Korean War period. Understood to be somehow ideologically tainted, family members had difficulties, for example, obtaining civil-service positions or even travel visas (S. J. Lee 2000; C. S. Kim 1988). It is not at all surprising that the Education Mother had quietly avoided telling me much about her father, having spoken of him for quite some time as having died in the Korean War. Nor is it surprising that it was only after many years of our talking together that the Education Mother would assert, "Yes, yes indeed, we are Korean War victims." Once her husband chimed in, "My wife's life is pretty representative. All the people of our generation have suffered about that much." She, in turn, continued with more stories of her "fantastically intelligent" father and what had become of him. She explained that he had sasang (ideology), meaning here Socialist ideology. "After all he was really smart. He was a landlord's son and really smart—people like that had sasang. Of course in theory sasang is a really good thing, everyone lives the same so it is better than capitalism." It is important to remember the 1990s context of this conversation; that is, increasing political freedom and the wane of the global Cold War combined to allow for these reflections.

Via a paternal aunt in Japan, the Education Mother did manage to send her father a letter years ago, close to the time she herself married. She described how thrilled her father had been to hear from his beloved daughter, and how much he had loved her. (He left when she was eleven years old. She recalled, "I used to bring him ingredients for soup and he always told me that it made the soup that much more delicious.") She told me how grateful he was that there were families who had been willing to marry their sons and daughters to children without a father (i.e., like the Education Mother), an inauspicious marriage condition in Korea. It is only now, in the millennial years, that the matters and struggles of wŏlbukja have really become public in South Korea. Quite remarkable, and telling of South Korea's ideological thaw, is that in the summer 2000 North-South family reunion, wŏlbukja families' applications for the chance to briefly meet with their wŏlbukja kin in the North were accepted (S. J. Lee 2000). Interestingly, the most positive appraisal that the Education Mother ever offered of her own mother came exactly on the heels of these warm reminiscences about her father's letter, as when she said, "My mother is good; it isn't that she isn't good." It was thus in the face of the gravest of historical circumstances that the Education Mother waxed sympathetic about her mother.

An Education Rescue Story

By all rights, the Education Mother's (only) son should have been college bound: The Education Mother and her husband had worked very hard, he was smart, the resources were there, and his sister was already securely attending a prestigious college. I offer her story—that of a mother who went to great lengths to put her son on track—as a class story: a mother's down-to-the-wire work for class reproduction (see Lareau 1989 and Reay 1998 on mothers' education involvement generally). We can recall that the Education Mother was matter-of-fact about the trappings of the (upper) middle class: savings, home/apartment ownership, travel abroad, membership in a health club, and so on—all things that she had attained. But she was not matter-of-fact about her thrift (*alttül*), careful financial work, capable child rearing, responsible husband, and the achievement of her own middle-class status amongst a number of siblings who were not making it (and were, furthermore, looking to her for financial help).

When the Education Mother finished telling how she had managed to set her son on a course headed for college (the once uncertain future that was by the time of telling already the secure past), she described how much she had come to hate her son in the immediate aftermath of it all. She came to resent him for doing that to her, making her suffer that way. I could feel her anger; I had never before heard her talk quite like that. But our conversation quickly returned to the upper-middle-class trappings of her life, to the concerns of that day: her daughter's health clinic, her plans for arranging her son's marriage, and the like.

On the day that the Education Mother told the story of her own son's education, we had been talking about her eldest brother, the brother whose life spirit (*ki*) had been quenched by her mother's ignorant ambition (*yoksim*):

> When I think back, she went overboard pushing him to study. But the fact of the matter is that you do need to go to college, but somehow [my son] wasn't really convinced of that.

Only moments earlier, she had conceded, "There is a path for those who don't study." Clear, though, was that she believed her own son needed to go to college. She acknowledged, however, that he was lacking in the "psychological and emotional makeup" well-suited to education: "With my daughter, she just studied; it was never a question of our saying anything. And he wasn't as talented as she was either. But he is smart. But then again he is lacking in ambition (*yoksim*)." We spoke that day about the full-time college-examination preparatory program that he attended after having not been accepted into college on the first round; *chaesu* (taking one or more years for continued study for the college entrance examinations after high school) is a routine practice in the South Korean education landscape (see Seth 2000). The ways of doing *chaesu* are highly stratified, and in this case the Education Mother's son's *chaesu* in a distinguished and expensive academy spoke to his family's privilege. The rest of our discussion that day was about the events that transpired when the Education Mother discovered he had been playing hooky from that elite entrance-examination academy:

I sensed that he hadn't been going to the academy. I called and asked the teacher to let me know if he was absent. My husband pleaded with me not to spy on our son this way, but I couldn't just leave things be. A boy needs to go to the military and he needs to go to college—even if it is only to eventually open a business . . . I couldn't just leave him be, so I went and found him. He had made friends with a bad kid. That kid's mother was even more distressed than I was. That friend of his was really walking a bad path. I was really on the verge, looking for him like a lunatic. But it was really hard to find him. His friend was from a family that was neither rich nor poor, but the mother wasn't able to be a housewife, because her husband wasn't a diligent worker. It's easy for kids from those sorts of families to go astray. Children from environments like ours, where the father goes to work and the mother stays home, don't end up like that.

I eventually found him in a Ping-Pong parlor; I had combed the whole neighborhood. I walked in and there he was, standing. I cried. I screamed and cried. In front of all those people there, I told him that I couldn't live on if he was going to keep on like this. My youngest brother's children [the only other prosperous household among her siblings] were by then all in college, and even if the colleges weren't particularly prestigious, I told him that I wouldn't be able to face them at the ancestral services (chesa) like this—that would be a fate worse than death. I told him that my brothers and sisters had absolutely no understanding of the effort, the work I had put in. I cried and cried. That was the saddest moment of my life. What with my husband having lived diligently and my having worked so hard.

[At the parlor] my son was hugging me and I told him that I simply couldn't let him be. He told me to stick by him because his spirit (ki) is weak. From then on I brought him lunch and dinner; I followed him, his every move. Even though that was the time when my husband had lost his job and was ill, I brought him [the son] everything: water, pulgogi [a popular and somewhat expensive Korean meat dish]. I brought it all to the academy, and I always timed it perfectly. He saw me, everything I was doing, and it made him study—seeing my doing all of that.

One of his friend's mothers teased me, "It's no use—he'll eat your delicious cooking and then he'll play hooky." But I know what is going on with my kids just by looking at them—I know when they have veered off the path. I lived like that for several months. And then he passed the entrance exam. After he was accepted, I hated him. When my stress was finally relieved that was all I felt: hatred for him. That guy (nom) made me suffer so . . .

The Education Mother's dramatic rescue story of her son's education comes into greater relief if we recall the education contours of her own family history—the stories of her mother and siblings. There we learned how education was charged for her, how it spoke to all aspects of her personal history: to her mother's twisted formation (for having been the daughter of an uneducated and abandoned woman, and for having by extension herself been uneducated and ignorant); to her own thwarted education (on account of her mother's gender prejudice, and on account of their economic instability); to her father's enormous intelligence and education (not unrelated to his *sasang* (ideology) that was implicated in his having left for the North); to her eldest brother's education that came to nothing; and finally, to her youngest brother's success in spite of his early education faltering. We can also recall the Education Mother's comments on *Adŭl kwa ttal*: that Hu-nam's success in education was unreasonable and that Kui-nam's education would likely not have taken him as far, and so on. It is clear the Education Mother was determined that neither her son nor daughter meet the fate of any of her siblings, or of the son in *Adŭl kwa ttal*.

More complicated in this transgenerational story that reaches back to her own maternal grandmother are the Education Mother's thoughts on maternal ambition: on the one hand, she credits it with having secured South Korea's development, while on the other hand, she blames her eldest brother's course on its twisted forms. Similarly ambivalent are her thoughts on the importance of women's education, more important than men's for being at the heart of family life, but potentially ruinous when women leave the confines of the household, deprive their children of maternal love, and even run from their marriages. How different would this story have been if it had been the daughter's education that had gone awry? No doubt, it would have looked different. For a mother's thoughts about her sons not having made it to college, I turn now to the case of the Janitor.

The Janitor and Her Sons Not Making It to College

Beginning the Janitor's story back in the village introduced in chapter 2, with the story of her siblings' education, we have the preamble to the education stories of her own children. These are stories on the move, revealing a rich contest of ideas about the meanings and values of education. While the Education Mother's account was situated in an intergenerational nexus and against a gendered and media family story, the Janitor's stands out for its attention to calculations of the worth of education capital and the status of occupations in changing times. Her ruminations are interestingly resonant with the thoughts of Mi-yŏn's brother in the eye of the IMF Crisis—thoughts on which this chapter closes.

A Family Story: Making It in Seoul

The Janitor and her family had been migrants to the village where I once lived and came to know four of her nine siblings (see chapter 2); they arrived there just before the liberation (1945), when the Janitor was fourteen years old. Although they had lost much of their former wealth over the course of the colonial period, they nonetheless joined the small propertied elite in the new village. The Janitor remembers hearing, in reference to her own family, that "rich people have come." Once prosperous and with *yangban* families of one surname (a common pattern of village settlement), the village had been ruined in the colonial period. The Janitor's family, a family with *yangban* pretensions that prided itself on having a family genealogy (*chokpo*) (the sine qua non of *yangban* identification), had moved there to take advantage of new economic opportunities.

The Janitor explained that she grew up around constant banter about *yangban* and *sangnom*, a somewhat derogatory term for *sangmin*, meaning "lower classes": "Even after the Korean War, there was still plenty of that *yang-sang* stuff." *Sangnom*, she elaborated, were people without family genealogies: "They might have used surnames—they would say they were Yi or Pak—but they had absolutely no idea which Yi or which Pak," that is, they were not really members of an illustrious lineage, as surnames in Korea are associated with distant patrilineal ancestral homelands. She then went on—knowing that I understood her—to name names: "You know, the one who runs that little store on the main drag, people like him . . . you know—you know more about that village than I do!" She laughed, then went on: "Ignorant people lived their lives without paying attention to any of this stuff; they just ate their rice." When she was young, she and her family referred to the *yangban* families as "such-and-such a household (*taek*)," but referred to the others by their first names, "without even a *ssi* (a polite suffix)," she added. "When all is said and done," she continued, "I guess it is a lucky thing that I was born into a house with a name, but when I was young I guess the only thing I really thought about at all was that I wasn't a *sangnom*." The Janitor made it clear, though, that the world today is changed. To illustrate, she repeated the popular phrase, "Today everyone is a *yangban*." She also put the same thought another way: "There are no *yangban* today. Money is all that matters."

When the Janitor was young, her father went to great lengths to set up a small school (*sŏdang*) for the learning of Chinese characters (*hanmun*). She said that they paid the teacher with rice, and that her mother had thus suffered from her father's ambitions as she tried to feed the family. She reflected that from today's perspective, her father's thinking was strange and anachronistic: sending his children to a *sŏdang* rather than to an elementary school (i.e., the Japanese colonial schools). "I don't get it," she went on. "Those characters came from China; why teach those foreign things?" She elaborated: "What good were all those Chinese characters he taught my brothers? It wasn't as if they were about to go off to China and use any of it!" On the other hand, she figured: "If a person at least went to elementary school, he could think about becoming a civil servant of some sort."

On several occasions the Janitor spoke of some of her sisters' resentment for being uneducated—resentful that their father had clung to his property rather than educating his children, through the proceeds from selling land. She too recognized that many of the *yangban* local elite with whom her father sat reciting classical poetry (*sijo*) did somehow end up educating their children, while her father did not. "The bottom line," she concluded, "is that he didn't know that Korea had changed." She said that if she really thought about it, the whole thing made her blood boil, and to add insult to it all, the only child that really mattered to her father anyway was the eldest son (in keeping with patrilineal logic and with primogeniture). On that score, there is more to the story, because in the final analysis, the eldest brother ran through the family wealth, emptying its coffers, and has long since been estranged from the family.

The Janitor reserved most empathy for the women who had been destined to marry the likes of her father: namely, the plight of the typical *yangban* daughter "who married into families like hers, and sat there rotting till they died." Such was not, however, her story. She went on: "Those poor *yangban* starved to death; they just put on those hats—*kat*, the ones made of horse hair—and sat there with their books." Saying this, she moved her body woodenly to dramatize their antics and airs. By way of contrast, she explained that "nowadays, people without money labor . . . even people who have been to college." The Janitor is just such a person, having labored. We can recall from the preceding chapter that it was the Janitor who described incapable men (munŭnghan) as just the sort who would let a college education, or yangban pretensions, get in the way of eking out a living.

After this digression on the past, the Janitor was quick to remind me that this world of status distinction (of this particular variety) was the stuff of yesteryear: "But we've followed the United States, and today we can educate our children, maybe more so than in any country in the world." Indeed, in South Korea today, the rates of college-aged who attend institutions of higher education are among the highest in the world. She continued, "We're like the United States now: those who want to get educated can and those who don't want to, don't." These were the Janitor's optimistic proclamations in 1996: that old distinctions were no longer meaningful; that education was open to all; and, moreover, that some of the good life can be had regardless of education attainment. These assertions in 1996 aside, the jury in South Korea is by no means settled on these questions, nor on the social reality on which they hinge. Rather, these concerns—the continuity of status capital, the equity of access to education, and the life promised those who do not make it to the higher rungs of the education ladder—continue to be vexing issues that are debated in the public arena, among families, and in the course of people's day-to-day lives. In the early 1990s, when I began this project, all of the women were each in their own way thinking about all of these questions. By the late 1990s they had joined most South Koreans in the certainty that some things had changed, but the questions were still very much the same, questions of social justice; "Plus ca change . . .," they seemed to be saying and feeling, perhaps a particularly 1990s structure of feeling, as reviewed in chapter 1.

The Janitor's thoughts on matters of opportunity and social (in)equality are inextricable from her housing history, and from thinking about her shantytown neighbors, the lives that hers had come up against. The Janitor's house is perched over a subway line and abuts an enormous apartment complex that only recently replaced a shantylike neighborhood; her house and a small corridor of other homes must have quite literally bracketed this makeshift neighborhood, whose residents were, she said, "the poorest of the poor—the lowest ranks of the class of sŏmin," meaning humble people, the class in which, as noted previously, she counted herself among the upper rungs. But by the time we were meeting, she lived just breaths away from the now highrise apartments that smacked of the middle class, with their apartment guards and family cars. She described that they looked no different than the notorious upper-middle-class expanse lying south of the Han River that the Janitor and her family could literally see from their yard, as they lived just at the northern banks of the river (see Lett 1998, 101–117, on housing and lifestyles north and south of the Han River and on housing choices generally; see also Nelson 2000, 39–47). The Janitor spoke variously of what became of those shanty villagers: "They've all become rich now . . . our government has done a good thing" with this urban renewal, but also, "People without money had to sell [i.e., their rights to those apartments— rights for having been displaced] to the middle classes. People without ability were forced out, but those with jobs can live really well now." As we talked on, it became clear much of what she wanted to say was that people today can generally eat, that rare was the person who needed to "eat off of others." Speaking about those who are still poor—people she described as "all originally country people, maybe one out of a hundred of them are originally from Seoul"—she said she wished she had the wherewithal to help them.

The Janitor was keenly aware of the differences on which her own fortune and those of her shantytown neighbors turned, just as she was of the differences between poor and prosperous farmers. Her own "advantage" was land—land in the countryside that they were able to sell to purchase modest property in Seoul. What had brought them to Seoul originally was the thinking of her "modern-style, not old-fashioned" mother-in-law. When a shamanic ceremony (kut) had augured that if the young couple— the Janitor and her husband—did not leave the land (the countryside), they would never bear a son, the mother-in-law had told them to go ahead and leave for Seoul. The couple already had five daughters at the time. But things were not easy in Seoul, and at one point they made a housing move that led to considerable losses. At the hardest moments in Seoul, the Janitor and her husband even entertained returning to the village: "In the countryside, we had a house on a mountain and my husband would say that we should just go home and grow fruit and raise dogs, but I refused. You know what they say, 'Send your children to Seoul [i.e., the proper place for educating children], and your horses to Cheju Island [i.e., the best place for raising horses].' " Another of the Janitor's advantages in Seoul was wealthy kin. The Janitor's husband also came from a yangban family; the marriage had been arranged. The Janitor described him as "the son of a family of higher standing than her own," who had only made it through middle school due to having been sickly. Once, when they came up short trying to purchase a house, they got help from her husband's maternal aunt. Although the Janitor is grateful to this aunt, over the years the class distances have not been easy to ford. "I really should visit her," she would say, but somehow couldn't bring herself to. She pointed to her surroundings as she explained:

> I'm really grateful to her, but it's hard to go there. She's rich and you know I live like this. You know, rich people drink coffee and juice and they are surrounded with delicious food so they don't eat much rice. When I go there she teases me for eating so much rice. So I never go there—it's strange, usually I am so comfortable, but somehow I feel so ill at ease with her . . . It isn't that she doesn't like me; in fact, she always praised me because I was pretty and because I worked so hard. And she doesn't really do anything to make me feel this way, but I worry that if I go there she will think that I have come to get a free meal from her . . . So, I end up not visiting her. I like my life here, just the way it is . . . You know, when they buy fruit, they don't just buy a few pieces of fruit, they buy the whole box. They don't take me seriously.

At one point, the Janitor mused that half of South Korea lives the way this aunt does, "surrounded by beautiful things and yummy things to eat." I protested: "Half!" So she retracted a bit: "OK, maybe one third, and the rest of us live in shanty neighborhoods (taltongne) . . . well, I guess this house and this neighborhood are on their way up from rock bottom, grasping for the middle class."

The Janitor struggled so hard to stay in Seoul, she explained, because the countryside was no place to raise children: "I knew that if I went back I would end up 'selling' my kids to the factories." There is some irony here because, in fact, two of her daughters did end up in factories, and because the children of her siblings who stayed in the countryside have ended up going further in their schooling. But the Janitor was aware that all education is not equal, that it took everything her brothers had to send their children to high schools in regional cities, but "no matter how smart a countryside kid is, at the end of the day, he cannot make it to Seoul National University . . . The level of the schooling in the countryside is too low, never mind the after-schooling that kids in Seoul who have money can afford—everyone else just falls behind."

The story of the Janitor's housing, employment, daughters, and of the hand-to-mouth way in which she kept her nuclear family going is long and hard to follow. Furthermore, it was not only her nuclear family that she supported. Their single room was her natal family's only room in Seoul and hence became the launching pad for anyone who wanted a go of it in Seoul. But her story is anchored by several things: by the fact of having had land in the countryside—although her late husband's eldest paternal uncle, at the helm of that patrilineage, prevented her from selling the land early on ("Had I sold that land twenty-six years ago, we would be really well off today")—that gave her a sense of security ("I always knew that if I needed to, I could go there and farm"); by the rice, though never abundant, that relatives sent from the countryside to help feed her family ("Without that, we would have really suffered"); by the fact of always having been able to own a room, though sometimes only by the skin of their teeth; and finally by a certain amount of luck with jobs, particularly one long stint at a company cafeteria, where she was able to even sometimes feed and bathe her children. In recent years she has thought to go and find that company president to thank him. She said, "Not that he really did anything other than employ me," but she feels really grateful for those years.

The Janitor's is a story, then, of shreds of capital—in the form of food, a sense of security, an initial lump sum that bought a modest house, and the occasional family help—that made a difference in the life of a woman who has labored, whose eldest daughters when young both labored for the family, and who has not been able to send any of her children to college. The Janitor, like all of the women in this book, has worked hard to make sense of—to theorize, in the sense described in chapter 1—her world. Her politics are complicated and inextricable from the vicissitudes of her life.

A Family Debate: Why the Youngest Son Did Not Go to College

My first encounter with the Janitor for this project was a summer evening that I spent with her and five of her children, who joined us intermittently. In my field notes from that day, I had jotted, "This has been my absolute favorite evening in Seoul!" The refrain for our conversation of that first meeting had been that the youngest son had not made it to college (he was then just past college age). Mostly, she touched upon this lightly, or even jovially. On a more somber note, though, the Janitor said, "My suffering (kosaeng) would make sense if I had at least educated one of [my sons in] college; but . . . my work has all been for naught . . . At least if you have graduated from college, you can get a ["real"] job, and rise up from there, to a taeri (mid-ranking office job) and on up from there."

During our meetings, the Janitor talked about the fact that South Korea's development has been accomplished on the backs of the hard labor of the likes of the members of her family: "All those exports made from our production labor!" At one point she interjected suddenly: "My eldest daughter tells me not to be so sad, because she will educate her sons, but I tell her, 'That's an entirely different matter; what good is that for me?' " These heartfelt regrets aside, if we listen in on the conversation from that first evening and to later conversations in 1995 and 1996, the Janitor is of conflicting minds on the matter of her sons not having been educated in college. In any case, she would have been elated had one of them made his way there. Noteworthy here, and recalling the Education Mother, is the extent to which the Janitor's desires are gendered: her daughters' education was clearly less critical.

Before proceeding with more of the Janitor's later reflections, let us listen in for a stretch on that 1993 evening. I submit that this conversation, uneven and undecided, reveals the universe of social reflection and even social debate that this book is intent on capturing—for such is the grist of South Korean social life.

This particular stream of conversation began when the Janitor announced that the youngest son, the baby of the family, was not smart enough to go to college. Her fifth daughter, who had recently returned from Japan and was just then about to begin working at a jewelry concession in a department store, disagreed with her mother: "It's that he doesn't want to go; he didn't even take the exam." The Janitor continued, now speaking of her two sons, the youngest two of her seven children: "All they ever do is drive [one was working as a driver at the time]. If they would just go, I would so gladly support them. All sorts of other people manage to go." It was then that she spoke of her life having no meaning because of their not having gone to college. The daughter who had recently returned from Japan interrupted: "They are wage earners; our thinking is different from yours," implying, "Isn't that good enough?" The eldest, and largely unschooled, daughter—who, about to give birth, had come home to prepare and, as is quite customary, planned to stay home for some weeks afterward—spoke up as if to both explain her mother to me, perhaps, and to defend her sister: "In farming villages, people think that if they don't educate their children they'll end up suffering like they did during the Korean War. It's totally different from the United States," where, she meant, it pays to be a farmer. But the younger daughter persisted with her train of thought, speaking this time about precisely the college-graduated salaried worker her mother had dreamed of for her two sons: "Unless you are exceptionally smart, you just get stuck at the bottom rung; I mean, after four years you might become a section chief and then a division chief, but from there a line is drawn, and it is hard to move any further up." This daughter did not make it entirely clear *how* the line would be drawn, but the Janitor—shifting gears from her earlier comments—continued the thought: "Yeah, either you need some pretty strong connections (*ppaek* for 'back' or 'backing') or you had better be really smart." The younger daughter then took things even further: "If you are just a regular college graduate, then after a while you end up quitting and going into business for yourself anyway. That's where you can make money. If you are a wage earner, you might be satisfied with your college degree, but when it comes to the work world, you will end up being ignored." She had thus sketched a veritable catch-22: the only place a college degree would matter would be a company, but for the likes of her brothers, without personal connections, they would not succeed in a company in any case. From there, the Janitor went on: "These days there are many college graduates doing nothing."

These thoughts about the meaning of a college education for people from humble families, run counter to the thoughts on which the Janitor had begun: that her life would be more meaningful had her sons' college degrees been secured. The younger daughter offered this by way of summary: "Business, or some sort of practical skill, those are the best—much better than college." It was then that the youngest son, stretched out nearly the length of the room, the object of the conversation, finally spoke up: "Yeah, a specialty college (*chŏnmun taehak*) would be best—then you could definitely get a job." The Janitor's desires aside, they had collectively been suggesting that there are real limits to the returns of a four-year-college degree for the likes of these boys, with their humble family background (see J. A. Choi 2002 for a fascinating discussion of class and education in contemporary South Korea).

Shifting the conversation a bit, the younger daughter then rekindled her mother's initial stance: "But Koreans simply like the idea of wearing a white shirt and sitting at a desk, holding a pen. A technician might have to touch oil! Heaven forbid that you would have to use your body!" About this daughter, the eldest would later say, and her sister would protest vehemently, "She wants to marry someone rich; she hates poor people." About this white-collar bias, the eldest daughter chimed in to explain: "It's all because of the Korean War: people think that the unlettered will suffer. As it is said the world over, 'Knowledge is power.' People think lightly of those who don't go to college." It was not entirely clear whether she meant to refer to the fact that it was the uneducated who became communists and eventually suffered, or whether she meant to imply more generally that the poor always suffer disproportionately. With this, however, the youngest son was moved to speak up again: "I think differently: it is college that I think lightly of!" Hearing this, the Janitor mused, "I should never have sent him to a humanities high school (inmungye kodŭnghakkyo) [i.e., a college-bound track]. Had I not, he wouldn't be goofing off now [i.e., he would have learned a trade]. It's just too hard to get him into college." With this comment, the Janitor returned to the point on which she had begun: that this son was not smart enough to get into college.

The Janitor thus wavered between asserting the value of a college education and acquiescing to the limits of its value. When the son declared that it was college he thought little of, she could only think that he would have been better off never even applying and instead getting a technical degree. The eldest daughter, obviously disturbed at the way things were unfolding in the conversation, turned to her youngest brother and interjected: "Wait a minute! Whose decision was it for you to attend a humanities high school?" He answered, "Mine," and explained that from there it would have been easier for him to attend college. In so asking, the eldest seemed to be reminding her mother that these strategies were really her brother's decisions—neither her mother's plan, nor her brother's failure.

The conversation then turned to the girls' education. The eldest had been hit by troubled family times and had not been much of a student to begin with, but her younger sister had been really talented at school and had nevertheless been sent to a commercial high school because of the Janitor's gender discrimination. The Janitor defended herself: "For girls it is a matter of finding a good husband, but boys rely on their education their entire lives." The younger daughter had decided to go to Japan because, in spite of having worked hard, she had been unable to pass the entrance exam for a two-year college. The Janitor had been really worried about her going to Japan, saying that she felt as though she were throwing her daughter away. She had pleaded with her to stay in South Korea, begging: "We can struggle here together." As the Janitor put it: "She had the heart to go to college, but things didn't go her way."

The younger daughter explained: "I didn't even want to go to a humanities high school. I was good in everything but English, and I had the mistaken idea that if I went to a commercial high school I wouldn't have to study English anymore." She went on to explain that, in fact, there had been a lot of English there. The eldest, as a young teenager working in a shoe factory, had tried to attend the factory's evening classes in order to obtain a middle school equivalency. Such programs were quite widespread, but often ineffective (H. M. Kim 1995; Kwon 1999). Without the necessary foundation in English and math, she had not been able to keep up, though the next eldest was able to obtain a middle school degree in just this fashion.

When the eldest daughter digressed to say that her teenage son spoke English well, her siblings teased her for this bragging. It was clear that these brothers and sisters were at home with this sort of banter. Having taken on the task of explaining her mother's education ambition, asserting that it was rooted in the countryside and the Korean War and so on, the oldest daughter insisted that she was not overly zealous about her own children's education: "I don't force my kids to study. Many people my age do, but who am I to predict what things will be like twenty years or so from now when they will be grown-up. I, for one, can't imagine that era, but somehow I don't think that a college education will be as important. Mostly, I just let my kids follow their own course." The Janitor echoed this sentiment: "Yes, we will follow the United States: it won't matter whether you did or didn't go to college. A strong body will be what matters." The Janitor's position thus shifted: from lamenting her sons' lack of college education to understanding that not all college educations are the same (even if college-educated, her sons would have been disadvantaged), to predicting a new world in which it would not matter so much anyway.

The Janitor's comment on strong bodies brought a different family legacy—not that of family elites and the like—to the room. The eldest daughter said, "My mother is so strong and healthy; that is her family's legacy." The eldest then went on about her mother in the countryside, describing that when her mother was a little girl, she had walked everywhere with wares piled high on her head. I asked her whether she had resolved to never marry a farmer, for so many of the women I spoke with had decided on that in their youth, and she answered, wryly, "If I had been thinking like that, I would have had the sense to study!"

Later that evening, the fourth daughter came home. This daughter was working for an American company, and the Janitor had been eager for me to meet her and possibly help her with her English. After scurrying to the bedroom to change out of her work apparel, she came out in sweats and immediately handed me her business card. The older of the two boys laughed at this, explaining that in his line of work, there are no name cards. They all chuckled when he noted that he did, however, have a beeper. At the time, the older boy's job was wallpapering—a service he described as mostly for the rich. Returning things to a more serious note, the eldest daughter then bragged about this brother, saying that he was a model son who brought all of his wages to his mother. She then complained about her youngest brother, who brought nothing home. The youngest protested: "I do so— once I brought home [a big sum]." They all then spoke on a bit about wallpapering, and the Janitor criticized it as such an extravagant thing (it was not uncommon for people to completely re-paper a whole apartment before moving in). The eldest daughter suggested it was only "a tiny minority" who lived like that, but the Janitor insisted it was more common, which recalls the Janitor's proclamation about "half of South Koreans living that way." Clearly she had a keen sense of exclusion from the ways of the wealthy, or even the middle classes.

Three years later, in spite of various concessions to her children's take on the world, the Janitor persisted on the meaning of college education. By then, both boys—the youngest recently having finished his compulsory military service—were working as drivers for a film studio unit. Together they aspired to buy a truck. They were happy, she explained, to be working on the road, to be traveling together. She persisted, though: "In this country you need to go to college because of the world of difference between what a college graduate and other people can do." To show just that world of difference, she stretched her hands as far apart as they could go.

Later that same year, 1996, the Janitor talked about changing times. Over the span of a short conversation, she wavered back and forth in her consideration of the access to and meaning of education. As suggested earlier, I take this sort of wavering not as the mark of indecision or personal confusion, but as a reflection of complicated times, which have rendered such calculations nearly impossible. Meanwhile, one of her daughters had married a civil service officer working in one of Seoul's small satellite cities. She explained that she was fond of civil service work because, being exam based, it does not discriminate regarding education level. With this comment, she sounded perhaps a note of sympathy for her sons. Shifting course again, though, she went on to say that "nowadays it is really only a 'bad kid' who doesn't at least graduate from high school." Then, on her earlier tack again, she described the economics of education exclusion: "Even now, there are kids hidden away here and there who really can't afford to go to high school." And flip-flopping again, "South Korea has really developed, and there are all kinds of people today out looking to offer aid . . . There are even rich people who answer the letters of poor people who write to the newspaper saying that they don't have the money to study . . . So today, if you are a good student, you simply have to write a letter and somebody from the media (*maesŭk'om* for "mass communications") will help. To tell you the truth, today the truly ignorant (*musikhan*) are those people who don't even know how to write such a letter."

The reader has seen that the Janitor can be radically populist at one moment, and apologetic for the powers-that-be at another. One final education story—the Janitor's unself-conscious thoughts about the brief interlude in which she attended North Korean schools as a young girl, during the Korean War—reveals the radical strain of her thinking:

> They [the North Koreans] took all of us [kids] to school and they told us that there were no *yang* [*yangban*] and *sang* [*sangmin*] anymore; they used the word "*tongmu*" (comrade) and said that all boys and girls were equal . . . What I will never understand, as long as I live, is why —with all those good ideas—North Korea didn't develop? It seems to me that those ideas should have made for such a good society. I don't know—I just don't get it. Maybe it was because they didn't have enough money. When it comes down to it, frankly speaking, South Korea got all sorts of help from the United States . . . You know it wasn't the North Koreans who did that killing here [in the Korean War], it was Southerners who killed their own people; the Northerners are really good people.

These comments run radically against the grain of South Korean anticommunism and prevailing historical perspectives under the Cold War era (while they recall similar comments of the Education Mother). The Janitor managed to be politically provocative without reference to any community of dissent in contemporary South Korean society. Hers are homespun politics, and remarkable ones at that. The Janitor's education stories, and the conversations of her family, help to establish the complexity of class maps (like those in chapter 2) and of class work. Her identifications, and those of her children, happen in narrative, life stories, and in conversations like those we have listened in on here.

I turn now to the contours and character of the education gamble, into the IMF Crisis era (1997–2001).

Post-IMF and Beyond: The Education Gamble

Education, we have seen, has always been a bit of a gamble. Certainly, such were the thoughts of the Janitor and her children as they calculated the costs of the sons not having been educated, and as they thought ahead to the lives of the next generation, the Janitor's grandchildren. But today, in the first breaths of the twenty-first century, one finds a South Korea in which the terra firma is shakier still. The financial crisis that was answered by a bailout of unprecedented size served to pose perhaps as many questions to South Korea's standard operating procedures as had the preceding decades of popular struggle. At the heart of those operating procedures was state-led *chaebŏl* (conglomerate)-centered South Korean capitalism (see E. M. Kim 1997; Woo 1991). The IMF Crisis made strange bedfellows of President Kim Dae Jung, a lifelong dissident (put under house arrest under Park Chung Hee and indicted, and nearly executed under Chun Doo Hwan for having "instigated" the Kwangju Rebellion), and the neoliberalism mandated by the International Monetary Fund. Byung-Kook Kim wrote of the "surreal" feeling of it all "with Kim Dae Jung—a politician known for nationalist and populist political inclinations—single-mindedly pursuing a neoliberal program of massive downsizing through a political mechanism consciously modeled after the social democracy of Western Europe within a fragmented Korean society of Confucian familism" (2000, 40). By the millenium one could not but sense the sea change: venture capitalism was everywhere, and *bench'ŏ* (venture), a veritable household word; the sense of the decline of the middle class was pervasive; education was being privatized to previously unimaginable degrees; South Korea was becoming wired as quickly as any corner of the globe; and the media had definitively declared South Korea's "stock market fever" (K. Lee 2001, 127).

In thinking about the Crisis, many people shared the sense that some South Koreans had been caught red-handed, that crony capitalism (its infrastructures, personnel, and ideologies) had tumbled the South Korean house. This thinking, however, in no way celebrated the justice of what would follow; the sense that the "rich are getting richer" seems evermore a feature of the South Korean present. Striking are these statistics: from 1997 to 1998 South Korea's poorest 10 percent suffered a 23 percent income reduction, and the next 10 percent a 10 percent income reduction, just as the richest 10 percent benefited from skyrocketing interest rates (B. K. Kim 2000, 78). The media has taken to reporting on South Korea's "downward leveling" and on the creation of "two nations" or a "20[rich]–80[everyone else] society" (B. K. Kim 2000, 87; see also Nelson 2000 on the IMF Crisis).

Today, as the IMF Crisis has been declared officially over, it is clear that while it is indeed so for some, for many (less advantaged) South Koreans the effects of the Crisis have by no means subsided (J. Song 2002).

The very meaning of heretofore markers and promises of the good life—an agreed-upon elite education, *chaebŏl* employment, study abroad—has been in flux, if not suspended. As I have been busily arguing in this book, the sense that the rug has been pulled out from under, or that sensible calculations have at times turned out to be way off base—be it educating your children in Confucian academies or not knowing when to sell your land, as in the stories of the Janitor above—has been a persistent feature of South Korean modernity. People are wondering: How changed is our world? How should we best prepare our children for a new world (as the Janitor's eldest daughter wondered aloud about her son)? And, as always: What shape might a more just social arrangement take?

Several recent news items speak to the education watershed in South Korea today (see S. J. Park 2001). First is the story of skyrocketing parental investment in extracurricular learning (*sakyoyuk*). In 1996, the top 25 percent of extra-education investors (i.e., parents) were spending 4.6 times that of the bottom 25 percent, while by 1999 this had risen to a 9.5 times difference (C. Yi 2000). The second concerns the ongoing story of the legality of extracurricular education (private lessons and home tutoring). In 1980 extracurricular education was banned in South Korea. It was banned as part and parcel of the reassertion of military rule by President Chun Doo Hwan. It is interesting, if not ironic, that at the height of insidious power politics, measures were promulgated that were nominally devoted to ensure equality of access to education. Also interesting is that one of the most rapid periods of the expansion of higher education is also the early 1980s. It is clear that these education reforms were carrot-and-stick measures. In 2000 the supreme court revoked these restrictions. These revocations have been understood to represent changing times: increasingly it is parental and student "rights" (*kwŏlli*) and the logic of the free market that are privileged. Surveys in 1999 revealed that 62 percent of elementary school students and 55 percent of all students were receiving some after-school education (Kang 2000). An April 2000 editorial opined that these neoliberal reforms have negative consequences for social justice in South Korea: public education is jeopardized, and the poor will get poorer and the rich richer. The jury is not out, however, on this liberalization (Kang 2000).

I turn now to Mi-yŏn's youngest brother to illustrate these education and social sea changes.

Mi-yŏn's Youngest Brother (Mi-yŏn's Mother's Youngest Son)

Having lived in his house as a boarder in the early 1980s, I have known Mi-yŏn's youngest brother since his early elementary school days. Foremost in my memory, try though I might, I simply could not get that little boy to engage me. As I described in chapter 2, language had not been a barrier in my playing with the poorer children who gathered in the alley next to his house, but somehow I could not get a smile out of this well-clad, pudgy little boy. Over his twenties, though, I have enjoyed many conversations with him, by e-mail, and in person, both in South Korea and in the United States. In my visits to her home over the years, his mother has usually seen to it that I had a few minutes to chat alone with him—vacating the kitchen table with the pretense of one or another thing to do. And I know that on occasion he has gone to considerable effort to time his trips home from college in synch with my visits there. And he has often driven me home when the evening grew late.

The early 1990s brought Mi-yŏn's youngest brother to the United States as a visiting undergraduate student; he had by then made the ambitious decision to repeat an undergraduate degree, the second time around in an engineering field. Through the early- and mid-1990s, at his request, I intermittently gathered the thoughts of technophile friends on the U.S. programs to which he might someday apply for graduate study. At some point, though, in the mid 1990s he began to wonder about a graduate degree, questioning his own earlier desire to become a professor, also becoming more confident in his earning ability with just a B.A. Steadfast throughout these years was his deep interest in the U.S. academy, his reverence for advanced degrees (even as he contemplated not pursuing one), and his considerable personal ambition. At each turn, Mi-yŏn's brother would carefully describe his plans to me; I always looked forward to our chats—his thoughts were so precise, considered, and interesting. But more than anything, I loved talking to him because of his unfailing concern for his mother: a pretty sight to my eyes.

By summer 2000, although his ambition was by no means flagging, much had changed. During that visit, Mi-yŏn's brother reported that he had recently quit his company, where he had worked for a couple of years. Two years earlier, he had told me that, with that job, he was putting off the decision about graduate school for a while. This time I chanced upon him in a rare week: a week off between jobs. When I arrived that early evening, he came out of his room to say hello but quickly excused himself, explaining that just then he was "chatting" (ch'aeting) by e-mail with a coworker from his former company, who was now working abroad. That evening Mi-yŏn's Mother did not leave the table but stood by, listening intently as her son described his employment plans to me in great detail; we were catching up. That his mother did not leave the area as we talked reflected, I think, her own considerable concern about his plans. In the job that he had just left, he had been an engineer in a forty-odd person start-up firm. When he had joined the firm, he planned to stay a couple of years and then head off for an advanced degree abroad; he had timed his quitting just as his stock options would become his own—but he did not quit to go abroad. Two years earlier he had been undecided as to whether to pursue engineering or business overseas, or perhaps both. Again and again that evening he stressed to me that the most important thing to him was the "freedom" to do what he wanted, to "venture" as it were. Clear that evening was that the venture capital world was his baby: he was among those following its every twist and turn—a member of that first generation of workers to really ride its waves. Now he had decided to look for a job as a venture analyst for a large investment group—a radical departure from his recent employment, which had been closely linked with his technical undergraduate training. He explained that the entire South Korea had become like Silicon Valley; the radical comparison—all of South Korea and a single American corporate-scape —actually seemed pretty apt to me after only several days in Seoul. The diffusion rate—of everything—in South Korea, and Seoul in particular, seems often beyond belief.

What surprised me most that day were Mi-yŏn's brother's radically transformed thoughts on study abroad (yuhak), in the United States—I had asked, since yuhak had been so much on his mind when we had last spoken about his future. Clearly, study abroad had sometime ago become passé for him. This is how he put it: "What I could learn under a professor in the United States in two years would be nothing compared to what I would get in the field, on the job, in South Korea." Later that evening, driving me back to my lodging, he ventured an excursus on South Korean education—or, for that matter, on education generally: "Education is really going to have to change because it is so behind. As it stands, it cannot keep pace with the world. If I were to take five years to get a Ph.D., I would end up behind beyond repair."

Just as I was reviewing this chapter in summer 2002, I received an e-mail from Mi-yŏn's youngest brother, writing to introduce his latest job as a venture capitalist—and to apologize for not visiting, although he had just spent several months in the U.S. "arm" of his company. He wrote: "And finally I am sure what I should do in my life. That's the global public/private stock market investment . . ."

As for Mi-yŏn's Mother, she wished that this son would follow a more traditional career path—stay put in some company, or "better yet, become a university professor." She hoped that he could "make good on all of the skills he has acquired—otherwise, what a waste!" Also, she was really troubled that this son was so interested in stock investments, all wrapped up over when to buy and sell. Most of all, she worried that thinking so much about money will ruin his health—as it has hers (a matter revisited in chapter 9). But that summer of 2000, he was resolute, saying to his mother, "You don't see me getting upset about it, do you?" Later in the evening, when she again worried aloud about his health, he leaned his head over to the nearby mirror (a mirror embossed with the insignia of his father's company): "Look, Mom, I've showered, I've exercised; look at my face—I'm even tanned." Smugly—smiling—he left the room, leaving us to talk, as he knew we would, about his father. Mi-yŏn's Mother, watching him walk away, said, "I wonder where I went wrong raising them—because all three of them care so much about money." But we cannot take a comment like this one completely at face value either!

Not entirely unlike her son, Mi-yŏn's Mother is not of a single mind on changes in South Korea. Several months later, in a conversation with one of my students serving then as a research assistant, Mi-yŏn's Mother spoke about post-IMF South Korea in terms of fundamental changes in the way people are coming to think about work; and she quickly turned to her son's case to further substantiate the point. She spoke optimistically—quite at odds with the media representation of the middle-class family in crisis with IMF-related unemployment—about company families in the aftermath of being fired. "As long as their wives are clever," she explained, "there are so many things they can do: open a restaurant south of the Han River, or even go and farm." When my student expressed her surprise, and said, "Farming?" Mi-yŏn's Mother affirmed that "people these days are following their particular inclinations." She continued that times have changed: "these days, as the very idea of 'high' and 'low' occupations wanes, people look for work that is well-suited to them—and so the feeling of our society [is changing]." Here it serves to recall her own son, who most of all wants freedom to do as he pleases. If Mi-yŏn's Mother had hoped that her son would pursue yesteryear's status track, she also celebrated exactly the new values he espoused.

In Mi-yŏn's youngest brother's IMF-era thoughts we find a contest over the worth and promise of education. Over scant years, he came to appraise education differently in accordance with transformations of the structure of the labor market, of public confidence in large business, and of social stratification. Not surprisingly, his mother was torn: dismayed to find him deserting his quite prestigious and conventional path, but at the same time exhilarated by new possibilities for a changed world. We can recall that the Janitor was similarly torn over the meaning of her sons' education and employment choices. More about Mi-yŏn's Mother on her sons' education can be read in chapter 9.

The education tales in this chapter have revealed the enormous parental (and class) work entailed in educating children. That work has also been revealed to be emotionally complex—education is an intergenerational project—and socially and politically fraught in changing times. In the following chapter, we will fan out to the consideration of social mobility, both including and beyond education.

5

SOCIAL MOBILITY
"Facts" and "Fictions"

In chapters 3 and 4 we observed the complexity of South Korean class and class mobility. The women's class locations and identifications, told obliquely through the stories of the networks through which I came to meet them, are, we learned, never static, and are inextricable from gender and from gendered stories. The education stories tutored us in the complexity of class work; it is there that people set out to effect their own or others' class mobility. In these stories, we also saw that gender—ideas about gendered ways of being and becoming—is always already part of the picture. We saw that mobility calculations have long been confused and are necessarily ambivalent because times are changing, and because the current moment itself is already always fraught. Hard to grasp, however, is the character of the ambivalence. The reader wonders whether there are historical coordinates that have structured the ambivalence, which have made for its particular character, content, and expression. It is the job of this chapter to answer: Yes, there are historical developments that bear upon women's narration of class, identification, and mobility.

Recalling Pierre Bourdieu, on structures and representations as necessary research "moments," from chapter 1, this chapter turns more self-consciously to both political-economic structures, such as the changing contours of the labor market and the workings of education capital, and representational economies, for example, the sense of the Korean War as a watershed, over South Korea's post–Korean War period. This chapter organizes the structural and the representational for this period through the story of the Laundress, the woman we have learned about thus far through the story of her ill-fated marriage and that of raising "tall trees"—the three sons she was determined to keep upright, to prevent from bringing harm to others (otherwise better dead, she had said dramatically; see chapter 3).

In keeping with this book's discussions of narrative and gender thus far, this chapter asserts their centrality for addressing even the seemingly most basic queries in the study of social mobility: how, when, and whether people's chances of social mobility have changed. Taking up numerous assertions about mobility, primarily founded on statistically collected data, my aim is by no means to discard the entire, and largely sociological, body of literature. To the contrary, I am grateful that others have painstakingly gathered facts and numbers important for this book's story. Facts and numbers, however, tell a partial story that has been largely deaf to women's roles, backgrounds, and identifications, and to narrative and the ways in which people recognize themselves. Recalling the education stories of chapter 4, how could we discuss the class identities and mobility of the Education Mother without paying attention to her economic activities beyond earned income, her gendered understandings of women's work, her family history, her labor for her son's education, and so on? Whereas chapter 4 began to assert the feeling of mobility narratives via education, its most critical coordinate, this chapter aims to organize the ambivalence we found there. This chapter thus lends equal importance to the work of socio-ideological regimes (in the sense of Bakhtin; see chapters 1 and 3) through personal understandings of changing times, and to the structural transformation of South Korea's economy. It is also this chapter's aim to familiarize the reader with the extant literature on these matters, for that literature not only anchors this book's findings and contributions but also reflects some of the very work of gender (and gendered bias) that this book is concerned with.

This chapter's title, with its "facts" and "fictions," intends to suspend simple understanding of both. The facts are always partial and as such can easily author fictions; and the fictions often reveal the work of narrative (e.g., of national memory) and are thus real parts of the social story I am interested in here. Taking them both seriously and skeptically, I do not mean to revere or undermine either.

Although this chapter offers numbers and figures that appear to set the scene and sketch the contours of this book's landscape, I resisted placing this discussion earlier because I wanted the reader to first become at home with the sensibilities, the structures of feeling, and the narrative tastes that this book is most of all committed to relaying. Believing that the narratives met thus far somehow exceed the picture drawn in this chapter, I am confident nevertheless that it will help to tell the story of class, mobility, women, and narrative in post–Korean War South Korea.

A Transgenerational Gendered Perspective

In examining postwar South Korea, we cannot but pause to consider the rapid decrease of farm work and the dizzying increases in urban production and petty-entrepreneurial work over the course of a single generation. As one sociologist observed, "after only three decades of industrial transformation, a nation of small cultivators became a nation of urban wage workers" (Koo 2001, 34). Indeed, South Korea is a popular example in the annals of development studies (Amsden 1989). Sociologists, however, have reached little consensus about the meaning of these structural transformations and the nature of their effects on individual and familial trajectories. In consideration of the reorganization of the labor market, even some of the most basic numbers are debated because analysts do not agree on how to characterize and classify post–Korean War jobs. Particularly contested, for example, are the boundaries between clerical workers and manual laborers, petty-entrepreneurs and informal economy workers, and capitalists and upper-level white-collar workers (see, for example, Janelli and Yim 1993, 236). The demarcation of these boundaries is problematic, not only for sociological studies of South Korea, but it is also at the heart of both neo-Marxist and neo-Weberian debates on class in general (Crompton 1993, 90–91,191). We can observe these debates for South Korea through several numerical contests. For example, Doo-Seung Hong and Kim Yŏng-mo calculate considerable increases in the numbers of the new middle class (Kim records increases from 6.9 percent in 1960 to 17.3 percent in 1980; similarly, Hong notes increases from 6.6 percent in 1960 to 17.7 percent in 1980 and 19.8 percent in 1990); however, orthodox Marxist Sŏ Kwan-mo records an increase of only 4.3 percent in 1960 to 8.7 percent in 1980 for the new middle class. On the other hand, Sŏ's estimation of the growth of the laboring class is much more dramatic than that of Hong and Kim (Hong and Koo record laborers at 22.6 percent in 1980, in contrast with Sŏ's figure of 37.2 percent) (Hong and Koo 1993).

Although sociologists of South Korea seek to understand employment in the context of society's evolving socioeconomic realities, they remain limited by not only a lack of quantitative consensus but also by the gender and production-focused biases of their primarily statistical measures. Also compounding the situation is that South Korean sociology, perhaps because of its historically orthodox Marxist bias, has paid relatively little attention to the study of social mobility. This book departs from the limitations of deriving class identities, social history, and social life from static maps of men's productive labor.

In so doing, this chapter builds on discussions in chapter 1 by approaching class through the transgenerational context of people's lives, including their families of origin and childhoods; taking women as critical agents in the production of family culture; and considering the narration of class mobility and identities. A transgenerational approach to social mobility pays attention to the particular class cultures and resource networks of families over time. In this way, I take up families not as uniform social entities but as social spaces through which class identities are transmitted (Bertaux and P. Thompson 1993, 7; P. Thompson 1993, 297 and 1981, 32). As Paul Thompson argues, "despite a general recognition of the importance of parental influence and other familial factors both in achievement and in the definition of social status, investigations of social mobility have been almost exclusively focused on statistical studies of *individual* occupational mobility" (1993, 15). Thus class identities are developed from and sometimes in reaction against family experiences. Furthermore, these experiences are subjectively remembered and recuperated in adult life and desires (Spence 1991, 236; Steedman 1986). The inclusion of women in discussions of class and social mobility demands much more than merely adding women's labor-force participation to the picture; rather, women must be appreciated as critical agents in the production of family's material lives and class identities, and in the work of class mobility.

Before proceeding with theoretical and historical discussions, I return to the Laundress, whose story continues in greater detail in the second half of this chapter, in order to sketch the challenges of understanding class in South Korea. Like most women of her generation, the Laundress belies easy placement in South Korea's contemporary class cartography. Upon cursory inspection, she (with her husband) is seen as a propertyless laundress whose observable living quarters and lifestyle are by most standards humble for contemporary South Korea; her husband works with her, having failed in other lines of work. The Laundress's monthly earnings after rent would not challenge these first impressions; nor would her education—both she and her husband are unschooled. The Laundress's class location and identities, however, become considerably more complicated when we take a transgenerational look at her story. We learn that her father had an elementary school education, an elite pedigree in the days of his childhood;

that three of her four brothers are college graduates, putting them in a privileged minority of their times; and that all of her three sons began college, two of them graduating—a considerable accomplishment for the sons of a modest laundress, although she had hoped to make a professor of one of them.

In the context of these education trajectories of her own patrilineage and of her all-male offspring, the Laundress's economic life seems anomalous. The picture becomes more complicated when we learn more about her male kin and their own horizons and limits. Her father identified himself as a *yangban* (hereditary elite) but worked mostly as a common urban laborer. The Laundress's one brother who did not finish college faltered in South Korea and then emigrated to the United States, where he now runs a not-so-successful laundry. Similarly, a generation later, her one son who did not finish college decided to emigrate. When I first met the Laundress, she was extremely worried that her youngest son, though then soon to be a college graduate majoring in education, would be unable to find work as a teacher because jobs were scarce and seemed to be reserved for those with connections and bribe money. As seen in chapter 4, the path to and promises of education must be examined at the crossroads of family specificities (e.g., family structure and the distribution of resources) and historical contingencies (e.g., the value of education capital and labor market composition).

In thinking about the class positions and identities of the Laundress or her family, it is important to consider both the social scientific and popular discourses that have obscured the contributions of her work, and the influences of her family of origin's class culture and resources. To argue that in the case of South Korea, social scientific and popular discourse combine to obscure the very parameters that make for a sociohistorically nuanced understanding of class, I begin with the developmentalist bias of much of the writing and understanding of social mobility. With these biases in mind, we will consider the "facts" that have characterized social mobility over the post–Korean War period.

The Recent History of South Korean Social Mobility

The Developmentalist Bias

In both scholarly writing and the South Korean imagination, there has been a tendency to overestimate equality of opportunity in South Korea's post–Korean War era. A "developmentalist bias" makes facile assumptions about individual mobility trajectories and well-being on the basis of South

Korea's dramatic "structural mobility"—the composite of employment shifts that emerge with urbanization and industrialization. This bias is reflected in the structures of feeling that fashion the present. In turn, class identities and horizons are fashioned at the crossroads of collective mobility histories —particular structures of feeling—and personal mobility stories. Briefly discussing the general study of social mobility will help to elaborate the parameters of the developmentalist bias in and about South Korea.

The general study of social mobility is divided as to the meaning of the sectoral redistribution of employment stimulated by industrialization, or structural mobility. Broadly, theoretical positions cluster around two main hypotheses. The first, purported by the so-called modernization or industrialization theorists, maintains that increases in structural mobility lead to a greater openness of society; its proponents argue that there is net mobility, after correcting for structural mobility, because of increases in education, mass communication, urbanization, geographical mobility, middle-class work, and the decline of ascribed attributes that are required for employment (B. K. Kim 1993, 22–31; Kurz and Müller 1987; Lipset and Zetterberg 1959). The second hypothesis, known most widely as the FJH hypothesis argues that, in spite of the structural change shared by the capitalist industrial economies, there are no *real* increases in people's mobility chances; that is, people's relative mobility chances remain static over time (Featherman, Jones, and Hauser 1975). Critical for the FJH hypothesis, whose research is wholly statistical, is the constancy of cross-national findings (for South Korea as an anomalous case, see Byoung-Kwan Kim 1993).

In the case of South Korea, a state-promulgated and state-centered developmentalist bias echoes the modernization/industrialization perspective. However, many aspects of social life—particularly in recent years—have fostered popular perceptions closer to the formulations of the FJH hypothesis, against "real" mobility. My own survey of the sociological literature on social mobility in South Korea suggests that there were relative mobility opportunities in the immediate aftermath of the Korean War but that these diminished over time. However, in order to grasp the popular sense of mobility opportunities over the postwar era, it is important to pay attention to the long-lasting effects of these early mobility opportunities. We will see these lasting effects at work in the Laundress's sense of her own and of South Korea's more general mobility history. Here we can also recall the Janitor's considerable confusion over the matter of mobility opportunity.

The South Korean developmentalist bias builds on several assumptions, the first being that structural shifts represent a vast extension of mobility opportunities, as people have left the agricultural sector for one or another urban (and often industrial) destination. In this vein, Nam Ch'un-ho warns, for example, to conclude from the dramatic shrinkage of agricultural labor and the increases in industrial production labor that rural migrants to the city uniformly joined the ranks of the urban industrial sector does a tremendous injustice to the enormous variety of the experience of rural exodus (1988, 85; see Brandt 1979; M. G. Lee 1979). Dae-Il Kim and Robert Topel similarly argue that South Korea's manufacturing growth was achieved by hiring new entrants into the labor force, while "migrants from agriculture entered the nonmanufacturing sector, replacing the young workers who were hired into manufacturing" (1995, 229). The second assumption of the developmentalist bias is that the individuals and households comprising South Korea's sectoral shifts have been in aggregate "upwardly mobile." The third assumption is that these shifts correspond to increases in mental labor (i.e., white-collar vs. manual or blue-collar labor) that require education credentials; this argument contends that these sectoral transformations both build on and foster widespread education opportunity (Chŏn and Kwŏn 1991, 532). The fourth assumption of the developmentalist bias is that these sectorial shifts both are predicated upon and fabricate a society that is not held back by rigid status hierarchies prescribing particular productive lives and class habitus to people (see Cumings 1997; Lie 1998). In sum, there has been both a popular and scholarly tendency to imagine the contours of individual mobility trajectories and meanings from the fact of dramatic structural mobility. Although this tendency to apply aggregate assumptions to the social life of individual and family trajectories is problematic, it is nonetheless critical to consider the "real" effects of this social portrait on people's class identities and horizons (for a comparative case see Sewell 1985, 268–269).

This developmentalist portrayal of South Korea as an open society relies on particular social understandings of the engine and timing of social and economic transformation. There are several sociohistorical breaks that are posited to have enabled various aspects of the transformation, including the end of Japanese colonialism (1945), the Korean War (1950–1953), land reform (1949–1950), and the rise of "modern" social relations (see Cumings 1997; Lie 1998). The Korean War, a colossal national tragedy, is an easily identifiable watershed because its death toll, destruction, and dislocations refigured the political, social, and economic landscape (Kendall 1996, 203). Byoung-Kwan Kim describes the destructive effects of the war: "Not only human lives, but also infrastructure, traditional residential arrangements of villages, industry structure, culture, and social order, including traditional rules that had shaped individual work lives, were destroyed by the three-year war" (1993, 247). Taken together with the end of colonialism, the war marks a threshold to modernity, signifying the end of fixed social and spatial ascriptions (see, for example, Brandt [1971] 1990, 18, 56–57). In addition to the refuge of people from local ideological strife, there was the demise of status distinctions both because of class struggle and the material destruction of the markings and trappings of these distinctions—the records and accoutrements of the rich (see Kendall 1985, 41). The war memory turns on the understandings of collectively shared impoverishment. Only a small minority went untouched by the dislocations and deprivations of this war. For the women in this book, it is the Education Mother and Mi-yŏn's Mother who most detailed the impact of the Korean War on their lives—as previously mentioned, both their natal families are examples of so-called divided families (for having come south, or for having relatives who left for the north) (see C. S. Kim 1988 and S. J. Lee 2000). Postliberation South Korea adopted the formal ideologies of a cold-war democracy, organized initially under a United States–centered military government, and later under the sway of U.S. political and cultural imperialism and military authoritarian development-focused regimes. It is important to note that these hegemonies were established against widespread popular socialist sentiments and struggle in Korea in the immediate aftermath of colonialism (Cumings 1981). Several of the women in this book, themselves old enough to have been exposed to socialist ideologies, spoke of the socialist alternative as one that had whetted their own childhood imagination; in this vein we can recall some of the thoughts of the Janitor and the Education Mother in chapter 4 (see also Mi-yŏn's Mother in chapter 9) (see also Abelmann 1996).

Land reform, which eroded the holdings of the largest landlords and turned large numbers of dispossessed peasants into independent farmers, is also critical to the public story of the erosion of village status hierarchies and the increases of economic opportunity (Janelli 1993, 22; Lie 1998). The promulgation and efficacy of land reform, however, were not entirely uniform or successful (Abelmann 1996). There is a widespread sense that historical processes converged to engender "modern" social relations which eliminated the excesses and exploitation of premodern social hierarchies. That is, this modern era "liberated" national subjects who could exercise their will to speed freely to the vortex of South Korea's vital economic development (M. K. Park 1995, 536). I submit that although we need to pay attention to the ideological effects of this developmentalist portrait—knowing that these have in part authored critical structures of feeling—we must remember that they obscure important continuities that prevailed in the contemporary era. Presumed watersheds are often permeable, and individual trajectories cannot be fully gathered from aggregate statistics. The Laundress's case—and those of all the women in this book—challenges us to be mindful of contemporary links to the past. In the Laundress's case, although her father's early rural emigration did not translate into steady factory work in Seoul's burgeoning industrial sector, his preliberation and pre–Korean War class and education capital nonetheless affected some of his children's achievement. The approach taken here reveals social historical processes that are otherwise easily obscured. I turn now to a broad discussion of mobility over the post–Korean War era.

Facts

Fragments of the postwar South Korean story enable us to sketch a portrait of collective social mobility, which can help us make sense of personal mobility histories as they take place and structure consciousness amidst ideologies or fictions of mobility.

I consider two main phases to the post–Korean War social mobility history. In the early postwar years, the dislocations of the war combined with the early phases of modern industrialization and the rapid expansion of education to effect opportunities for some open (or relative) social mobility. Over time, however, with the slowdown in social and economic change, these opportunities evaporated. The ideological effects of this history are as follows: the early years of relatively open mobility opportunity, bolstered by the state's ongoing developmentalist rhetoric, fostered an ideology of individualistic open mobility—the sense that one's efforts could ford considerable class distances. This ideology long outlasted the social realities and fictions that produced it, managing to persist—if awkwardly and at times intermittently—even in the face of considerable collective and personal counterevidence (as we encountered in the Janitor's narration in chapter 4). It is these awkward ideological effects that we will find in the Laundress's social mobility narrative, and throughout this book. Beginning in the 1980s, then throughout the 1990s and into the millennium, however, increasingly visible class distinctions and fixed class subcultures contributed to a growing sense of limited mobility horizons, challenging the developmentalist ideologies of open mobility. This said, however, we have also seen that some post-IMF developments foster yet new senses of mobility opportunities; here we can recall conversation with Mi-yŏn's Mother and her youngest son in chapter 4.

Several statistical studies confirm the relatively open mobility in the years immediately following the Korean War. Based on a work survey gathered nationwide in 1983, Byoung-Kwan Kim reports that from 1954 to 1963 there were much greater chances of dramatic labor mobility than in any period thereafter (1993, 244). It is unfortunate that much of the recent work on social mobility in South Korea draws on this same 1983 survey. The concerns and scope of that survey—intragenerational, occupational mobility—were limited such that surveyors did not gather, for example, information about the workers' parents. Hagen Koo similarly documents greater egalitarian income distribution in the immediate postwar era through the 1960s (1984, 1031,1035). We can attribute the relatively more open and egalitarian early years of the postwar period to several factors, including: the effects of the war, the structure of industry, and changes in status hierarchies. Koo maintains, for example, that the distributive figures for this period are good because of the rather sudden increase in full employment following the disruptions of the Korean War in conjunction with the sudden rapid growth of the industrial sector (1984, 1031). Characteristics of employment and industrial structure in that era were also relevant.

This early period allowed for greater open mobility because of the relatively unstructured first phase of industrialization in which career paths were not yet systematized (B. K. Kim 1993, 246, 248). In this vein, we will see that the Laundress admired people who made something grand of early work opportunities in Seoul. Koo supports this contention with his argument that work thereafter became increasingly credentialized and thus reliant on education capital (1984). As a result, the gap between manual and nonmanual labor increased (B. K. Kim 1993, 244), as did income differentials between those with and without a college education (peaking in the mid-1970s, Koo 1984, 1035). Finally, real advances in the long struggle to abolish status hierarchies—a struggle that began in the last century and was thwarted by Japanese colonialism—also bolstered mobility in this early period. Korea's independence (from colonialism) opened a social space for individuals' social capacity (vs. ascribed status positions); to what extent, however, South Korea's postcolonial, divided reality continued to thwart this project (as the Laundress will query) remains an important question (M. K. Park 1995, 536). Over time, however, the horizons of mobility narrowed and class differences became more distant. The Laundress's story—

the larger promise of her educated brothers than of her educated sons—is telling of this trajectory.

Studies of mobility through marriage concur with these findings. The immediate postwar years saw the highest chances of both men's and women's upward mobility through marriage, while later, increasing education homogamy prevailed (K. S. Pak 1993, 51; S. C. Pak 1991). It is not surprising that mobility through marriage should accompany increasing openness of occupational mobility, because with men's expanded job horizons, women could bargain on the potential of a man's personal and education attributes independent of his family background (Kendall 1996, 102). Indeed, stories of parents marrying their daughter to a promising son of a poor family are not uncommon. Conversely, there is the familiar story of the pretty and proprietous girl who wins a man above her social standing. In such cases, her charm and beauty are considered critical attributes for the attainment of upward mobility. We will see that the Laundress regrets not having made such a marriage. It is also not surprising that apparent mobility through marriage should accompany this era of radical postwar dislocation because the immediate family circumstances of many young people were discordant with their class upbringings and identities—as was the case with the Laundress.

The narrowing of education-mobility opportunity over the postwar era similarly echoes the trend toward a less open society. Although studies report increases in both education opportunity (Chŏn and Kwŏn 1991, 532; Oh 1975, 116; You 1981, 68) and in the value of education capital over the early years of the immediate postwar period (especially in the 1970s, Koo 1984, 1034), they caution that such figures do not necessarily indicate increases in open mobility, because of the concurrent escalating correspondence between social background and education achievement (see H. J. Cho 1995; Chŏn and Kwŏn 1991, 532; You 1981, 68). The value of education was also compromised because society was increasingly unable to subsume the surge of high school and college graduates in jobs commensurate with these education credentials (Oh 1975, 116–117, 132, 146). Several studies argue that increases in education for women are even weaker indicators of open mobility, because their education attainments are more closely determined by class background than those of men (K. S. Pak 1993, 53; Sŏl 1994, 249).

In the 1980s and 1990s an increasing sense of the collapse of real mobility opportunities strengthened an emergent class-consciousness. Economic slowdown in conjunction with political and discursive transformations limited both actual mobility opportunities *and* the belief in them. First, there was the slowdown of structural changes—the stabilization of South Korea's occupational structure, rates of rural exodus, industrial expansion, and GNP growth. Second, the inflationary economy of the 1970s and 1980s led to an increasing gulf between landowners and the propertyless; there was an escalating sense among many people that it was too late even to dream of buying a domicile in Seoul (one of the Laundress's greatest sadnesses) (Han 1993; Koo 1984, 1034). Third, with the rapid expansion of education into the 1970s and through the 1980s and 1990s, the value of a college education declined, guaranteeing neither employment nor a middle-class life (Sŏl 1994, 252, 266). These shifts have called attention to the advantages of class resources (economic, symbolic, and social) beyond education and employment (Chang 1991; Koo and Hong 1980). In this vein, Koo refers to the frustration of the middle class, which is better educated than—but deprived relative to—the capitalist class (1987, 109). In his observations of the 1950s and 1960s, Byung-hun Oh made the same point about the salaried middle classes in relation to the nouveaux riches (1975, 136). Fourth, unleashed from both the constraints of decades of authoritarian regimes and the austere culture and ideology of dissent (Abelmann 1996), the lifestyle and consumption of the upper class became increasingly visible in the 1980s and 1990s (Cotton and van Leest 1996; Janelli and Yim 1993, 87, 99, 198; Janelli and Yim n.d.; Nelson 2000; Ogle 1990; Paek 1993). Taken together, these increasing inequalities and visibilities have made for heightened awareness of inequalities of opportunity and of the advantages of class resources. Certainly, in chapter 4, the Janitor was acutely aware of such inequality and of the workings of class resources.

For those people dissatisfied with their lifestyles and horizons, there is a keen sense of having somehow missed the boat—of not riding the waves of the times (Abelmann and Lie 1995; B. Song 1985). Indeed, the combination of real mobility opportunities in the early postwar years and enormous postwar structural growth made it so that in some cases infinitesimal differences of fortune or achievement produced vast gulfs in standards of living and class horizons, making for the melodrama of South Korea's mobility that I argue in this book (see also Glaser and Strauss 1971, 171, on the importance of "temporal aspects of social mobility"). There is a growing sense that those who have made it have done so backed by privilege and illegitimate deeds. Interestingly, this is reminiscent of the popular sense during the colonial period that individuals succeeded only through collaboration with the colonizers (M. K. Park 1995, 537). People have become increasingly incensed at the favoritism, graft, network hiring, and kickbacks that spurred the development which has been so publicly celebrated. In response to an outraged citizenry, the "democratic" regimes following the widespread civil unrest of the 1980s had to bow to popular pressure and expose the enormous social economy of political patronage (Jung and Siegal 1985, 380). These sentiments reflect many South Koreans' strong sense of social justice, a "strong principle of meritarian justice" (Jung and Siegal 1985, 403), as well as their approbation at relative impoverishment (B. Song 1985). It is not an exaggeration to say that this combination of factors has made many South Koreans dissatisfied with their place in life and convinced that their attributes and achievements should have taken them further. To some extent the Laundress embodied these frustrations. As discussed in chapter 1, these sorts of frustrations are particularly piqued in the 1990s, the decade of this book's research.

This portrait of social mobility over the postwar period reveals that social mobility and its ideological effects are hard to measure and document. Class positions—the units of analysis in the measurement of mobility—have ambiguous social meanings that demand considerable refinement. Furthermore, even with some consensus on class categories, mobility itself is difficult to measure. We have observed that in spite of the real and ideological play of watersheds over the immediate postwar era, the extent to which these transformations really signify long-term changes in opportunity structure is unclear. For example, apparent education or marital mobility does not necessarily signify society's openness because it is often long-standing class resources that dictate class location, and such resources might have been masked by temporary social dislocations. And, we can query whether "premodern" status distinctions really had no sway in the postwar era, or whether wartime dislocations and the land reform truly disrupted class standing and resources. This caveat aside, however, I am skeptical of analyses that are quick to equate South Korea's middle classes today with *yangban* (e.g., Lett 1998, 14, 38–39, 41, 67, 224–228). Anthropologist Denise Potrzeba Lett, for example, writes of a "culturally inherited disposition on the part of Koreans to seek high status" (1998, 2); I worry that such analyses can fall prey to a troublesome cultural determinism. The evocation of *yangban* values or attributes in contemporary narratives, for example, must be understood in their narrative context rather than as the reified reproduction of premodern status hierarchies (see D. S. Hong 1999, 677–678 for a discussion of Lett; see also Janelli and Yim 1993, and Kendall 1996, for similar cautions about culture). Finally, individual mobility comes to life, in part, in the narratives of its representation, which are inextricable from the collective histories and public ideologies that have inscribed recent history.

I turn now to a consideration of women and class in South Korea in order to expand upon this perspective on mobility. Understandings of social mobility are transformed by moving beyond men's productive labor to include women and households.

Putting Women in the Picture: Mobility Revised

I explore women's contribution to class culture and reproduction so as to fine-tune our understanding of post–Korean War social mobility and contemporary class identities. The vast majority of statistical studies of mobility record the formally productive activities of men, subsuming the class positions of households under the productive lives of their male household heads—what Abbott and Sapsford call the "malestream position" (1987, 10) (e.g., Goldthorpe 1983). These gender and employment biases ignore the important contributions of women, including their own employment (when relevant), the non-wage earnings they often control and contribute, and their symbolic inputs as well (Abbott and Sapsford 1987; Crompton 1993; Sørensen 1994; Walby 1986, 31). When women are included in the discussion of mobility, it is often only those women who work in the formal economy (Walby 1986, 26–27). Also excluded are those women who do not marry. These gender and production biases lead us to query to what extent women can have class identities—and correspondingly, social and political consciousnesses—apart from their husbands, and to what extent men's and household identities are fashioned by women. As Annemette Sørensen summarizes, there is a vast divide between those studies that integrate women merely through the consideration of their individual class position and those works that shift the focus of analysis from the individual to the family (1994, 31–33). Traditionally, scholars who wanted to incorporate women into the measure of family class standing considered whether it was the woman or man whose employment determined the identity of the household.

In recent years, however, some studies undertake a so-called joint classification of the household, thus observing the joint contributions of men and women (Sørensen 1994, 41–44). Certainly such measures would be critical for a number of the women featured in this book, including the Laundress, the Janitor, Hye-min's Grandmother, the Education Mother, and Miyŏn's Mother.

A gendered understanding of social mobility and class identity shifts our attention in several ways. Households are considered not as composites of individuals uniformly characterized by men's productive activities at a particular moment in time but as often the meeting place of fractured class memories, identities, and horizons, as discussed in chapter 1. Furthermore, familial configurations—within and beyond the residential household—contribute to the production and maintenance of the household's class identity and habitus. That is, economic and extra-economic inputs from beyond the residential household determine household standing; although somewhat diminished today, these inputs have been extraordinarily important over the course of South Korea's recent history, as we have already observed for the Janitor. Interesting in this regard are Myung-hye Kim's findings that extra-household inputs are more important for higher-income than for lower-income families in South Korea (1995). The kinship and cultural configurations of South Korean patriarchy as both a social and ideological system are critical for understanding the ways in which women contribute to class standing and reproduction: women's virtue as a sign of household status and the general patrilineal organization of society.

Regardless of whether married women formally participate in the labor market, and in spite of South Korea's patrilineal, patriarchal social organization and cultural orientation, women can bring numerous class resources to marriage: their own class backgrounds (including their mothers' and fathers' productive activities), which can include both symbolic, and in some cases material, resources and capital (Abbot and Sapsford 1987, 6, 92); their own education histories and resources; and their own pre-marriage work histories. All of these, we will see, were critical resources that the Laundress wielded in her married life. Also, women who work after marriage, like the Laundress (as well as Hye-min's Grandmother and the Janitor), bring their incomes and maintain their work identities. Furthermore, as we have seen, "nonworking" women often contribute extra-wage incomes and investments. This is the case foremost for the Education Mother and Mi-yŏn's Mother. Thus women's class (economic and symbolic) and education resources, and their past and present employment experience combine with their current wage and non-wage incomes in the production, expression, and maintenance of their own, their husbands', and their households' class locations and identities.

The Western social mobility literature is surprisingly silent on the intergenerational mobility of women—the position of their current households measured in relation to their natal households and the productive activities of their parents. This bias is even more extreme in the South Korean case, where the weight of patrilineal social organization and cultural ideologies can obscure the importance of a woman's natal family both in theory and in daily life as well. Anthropologist Laurel Kendall has offered important evidence of women's postmarital ongoing ritual, economic, and affective ties to their natal family; her studies have refashioned the family in the ethnography of South Korea (1985, 21–22, 150, 157, 159, 163, 169; 1996, 173; see also Janelli and Yim n.d.). Kendall's description of three sisters' households in relation to their mother's household speaks volumes: "The three daughters' households revolve around Ŏmŏni's [Mother's] household like planets around the sun" (1996, 221). Sadly, even studies that pay some attention to intergenerational mobility of women mirror these biases, because they limit their scope to the correspondence of women's husbands' and women's fathers' occupations *only* in the case of working women (U. Cho 1990; S. C. Pak 1991). Confirming the sense of increasingly fixed hierarchies described above, these studies demonstrated high levels of correspondence between women's fathers' and husbands' class positions for the growing new middle classes (including professionals and office workers), reaching, for example, a 42 percent convergence in 1990 (S. C. Pak 1991). These research biases and limitations are unfortunate because the relationship between women's work and their fathers' work, and the relationship between the work of the husbands and fathers of unemployed women, are also significant measures of women's (and households') mobility and class identities.

It is important too to consider the contribution of women's pre-marriage education resources and identities to their class identities after marriage. Women neither forgo their own education attributes, nor acquire their husbands' education credentials, with marriage. This said, however, in many cases women's pre-marriage education is a vague indicator of social standing because of the general exclusion of women from formal education until recent decades—certainly the case for the Laundress (P. Thompson 1993, 32). The education levels of older women in particular often do not bespeak their family backgrounds, and thus we cannot necessarily count their education hypergamy as evidence of upward mobility (this is to some extent the case for the Janitor, the Twins' Mother, Mrs. Pak, Mi-yŏn's Mother, and the Education Mother; such is the case of women whose husbands' education levels are not unlike their brothers, the Laundress being a counterexample). Younger women's education levels come closer to reflecting the class positions and identifications of their natal families; their work experiences and aspirations, however, typically do *not* represent these education levels

(K. S. Pak 1993; Sŏl 1994, 249). That is, until very recently, women's high levels of education (particularly college) have seldom translated into high-level participation in the labor force. Although education resources are signified differently across the generations, we can see that patriarchy operates in both cases, either to withhold education or to withhold job opportunities commensurate with educational achievement. Interestingly, however, women's education has become increasingly important to family class reproduction. A woman's education resources contribute to the maintenance of her family's class distinction and ensure and enhance quality education for her children—something we have seen in the education stories in chapter 4 (M. H. Kim 1992, 168; 1993, 80; O. Moon 1990).

Although women's work experiences both before and after marriage are critical to their class ideologies and horizons after marriage, their labor-market experiences before marriage have been largely ignored in the general social mobility literature (Abbott and Sapsford 1987; Martin and Roberts 1984). In the South Korean case, lower-class women have been consistently employed and central to the household's basic economy (M. H. Kim 1993; S. K. Kim 1997), and in recent years, women's formal labor-market participation has increased across the class spectrum (although with the IMF Crisis there has been a downturn). Interestingly, studies demonstrate considerable discordance between wives' and husbands' employment, particularly in Seoul, where they occupy similar labor niches in only 32 percent of the cases—leaving room for variable class identities within families (S. C. Pak 1991). This is not surprising, because of the aforementioned gaps between women's education qualifications and employment horizons such that their jobs and class identities can be quite distant.

Beyond women's formal employment, their informal labor and extra-wage contributions are also critical to households' class positions and identities at both ends of the class spectrum: women's contributions may include piecework at home for the lower classes, and for the middle and upper classes, real estate and stock investments as well as extra-economic contributions. For the lower classes, it has been documented that women's incomes exert considerable influence on household identity (M. H. Kim 1995), although women's contributions are not necessarily evenly evaluated by both husband and wife. One study showed that women estimate their effects on social standing to be larger than men do, and that men think household standing is more affected by women with high-income streams (Park and Hong 1994). For the upper classes, it is well-known that women's non-wage earnings often far exceed those of their even high-earning husbands and strongly affect household identities and horizons (the case for the Education Mother and Mi-yŏn's Mother, the most prosperous households featured in this book) (M. H. Kim 1995, 77, 79). As Myung-hye Kim argues, it is a gross distortion to refer to "unemployed" upper-middle-class women as "housewives" (1995, 82).

Finally, in addition to being economic contributors, many (married) women are the managers of patrilineal kinship groups and the nurturers of social networks that are critical to the production and reproduction of class standing, including their children's employment and marriage opportunities and their husbands' professional standing and advancement—what Hanna Papaneck calls "family status-production work" (1989). These contributions are particularly critical in the case of South Korea's upper classes (M. H. Kim 1995, 72, 75–79; E. Yi 1993; see Lett 1998, 72–79, on the family labor entailed in the maintenance of the middle class). We can thus observe the ongoing legacy of women's symbolic contributions to the maintenance of premodern elite status (H. J. Cho 1998b; Deuchler 1977; Haboush 1991).

This review of social mobility and gender for South Korea has sketched a range of parameters that contribute to a more nuanced rendering of class identities and social mobility histories. Based on these discussions of women's often autonomous class attributes and contributions, it would be a mistake to conclude that in order to remedy the existing social portrait we need to only include women separately in statistics. Rather, we need to reconfigure our understanding of men's and households' class standing, mobility, identities, and horizons as well because they cannot be isolated from the economic and symbolic contributions of women (see also Abbott and Sapsford 1987, 54, and Sørensen 1994).

I now return to the Laundress to illustrate the importance of transgenerational family history, family form and networks, employment history, and narrative to the understanding of her and her family's class identities and horizons.

The Laundress, 1990s

In my talks with the Laundress, each time over her black sewing machine, the lightbulb dangling above us, I learned of her son, the Chinese language teacher and friend of Mr. Kang's, described in chapter 2. In the later years of this project, the Laundress would take care of the infant of that oldest son. The second son began, but did not finish, college, then emigrated to New Zealand, where he started a small business. The third son, who had just finished his compulsory military service when I first met the Laundress, was studying to become a teacher at that time. Over the years we talked, the Laundress worried as to whether he would ever find a job, and eventually he did. With no formal education herself, and having labored and lived modestly her entire adult life while suffering the abuses of a violent husband, the Laundress prided herself on having raised three successful sons and two teachers. She reported that neighbors praise her for her accomplishment. We can recall her eldest son's sense—and her own—that her name should be recorded in the annals of history. Central to her class identity is her success in educating her sons against considerable odds.

The Laundress's pre-marriage class and education, and her occupational and material resources have been critical to the course of her adult married life and the nature of her class identities and horizons. As an elementary school graduate, the Laundress's father was one of the most educated people in their small, unprosperous coastal village. Her father's family claimed to be *yangban*, which she took to mean "that at some point in the past we did not live so badly." She recalled that her paternal grandfather had once even owned some land. It was perhaps these attributes that facilitated her family's early exodus from the village—they were the first to leave. The extended family (her parents, paternal grandparents, and paternal aunts and uncles) left so that her father could avoid labor conscription to Japan; their rural emigration was thus an effort to secure a better future in the politically turbulent times of World War II under Japanese colonialism. Most of the remaining village families, the Laundress explained, emigrated later under less auspicious circumstances.

The Laundress imagined that her family history might have been different, however, if her father had been afforded more education. It was her *yangban* grandfather's drinking, she explained, that prevented her father from going further in his schooling. In Seoul, the family did hard labor (excepting the times her father started small business ventures): "What else could people like that do?" She attributed her father's zeal for his sons' education to his own resentment of his father's drinking, which had so limited his own horizons. In Seoul, every comfort was sacrificed to scrape together her brothers' school fees. Although the Laundress and her sister remained uneducated, they were not excluded from her father's and natal family's *yangban* history and identities. Most of the time she attributed her and her sister's lack of education to her family's patriarchal ideologies, but sometimes she explained it as a contingency of timing—that her father had failed in business just at the time she might have gone to school. In this way, mobility stories straddle the vicissitudes of timing. With three of four brothers college-educated, the Laundress never even entertained the idea of not educating her own children: "It was my own thing entirely—it had nothing to do with my husband."

Although completely unschooled, the Laundress is literate and adamant about the importance of keeping informed; she was an avid reader of fiction in her youth, and throughout her busy adult life she has always made time to peruse the newspaper headlines and read the editorials, which she considered "the most important part of the paper." It is because she reads and keeps up, she explained, that she is broad-minded; she thanked her upbringing for this: "A person can become broad-minded either from education or from upbringing." She frequently complained to me about housewives who are completely ignorant of the world's goings-on, including many of the women in the neighborhood group she gathers with periodically and her brothers' wives. She does not feel a bit inferior to those high school- and college-educated housewives who "know nothing": "What have they made of their opportunities?" She said that these women—"and even my husband!"—have no idea she is entirely unschooled. Furthermore, she was confident that if she had been educated, she would have become a "truly great woman": "If only I had not missed my time (ttae) in life to study." Mi-yŏn's Mother echoed these thoughts on her life (see chapter 9). It is widely understood in South Korea that there is a proper "time" in the life course for studying, and that beyond that time, education becomes near impossible. She did, however, in a different vein, wonder why she was not one of those little girls one reads about in primers or novels who get themselves educated against great odds, the girls who "beg at the school window to be let in." Although she was self-conscious of family assets beyond education (of her family's transgenerational class history), she often spoke of her achievements in isolation of these contributions.

In sum, when thinking about her upbringing and education, the Laundress bears and claims, if obliquely—and not necessarily consciously—her grandfather's *yangban* identity, her father's education values (although he was himself a laborer), her literacy and self-styled worldliness, and her brothers' education achievement and social standing. Interestingly, this aggregate of class capital surfaces neither in her own or her husband's current occupational status, nor in her late father's occupational or social standing. Furthermore, it surfaces only intermittently in her own mobility narrative. We can see, however, that her own class identities and horizons are fashioned through multigenerational memories and family history, the class maps of her natal family (her brothers), and cultural capital independent of formal schooling. Although these features are quite invisible in any of the standard indicators of class or mobility, they are critical to an understanding of the class identities and horizons of the Laundress and her family.

Also noteworthy is that none of these class attributes can be discovered through consideration of her husband; it is no exaggeration to say that the Laundress has resided in a class space almost entirely independent of her husband. Her husband, also unschooled, was from a family with "no *yangban* pretensions" and was really poor ("poor even among poor of that era"). She recalled that she was so naïve at the time of her marriage that she did not even think to check into his education or employment history (see chapter 3). His shared religious background (Catholic), the seeming promise of his job at an American military base, and the apparent prosperity of his brother (who negotiated the marriage) had sanctioned this otherwise unlikely match. Stories of marital misinformation are not uncommon in yesteryear Korea (see, for example, Kendall 1988, chapter 3). And the Laundress could not believe that she had turned away educated and skilled suitors who were "attracted by my beauty." She thought of her husband, whom she explained has been discriminated against as a *sangnom* (a derogatory term for commoners), as having suffered the injuries of class (see Sennett and Cobb 1973). She described that he was wracked with "useless pride" and "the sort of personality that inhibits a man from developing (*paljŏn haji mottal*) or making anything of himself" (here we can recall the Education Mother on her brother). She went on to detail problems with his human character (*in'gansŏng*), his lack of schooling (which prevented him from "stretching himself"), and his home environment (*chip hwan'gyŏng*). Indeed, she attributed his abusive nature, senseless pride, and character flaws to his extreme childhood poverty. Moreover, all of these were aggravated because he had married above his station—"something that is damaging to a man's pride." She also reserved some sympathy for him because of his family's religious roots: they were Catholics who had fled persecution into remote mountainous villages generations earlier (Catholics represent only a quarter of South Korea's Christian population, per Korea National Statistical Office 1995). She told me that her husband once said to her, "You are a woman with little ambition (*yoksim*) to have ended up with the likes of me!" Throughout her marriage, as we learned in chapter 3, she struggled for domestic harmony so as to foster a healthy environment for her children. She worked hard to nourish her husband's frail ego and to preserve his stature in the eyes of her children.

The occupational and material resources the Laundress brought to marriage also contributed to her married adult trajectory and identities. She began working as a young girl, selling vegetables on the city streets. At seventeen she found work at a Western clothing factory, where she started as an errand girl (shining shoes and so on), and later found her "life's work" as a sewing machinist. Because she made significant contributions to the family—she often spoke of having provided clothes for her younger brothers and sisters—she felt "useful" and never thought to consider her life as pitiable. She worked at the factory until her marriage, at twenty-four. It was her sewing-machine experience, "my skill," that led her and her husband to open the laundry, where she also mends clothes, after his early employment ventures all came to ruin. The laundry, "something one could do with very little capital," was her idea, and she was matter-of-fact about being the one who got it going and made it work. She decided that her husband would never amount to anything on his own but that, under her supervision, he could be diligent. Hence, the couple's self-employment—steady but modest—can be credited to the Laundress's pre-marriage work experience, continued diligence, worldliness, and savvy manner with her clientele (this sense is echoed in Hye-min's Grandmother's accounts of her work life as a small shopkeeper; see chapters 3 and 8).

The Laundress's material resources during childhood were limited. In Seoul, her grandparents and parents pooled their earnings, and as the eldest daughter, she also contributed hers. Sporadically, however, there was some extra cash when one or another of her father's business ventures was going smoothly, and there were even several years when the family owned a home. In fact, it was with money from her own parents that she and her husband bought a modest home when they were newly married. She explained that although women are understood to sever material ties with their natal families, in fact, the relations are ongoing: "How can a daughter really become a stranger (nam)? Of course they tell us to go to that house [the husband's] and die there, but . . ." Shortly after marriage, however, a business venture shared by her father and husband collapsed, and both she and her parents lost their homes. Since that time, she and her husband have not owned a domicile. Although the inputs from her family have been modest over the years, her squarely middle-class brothers have helped out from time to time with her sons' tuition. The Laundress is certain that she would have educated them in any case but that "without those resources, it would have been that much harder." There were also small material contributions from her husband's siblings, two of whom were somewhat prosperous as young men, working at the American military base. In fact, she first met her husband because he had been living with one of these brothers, who had procured him an American military-base job, but he made little of it and eventually quit. The Laundress's husband had not been, she regretted, the type to have ridden on opportunities afforded by American military-base employment to land a lucrative career—an often told tale (see Cumings 1997, 299–309, for a vivid description of these sorts of opportunities).

In the scheme of things, the Laundress has received few lasting material contributions from her own or her husband's family, and in her stories, she paid scant attention to what she has received. She complained that her eldest and most prosperous brother has shared little of his wealth with family members: "Both he and his wife are not the sorts who suffer for the extended family (chiban)." Because her youngest brother looks after her elderly mother she disparaged her eldest brother (who, according to cultural dictates, should assume this responsibility) as too "narrow hearted." The matter of distribution of family labor was a point of considerable contention for several of the women in this book, including particularly the Twins' Mother and the Education Mother (see chapter 8). The Laundress complained several times about the televised ceremonies that award prizes to widows who have remained chaste (a virtue in the Confucian worldview) and successfully raised and educated their children alone. She explained that these women are typically widows who received all sorts of real financial help from their natal families: "How can their situation be compared with mine?" The patriarchy and patrilineal bias of families have impacted her sons' lives as well. Her first son's wife lost both of her parents when she was quite young, and in a recent distribution of her parents' assets, she was given nothing—in spite of contemporary changes in the inheritance law that should have ensured her an equal share. Although the Laundress's first domicile, as well as her husband's first post-marriage productive activity, was secured by her own parents, she nonetheless considered herself a woman who has made it on her own.

The Laundress's perceptions of postwar social mobility are crafted between the specificities of her own story and the collective narratives of South Korean development. She explained, "Poverty then and now is the same, except that it is perhaps a bit more visible today because of television and the like." She explained that although there are more jobs available today, education seems to guarantee less and less: "A college degree, as long as it is not from some flimsy (sisihan) school, is an absolute necessity, but it does not promise anything." Here she echoed the ambivalence about education we found in chapter 4. Although her oldest son, who graduated with a high school teaching degree in Korean (language and literature), managed to find a job easily (albeit a job at a low-ranking high school, as she was quick to point out), she worried that with the same credentials her youngest son might not find a job. She explained that she and her husband have neither the connections nor the money to have made bribes to procure their sons' teaching jobs. That such bribes have been quite customary is widely understood in South Korea. She was even more pessimistic for those without education. She thinks that people like her middle son and brother, who did not earn college degrees, for example, are better off leaving South Korea for countries with greater opportunity. She thus applauded her son's emigration to New Zealand: "I tell him, 'Go there, suffer, and live well.' What options does he really have?" She was heartened to have heard that in New Zealand the discrepancies between the rewards and prestige for white- and blue-collar workers are not as large as they are in South Korea. But for the brother who did not finish college and followed his wife's relatives to the United States, she speculated that by the time he and his family arrived in the United States, the economy was such that it was "too late" for a newcomer to really succeed (New Zealand, in contrast, struck her as still a promising frontier). In a similar vein, she was convinced that it was getting harder and harder these days for a poor child to succeed in school in South Korea: "It used to be that the poor children did best." When her own children were in school, they could not afford any of the after-school training and programs that are the sine qua non of middle-class schooling in recent years, but they made up for their disadvantages in part by directing their studies not to their passions and interests but to the least competitive college entrance examination subjects of the time—teaching and Korean language.

Although the Laundress was proud of her work history, confident that it is easier to get ahead through self-employment (small businesses), and convinced that such work is "more independent and fun," she realized that "it does not bring social recognition." She asserted that it is white-collar occupations reached through education credentials—the ones she charted for her children—that win a person respect. For a woman in her shoes, the only way to win recognition, she explained, is to educate her children well.

The Laundress thinks that in the past, there were real windows of opportunity, like the one at the American military base that her husband managed to miss ("Some people got really rich off of those jobs") or the chances to go work in Saudi Arabia. She really admired those "great" men who went to Saudi Arabia, who knew how to "seize the opportunities of their place and times" (men like the Moviegoer's husband; see chapter 6). But as with the case of her husband, she knows that for some people the degradation of poverty itself can stop a person from seizing such opportunities. She realized that even the timing of rural emigration (very early in the case of her own family) can affect mobility trajectories; she noted, for example, that her husbands' siblings who remained in the countryside have not fared as well as those who came to Seoul (for similar discussions see Hye-min's Grandmother in chapter 8). Although the Laundress acknowledged that real estate investments have afforded people incredible opportunities, she said that one needed both money and smarts to be able to play in that arena (thus echoing the thinking of several of the other women in this book, including, Mrs. Pak, the Janitor, and Hye-min's Grandmother).

Central to the Laundress's sense of narrowing horizons in the days we spoke was the drastic housing situation in South Korea, whereby those without capital could barely dream of purchasing a domicile in Seoul (see Nelson 2000). Once the Laundress spoke about not having had a daughter in terms of housing:

> I didn't think about not having a daughter—not because I wouldn't
> have wanted one, but because my circumstances didn't allow me to
> even think about one. It isn't about whether sons or daughters are
> good—it is about the fact that I raised my three children in one room.
> If we had had a daughter, it would have been even more difficult—
> I couldn't have had her sleep with the three boys. It was a good thing
> I didn't have a daughter.

Several years ago she and her husband purchased an apartment outside of the city, but they could not afford to live there because they purchased it with the *chŏnse* (renters' lump-sum down payments that are often exorbitant) paid to them by the tenants to whom they immediately rented the apartment. The Laundress was dismayed that after toiling a lifetime, she was still not able to afford a "room of her own." She mused that it would take decades for her eldest son and his wife (who both work) to be able to afford an apartment. When we spoke in 1996, she was watching this son's infant—leaving her sewing till the late night—because, she said, the only thing she could contribute to the couple's housing quest was "my own body's labor." One of the things about young women those days that angered the Laundress was that they "pretend to work because they want to."

Young women should, she explained, tell it like it is: "After all, they work because otherwise their families would have no chance of affording an apartment and a middle-class life." Interestingly, with this complaint, she showed she was offended by women's false claims both because she thought they should take care of their children, and because such claims obscured the reality of the narrow prospects for less advantaged people in South Korea in the 1990s.

In sum, although her sons have garnered the education trappings of the middle class, in 1990s South Korea—after decades of real-estate inflation, with declining values of a college education, and escalating unemployment for the college-educated—they were not ensured the middle-class life she had toiled to provide them. She was hopeful for her eldest son, who found a job early, reconciled to her second son "suffering" abroad, and was worried as to whether her third son's education qualifications alone would procure him a job.

The Laundress's narrative is distinguished by several obfuscations that reflect the mobility and gender ideologies of her times. Although her mobility story reveals the importance of transgenerational class and cultural resources, her narratives of personal triumph often ignore them. In this way, she brings individual ardor and attitude to the center of her explanation. This is not to say that the Laundress thinks of South Korea as an open society. To the contrary, she is fully aware of the particular moments and spaces that have facilitated mobility opportunities. Similarly, in spite of the fact that the story of her own family mobility reveals the absolute centrality of her own contributions, in her day-to-day family and work life she has worked hard to make her own real inputs—work, decisions, know-how, and intelligence—invisible. She has done this in the interest of nurturing her husband's ego, fostering domestic tranquility, and ensuring her sons' healthy development and education. She has thus reproduced patriarchal social relations by supporting her husband's role as family head. Women, she thinks, need to make everything work and to manage their husbands' delicate egos (see chapter 7 for further discussion of this theme). She seemed to reserve more sympathy for men burdened by twisted characters than for women, whom she thinks "should rise above their circumstances." The Laundress often explained the variable class fates of the members of her family, such as those of her father's brothers, her own siblings, or her husband's siblings, in terms of their diligence and upbringing, and according to the attributes of their wives. She was matter-of-fact, as were most of the women I interviewed, that it is women who determine the course of families: "When a woman marries poorly, she is the only one who suffers, but when a man marries badly, it is the whole family that suffers."

While the Laundress felt triumphant for having succeeded in spite of her husband's abuse, she had little sympathy for women who have not been equally triumphant: those who have not exercised their education (e.g., the housewives in her midst) or those who have been inhibited by their lack of class resources. She once criticized the weakness of character of a woman whom we had talked about (a story that I had told her) who did not seize opportunities to marry up because she was too ashamed of her humble origins. Although the Laundress was fully aware of the importance of class background and capital, she seemed to think that women should be able to succeed (for their families) through their own self-styled grit, determination, psychological acumen, and worldliness. Thus, although she labored her entire adult life alongside an abusive husband in order to care for her family, she objected to women's employment for the sake of personal fulfillment, and she was adamant that a "family cannot have two heads." In her stories and ideologies, patriarchy figured culturally and ideologically beyond its more obvious structural and organizational effects.

The Laundress, Summer 2000

A visit with the Laundress in summer 2000 revealed her persistent sense of social inequality and her thoughts on women's changing social roles. The Laundress emerged as both profoundly socially critical and as a seemingly staunch defender of patriarchy. She is, I think, neither and both—much as we have seen in the complexity of her sense of her own personal and family course throughout this chapter (echoed also in the competing calculations of the Education Mother and the Janitor in chapter 4). Here I take up her 2000 thoughts on her current phase of life, on recent social change, on her sense of her social position, and finally on women generally.

The Laundress considered herself "old now" for, as she put it, "I've finished doing what it is that Korean women do: I've raised my children, I've married them, and now I'm done." The research culminating in this book began with women at the life-course moment just before this benchmark. She explained that she has nothing to think about now other than "passing the rest of my days comfortably." To that, she added, noting that her parents had by then passed on, "I have no debts to repay and no desire for any wealth." Her work is done, and her scorecard even, is what she seemed to be saying. These were not sad thoughts of old age, but rather contented ones, quiet ones to say, "Mine has been a hard life, but I've done my work, and now I can think about myself." This said, however, the Laundress's life has been too hard for smug reflection: "These days, I hate to look in the mirror. I'm so old. I have so many wrinkles. I used to like having my photo taken, but now I can't stand looking at a photo. People used to say that I had aged well, but I don't hear that anymore." The Laundress offered a well-worn South Korean expression: "When I was young, I had health but neither time nor money, but now that I am old I have some time and some money, but I don't have the health to be able to enjoy any of it. I've worked so hard—there are no words to describe it; my generation has lived so hard." Although she and her husband can no longer live on what they make, and receive help from their sons, they keep on working: "For us, it is more comfortable to work than to quit and relax."

The Laundress was a hard judge of post-IMF South Korea. Laundries were hit hard by the crisis. "People say," she said, "that things will get better in two to three years, but I don't see that happening." She echoed the views of many that the rich-poor gap in South Korea had only been exacerbated: "These days, people with money use even more of it, and people without money use even less of it. So, the stores with luxury items are doing better than ever, and those without them are doing worse than ever." Although her youngest son did manage to procure himself a teaching position, the Laundress's worries were realized in the employment of that son's wife; although trained as a teacher, she failed the certification exam and was about to take a job at an extracurricular academy (hagwŏn) (i.e., for tutoring). Although the Laundress was proud that her children went through schooling with no extracurricular training or tutoring, she explained that educational pressure today was even more extreme: "Extracurricular activities these days have absolutely nothing to do with developing a particular talent of one or another student. No matter what, parents send their kids to piano, art, and so on, with whatever time that they aren't in school." The implication here was that families like hers in the days of her children's childhood would have never been able to afford all that. She is against such extracurricular education for her grandchildren, but she decided that she would say nothing to her children: "It's none of my business and I've decided not to control their lives in any way."

These critical thoughts aside, however, at several points the Laundress offered that she is really in no position to care about changing times. Implied here, however, quietly, was both her keen sense of her very lack of power and the extent to which it is unlikely that any social change would register in her humble life: "For mere citizens like me, what changes would really matter so much anyway? It is only the wealthy who worry about those things." On the question of North-South unification, she began her thoughts, "Humble people like me don't want to think about that," but went on to say that she was disappointed in politicians, that she was initially happy when Kim Dae Jung became president, but that in fact "there is no change."

It was about women, work, and child care that the Laundress spoke most passionately that day. She lamented, as she had earlier, that women have to work in order to live—in the case of her children, in order to ever be able to purchase housing. The Laundress remembered hearing rumors when she was young about working couples and household appliances in the United States; she could not quite believe that what seemed so odd to her in those days had become the South Korean contemporary reality:

When I was young, women didn't work, and if you were privileged, you had some maids. In those days, we heard rumors about the United States—that with washing machines, vacuum cleaners and the like, there was nothing that people had to use their own strength for, but that both husband and wife had to work to make ends meet. At the time, I thought that was so strange. But that has become our reality today: we now have all those appliances, and both husband and wife have to work.

In the case of her eldest son, the Laundress was particularly happy to watch his young children: "There was no place that they could have comfortably left their children." As for her second son, however, she has told him and his wife that she will not be able to care for their children, not because the will is not there but because her health is not up to it: "It's not that I won't watch them; it's that I can't watch them." She explained how hard it is for parents of young children when the grandmothers cannot help out: that they cannot work with an "easy heart" and that they do not have the flexibility to stay late as is demanded of so many jobs. Nonetheless, in the Laundress's ideal world, women would be at home. Although she acknowledged that men must make some accommodations for working women (like her!), she is vehemently opposed to any radical reorganization of the domestic realm:

A woman can't be the same as a man. How could a housewife be the same as a man? The housewife is the protector of the household. And even if a woman works, she is a housewife when she comes home. A woman can't be thinking, "I worked all day, just like you [i.e., her husband] did," but these days that is how things are heading. [That sort of thinking] isn't good for the couple, or for their children's education. That is how the family comes to ruin . . . Men have changed—they aren't as inflexible as they once were—and of course they should help out because life is hard. It's only natural for them to help out. But it shouldn't be, "Today is my day; tomorrow is yours . . ." Women should just know that [the work] is theirs to do.

The Laundress blamed the United States for the culture of divorce that has found its way to South Korea. Echoing her thoughts from years earlier, she offered that a household can only have one head and it is because young women do not understand this that the divorce rates have escalated. She went on, horrified, to report: "In the case of divorce, it used to be that both parents would fight over the children. In divorces these days, though, neither parent wants the children. It used to be that women thought, 'These are my children; no matter the suffering, I need to raise them.' Nowadays, they think, 'Why do I need to sacrifice for someone else?' That is the sort of thinking that makes the divorce rate high." As for feminists and feminist organizations, the Laundress thinks little of them. Here, though, she struck an ambivalent note, for she was most critical of the fact that, in spite of few real changes for women, those organizations keep proclaiming profound change: "The only thing that has changed in terms of women's status is that more women say that it has changed." Interestingly, these comments served as both an indictment of women's organizations and of society more broadly. But she ended that part of the conversation on a conservative note: "Women aren't really doing very much, even if those women's organizations think that they are doing something. They just put themselves out there and cause confusion. And then the divorce rate goes up, and there are more and more women who don't raise their own children."

The Laundress's narratives illustrate that in any consideration of a household's mobility, it is critical to observe a woman's economic, symbolic, and memory resources. Women are "classed" subjects before and during marriage. We have seen that many aspects of the Laundress's pre-marriage life are relevant: her natal family's class standing and even multigenerational class memory, her educational experience and values, and her family's material resources and contributions. In one sense, although the Laundress is a propertyless and unschooled woman whose tiny business might not even render her a petite bourgeoisie, she shares the horizons and identities of her college-educated brothers. Furthermore, we have seen that her class identity and aspirations are quite independent from those of her husband. And although she does not share the luxuries of her neighbor and sisters-in-law housewives (property, freedom, and time), she was sure that hers is the more worldly and impressive existence. We have also seen the important play of patriarchy, as it affects the education, early economic activities, family networks, and gender ideologies of women.

The Laundress's mobility story underscores the complexities of her own and her family's class identities and mobility horizons. Through the Laundress's social mobility history and its narrative evocation, we can observe: the limitations of subsuming her own or her family's class position under her husband's occupation; the importance of a transgenerational perspective to the understanding of the particular shape and culture of families; the subjective nature of the Laundress's understanding of social mobility; and the centrality of gender norms and ideologies to both her life path and her understanding of that path. The Laundress understands that many personal resources are flexible in their determinacies; that is, they are potentially but not necessarily enabling—or, alternately, potentially but not inevitably damaging. It is, then, the fabric of personal destiny, personal proclivities, social life, and structural factors that set these determinacies. Her story challenges the clean break with the past that is often assumed by developmentalist understandings of post–Korean War South Korea.

Class identity and horizons are neither the exclusive province of men nor of temporally isolated individuals. Gender, families, households, transgenerational factors, and nonmarket elements are critical to any understanding of class and social mobility. People's class identities are delicate matters that reside between genealogical memories and genealogical experiences, and the goals and aspirations for the next generation. The productive activities of any woman's husband are but one narrow measure of her own or her family's situation. This is especially the case for South Korea's postwar history, in which rapid structural change and early mobility opportunities have made family situations at one moment or another mere way stations between transgenerational memories and imaginaries.

Whereas in this chapter I have juxtaposed the "facts" and "fictions" of social mobility as critical—and sometimes competing—contexts for understanding women's senses of the course of their lives, in the next chapter, I take up a parallel tension in women's discourses on personality. In the same way that we have seen the Laundress wax and wane on her own agentive role in things, so too do most women through the discussion of their own or others' personal style.

6

PERSONALITY SPEAKING

When I was in a good mood, *everything derived from myself.*
I had pulled myself up out of nothingness by my own bootstraps
in order to provide men with the writings they wanted.

In hours of gloom, *when I felt the sickening dullness of my own*
goodwill, the only way of pulling myself together was to lay stress
on predestination: I would summon the human race and foist on it
responsibility for my life.
—Jean-Paul Sartre, *The Words* (emphasis added)

In chapter 5 we left off on the difficulties of assessing social mobility—on the Laundress's various accounts of educating her three sons: various for the extent to which she appreciates her extended family's contributions, and various for her account of the meaning of that education in South Korea. In both senses, we observed how her view of her own role, or agency, varied. I argued in chapter 5 that the tension between structural constraints and her own contribution to things reflects larger social debates on the course and character of South Korea's rapid social change or "development." Similarly, in the education stories in chapter 4, which followed several people's varying accounts of themselves as authors of their educational pasts, we met accounts that quickly turned to stories of constraint beyond the province of individual agency. And before that, in chapter 3 we observed that the key words of the women of this generation turn on conflicting understandings that in large part speak to social transformation, a story that can be profoundly personal, and at the same time impersonal in that it seems to happen to (or even against) people. Therein we observed the heteroglossia on the matter of individual authorship. Finally, discussion in chapter 1 of a melodramatic sensibility, and of narrative generally, began this book's examination of the inextricability of the personal from the social, a cornerstone in the examination of the workings of gender and class. In keeping with these discussions, this chapter takes up a related discourse that we have already encountered: namely, that of personality, which is also seemingly personal, but in fact, ever so social.

This chapter reflects my interest in the centrality of personality in social mobility stories as a window to the idioms and epistemologies of selfhood. I argue that the idiom of personality that is so pervasive in the social mobility narratives of the middle-aged South Korean women in this book constitutes a discursive space through which competing epistemologies of selfhood are articulated. While in some narratives, personality weds individual proclivity to the contingencies of social life and even historical causality, in others, it is the province of unbridled individual agency. Thus selfhoods are variously fortified by agency, or overdetermined by larger social and historical forces. And in most cases, these more and less agentive voices combine in the same woman, as we saw in the case of the Laundress in the last chapter. In this way, I understand agency as a particular narrative convention and historical epistemology. I pay particular attention to those narratives on personality and epistemologies of selfhood in which individual agency is subordinated to or blurred with social and historical processes. It is in this vein that women narrate the sociocultural development of personality in the context of particular genealogies, family settings, and historical times. I consider agency not as a property or power exercised against structural determinacy, but rather as a feature of discourses on personality and thus of the epistemologies of selfhood.

Following a theoretical discussion of selfhood and personality, I turn to the Moviegoer, the woman who spoke variously in chapter 3 about not having made money: On the one hand, she lamented that she had been foolish (mŏngch'ŏnghada) but on the other hand, she was quietly secure that she was not like those other women who put on airs (challan yŏja). Thus she wavered in her self-estimation according to competing social values. We can recall that she contrasted herself both with her husband and with other women in her midst, including the long-term friend on a visit, the one who had recently become an insurance agent, who dropped by during one of my visits. We can also recall that it was the Moviegoer's husband who greeted that friend by teasing his wife for having been stupid (pabo katta) for staying with him, for putting up with him for all these years. I first consider the Moviegoer's thoughts on her personality as they articulated with the central theme of her narratives: namely, her having never extended her family's economic standing. I then take up the Moviegoer's thoughts on her husband as well as some discussions that I had with him. In so doing, I draw upon a theme from chapter 3, the often gendered contrast that women draw between themselves and their husbands. I elaborate this theme in chapter 7, which considers women's thoughts on the men in their lives in relation to larger social discourses on men and masculinity in Korea's twentieth century. Finally, I take up the Moviegoer on a soap opera *Kashi namu kkot* (The thorny branch flower), which echoed aspects of her own life.

Selfhood and Personality

I turn to theoretical discussions of selfhood and personality in order to set the exploration of personality in the context of this book's focus on social mobility stories. Anthropologists have long been interested in demonstrating that "modern" Western selfhood is not a human universal (Mauss [1938] 1985; M. Rosaldo 1984; R. Rosaldo 1980; on "modern" subjectivity, see Foucault 1972, 95–96, and Taylor 1985). In contrast to the clear demarcations between "private selves" and "social persons" in the prevailing sense of Western selfhood (M. Rosaldo 1984, 145–146) (and in the prevailing sense of melodrama—see chapter 1), many anthropologists have found "collective, relational" selfhoods among their informants (Battaglia 1995, 7). In drawing such a contrast, anthropologists affirm that subjectivities are *already* cultural, and that "culture, far more than a mere catalogue of rituals and beliefs is instead the very stuff of which our subjectivities are created" (M. Rosaldo 1984, 150; see also Shweder 1990, 24). Although I agree with the premise that subjectivities are culturally circumscribed, there is a certain danger to this line of argument: against a collective selfhood in the field, "modern, Western" selfhood is rendered epistemologically unified or fixed —a straw man against which to pose temporal and cultural others. A narrative perspective on selfhood alternatively allows for the coexistence of epistemologically varied selfhoods. By assuming various and blurred epistemologies in the (traditional anthropological) field against a unified selfhood in advanced capitalist societies (including South Korea), we impoverish our understanding of selfhood everywhere. Such a contrast is drawn by reifying selfhood, wresting it from its narrative constitution. I suggest rather that selfhood is everywhere constantly and variously emergent (see also E. Bruner 1986, 12, and Lewis-Fernández and Kleinman 1994, 68). I share Debbora Battaglia's perspective on selfhood as a "chronically unstable productivity brought situationally . . . to some form of imaginary order, to some purpose, as realized in the course of culturally patterned interactions" (1995, 2). In other words, although selfhood is always in flux, it is necessarily reified from time to time in the context of particular social relations. Thus Battaglia is interested in "what *use* a particular notion of self[hood] has for someone or some collectivity" (1995, 3). Similarly, historian Joan Scott argues, "Subjects . . . are not unified, autonomous individuals exercising free will, but rather subjects whose agency is created through situations and statuses conferred on them" (1992, 34; see also Ong 1990, 272).

Over twenty years ago, Amélie Oksenberg Rorty elaborated a perspective on and a vocabulary for selfhood that are helpful for clarifying an emergent, discursive approach (1976, 319). Rorty distinguished characters and persons in Western literary and social history in order to articulate the "archaeological layers on which our [contemporary] practices rest." She considered these "layers" not as historical phases where one is replaced by another but rather as coexistent in the present: "We are different entities as we conceive ourselves enlightened by these various views" (Rorty 1976, 302). I take up some of her categorical distinctions because they are helpful for elaborating the competing epistemologies of selfhood I found in South Korean social mobility stories. By using these terms that are derived from Western literary history, I do not mean to suggest that Korea's literary or social history can be subsumed entirely in Western patterns or precedents—a caution I also offered for melodrama. I suggest, however, that many of the historical processes that shaped the transformations which Rorty outlines are ones that have been broadly at work in Korea over the course of its rapid twentieth-century history.

Among Rorty's terms and epistemologies for selfhood I draw particularly on her distinction between characters, as sites of historical and social constraint, and persons, as centers of agency. Characters have dispositions that "determine[s] their responses to social and environmental conditions . . . To know what sort of character [somebody] is, is to know what sort of life is best suited to bring out his potentialities and functions" (Rorty 1976, 304–305). Destined to live out their disposition, in times of "great social change"—in which changed social circumstances have made anachronisms of particular dispositions—characters can be easily made tragic (Rorty 1976, 305). Thus characters who merely "choose from their natures or are chosen by their stories" do not exercise free will.

As the reader has already seen, characters—social positions and dispositions that fare variously in the tumult of social change—abound in South

Korean social mobility stories. These include status characters, such as the sŏnbi, usually an impoverished Confucian scholar who eschews manual labor, simultaneously bringing glory to his lineage but hardship to his family (see Lett 1998, 29–30); the farmer, or ch'onnom (country bumpkin), whose life is but an extension of the prerogatives of the land; and the chŏnt'ongjŏgin yŏja (a traditional woman; see the Laundress in chapter 3), whose code of propriety and domestic horizons prescribe a predictable life. Korean kinship and patriarchal norms also fashion characters, among them the chaste widow, the filial son, and the devoted daughter-in-law. Characters are thus easily understood as social products unfurling in the vicissitudes of particular social times. Chong-un Kim (1983, vii–xxxviii) offers a pithy review of some such "characters," including "the walking wounded," "the inspired rebel," and "the victimized aesthete." Laurel Kendall makes a similar case for "the matchmaker" (1996, 133–135). In chapter 2 we met a number of characters in the negative stereotypes assigned to overly ambitious, instrumental, or greedy women (e.g., pokpuin, Madam Ttu).

On the other hand, Rorty's persons, "the unified center[s] of choice and action," are responsible for, and act out their roles (Rorty 1976, 309). They are private and principled moral centers: "It is the intentions, the capacities for choice rather than the total configuration of traits which defines the person" (Rorty 1976, 311, emphasis added). Central to the conceptualization of persons is Christianity's "conception of unitary and equal persons"—that "a person's moral essence becomes completely internal and private" (Rorty 1976, 310–311).

Between characters and persons, the rhetorics of selfhood can sympathize with "character-istic" dispositions; condemn characters for their lack of agency; and celebrate persons' agency. Broadly, selfhood is always in flux and thus calls for a situational approach. Here the reader can also recall from chapter 1 the discussion of melodramatic mode that manages to sustain a provocative tension between character and person. When we understand selfhood as a vexed archaeology—not uniform but rather "latently in conflict" (Rorty 1976, 319)—we must relinquish several ideas, including fixed identities (e.g., class); reified distinctions between the social and personal; and a notion of agency as independent of narrative. In this context, personality is a narrative domain that both constitutes and is constituted by such competing selfhoods. In a similar vein, Sartre wrote of alternating moods: "the sense of everything deriving from myself" on the one hand, and of "predestination" on the other ([1964] 1981, 172).

Personality emerges in these women's social mobility narratives as both socially circumscribed and thus exterior, and privately fashioned and thus interior. Dichotomies such as social/personal and interior/exterior are obviated in these narratives, as we saw in chapter 1 for melodramatic texts. Thus I diverge from anthropology's "culture and personality" approach that long "relie[d] on a division of the self into the social and the psychological" (O'Nell 1996, 182). Instead, I take up personality in the manner in which Lila Abu-Lughod and Catherine Lutz take up emotions—not as public representations of private worlds but rather as productive of the social world: "Emotion [or personality] talk must be interpreted as *in* and *about* social life rather than as veridically referential to some internal state" (Abu-Lughod and Lutz 1990, 11; see also O'Nell 1996, 181–190; Schwartz 1992, 340–341; Shweder 1990, 27; G. M. White 1992, 31). I thus take personality as what Geoffrey M. White calls "ethnopsychological discourse," relevant to both the "nature of local subjectivities" and "social institutions" (1992, 22). This approach—enlivened in the discussion of the Laundress in chapter 5—thus redresses social psychologist Alan C. Kerckhoff's critique that in recent years, structualists and "work and personality researchers" have not been able to integrate analyses of the "social psychology of social mobility process" (1989, 21; see also Kohn 1989, 26; see Elder 1974 and Newman 1993 for examples of such integration).

Another discourse in Korea that shares many of the features of narratives on personality is the well-developed discourse on fate (*p'alcha* or *unmyŏng*), which is often spoken of in relation to women (D. Janelli 1982; Kendall 1985, 94–98). This discourse on fate is one that does not deny personal style or the workings of history. Like the discourse on personality, *p'alcha* or *unmyŏng* are socially and culturally circumscribed ethnolinguistic and ethnopsychological constructs that do not necessarily preclude the workings of the history or social circumstances that I find similarly at work in the discourse on personality. Dawnhee Yim Janelli argues that "the concept of *p'alcha* emphasizes social irregularities [e.g., women whose social positions are anomalous] . . . [and] explains these misfortunes in an appealing way" (1982, 68; similarly, on luck see Flanagan and Rorty 1990, 4).

Personalities are thus articulated in relation to a historically specific and discursively constituted social field of possibilities. We have already seen how socially embedded discourses on personalities offer important commentaries on rapid social and economic transformation; in these discourses particular personality traits are considered variously well-adapted, and are therefore differently rewarded (Turner 1988, 8; for South Korea see Brandt [1971] 1990, 83, 108). Ralph Turner elaborates the important distinction between "favored" personality configurations that facilitate social mobility, and "exemplary" personalities that are "represented as admirable" (1988, 5). The Moviegoer, as did many of the other women, often wavered between favored and exemplary personalities in her estimation of herself and her readings of the social world.

The Moviegoer

I began the process of ruining myself in the received style, like any other spooney. I had not, it seems, the originality to chalk out a new road to shame and destruction, but trod the old track with stupid exactness not to deviate an inch from the beaten centre.

My thin-crescent-destiny seemed to enlarge.
—Charlotte Brönte, *Jane Eyre*

Many of my discussions with the Moviegoer were about movies; she amazed me with her vivid reminiscences of the melodramas she had watched in her youth, and frequently urged me to see Western classics I had—to her surprise —missed, from *Waterloo Bridge* to *Ben Hur* (on *Waterloo Bridge* in the South Korean imagination, see H. S. Chung n.d.). The Moviegoer lives in a medium-sized apartment in a high-rise with a corridor view of Seoul's Han River. As described in chapter 2, her husband had bought the apartment with his severance pay from a regional chemical company where he had spent most of his career working as a chemical engineer. In the decades since, he has had several work stints in Iran but now finds it hard to do anything professional in South Korea because he is older and does not have a college degree. The Moviegoer was sad to find her husband doing common labor for paltry wages, after all those years of skilled work. Counting herself in the "lower middle" or maybe "middle middle class," she was a housewife who not only did not work but also made no investments to raise her family's material standard of living. Neither is she one of the *challan yŏja* (women with excessive *yoksim* or desire) the women of her generation speak of (see chapter 3).

The Moviegoer's apartment, except for the photograph of the chemical plant where her husband worked, was decorated with Christian paraphernalia: etchings of Jesus (in the most prominent one, he is at the helm of a boat in turbulent waters), crosses large and small, and framed Bible passages. The Moviegoer was a devoted Christian and churchgoer who said that without faith, she would have already committed suicide many times;

the church was her solace, the place where she went to comfort herself—"It is all I have." As the eldest in a family with only daughters, she took care of her own mother at home, a senile, difficult woman the Moviegoer claimed to have "hated my entire life": "Friends tell me that if I could only bring myself to love her she would finally die, but how could I do that?" We can recall her chapter 3 conversation with friends about Alzheimer's disease and women's suffering. She considered this predicament—being in her late fifties and unable to leave the apartment except to go to church because of having to care for a mean and crazy old woman—her *han* (built-up resentment): "I have lots of it [*han*], for all I suffered in my youth and still not to be free at this age!" Some readers might be surprised to find the first mention of *han* beyond this book's halfway mark, because in some cultural and academic circles, *han* is considered a preeminent, and uniquely Korean, structure of feeling, especially for women. I have surprised many South Korean friends and American scholars of South Korea by telling them that in fact I have seldom encountered the word in both my earlier studies of relatively dispossessed farmers and in the research with middle-aged women culminating in this book. I am struck that *han* is more a feature of a general cultural imaginary on women and the dispossessed, than it is a feature of the discourse of these people (on the discourse of *han*, see Grinker 1998). To be more bold, I would argue that although the construct has become a cornerstone of various public cultural nationalisms, it is best appreciated for having been naturalized in a particular cultural history rather than for stemming "naturally" from women's experience.

The Moviegoer has three children: her eldest daughter (whose infant daughter she cared for), who worked as a social activist educating laborers with her husband—the daughter through whom I came to know the Moviegoer (see chapter 2); a second daughter, a longtime Christian feminist activist, who was at the time "too old to be single" ("I tell her that I've left her marriage up to God") and who was studying to become a minister; and a son who, although an "activist in his heart," had taken a more conventional path (he worked for a large corporation and had just then recently married). Although all three of her children were college-educated, the Moviegoer did not really congratulate herself for this accomplishment: "Anyone in my [class] position could have done as much." There were times, however, when she admitted that her daughters, "who are doing something for the world," answered to her own youthful hankerings: "I had this vague desire—but never a concrete plan—to do something for the people who had it hard in the world." When people ask about her children, who—by conventional standards—were not necessarily so successful (at least the girls), she told me that she wished she could bring herself to answer with pride, "My kids live well and with a [social] conscience."

On Not Having Made Money

The Moviegoer was often self-critical. At the heart of her reflections were musings as to why she never thought to work, or to somehow better her family's circumstances, as so many women of her generation and standing have done. Her regrets in this regard were not, however, so straightforward, as we began to learn in chapter 3. In part, she posed this question repeatedly because she knew that such women (the kind who make something out of their own or their husband's money) would have made her husband happier. For her and her husband to live together, "both of us have had to bear with things (ch'amta)": while she thought of her husband as having desire (yoksim) and ambition (yasim), she considered herself lacking in motivation. Nonetheless, she felt lucky to be married to her honest husband—a hardworking and income-earning man who had given her a comfortable life. Above all, she found it remarkable that he "allowed" her to care for her mother at their home.

The Moviegoer blamed a combination of her personality, upbringing, and ideology for her inability to better her family's circumstances. Constantly ridiculed by her mother as a child, the Moviegoer described herself as lacking in confidence, courage, and yoksim. Her mother, a "typical" yangban woman ("the kind who knows nobody but herself") had no ability to share or give to others (pep'ulda): "Yangban live off of others' labor, and care little about others." The Moviegoer's mother was deserted by her husband, who left her to philander, and later to take a concubine: "Some of that frustration was what she took out on me, her eldest child." Her mother also suffered from not having given birth to a son.

According to the Moviegoer, one of the problems with yangban men in those days was that they were forced to marry uneducated, yangban country girls of whom they grew tired when they went off to the city, where they found worldly and pretty "modern" girls (see also Kendall 1996, 101). These marriages were precisely the "terrible" marriages that were featured in many of the melodramatic films and soap operas the Moviegoer so enjoyed. She confessed that when she really thought about it, her mother did not even seem like much of a yangban at all: she lacked the well-mannered behaviors associated with yangban; instead, she was mean and treated the Moviegoer "like cold rice" when she was young. For the Moviegoer, yangban is variously signified, as it is so often (see chapter 7 for an extended discussion of this point). Here, the Moviegoer explained that she herself was literally robbed of a healthy subjectivity by this *yangban* woman who had been abandoned. Upon further reflection, the Moviegoer mused that her mother was also not a "typical traditional woman"; she was neither gentle (*yamjŏnhaji anta*) nor warm, nor did she sacrifice herself for others. This example reveals that both "*yangban*" and "traditional" are flexible signifiers: as a character type, *yangban* women suffer particular destinies; but out of step with changes in social hierarchy, *yangban* are undeserving of social respect. Interestingly, the Moviegoer reserved "traditional woman" for a gender character that was unmarked by class, and in her narrative, her mother straddled more inevitable determinations of character and less pitiable flaws of persons and personality.

It was not only the Moviegoer's lack of drive and confidence that destined her to be a housewife who was unable to improve her family's status, but also her lack of skills and education. She blamed these failings on her childhood poverty and, in turn, on her father. A good-for-nothing and a philanderer who neglected his wife and his family, she described that her father had been fashioned by the ideas of the Korean Enlightenment Period (late nineteenth century): "All Western style but no content." Although he paraded about in showy suits and ties, he was really "neither this nor that," as the Moviegoer would say so many times: for example, he was neither a *sŏnbi* (proud of his lineage and classical Confucian learning) nor a laborer who could make something of himself in the new age. He was nothing but show. He brought neither propriety nor prosperity to the family, and the Moviegoer's only fond memory of him was when he took her to see the film *The Count of Monte Cristo* (one of her all-time favorites) when she was still single and working in a factory in a regional city; ironically, this had been one of the times when he had left his wife behind in the village.

During the Moviegoer's childhood, her family lived off of her eldest paternal uncle, who presided over the so-called *k'ŭnjip* (big house) at the helm of the patrilineage. Although her *k'ŭnjip* had some land, it was not especially prosperous. When the Moviegoer thought about her marriage, she occasionally felt bad for her husband because she had not particularly wanted to marry him (or anyone for that matter) but had merely desired to escape her parents, her factory job, and her youth. It was sheer luck, she figured, that brought her such a capable man and responsible husband.

The third ingredient that contributed to making the Moviegoer a woman who did not better her family's circumstances was her sense of herself as a "traditional Korean woman" (the kind her mother was not) who simply wanted to do well by her family and to raise her children well. As we can recall from chapter 3, this was why she considered herself lacking (mŏng-ch'ŏnghada) or stupid (pabo katta), for not being like those intelligent or clever distinguished women (ttokttokhan challan yŏja). Her children, we can recall, described that there was something cramped, stifling, or frustrating (tap-taphada) about her manner and lifestyle. The Moviegoer also frequently used taptaphada to describe the staid lives of characters in television soap operas in which nothing happened and the protagonists floundered in situations of their own making.

The characters of the Moviegoer's stories are recognizable: the yang-ban, the traditional woman, the nontraditional woman, the challan yŏja, the enlightenment man, the sŏnbi, and so on. These characters were fashioned both in a Confucian patriarchal complex and in the vicissitudes of the twentieth century. She narrated her own personality as having been developed by and in reaction to this medley of characters. Although she characterized her personality partly in terms of her own frustration for not having contributed to the family economy (that is for her lack of agency), she also described her personality in terms of morals and choices: "living before God," rearing families in love, and contributing to make a more just society. She was critical of the fact that moral people were not given social rewards, and of the topsy-turvy world of South Korean capitalism—a world in which sloth, exploitation, and ancestral misdeeds (e.g., collaboration with the Japanese colonizers) had been rewarded by wealth and power.

The Moviegoer's story was neither one of unbridled agency nor merely the stifling (taptaphan) one she sometimes purported it to be. Rather, her social mobility narrative, and its discourse on personality, combined multiple selfhoods. In the case of her own family mobility history, it was a story of what "might have been" for her family had her own personality been different. It was also, however, a story of the social failings of the contemporary era, which she described as remaining under the sway of unjust social hierarchies. The Moviegoer placed women at the heart of Korean social (mobility) history and was adamant that it was women who were in charge and should take charge of the home, on the grounds that personality was largely fashioned in the home.

On Her Husband

As with many of the women (see particularly the discussion of the Twins' Mother in chapter 3 and of Mi-yŏn's Mother in chapters 7 and 9), the Moviegoer was keenly aware of herself in contrast with—and, as such, seen by—her husband. Although the Moviegoer rarely ventured beyond her apartment and her church, she nurtured her vivid imagination and love of stories through her passion for novels, soap operas, and movies. When the Moviegoer's husband would overhear her effusive storytelling during our discussions, he chided her, "Why are you going on about that?" He had purportedly no interest in stories. He was a man who, the Moviegoer lamented, "could not even stay awake at a movie." For her part, she was not embarrassed about her love of stories; in fact, she once retorted to her husband, "How can you take that away from me? It is all I have!" The Bible, which she proclaimed as "the world's best-selling novel," was one of her favorite sources of stories. What did move her husband, she described, was his interest in personal mobility and in the nation's political stability. It was in the context of this contrast that she explained her lack of ambition (yoksim) and her rather staid lifestyle were particularly ill-suited for him. The Moviegoer knew that her husband was from a poor family and that he would have liked a prettier, more charming, and, most of all, economically more ambitious wife. The Moviegoer agreed with her husband that both she and her mother were "women without feminine charms (aegyo)"; she managed a half smile when she said this.

A brief glance at the personal history of the Moviegoer's husband is revealing in the light of the Moviegoer's sense of her style or personality, and of her marriage. The Moviegoer retreated to the kitchen when her husband and I chatted in the living room. When her husband first left his remote countryside village, he promised himself that he would not return until the day he could fly back in a helicopter—just like the ones he had seen in his childhood when the American military had been stationed nearby. Although that day never arrived, he did manage to finish high school and become a respectable wage-earning technician. None of his achievements, however, ever lived up to his sense of his own promise, and he had many regrets about might-have-been lives that did not come to pass (e.g., going to the United States, or staying in Seoul and working his way into the government). The Moviegoer's husband described an interesting decision he made early in his life: to abandon the traditional lettered life of his sŏnbi (a poor Confucian scholar) father, who was not amounting to anything in the "modern" era, and instead to follow the ways of his father's oldest brother. This uncle, although technically at the head of his father's patrilineage, in fact occupied a precarious position. The first wife of the Moviegoer's grandfather-in-law had been unable to bear children, and in a measure to secure a son, he had born this uncle with another woman. Shortly thereafter, however, his grand-father became dissatisfied with this woman, who was of low standing, and brought in another woman from a *yangban* family—the woman who bore the Moviegoer's father-in-law and five subsequent children. Thus the Movie-goer's husband's eldest uncle was technically not even in the family regis-ter. Although the uncle (son of the low-class woman—who was eventually kicked out of the household) had little scholarly ability or refinement, dur-ing the colonial period, he managed to travel to Japan and to succeed in busi-ness there. The Moviegoer offered a roundabout commentary on her hus-band's sympathies (i.e., in favor of the uncle over his own father) when she derided the uncle as "a collaborator with the Japanese."

The Moviegoer's father-in-law, having no real occupation himself other than the preoccupation with classical learning, relied on the earnings of this half brother (although not even formally recognized as such) for his family's survival. In an act that the Moviegoer's husband praised for its ex-traordinary generosity, his father decided to have the uncle formally regis-tered as the eldest son of his father, placing him, at his own expense, at the much-valued helm of the patrilineage. It was this eldest uncle, a man the Moviegoer's husband admitted was a bit of a brute, whom he decided to model himself after. He described his own father as an anachronistic figure who had amounted to nothing.

The irony of this family arrangement, not lost on the Moviegoer's hus-band or the Moviegoer, was that it was his own father's "enlightenment" (i.e., open mind) that had enabled the uncle's very social space. The Movie-goer's husband left the village shortly after the end of the colonial period to live in the sumptuous Seoul residence of this uncle so as to procure an education. As it turned out, though, the Moviegoer's husband's education dreams were never fulfilled beyond high school because during the ideo-logically charged Korean War, the sumptuous quarters and social standing of his collaborator-uncle were destroyed; with this, the Moviegoer's hus-band's world also turned upside down. Thereafter, the Moviegoer's husband followed a local schoolteacher, from his home village, who had invited him to join a rural ammonia plant. This schoolteacher, quiet and more like his own father, was a far cry from the flashy figure of his uncle. The Movie-goer's husband considered this move to have been the grave mistake of his life, for he ended up leaving Seoul, the heart of South Korean social and po-litical life, where he believed he could have eventually secured an impressive political career. It was a backward move, returning to the countryside and following local lines of authority—hardly the path he had envisioned for himself. Such is the Moviegoer's husband's personal history that figured as the backdrop to his disappointment in his wife—a disappointment that I mostly heard about from her. Her sense was, I think, that her husband wished that she might have helped him realize the material dreams befitting the course of his much earlier life—a tall order, really.

The Movigeoer's husband's early ambition and emulations of his collaborator-uncle aside, in the years that I was meeting with the Moviegoer, his social position was in fact quite delicate. Indeed, it was the very instability of his social position that made it difficult for the Moviegoer to think about herself in any one way or another in relation to her husband (see chapter 7 for discussion of women's difficulty in taking a critical stance on the men in their lives). Alongside the Moviegoer's Christian wall-hangings in the living room were two framed blown-up photographs of the ammonia plant where her husband worked (a daylight and a nightlight view), in what had been a state-of-the art operation, a cog in the wheel of South Korea's technological development. However, during the early months when I was interviewing the Moviegoer, her husband had sat hunched over a glass-surfaced coffee table covered with plastic lace, trying to decipher the English language blueprints of the plant that a Japanese company was going to build in Mongolia. He and several other men he had worked with over a decade ago had been called to go to Mongolia for a half year or so to help set up this plant.

As the Moviegoer's husband painstakingly translated the English and the numbers into registers familiar to him, he made a discovery that kept him muttering to himself in amazement week after week of my visits to his wife. The Japanese, he had learned, were building an ammonia plant at the technological level of the one he had been a part of now for decades in South Korea: they were knowingly building a dinosaur, and a toxic and dangerous one at that. He had been called to serve not as the vanguard worker he had once been, but as an engineer of anachronism who could make sense of plans that were illegible to the more modern, better-trained Japanese, who to boot would not dream of hardship stints in the likes of Mongolia. Over the months, his sixties-something cohorts one by one abandoned the project; their every-several-day gatherings in coffee houses had proved pointless. Limited though he was in English, he fared better with the English than they did. Finally, he was left alone to make his way through the blueprints. Not long after I left, the whole project fell through. Even his chance at fossil employment had failed.

Not surprisingly, the Moviegoer and her husband parted ways in much of their thinking about their children. A once aspiring civil servant—or even politician—the Moviegoer's husband hated the civil unrest and student movement that had destabilized the 1980s and in which his daughters had become embroiled. The Moviegoer's husband calculated that while he had been busy serving the national economic vanguard of South Korean contracting in the Middle East, his daughters, uncontrolled at home by his wife, had contributed to national instability. The Moviegoer said that the conflict between her and her husband over their daughters' years of student activism was "one for which there are no words . . . No one can know what I went through." Away in the Middle East for much of that period, the husband blamed his wife for not raising their children properly. Although the Moviegoer was frightened for her children, and sometimes wondered "why it was our own children who have to be the ones involved in the student movement," she was secretly proud that they were "living for others," for people who were poor, as she had been in her youth. Regarding their only son, the Moviegoer's husband hoped that he would eventually go into business for himself and be highly successful, but the Moviegoer—in a perhaps ironic defense of her husband's life (but not of his dreams)—offered, "What is the matter with living the way my husband has lived, as an honest wage-earner?"

Just as the Moviegoer was secretly proud of her activist daughters, she was also quite self-assured about some of her own ways and proclivities. It is, as we have seen for many of the women, misleading to take her self-criticisms at face value. The Moviegoer was, for example, as we learned in chapter 3, firmly convinced that raising children was the most important work of all, and she passionately criticized the widespread idea that the only "great women" were those who made money. "These days," she complained, "people consider women like me to be foolish (pabo katta)—even my own daughters think a bit like this." She was adamant that women who want careers should not have children, because children only grow up properly when supported by maternal love—the kind she had not received. Even her own daughter, she said, should not have had a child. In fact, the Moviegoer said that she would never have consented to look after her granddaughter had her daughter's work not involved helping the poor. In South Korea it was, and is, radical for a mother to talk like this. Indeed, when she said this in front of several contemporaries, they were horrified and told her to hurry up and encourage her daughter to bear a son, or at least a second child. To this day, her daughter has only one child, a daughter—the daughter she hopes to take to the United States—and no intention of having more.

As for her own lack of ambition (*yoksim*) and her kindness (we can recall from chapter 3 that when a friend once called her "kind," the Moviegoer retorted humbly and humorously, "Not kind; just stupid"), the Moviegoer said that this was really the way "we should live in front of God," and that it was not such an easy thing to do. And for the very rich, she reserved no sympathy. She repeatedly lamented that South Korea was a society in which diligent people who lived honestly were not rewarded, and where the immoral triumphed. Her greatest antipathy was for the Koreans who collaborated with the Japanese during the colonial period (*ch'inilp'a*), whose offspring she noted, "continue to live well to this day, while the descendants of independence fighters remain poor," which recalls her thoughts on her husband having followed his collaborator-uncle. She explained that society should reward the honest and diligent, and permit everyone to live well regardless of their education level and connections.

But the *ch'inilp'a* (collaborator) descendants were not the only index of South Korean inequities: "South Korea is not the sort of place that appreciates quiet diligence," and, because it is a country that "knew *yangban-sangmin* (elite-commoner) distinctions in the past," there is a legacy of "people who are themselves idle but live well off other people's labor." Her laments became more personal as she talked about how the members of her own family fared in South Korea's unjust social landscape. She was, for example, dismayed that she could not afford to buy her son a decent apartment in Seoul, taking this to speak for a great social problem: corrupt land speculation and a housing market crowded with large, luxury apartments that should never have been built (see Nelson 2000). Furthermore, she thought that the South Korean state should support welfare institutions and provide services to help her care for her senile mother. Finally, she called for a change in values such that people would recognize her socially conscious daughters as "successful." As her friend said about her in chapter 3, "You can tell she is the mother of student activists, what with the things she says!"

Through the months in which I met with her, the Moviegoer talked about the days of her husband's great ambition, of her inability to match it and so on, all the while checking the nearby living room periodically to see if her husband had not fallen asleep over the blueprints, to remove his glasses, and to cover him with a colorful afghan if he had. For the Moviegoer, who secretly admired her daughters' activities in the student movement and supported their continued political activities, her husband's situation—suffering for want of a college degree, unemployable after a lifetime of hard work—was emblematic of an array of social ills she never tired of detailing. As it became harder and harder for her family to maintain middle-class trappings, she had begun to think that she really had failed her family with her economic inactivity. This is precisely the sense in which her husband's precarious position made it difficult for her to retain a clear sense of self-confidence for not having participated in the family economy.

This discussion of the Moviegoer's husband reveals that the personal styles of this couple—most often posed against one another—are deeply socially embedded, in historically situated personal histories and in more overtly social stories.

Plausible South Korean Women: The Moviegoer on a Soap Opera

My earliest meeting with the Moviegoer turned out to be an extended discussion of *Kashi namu kkot* (The thorny branch flower), a soap opera that was popular with middle-aged women in 1993; as a matter of fact, it was our shared interest in this soap opera that occasioned our first encounter—her daughter (my friend) had arranged it. I did not then yet know of our also shared love of movies. I take up our conversation here because it so echoes the Moviegoer's narratives of her own life and of women in South Korea more generally.

Kashi namu kkot offered elaborate and exaggerated portrayals of five women: two twenty-something second-cousin young wives (still childless), their fifty-something first-cousin mothers (yet to be grandmothers), and the shared (!) mother-in-law of both wives (their respective husbands were half brothers). Although the Moviegoer did not identify with all five women equally, and did in fact identify quite strongly with one of the fifty-something mothers, she was steadfast that all of these women (and the soap opera's men as well) were plausible (*issŭl su innŭn saram*, people who could be) for South Korea. I challenged her as to their plausibility because, in not atypical soap opera fashion, some of the portrayals were so very melodramatic; in fact, it was for this reason that a number of my same-age acquaintances took no interest in the soap opera at all. If memory serves me, I think I had begun watching it because one of my other interlocutors had been following it as well. In the Moviegoer's take on *Kashi namu kkot* we will find characters, persons, and personality much as I have discussed them in this chapter and throughout this book. I first review the soap opera's plot before turning to the Moviegoer's thoughts on the program, which she watched intermittently and followed through friends when she could not get to it. I then draw upon an interview with Nam Chi-yŏn, the writer of the soap opera, for its resonances with the themes, vocabulary, and arguments of this book. For the Moviegoer, soap operas were the source of stories—her mainstay. In the rhythm of her daily life, soap operas provided stories for those many times when she was simply too tired to pick up a book.

At the heart of this soap opera were two female second cousins who had married into the same family. Kyŏng-ch'ae, the daughter of an upper-middle-class snooty and disagreeable woman, married Yŏngbin, the white-collar successful son of a lower-middle-class family. Tong-ju, the daughter of Kyŏng-ch'ae's mother's first cousin—the lower-middle-class wife of a building guard (employed by Kyŏng-ch'ae's father)—married Su-bin, whom she met as a jewelry peddler (nojŏmsang) at the gate of her woman's University in Seoul (likely Ehwa University—South Korea's most prestigious women's college). As a peddler pushing a cart, Su-bin was a low-level worker, entirely unbefitting as an educated and refined young woman's husband.

The soap opera revolved around several plots: (1) Tong-ju's determination to educate her husband—eventually he was admitted to the competitive Chinese medicine (hanyak) department of a national university; (2) the bitter class conflict between the mothers of the two young women, as Kyŏng-ch'ae's mother belittled her "poor cousin" and Tong-ju's mother was forever hurt by her cousin's airs and exclusions; furthermore, their class conflict was fueled by and through their hopes and dreams for their respective daughters; and (3) the young wives' relationships to their shared country-bumpkin mother-in-law who was portrayed (recalling the depiction of Hu-nam and Kui-nam's mother in Adŭl kwa ttal from chapter 4) as reproducing all the excesses of Korean patriarchy. The soap opera proceeded such that Tong-ju successfully educated her husband while Kyŏng-ch'ae's husband not only failed (in business) himself but also managed to bring his entire nuclear family to ruin. In the final scene, Kyŏng-ch'ae's mother tearfully repented her greed with her hand placed on a Bible just barely in sight. Nam, a Christian writer who explained that she had to be careful to not make the drama's religious colors too prominent, wanted to show her viewers that "money is not everything."

Interestingly, although Kyŏng-ch'ae's mother was vilified for her greedy ways, Tong-ju was the drama's heroine for her arduous efforts to educate her husband. The Moviegoer was sympathetic to almost all of the characters: in large part because tortured times explained the twisted personalities of the less admirable and likeable among them (this recalls, for example, the Moviegoer's thoughts on her own mother and, in turn, on the genesis of her own failings). The more admirable among them spoke for the Movie-goer of the very coordinates of Korean motherhood, most notably Tong-ju. Finally, those with whom she could most directly relate, particularly Tong-ju's mother, were, in the idiom we have explored in this chapter, simultaneously characters and persons—products of their times who were nonetheless reaching for more. The Moviegoer stopped her stream of detail on these people and their goings-on several times to say that this soap opera "is a portrayal of this society, *as it is.*" Similarly, our conversation paused here and there when she acknowledged, with a deep sigh, "Yes, indeed, all of those types are out there." In so doing, she begged to differ with my own sense of the extremes and flourishes of the drama's plot and portrayal.

Taking up the women in turn, I begin with Tong-ju, the object of the Moviegoer's great admiration. If Tong-ju corresponded to a "traditional mother image" (*chŏnt'ongjŏgin ŏmŏni sang*), the Moviegoer was nonetheless clear on one implausible feature of the soap opera—that Tong-ju was a special *young* woman in that "kids today wouldn't even look at a guy like that [i.e., Su-bin]." What made Tong-ju traditional-mother-like the Moviegoer described was that foremost she supported her husband "as a mother would." Furthermore, for the Moviegoer, Tong-ju embodied this image because of the way in which she put up with her insufferable mother-in-law. What was notable about Tong-ju for the Moviegoer was her ability to have discovered "a pearl in the dirt" (i.e., a diamond in the rough). The Moviegoer explained that Tong-ju had been able to appreciate Su-bin's "hidden talents" in the design of the jewelry on his humble cart. And her support was unfaltering, even after Su-bin failed the entrance exams twice. The Moviegoer found the performance of the actress who played Tong-ju drab, dark, and unlively. But, on second thought, she decided that Tong-ju was played in a fashion "befitting of an Ehwa Woman's University student," meaning mature and intelligent, and moreover, she acknowledged that Tong-ju reflected the "atmosphere" of the family in which she, Tong-ju, had grown up, one that would likely have been somewhat dark for having struggled financially.

As mentioned, the Moviegoer related most to Tong-ju's mother, the woman of her own generation, who had lived hard. She described that family as "poor but diligent." Tong-ju's mother also made her the saddest (*sŏp-sŏphage*) because of the reality of her situation: "They have no money, but somehow they manage." The Moviegoer could understand how Tong-ju's mother bore grudges, "because her husband was so incapable (*munŭnghan*) and because in spite of managing to send her daughter to college, that daughter had married the likes of Su-bin." The Moviegoer could also relate to that mother's threats to cut relations with Tong-ju were she to marry Su-bin, and again when she could not act on her word, and yet again when she eventually even helped out with Su-bin's school fees. As for the fact that Tong-ju's mother actually supported the very son-in-law she had objected to, the Moviegoer offered (not unlike she had for Tong-ju), "That is the mother image (ŏmŏni sang) of our country." The Moviegoer could also empathize with all that Tong-ju's mother had endured, what with her husband beholden to her cousin's husband, and the way Kyŏng-ch'ae's mother would show up unannounced and strut about her house. We know that the Moviegoer had little tolerance for those people who think they are somehow above the common folk with whom she was quick to defend and identify.

As for Kyŏng-ch'ae and her mother, quintessentially spoiled rich girls, the Moviegoer was not fond of them but could nonetheless understand and explain them: Kyŏng-ch'ae's mother stood perfectly for "our country's evil wealthy class (akhan puyuch'ŭng)"; hers was new wealth, "not the generation-after-generation wealthy who live modestly, but the low-level nouveau riche from real estate." Kyŏng-ch'ae's mother was hardly a stranger to her: "I have friends like her, friends whose children went to Seoul National University and who can't stop themselves from bragging about it." Kyŏng-ch'ae's mother's exaggerating her material successes to her first cousin, Tong-ju's mother, was, the Moviegoer explained, because of "conflict in the family from prior generations," conflict about which we never learn directly. "Kyŏng-ch'ae's mother has something hidden, and so when she married rich she couldn't help but flaunt it." She continued that Kyŏng-ch'ae's father was also entirely believable, portrayed as somehow untouched by the material world. Indeed, it was only his wife who flaunted the excesses of their new wealth (which recalls the soap opera portrayal of Hu-nam and Kui-nam's father in Adŭl kwa ttal, as discussed in chapter 4). The Moviegoer explained that this character was aware of the problems with his wife but, for the most part, did not interfere, although, "one word at a time, he does scold her."

Kyŏng-ch'ae, the Moviegoer admitted, was the sort of person "you hate," but she too was believable: "She wasn't raised well. Because there was no household education (kajŏng kyoyuk), she turned out spoiled and unfeminine." The Moviegoer went on to explain that while Tong-ju "can take it," meaning the antics of her difficult mother-in-law and hard marital circumstances, Kyŏng-ch'ae had no ability to deal with things.

Finally, on the most exaggerated of all the portrayals in the soap opera,

Tong-ju's and Kyŏng-ch'ae's shared mother-in-law, the Moviegoer was matter-of-fact: "For an ignorant (musik han) woman like her, we can easily understand how she could have elevated one son [Yŏng-bin] and not the other [Su-bin]." She is just the sort of person who "makes people uncomfortable," the Moviegoer explained. Although the soap opera never says so explicitly, the Moviegoer could gather that Yŏng-bin was "definitely a graduate of Seoul National University—we just know"; and with the older son but a seller of wares, the contrast was, she explained, pretty stark. Also, though never made entirely clear in the program, viewers "do know that the boys are not full brothers." The Moviegoer surmised Su-bin was actually a son that her late husband had brought to the marriage. Furthermore, the mother-in-law's being a widow could also explain her antics.

The Moviegoer's greatest interest in the soap opera was the fate of Tong-ju and Su-bin: "Would he succeed in entering and graduating from college?" Not surprisingly, the Moviegoer found vicarious pleasure in the soap opera's dramatic reversal of fortunes: that Kyŏng-ch'ae's family "would come to ruin." Actually, she had missed the final episode in which this came to pass: Kyŏng-ch'ae's mother apologized to Tong-ju's mother, it was revealed that Tong-ju's maternal aunt had arranged employment for Yŏng-bin after his colossal business failure, and Kyŏng-ch'ae's mother "came to believe" in Christianity. It was in fact Tong-ju and her mother who triumph in this soap opera, in the end echoing the Moviegoer's intermittent sense of her own ethical and social triumph as a mother and survivor in contemporary South Korea.

Writer Nam Chi-yŏn is a woman of the generation explored in this book, and her cultural logics resonate with those at the heart of this book. Her discussion of the inspiration and plot development of the drama in the soap opera all circled around the yoksim of her brothers and sisters. Echoing the remarks of the Education Mother in chapter 2, Nam explained that for contemporary South Korea, the old proverb "Your belly aches when things go well for your cousin," should be modified today to include the intense jealousies even among siblings. We discussed the considerable competition between her own female siblings and the incredible lengths to which they went to educate their children so as to "ensure their marriageability." A number of her sisters' sons and daughters studied for the college entrance exams for as much as three and four years, aiming to enter the most prestigious schools. She said, "People suppress their competitiveness, but in terms of basic instincts everyone is the same—particularly women . . . South Koreans are the most extreme example of these tendencies in the world." Having been widowed as a young woman, Nam explained, was the source of her own *yoksim*: her ambition led her to successfully educate her daughters and make them into prosperous housewives. "It is a scary thing, but if you lose your husband young, then you become a 'woman with a strong fate' (*p'alcha ka seda*)—a woman who runs into difficulties in the course of life—but for your daughters you want them to live easily, to marry into good and prosperous families." In short, her own career as a soap opera writer—a career that she complained had by then thoroughly exhausted her—was born of *yoksim* that was in turn the product of a character fashioned by her fate as a young widow. Nam spoke of her efforts in *Kashi namu kkot* to "include something for everyone—rich and poor, old and young." Nam's self-professed familial wisdom on *yoksim* invested the drama with precisely the melodramatic and social tension that pervades the structure of feeling in the women's stories populating this book's pages.

We have seen that the Moviegoer articulated her personality both positively and negatively vis-à-vis images of others. The Moviegoer's "other" is desirous, capable, and ambitious while simultaneously socially irresponsible, narrated in terms of her own lacking in desire and ability to extend the family economy. However, her "other" was never uniformly appraised in a positive manner: the more socially well-adapted personality was not necessarily morally superior. To the contrary, she seemed to understand the very efficacy of these personalities as the harbinger of unjust times and social realities. For example, the "more successful" others were, if anything, symbols of social injustice. In addition, the element of her own personality of which the Moviegoer was most self-critical—lack of ambition—had ironically resulted in positive outcomes for her life: an alternative and superior social vision. In this way, personality was a domain through which social justice could be articulated. Here we can recall the open quality of melodrama, forfeiting both narrative and moral closure (see chapter 1).

Rather than ask whether one or another woman has exercised agency in the social mobility of her life, I have instead turned to selfhood as composed of competing epistemologies constituted in narrative that are variously agentive. This approach echoes Battaglia's call for attention to "the social conditions of [agency's] appearance or obfuscation" (1995, 2, 4), as well as Rorty's observation that "humans are just the sorts of organisms that interpret and modify their agency through their conceptions of themselves" (1976, 323; see also Pile and Thrift 1995, 5). These social mobility narratives—including their attention to the development and effects of personality—were also commentaries on social justice, insofar as they precariously straddled historical and cultural circumstances, life chances, and social outcomes. In this way, in keeping with the melodramatic mode, the discourse on personality can become a moral and political domain through which people judge the reward structures of their place and time. As such, social mobility narratives are not unified portraits of the simple exercise of personal will, of unlimited agency, or of how "individuals" cut a path through the chaos of rapid social transformation. Rather, combining laments of circumstance and celebrations of agency, these stories are often simultaneously tortured and triumphant, structured and selected, fated and fashioned. Agency is thus articulated in the context of moral debates on society and its times. When agency and circumstance are understood as mutually inextricable from fate, it is not productive to distinguish between the personal and the social, the internal and external, or the domestic and public. These logics are certainly at work in both the narrative of *Kashi namu kkot* and the Moviegoer's reading of that soap opera, as well as in her own social mobility stories. In keeping with discussions begun in chapter 1, it is no surprise that this soap opera's melodramatic sensibilities so resonated with the Moviegoer.

In chapter 7 I turn from personality to another window on social mobility stories: masculinity and its articulation with social displacement, a theme that we met in this chapter in the shape of the Moviegoer's husband.

7

GENDERING DISPLACEMENT

Men, Masculinity,
and the Nation

It is no surprise to find men with little subjectivity (chuch'esŏng) because, after all, during the Korean War where were the men? Just hiding in outhouses.

—Mi-yŏn's Mother

This chapter focuses on a prevailing national and historical narrative: that of male subjectivity (chuch'esŏng). I consider how male subjectivity—particularly its loss or displacement—works as an actor in the narratives of the women in this book, and in South Korea more generally (see Em 1995; Jager 1996a; and Schmid 1997 on Korean gendered narratives of nation and history). Beginning with a discussion of male displacement, I then introduce three films in order to elaborate and illustrate the popular and public narration of the loss or displacement of male subjectivity. Next, we will consider gender in national narratives more broadly, and finally the play of these gendered national narratives in Mi-yŏn's Mother's mobility stories.

Men's Displacement

The displacement of male subjectivity is one stream of national narratives with of course its own particular historical, generational, gender, and class coordinates. For the women in this book, male subjectivity refers to both the personal attributes of the men in their lives *and*, metaphorically, the national and historical narratives. It is in this sense that I choose not to translate "chuch'esŏng" as "ego"; although in many contexts "ego" would make sense, such a personalized term too easily forfeits its national and historical references. In Korean, "subjectivity" registers very differently than it does in English: it operates in both the personal and the national range of meaning. A person without chuch'esŏng refers loosely, for example, to one with little spine, confidence, or sense of self. In another vein, South Koreans equate chuch'esŏng with national subjectivity or sovereignty. And yet again South Koreans recognize chuch'e sasang (the ideology of chuch'e) as the North Korean official ideology of state autonomy (see Em 1993 and Robinson 1984 on chuch'e).

I focus particularly on the loss or displacement of male subjectivity not because all men—or even all of the men who figured in the lives of the women in this book—were displaced, but because this mode of representation is frequently at work in the narratives and gender subjectivities of the women in this book. Specifically, male loss or displacement—physical, material, cultural, and social dislocations—constitutes a grammar for articulating the costs of colonialism, the Korean War, and rapid social transformation in South Korea. I do not mean to say that men suffered greater losses—real or symbolic—over the course of Korean contemporary history than did women, or to suggest that the only way to narrate loss or displacement is to focus on men. That chŏngsindae (comfort women), for example, have recently become more of a public narrative in South Korea, is a good counterexample (see Kim-Gibson 1999; C. Choi 1997; Soh 2000; see also Jager 1996b on female subjectivity in the narration of the division of the peninsula). I did find, however, considerable interest in the historical loss and suffering of fathers and husbands. In this vein, we can recall the Moviegoer on her husband, in chapter 6. The stories of men at the center of their place and times, articulate this theme as well in that they ask what it has taken to preserve subjectivity in twisted times, or during immoral orders, a prevailing theme in Mi-yŏn's Mother's discussions of her husband in this chapter (see also chapter 9).

It would be problematic to claim that all talk of men and displacement refers obliquely to national suffering or loss. My suggestion, rather, is that in a patrilineal, patriarchal society such as South Korea with its history of national loss and displacement, it is easy for male subjectivity to take on particular representational salience. In this context, it is revealing to consider how private histories can sometimes speak to these narratives (see J. J. H. Lee 2002). For South Korea, I think that for the generation that came of age in the 1950s and 1960s, this articulation is particularly piqued because of the vivid experience of the Korean War, the recent memory of colonialism, and statist narratives and projects of national renewal and development (see

Jager 2003). As discussed in chapter 1, for increasingly post-nationalist and perhaps post-development generations, this and the other narratives in this book grow perhaps ever more remote (see Jager 2003 for a fascinating discussion of the pathbreaking aesthetics of Kim Dae Jung's presidency).

Although male displacement may be at the heart of the story, displacement is spoken of here in various gender terms: that is, "male" and "female" traits are attributed to both men and women because of competing ways in which the understandings of domestic and social reproduction are gendered.

Addressing gender as a public sign-system or register, which is in turn producing private subjectivities, it is often most effective to look beyond positions or ideologies, to forms and symbolic systems of narrative. Such a perspective is important in the consideration of women, whose personal narratives refer less often to public narratives and periodicities.

Before elaborating on these gender sign-systems, I turn to *Romaensŭ Ppappa* (Romance papa) and *Pak Sŏbang* (Neighbor Pak) from 1960, and *Pŏng'ŏri Samnyong'i* (Deaf-mute Samnyong'i) from 1964, films from South Korea's so-called Golden Age of Cinema spanning the late 1950s to early 1960s, before the filmic eclipse under the state censorship of President Park Chung Hee (on this film history, see K. H. Kim 2002; Y. Lee 1988; Lent 1990; on Golden Age cinema in particular, see C. Choi 1998; K. H. Kim 2002; McHugh and Abelmann n.d.). These films are all part of the viewing canon of the generation of women featured in this book (on South Korean so-called women's films, see S. Kim 1998). I call these films that captured youthful imaginations (both American and South Korean) "melodramas of social transformation," particularly the displacement effected by change in the configuration of status hierarchies. Across the three otherwise diverse films I take up here, "male subjectivity" is the thematic protagonist.

Melodramas of Social Transformation: "Male Subjectivity" on Screen

The film melodramas of social transformation examined here maintain a creative tension between patriarchy, namely the excesses of male privilege and power, and the dislocation of men on account of radical social transformation. In each film, then, the staging of patriarchy—at moments very "real" and heavy-handed—is undermined once the camera turns to the man as the pawn of larger social forces. Echoed in these films is precisely the tension between the personal and the social enlivening the discourse of personality, as discussed in chapter 6. Patriarchy is thereby effectively reduced or even mocked; therein it can become a constellation of humorous antics or a complex of pathetic machinations (for a related discussion on *Obalt'an* [A stray bullet] 1960, director Yu Hyŏn-mok, see E. Cho n.d.; on *Hanyŏ* [The housemaid] 1960, director Kim Ki-yŏng, see K. H. Kim n.d.). For the women in this book, it has been hard, I argue, to name patriarchy as such for precisely this reason: the hand of history is, in this narrative complex, taken to mollify that of patriarchy, however real its local workings might be. Simply put, in the name of larger concerns, women have found it hard to pin blame on the failings of individual men. In my recent research on Korean American immigrants and their children (described briefly in the preface), one of the mothers, pained and teary by that point in our conversation, said, "As many years as my father has been dead, I still really hate him—to this very day." In writing this book I have often thought back to her comment because it was, I think, very difficult for a woman of her generation to express herself in such stark terms. None of my other research interlocutors were quite so bold about their fathers.

Before turning to the films, let me briefly consider their times. Much as the 1990s stood precariously between the enormous promise of social reform and considerable disappointment (as reviewed in chapter 1), so too were the early 1960s (the heart of this cinematic moment) fraught, coming as they did on the heels of a watershed year in postliberation history, 1960. Four-one-nine (for April 19, 1960), the outbreak of student protests against the Syngman Rhee regime (1948–1960) and its suppression, leaving more than a hundred dead and a thousand wounded, is reviewed here briefly to underscore a historical moment ripe for a sympathetic appreciation of men's dislocation and troubles.

By the late 1950s the Rhee regime was strained. The fault lines were many: Rhee's autocracy had become increasingly apparent, especially in the light of a stagnating economy (Lie 1998, 33); high school and college attendance had quadrupled from 1948 to 1960 (Cumings 1997, 339), making for an intelligentsia that sustained democratic ideals as well as economic desires; there was conflict over revisions to tighten the already draconian national security law; and many opposed the prospect of a normalization treaty with Japan (Lie 1998, 36; Cumings 1997, 343). The 4-1-9 student uprisings were victorious: they toppled the regime. By the end of April 1960, Rhee took exile in Hawai'i, paying perhaps ironic tribute to the graft economy of American aid that ran the country under his aegis. The uprising bore fruit in the brief democratic regime of Chang Myŏn (1960–1961) only to be eviscerated by the military coup of Park Chung Hee, on May 16, 1961, another landmark date in South Korean history (see S. Kim [1965] 1990 for a fictional portrayal of post-4-1-9 social frustrations). Park's regime combined staggering economic growth of remarkable dimensions with a stunningly autocratic regime to match, including ideological control and unrivaled labor suppression and working conditions (Koo 2001). This history suggests that the salience of the memory of these films in the 1990s was not only that they happened to recall these women's youths but that they also spoke to the sensibility of the 1990s (see K. H. Kim n.d. for a fascinating comparison of Golden Age and late 1990s film).

The 1960 Romaensŭ Ppappa (Romance papa), directed by Sin Sang-ok, features a new urban middle-class bourgeois family with all of its trappings (see C. Choi 1998 on class, mobility, and modernity in Golden Age film). Played by Kim Sŭng-ho—one of the favorites of women of this generation, famous particularly for his fatherly roles—Romance Papa is a warm and jovial figure promoting domestic harmony. The opening scene captures the patriarchal tension I have just described, which runs throughout the film. Three of the family's five children, in their teens and early twenties, are playing a trick on their parents: running between them to gather stories of their romance and marriage and, in turn, reporting to each of them entirely distorted versions. Amid giggling and girlish antics, they feed their father lines to warm his heart: telling him that their mother has called him "her man, her ideal" (kuwŏn ŭi namsŏng). The father's well-fed physique seems to bloat with these words as he basks in the glory of his dominion. Moments later, behind the screen of the sliding door, the children peek in on their father as he reports to their mother all that she has said, only to be put in his place by the trim woman at her sewing machine, who, hardly missing a stitch, cocks her eyebrows and asks what he has been doing feeding such nonsense to the children; the children laugh and squirm (see An 1998, 32–33, on humor in this film). No sooner have the children witnessed this little scene that they have so lovingly staged than do they whisk their Romance Papa away and break into song, Schubert's Serenade. The father joins in and bourgeois harmony is restored, to the fitting accompaniment of Western classical music.

The film's next scene shows the family's eldest daughter newly married. She and her husband are living with the family briefly, as would have been customary. Her younger siblings are tickled by the transformations they find in their newlywed sister, acting the part of a somewhat anachronistic bride. When made to explain to her family why it is that she has scrambled into the house to fetch an umbrella for her husband on an unequivocally fair day, she offers, a bit sheepishly, that her husband thought it might rain. This time it is her father who stages patriarchy: "Yes, yes, well, your husband is the heaven," says Romance Papa, evoking the Confucian maxim of heaven and earth on the sexes that could only ring as "traditional."

It is not long in coming that this domestic scene is delivered to a wider world, the public world of men. Foreshadowing instability in that wider world, is a scene in which the second son, who we have learned is studying for the college entrance examinations, has a wrestling match with his father in the enclosed courtyard of their home, the stagelike *madang*. When the father topples, the mother and two daughters run to his aid. The unstable economy soon topples the father's world, as well, as he loses his bank job, which had been seemingly secure, to "make room for younger people." As the father leaves the bank, he is shown confiding in a younger employee that he will not tell his family what has happened. Herein begins the most centrally staged narrative of the film: the pretense of the stable work, in fact eviscerated in changed times. The film's stagings of patriarchy described have set the dramatic tension that runs the length of the film. Not long thereafter the father runs into his eldest son, an aspiring playwright, at a bar. Man to man—importantly, man to eldest son, the building block of Korea's patrilineal social organization—they confide in each other: the father that he has lost his job but plans to not tell the rest of the family, and the son that he has in fact dropped out of college to pursue acting and writing. The son asks, "But what will you do all day?" He tells his father that he will give him money, that "it's my turn now."

The film follows the father as he tries to find a job through old friends and acquaintances. Finally out of luck, he ends up at Pagoda Park, in the heart of Seoul, where older men have for decades passed their days beyond the age or inclination of employment. When a man asks him for the time, Romance Papa suddenly realizes that he is still a man of property, and he decides to hawk his valued pocket watch, a sign of the bourgeois modern.

From here, the plot winds among the loving efforts of Romance Papa's family to help him proceed with his artifice as the bourgeois provider. By this point the entire city has become the stage for his pretense. All dressed up in the requisite suit, tie, and hat, and sporting a briefcase, he has no place to go: a figure we have already met in descriptions, for example, by the Moviegoer of her father.

Behind the scenes, the wife and children—who have learned about the situation from the son-in-law, who discovered it through his own work—proceed to take on piecework and part-time jobs to make ends meet. When

Romance Papa is aghast to find their services advertised at the prosperous gate of his home, the children tell him that they have initiated this because they are bored (simsim haesŏ). The mother's first response to the news was to tearfully muse about how hard it has been every day for her husband to stage his façade; she and the children all cry. The high-school-aged son declares that now, just as the wrestling match had foretold, his father really has no power (kwŏllyŏk).

In the film's climax—a birthday celebration for Romance Papa—the son-in-law has retrieved the watch and they all present it to the father. In this loving way, Romance Papa comes to know that the whole family has been in on his secret all along, but that even without the paycheck, he is still the Romance Papa. This birthday scene is played as a resolution: the symbolic watch has been restored, and the father's position secured, even without a job and paycheck. Interestingly, and entirely unrealistically, it is as if the restored male ego alone will safeguard this family and its lifestyle. Thus, in the final analysis, it is male subjectivity itself that plays the protagonist and sustains this plot structure.

Like Romaensǔ Ppappa, Pak Sŏbang (Neighbor Pak), released in 1960 and directed by Kang Tae-jin, invites reflection about men and changing-status hierarchies and social morality. Pak Sŏbang features a father (also lovingly played by Kim Sŭng-ho) who is portrayed as somewhat of an anachronism: he is a handyman whose specialty is fixing the flues of Korean ondol floors, through which hot air passes to heat traditional homes. "Sŏbang" most commonly refers to a son-in-law; when applied, as in this case, however, to a middle-aged man, it refers both to his familiarity in the neighborhood and to his modest social standing. Until the film's final scenes, he is featured in Korean dress, often, though, with a Western hat and black shoes. Although by no means a traditional elite, he is well respected in his urban neighborhood (one that acts much like a village) because his children are well mannered, educated (at least through high school), and employed—his second daughter, Myŏng-sŏn, is an office worker at Northwest Airlines, where she is called "Missǔ [Miss] Pak," and his son is a white-collar worker in a prosperous pharmaceutical company.

Charmed by his provincial manner, one of Pak's customers invites him in for "Western liquor" and a snack. He comes up from the flooring, wiping his feet and hiding them from the woman, to sit in a chair at the table with her—traditionally, Koreans ate seated on the floor at low tables. The woman chortles, albeit lovingly, at his unfamiliarity with a Western table setting (see C. Choi 1998 for a discussion of the representation of things

Western in South Korean film). (Later, in the company of his neighborhood buddy, Mr. Hwang, Pak reports on having imbibed Western liquor, and Mr. Hwang ventures that such drinks are "for long-nosed people, not for us.") The lady of the house then proceeds to report that her maid tells her his family and the successes of his children are the envy of the entire neighborhood. As we have seen, in times of flux it is difficult to locate a family's standing; in the case of Pak's family, his occupation, family cohesion, social graces, and the promise of his children's success are all critical and competing elements. Much later in the film, at a birthday celebration for Pak, Mr. Hwang, seeing the warm family-gathering and the family's presentation of a watch (echoing *Romaensŭ Ppappa*), tells him: "You have risen in the world (*ch'ulse*)."

Pak's traditional patriarchal familial role is portrayed endearingly precisely because of his anachronistic ways and line of work. It is as if, as in *Romaensŭ Ppappa*, the family plays along with his domestic authority because his social authority has been displaced. This works so that the postures of patriarchy seem to be just that, postures. There are numerous interesting juxtapositions of serious postures and posturing: such as when Pak's wife mutters under her breath about her husband's constant meddling in their daughters' affairs, "I don't know when he'll grow up," and at another point telling him not to be so childish. But this does not stop the eldest daughter's immediate and quite serious query to her mother about her marriage plans: "Have you mentioned it yet [to Pak]?" His patriarchal role is thus not entirely chimerical. Similarly, when Pak first meets his second daughter's intended, he sends him off in a patriarchal gesture. Moments later, however, we hear him lovingly admit to his son: "Earlier I sent him off, but let's see what happens." There are, however, other moments where Pak retaliates, such as when he catches Myŏng-sŏn just as she is about to go off mountain climbing with her fiancé, although the family had sent Pak to the bath house, to avoid the encounter, but it was closed. Condescendingly, the daughter explains to her father, "People who use their heads [i.e., white-collar workers] need *rek'ŭreisyŏn* (recreation)" and the fiancé then elaborates the meaning of the English loan word. Grabbing his cane and helmet, to join them, Pak retorts that he too needs a respite "because I use my head to clean the flues." A comical mountain-climbing scene follows, replete with yodeling and Pak's near disaster.

In scene after scene, the family is scrambling to hide things from the father, particularly things associated with the romantic exploits of his two daughters. This all transpires in the context of Pak's ambivalence about the new culture of dating and romance. Much of this is played out in humorous almost slapstick scenes in which the traditional home becomes a labyrinth for the children to evade the anticipated gaze of the "patriarch." Again, though, between the comic dramatic style and the anachronism, it is hard to view Pak as traditionally patriarchal. The film mise-en-scène thus allows for a staged patriarchy in skeletal antics and gestures. Pak's posturing is showcased most vividly in his drunken sprees in which the lubricant of liquor renders patriarchal flourishes, again signs of anachronism. One of the film's most highly stylized moments, a cinematic aside or meta-commentary in which a captive rat circles his wheel to high-pitched music, refers, I think, to Pak's predicament, though the scene appears exactly at a moment in which he has just hit his eldest daughter, and could thus, perhaps, refer to her situation as well—or to their predicament together.

Much of the film's plot development circles around the romantic exploits of the two daughters, but the central pair in the film is the father and his only son (played by major film star Kim Jin-gyu, who also played the son-in-law in Romaensŭ Ppappa). Here too we find interesting twists on patriarchy. There are many points in the film in which the father and son are portrayed almost as lovers, encircled in greenery, holding hands, in teary raptures, and with requisite musical accompaniment. Early on in the film we hear the father proclaim, in the midst of his consternation about the romance of Myŏng-sŏn with her coworker, to his son: "You are the only one I trust." When the son responds to his father, "If you were to die, it would be Yŏng-sŏn [his eldest sister] and Myŏng-sŏn who would grieve most," Pak replies, "I'd have to die to know that!" Pak even abrogates conventional patriarchal authority when in one scene he invites his son to smoke in his presence; the son, though, refuses.

The son is asked by his boss at the pharmaceutical company to consider a placement abroad in Thailand. After the warm familial birthday celebration for Pak, previously described, the son breaks the news about Thailand to his father, who asks, "Are you the only one they can send? If you leave I have no one else to trust—don't leave!" The son pleads, explaining that this is the only way for him to advance, to rise up in the world (ch'ulse), but Pak persists: "What if you die in a plane crash? The neighborhood people all say that you are filial . . . I didn't raise you to go abroad."

The classically melodramatic climax of this film—with the requisite violin crescendo, thunder, and lightning—is Pak's meeting with the villainous aunt of the orphaned young man who would like to marry his second daughter, Myŏng-sŏn. Myŏng-sŏn begs her father to wear Western clothes for this meeting, but he stubbornly refuses. It is this stubbornness that is lovingly highlighted throughout the film. The aunt, who has recently returned from Hawai'i, where we gather that she has emigrated, has called him to her sumptuous home because his daughter's intended is her ward. Pak enters the home to the sound of a bulldog barking, foreshadowing the woman to come. The home is foreign, in every nook and cranny, from the television to the Japanese-style floral arrangement. The aunt has called him there to inform him that the likes of him and his family are unbefitting of her nephew and of her family's social standing. Before explaining her real motives, though, she goads him, asking if he knows why she has called him; and he speaks naively of his daughter's charms and of the praise she has garnered in their neighborhood. Earlier the aunt had chided her nephew about the status and heritage of his intended: "Family, prestige, blood—do you know nothing of these?"

In an interesting allusion to the earlier scene with the neighborhood woman, when the aunt offers Pak tea, she silently ridicules his ignorance as he opens the tea bag into the water. Gone, however, is any neighborhood mitigation of class difference. She tells him that he is ignorant and unlearned (musik) and that "laborers are meant to marry laborers." At this point a melodramatic storm and its musical accompaniment envelop the scene. The nakedness of this scene is epiphanic for Pak; the humiliation of this encounter—in such stark contrast with the loving coddling of his family and neighborhood—becomes a call to action. He is thrown out of the home, reeling, and the longest and most melodramatic shot of the entire film captures him silently leaning against the high walls of that house, that fortress. To the filmic accompaniment of scenes from his past, he walks away, stooped over, reminiscing about the hardships of laboring and of rearing his children. He goes to his neighborhood bar and sits alone as the furious thunder and lightning storm rages on.

After the bar he meets his son and immediately asks him what it is that one does with a tea bag. He then weeps in the knowledge of his humiliation. His response: to tell Myŏng-sŏn that she must go to college as he cries over his "sin" for not having educated his children "as others have." He proclaims, "Others say that you are the children of a good family, but you are nothing but the children of a flue repairman. People look down on you. How will I ever be able to bear the burden of my regret?" He vows to work himself to the bone to send his children to college, calling himself "this dad who couldn't educate you to college." The children assure him that their lives are just fine, but he persists with declarations of his humiliation. In a mid-1990s magazine column that featured people's favorite classical films, one man described the tea scene in Pak Sŏbang this way: "You can't help but laugh at this event—a Korean-style tragedy scene . . . but I cried and cried over that father's love for not wanting to pass down that ignorance and poverty to his children" (N. J. Kim 1996).

In the storm of this melodramatic moment, Pak decides that his son must go abroad, that he must allow him to garner the capital of a new era. He tells him, "Go and succeed in Thailand," and walks off to a melodramatic dirge. Unlike the chimerical resolution of Romaensŭ Ppappa in which the restored male ego insures domestic tranquillity, in this film's epiphany, the father is made cruelly aware of his displacement—albeit, and importantly, away from the local eye of his family or neighborhood. And he retaliates with decisions in step with the times. In this way, he safeguards his ego and makes the patriarchal proclamation that sanctions his son's departure. As with Romaensŭ Ppappa, although perhaps more pointedly, it is the father whose restored ego or subjectivity insures domestic harmony and, in this case, upward mobility.

The film's penultimate scenes are the son's wedding and his immediate departure for Thailand afterward. In these scenes Pak is featured in a Western suit. The wedding is a teary celebration of the son's filiality: the son proclaims his sadness to be leaving, others sing of his filiality, and the father and son leave the festivities for a teary embrace. The son tells Pak to live with hope. As the plane takes off, we see the son crying inside. Pak retreats to melodramatic music, muttering to himself that the plane better be strong and that his son should return with children, then walks off down a peaceful tree-lined street of Korea's yesteryear.

This film's melodramatic flourishes and plot structure dramatize South Korea's social transformation and the vicissitudes of personal mobility. The film's tensions—the parallel sway and anachronism of patriarchy, Pak's simultaneous triumph and defeat, and the competition between nostalgia and a brave new world—invite a rich array of commentary and reflection on a changing world.

Finally, I briefly introduce parallel themes in Pŏng'ŏri Samnyong'i (Deaf mute Samnyong'i), also from 1960, directed by Sin Sang-ok, a film based on Na To-hyang's 1927 colonial-period short story. The film's three main protagonists are: the ill-mannered good-for-nothing son of a refined gentleman with yangban pretensions; this son's bride, the daughter of an impoverished yangban widower (in the short story a widow), chosen precisely because of her elite origins (played by Choi Ŭn-hŭi, who acted as the eldest daughter in *Romaensŭ Ppappa*); and Samnyong, the deaf-mute loyal servant of the family who has long born the brunt of the son's crass and cruel behavior. Here too the thematic protagonist of this film is the son's ego or subjectivity. Central to the plot is his status anxiety, his keen awareness of somehow falling short of the requirements of a *yangban* son. The wife and deaf-mute showcase the complexity of his status anxiety: the deaf-mute because his low status and handicap render him an easy target for the son's status insecurity, and the wife because he imagines that she is—by her very being—ridiculing him. In the short story, Na makes clear that the father is a newcomer to the village and that, although known as a *yangban*, he needs to work hard to maintain his status in the eyes of his fellow villagers ([1927] 1974). The story describes the father as having "always bewailed his own low social rank, so it was only to be expected that the first requirement for a wife should be that she must be high born" (Na [1927] 1974). The marriage to the impoverished *yangban* daughter is symbolic because we know that money has been exchanged to procure her; this makes for insecurity for both the son, who was not meritorious without money, and the son's wife, who needed to be exchanged for money. In the short story's opening lines, Na sets the story in further historical perspective by telling the reader that the location of the tale has in but fourteen years been entirely transformed, wholly incorporated in an expanding Seoul: "Today we find it a neglected slum, the abode of laborers, but at the time its inhabitants considered themselves of some rank" ([1927] 1974).

Several scenes in the film portray the transformations of the times. In the earliest days of their marriage, when the bride refuses to show her face to her groom's friends in the wedding celebration, we hear the son snicker to his bride, "What is so *yangban* about that?" On their nuptial evening, the bride wants the candle extinguished before disrobing, but the son makes it clear that he intends to uphold no such propriety. The bride begs: "Are there no manners to be observed even by husband and wife?" Within moments, he lets her know that he can satisfy his needs with other women and leaves her chamber for a jaunt with one of the housemaids. Throughout the film, he and the maid, a married woman, meet for sex, often in the village mill (analogous to the barn in American film). A frequent refrain in the film, though not in the short story, is the son's obviously insecure charge to his bride that she is somehow ridiculing him, or holding herself above him, because he is inferior or stupid (*monnan saram*). In one scene, the father has instructed the son to visit his bride's father, as would be proper. No sooner have they begun the trip, with Samnyong in tow, than the son taunts his bride, "You really thought I would just follow you there," and runs off. When the son comes home more than a day later, the bride and the deaf-mute already returned, the father scolds his son. The son then accuses his bride of coming home early so as to belittle him in the eyes of his family. In a scene in which his paternal aunt reprimands his actions and warns him to pull himself together, she calls him an "uneducated brute" (motpaeun nom), and as if to prove it, he proceeds to wreak havoc with the room: kicking in doors, smashing porcelain objects, and so on. Earlier, in another defiant moment, when his mother points out that he should have bowed to this aunt when he greeted her, he quipped, "I said 'hello.' Why must I bow?" In this way he wavers: at one moment brash, in a total condemnation of all propriety, in another self-deriding for his own obvious personal failings. In the short story, the old master's wife and paternal aunt blame the father for having indulged his only son, a son who is furthermore a so-called samdae tokcha (a third-generation only son: that is, his is the third generation for which there has been an only son).

The film proceeds with numerous violent scenes between husband and wife. Once, the son grabs some of his bride's most precious items to sell in order to pay off his mistress, who has threatened to leave because her husband has plans to leave the village in search of work. When the bride protests, he reminds her that the items were originally given to her by his mother. The marriage unravels dramatically and, with it, the entire decorum and standing of the family itself. Two events are precipitating: the son's wrath at Samnyong, who he decides is having an affair with his bride; and a public village trial (absent from the short story) over a brawl between the son and the husband of his mistress. From the earliest moments of the film, Samnyong is infatuated with the bride, her beauty and refinement. What wins his heart are the cruel circumstances that have befallen her. Samnyong's efforts on her behalf—early on, the silly slapstick antics he offers to make her smile, and later, his wellspring of empathy—drive the film. Almost comical is a dream love scene in which an eloquent Samnyong woos the bride.

Samnyong's role, played by Kim Jin-gyu—the son-in-law in Romaensŭ Ppappa and the son in Pak Sŏbang—serves more, however, than simply to highlight the brutality of his young master or the elegance and pathos of his young master's bride. As a deaf-mute he observes neither the rules of social standing, nor those of gender and is thus free to roam the entire village, to bare it for the camera's eye. We find him, for example, at the spring with the village women and maids, where he carries a water jug on his head as only a woman would, and is thus privy to their gossip, and in the private quarters of the new bride. In the short story, Na describes that "few people were allowed in the private rooms where she lived with her husband. But this restriction did not cover the deaf mute, Samyong [sic], who enjoyed all the innocent freedom accorded to a house dog" ([1927] 1974). Much of the film follows Samnyong as he meanders the paths of the village, and the stream of village talk. To that talk, Samnyong contributes his own news, "spoken" through exaggerated pantomime, once demonstrating with a radish how the son has beaten his bride. As such, Samnyong's silence itself reveals village goings-on. He is always present: for example, to rescue his young master when he has been nearly beaten to death by his mistress's husband. When Samnyong lies about the brawl to the Japanese colonial village tribunal—the only scene in the film that sets the movie in its historical period—on behalf of his master, the bride affectionately consoles him, "I know why you lied; you speak with your eyes." This is the moment that fades into the dream scene mentioned.

In the film's final scenes, the son has become wholly convinced of an adulterous affair between Samnyong and his bride. The old master fears for Samnyong's life and tells him to leave, an old gentleman's desperate measures as he realizes he can no longer prevent the demise of his household. Meanwhile the bride has tried to hang herself, but Samnyong saves her. Later the father counsels that she too must live out her destiny. In the film's tragic ending, the mistress's husband has set the house on fire. Samnyong saves the bride, and in response to the bride's request, enters the flames to save his wayward young master. As the film ends, Samnyong, the young master, and the young master's mistress have all died. The bride, and the old master and his wife have been spared. In the short story, Samnyong is there to plunge into the fire—although he has been cast out of his only home. He first saves the old master and then enters the flames again to find the bride but encounters the son along the way. Throwing him off, he continues his search for the bride and dies, ablaze, with her in his arms as "a smile of happiness flickered about his lips" ([1927] 1974).

Uniting all three films and many more of this era is the delicate play of male subjectivity amidst societal precariousness and considerable status anxiety. The medium of film is apt here: it allows patriarchy to be staged such that it emerges simultaneously as exaggerated, absurd, and pitiful, but nonetheless powerful. Each of these films sets its primary male protagonist —the unemployed father in *Ramaensŭ Ppappa*, the endearing father in *Pak Sŏbang*, and the insecure son in *Pŏng'ori Samnyong'i*—in challenging times.

In each case, the character's execution of patriarchy is mollified by the humiliation meted by turbulent times: Romance Papa is fired, to make way for younger men; Pak Sŏbang is humiliated for his ignorance of a changing world; and the *yangban* son in *Pŏng'ori Samnyong'i* suffers the indignities of a marriage to a woman of "real" *yangban* background. Each man thus stands for more than his personal predicament. I submit that the ambivalent male gaze of these three popular Golden Age movies speaks to prevailing and long-standing ways in which displacement has been gendered and narrated in South Korea generally, and particularly for the generation of women featured in this book (for related discussions of male gaze see E. Cho n.d.; McHugh 2001 and n.d.).

Gendering the Nation

I now examine gender sign systems in the colonial and postcolonial transformation of status systems. The rhetoric of both late-nineteenth- and early-twentieth-century Korean reformers and of the Japanese colonizers—and, later, both the postcolonial state *and* counter-hegemonic nationalisms—portrayed the premodern Korean elite class (*yangban*) as both feminine and masculine: as ineffective and effete, hence failed at or unworthy of autonomous, or national, modernization; *and* as patriarchal and antimodern (see Schmid 2002 on early-twentieth-century discourses on *yangban*; see Robinson 1991 and H. J. Cho 1998a on twentieth-century representations of Confucianism). Thus, *yangban* were rendered both effete *and* patriarchal signs against the modern. This gender sign system has been variously engaged over the postcolonial era in ceaseless contests over cultural identity and national sovereignty. In broad strokes, the hypermasculine modernizers of South Korea's successive military regimes depicted *yangban* and Confucianism (despite the inaccuracy of conflating the two) as historically effete for being agents of Korea's loss of national subjectivity, while social reformers looked to *yangban* culture additionally for its patriarchal excesses (see Robinson 1991 on contradictory representations of Confucianism; see Jager 2001 and S. Moon 1998 on President Park's masculine nationalism). The contemporary era, however, by no means conforms to a simple contrast between military modernizers and social reformers.

For diverse audiences, and at diverse times, the decline of *yangban* status and culture, coded as Confucianism, has rendered patriarchy a sign of Koreanness (vs. Japanese/Western). Not surprisingly, this rendering is gendered and classed, mapping itself differently onto men and women. Further, I suggest that there is a sleight of hand, and one by no means unique to South Korea, in which "traditional women and womanly virtues" and, by extension, the propriety and communitarianism of the "traditional" household come to stand for Koreanness (see Jager 2003). As to why this sleight of hand here, it is often normative to assign "culture" to women; and for Korea in particular, the assignment of premodern patriarchy to women shifts the attention from the excessive exercise of authority to the more socially palatable coordinates of women's compliance and femininity.

The picture I am drawing, however, is further complicated because the contemporary woman is often vilified against a celebration of "traditional" femininity. Furthermore, women can be vilified as keepers of a familistic modernity in which women work only for their families' well-being against broader social interests. Women are thus, as discussed in chapter 1, easily charged with complicity with systems of power, for assuming dominant values and promoting prevailing prestige systems; and for privileging the home, or the family collectivity. There is, however, yet another complication: namely, in the face of the sorts of displacement at the heart of this book, the patriarchally organized private household can be figured as a refuge for the male ego. Thus it becomes a sign of Koreanness, a "Korean" safe-hold in the face of colonialism or Western modernity. In this sense, it is not only the patriarchal organization of the household or domestic economy that is a sign of Koreanness, but also the household as a refuge collectivity—an alternative system of social organization and power distribution. Women are thus posed to operate both as masculinized enablers of male refuge, by bolstering the family through their in-fact very "public" private work to sustain the household, and simultaneously as feminized cultural workers in the reproduction of patriarchy. It is in this context that women can even be rendered "masculine" agents of the very systems of power (and of representation) that have been figured to displace or marginalize men, as in colonialism and capitalistic modernity. Also, when women cannot enable or enact this male refuge, they can be feminized, not as previously portrayed, as protectors of the patriarchal household in vulnerable national times, but as antimodern, "traditional," anachronistic, and unproductive in their femininity. These representations of women are, to say the least, hardly flattering.

As described in earlier chapters, there is a tendency for women to locate the extremes of desirable and undesirable femininity in other women: the extremes of womanhood are always elsewhere or in another. Not surprising, then, is that women's identifications and dis-identifications are often confused or in flux. What I have sketched here are sign systems that are enormously flexible, although by no means random. Gender sign systems are indeed flexible when the excesses of patriarchy can be encoded "female"; they are also flexible when women's assumption of male roles can enable the refuge of men and the protection of male egos; and finally, they are flexible when women as enablers of the patriarchal household are figured as agents, not objects, of power.

These South Korean gender sign systems thus reveal women's necessarily complicated gender identities and identifications: the case for the women in this book. I turn now to this complexity through the consideration of Mi-yŏn's Mother's thoughts on her father, husband, and two mothers.

Mi-yŏn's Mother: Narrating Gender

We can recall from chapters 2 and 3 that Mi-yŏn's Mother lived in more sumptuous quarters than those of the other women featured in this book. We can also recall that in spite of having worked very hard to ensure her family's mobility, Mi-yŏn's Mother had considerable ambivalence about this very labor. In chapter 4 we also learned about her confusion over education, study abroad, and her son's career trajectory. And we listened at some length to Mi-yŏn's Mother's thoughts on *yoksim* in chapter 3. In this chapter, I focus on Mi-yŏn's Mother's gendered reflections on her three parents and husband. In chapter 9 we will return to many of these details for a focused consideration of Mi-yŏn's Mother's struggles over the meaning of life and manner of living.

Mi-yŏn's Mother's father, a refugee from the northern provinces that became North Korea, and the educated son of a wealthy land-owning family, lost all ability and drive in the retreat southward. Living for the day when the country would be united again, when the wealth of his northern village homeland would be his again, he was—unlike the other male relatives of his generation—completely unable to reproduce his class-standing in the South. He wanted to feast on the delicacies of the old days but rattled on about his disdain for money, had no business acumen, and never succeeded in bringing in any money. Relatives tried to help him, giving him positions in family companies, but his "*yangban* pride" got the better of him. As the reader will learn in greater detail in chapter 8, this was actually a family with newly acquired wealth, newcomers to *yangban* pretensions. Although Mi-yŏn's Mother periodically referred to her father as a *yangban*, she once clarified it this way: "It wasn't his having been a *yangban* that was the problem;

nor was it that he was particularly *sŏnbi*-like (scholar-like)—really there was no illustrious family lineage (*kamun*) or anything like that. The problem was that he had lots of learning." Mi-yŏn's Mother spoke about the incapable (*munŭnghan*) men of her father's generation—here her comment about "men with little subjectivity (*chuch'esŏng*)," which began this chapter, is apt. Mi-yŏn's Mother described that she was "*no k'omentŭ* (no comment)," meaning to be disparaging, about the fact that her father brought in no money. She went on: "He was incapable (*munŭng haetta*), so when I was in middle school, I just picked up and left for Seoul." We can also recall the Moviegoer, from chapter 6, speaking harshly of her father but also describing his sort as a "type of man" of the era: all appearances, all dressed up but with nowhere to go—the fate also of Romance Papa.

Mi-yŏn's Mother spoke of her "incapable" father in feminine terms. She often recalled this particular memory of him: when he came to pick her up from elementary school on rainy days, she would find him standing there, in his tattered clothes, with his makeshift umbrella, surrounded by young maids who had been sent by wealthy families to pick up their charges. Mi-yŏn's Mother was embarrassed by this father who just stood there "stupidly, beaming with love." "It would have been one thing if it had been a good umbrella . . ." Furthermore, because Mi-yŏn's Mother was his firstborn, he spoiled her. Mi-yŏn's Mother often turned her palms to the sky, bouncing them upward to refer to this precious treatment—pampering that had embarrassed her. She described how she was coddled, adored, and even addressed in honorific language (unusual for children). It was this indulgence, she insisted, that ill-prepared her for the ways of the world. Mi-yŏn's Mother described how it wasn't until the painful early years of her marriage that she came to realize her own ignorance of patriarchy:

Once I put a "question mark" [in English] to my husband: "Can't men and women be the same?" He said, "No," and explained that women must bolster their men, but I didn't agree. When I was in school I thought that men and women were the same, but at my place of work, what a difference! And oh, after marriage this was all the more clear. My family (*chip*) was wrong: Love is a good thing, but theirs was too much. You need to suffer (*kosaeng*) some.

Mi-yŏn's Mother said that after marriage, she had "no energy (*kiun*), no sense of vitality (*saengdonggam*)." Her earliest brush with overt gender discrimination, however, was when she and her family took shelter with a former tenant farmer during the Korean War. Mi-yŏn's Mother was shocked by how the tenant farmer's mother treated her daughter-in-law. For example, the mother-in-law, as the senior woman in the patrilineage, measured out the rice each meal, not the wife. As Mi-yŏn's Mother explained, "We were rich. We didn't know anything about that sort of behavior." In her memories of her family during her earlier childhood, the relaxation of patriarchy was a marker of class privilege. Interestingly, later this relaxation spoke to her father's inability to provide for the family, a lack she abhorred.

Over the years, however, Mi-yŏn's Mother has come to think differently of her father, of the way he "resisted" the new era as he held fast to divergent values. His household in the North had been, she described, a collectivistic one that distributed wealth and resources throughout the extended family and beyond into the larger community. She had come to understand that, as the "son of a yangban," her father had been unable to muster an interest in laboring. In her discussions, she thus meandered between competing and necessarily gendered ideas of the ideal work life. She explained that her father's innate personality and his yangban upbringing made him munŭng (incapable). Not only did Mi-yŏn's Mother come to understand her father differently, but so did her once-wealthy relatives in Seoul (see chapter 8): "In those early days some relatives used to ask me why my father didn't work, but now as they get older, they understand why it was that he couldn't go off and do hard labor." For Mi-yŏn's Mother the idealized homeland and mores of her childhood stood for a "Korean" alternative to the ills of contemporary South Korean modernity (see K. S. Chang 1997 on nostalgia for the [largely mythical] extended family more generally). As Mi-yŏn's Mother aged, she came to narrate the effeminate figure of her dreamy father—who loved poetry and indulged his children to the point of embarrassment—precisely in terms of the male displacement featured in this chapter. In her father, Mi-yŏn's Mother came to celebrate what we might call a feminized portrayal of "Korean tradition." There is irony here, for Mi-yŏn's Mother has lived much of her life in defiance of this father. She resisted his advice and style—most of all in her self-conscious choice of a husband who embodied all of the masculine drive and desire that befitted her sense of changed times. Once, noting that her eldest son looked exactly like her late father, she said, "I guess God punished me for having sinned, for having hated my father that much."

But Mi-yŏn's Mother did not think of her father's effeminate ways as entirely of his own making. She described that it was the style and activities of her two mothers that enabled her father's refuge from the real world, caught in the anachronistic trappings of "yangban lifestyle." Her "two mothers" included her so-called Big Mother, her father's legal wife, who had been unable to bear a living child, and her biological mother, the woman who bore her father's four children. I refer to the legal wife here as Big Mother (k'ŭn ŏmŏni) because this was the way in which Mi-yŏn's Mother spoke of her. This usage of the term, however, is not standard. "K'ŭn ŏmŏni" typically refers to the wife of a person's elder or eldest paternal uncle. Mi-yŏn's Mother's usage was likely an allusion to the k'ŭn manŭra (senior or big wife) as distinguished from the chagŭn manŭra or chagŭn kak'si (small or junior wife), to mean a concubine (chŏp). Mi-yŏn's Mother said that these "two mothers" worked together "as a couple" to tend to her father, describing that "between the two of them they did both male and female work."

Big Mother, "a woman who could hold a candle to any man," took to the streets as a petty vendor to secure the family's livelihood, while Mi-yŏn's Mother's biological mother (whom she described as "a woman among women") sustained the trappings of village life and a patriarchal household. Mi-yŏn's Mother reported that early on, Big Mother said this to her biological mother: "This is our fate (unmyŏng), so let's try to make something out of this household." According to Mi-yŏn's Mother, Big Mother had the "'style' [in English] of a male type—she was both father and mother to me." Once, after we had been meeting for a very long time, Mi-yŏn's Mother described that her mothers were "like a same-sex couple (tongsŏng-aeja) in the United States: dividing labor the way a man and a woman would." Later, when Mi-yŏn's Mother was struggling with small children and an inattentive, noncontributing husband, Big Mother helped her to run a boardinghouse, which launched the capital that Mi-yŏn's Mother extended through frequent moves and the purchase of stocks and real estate: "It was almost as if she was our maid. Because of her infertility she slaved in gratitude." Mi-yŏn's Mother continued: "She worked till she sweat blood (p'inanŭn nodong). But it wasn't as if she was really making money like a man. So honest and hardworking, fit to be among Buddhas. I feel really sorry for her. How good she was!" Mi-yŏn's Mother described how when they were doing construction on their home and the entire first floor was torn up, Big Mother slept downstairs, in the cold, in order to guard the house. These accounts, however, are a bit anomalous in that Big Mother's position was in fact secured as the legally registered wife.

Over the years, just as Mi-yŏn's Mother has come to reevaluate her father—from a despicable figure to a pathetic one victimized by the march of history, and again to an icon of resistance—so has she her mothers. She contrasted her own style of relating to men with that of her biological mother's: "My innate style isn't the sort that lays on the charm (aegyorŭl purinŭn sŏngkyŏk ŭn anida), but my mother had more of that than I do. To men, I can seem cold and indifferent. Men see young pretty girls in their midst, but come home to their wives, who wear shabby clothes." She also mentioned this "lack of charm" in relation to her difficulties with her mother-in-law and her philandering husband, suggesting that she had been ill-prepared to win their favor. Mi-yŏn's Mother had thought of her biological mother as unsociable and not adept at the ways of the world, but she saw things differently when, in her later years, her mother became active in a church. She realized that all along her mother had possessed considerable social abilities (sahoesŏng): "But they had never surfaced because all she did was cater to my father, who, after all—what, with two wives and all—was somewhat conservative. I feel truly sorry for my mother, a woman having to live with another woman, and sacrificing everything for the children! If I think about it, it makes me completely crazy." Mi-yŏn's Mother explained that people sometimes referred to her biological mother as a "junior" or "small" wife (to mean "concubine"), which really infuriated her. "Once, when we were doing some health-insurance paperwork, we discovered that she wasn't even recorded properly in the register, listed merely in the manner a boarder would be . . . It's unthinkable, something that by today's standards just couldn't be, a life like hers!" Mi-yŏn's Mother's comments here are perhaps a bit naïve or even staged, recalling those about Big Mother having been able to stay with the family. That her biological mother, who was not her father's legal wife, would not have been registered as a wife makes perfect sense. Mi-yŏn's Mother surmised that her biological mother's eventual death from stomach cancer had its origin in the "scars to her heart from her early marriage years." It was also to this mother that she credits her drive (yoksim); just witnessing her biological mother's life gave her ambition: "That she came from a rich family and still ended up like that gave me yoksim."

As a young woman, Mi-yŏn's Mother consciously fashioned herself after Big Mother. Her biological mother had seemed so limited, tied to her kitchen and the petty patriarchy of her father's dreamy world. Big Mother, on the other hand, struck her as a survivor, a woman of her times, an economic woman, a provider: "Had she been born a man she would have been a match for Chŏng Chu-yŏng," referring to the founder of the Hyundai Group. She explained, however, that over time she'd decided it was her biological mother's generosity that had allowed Big Mother, a barren woman, to live with the family and even enact the social role of mother. Again, these comments ring a bit odd: although it is true that some wives were sent back for infertility, in this case it was Big Mother's, the legal wife's, largesse that allowed Mi-yŏn's Mother's biological mother to reside with the family. For a long time Mi-yŏn's Mother thought of her biological mother as stupid (pabo), but now she thinks with great sadness of her biological mother, as "a true woman, a kind small bespectacled woman. The prototypical kind Korean woman . . . She was good at knitting and cooking, and she was pretty. If only she could have been rich." Although Mi-yŏn's Mother spent much of her life admiring Big Mother's health and spirit, and emulating it in her own economic activities, she reflected that Big Mother had also made her weary.

When we spoke a year after Big Mother's death, Mi-yŏn's Mother was still carrying a piece of paper in her pocketbook on which she tallied Big Mother's "good" and "bad" traits in vertical columns. On the "good" side she listed: "good manners; makes proper greetings; a sense of humor; intelligent; prepared; honest; diligent; exacting." On the "bad" side she detailed: "too calculating; miserly; overly ambitious; doesn't know how to have fun; doesn't have a leisurely spirit; stubborn; isn't spiritual." She once explained Big Mother's strength and resolve by describing how she had "oddly" abhorred television cooking programs; Big Mother felt strongly that cooking was not something to be done through words—"that is how strong she was!" Similarly Big Mother refused to spend money on doctors, convinced that she was the one who knew her body best. Oppressive for Mi-yŏn's Mother were household details: like the fact that Big Mother planned the side dishes so many days in advance. Interestingly, she recorded Big Mother's drive and desire in both of the columns; it was on the debit side because Big Mother set an example that she felt incapable of living up to; because Big Mother made her feel guilty for not rising at the crack of dawn and for her retiring nature; and because she had misgivings about Big Mother's maniacal focus on money and material accumulation. But she also considered Big Mother's life a tragic one: "Life is really about ups and downs. The worst thing is if in the end, as in the case of my Big Mother, you end up alone with no money. My Big Mother could have lived so well if she had just gone off on her own and worked, but instead she sacrificed herself and didn't make any money for herself. If she had, she would have ended up better off than any of us."

Mi-yŏn's Mother cried as she recalled Big Mother's final departure from her house, when Big Mother was going senile and prone to rising from bed and screaming out all night long. "When she walked down the garden steps for the last time, she chuckled as she sang, 'When will my feet touch these stairs again?' " Although it was easier for Mi-yŏn's Mother to criticize her biological mother—an incapable woman from the mind's eye of her youth— her criticisms of Big Mother were quiet, deep, and mature. In a word, Big Mother set an example of womanhood and adulthood that Mi-yŏn's Mother would come to see as near oppressive: shoes she could not fill, and even traits she would come to doubt.

Mi-yŏn's Mother's list of pros and cons about Big Mother is a veritable template of Mi-yŏn's Mother's lifelong ruminations on gendered ways of being in South Korea. In her mothers, Mi-yŏn's Mother met fascinating templates of "female" and "male" that have refused to stand still over her life's reflection and reappraisal. Hae-joang Cho writes aptly of South Korea's "three generations of daughters who flatly refuse to live like their mothers," suggesting that such intergenerational refusal speaks to South Korea's enormous social dislocation and to the way in which cultural transformations have been mapped on women (2002, 167).

Mi-yŏn's Mother's husband epitomized the less desirable traits of Big Mother. Salve for hurt from the incompetencies of her father and "masculine" above all else, the strength of his courtship and his masculine resolve to marry her were what attracted her most: "It seemed a waste to leave him for another woman to find." Mi-yŏn's Mother explained men: "If they have a goal, they just go after it. My husband is the sort who keeps his 'style' [in English] wherever he goes. He would live well in any corner of the globe." She spoke of him as an "American-style man who knows nobody but himself, his own pleasure, and money." She also described him as "terribly manlike and machinelike." And she disparaged his lack of interest in collectivities, familial or otherwise, and caring only for his own well-being. She claimed her daughter, Mi-yŏn, "because she didn't want my life (in-saeng)," opted for a dentist, a dull and quiet fellow, "terribly thin and pale and too doting for a man," having rejected a promising lawyer whom she suspected of being a womanizer like her father, and an aggressive social climber (again, like her father).

Mi-yŏn's Mother did nevertheless on some occasions praise her husband: his health—so remarkable; his subjectivity—so intact; and his drive and desire, and the pleasure he takes from life (even in womanizing)—so admirable. For his part, she described his criticism of her hesitant manner, her burdened existence, her inability to make others feel joyous, and her inattention to her femininity. Although Mi-yŏn's Mother said she hated him for these ugly allegations, his philandering, his squandering of family funds, and his abandonment of the family, she acknowledged that she did in fact feel weak and unspirited and would give anything for more vigor. When she watched a television program on "depression," the construct of which was quite new for her, as it would have been for many women of her generation, it all sounded so familiar, and she was amazed to hear about so many women who shared her feelings. In light of her struggles with psychological well-being, she thinks of her husband's health as remarkable, especially because of his own complicated personal history as the son of a woman who was abandoned by her husband for another woman and for hailing from the underdeveloped and discriminated against southwestern Chŏlla provinces. "If only," she mused, "I could be like him, never wasting a morning moping about or suffering a sick spell."

Those who do not know Mi-yŏn's Mother well—who see the trappings of her large home, who note the achievements of her children, and who know of her toil (in running a boardinghouse in the early years, in buying and selling real estate, in managing her children's education, and even in supporting her husband's career ascendance with innumerable behind-the-scenes efforts)—might be shocked to learn that all of her activity and ambition has weighed heavily on her, both emotionally and ethically. Once she described to me how she had dragged herself to the lottery for a newly constructed apartment South of the Han River at the request of her husband, and how this activity, which she had done so many times before, seemed suddenly so oppressive, even terrifying. She surprised herself, in her later years, for identifying more and more with her biological mother: she thought back to her —feminine and weak, "trapped at home" making homemade *mandu* (meat-filled dumplings) that were shared by the whole family and village in those "days when people knew love." Similarly, she reminisced about her loving father and his affection, which had for such a long time only struck her as weak and unflattering. Once she explained that she had come to understand her father's enormous affection when she saw her cousin and his wife, who had had a child late in life; their boundless love for this child awakened her to her own father's love.

Considering her changing perceptions of her family and past, it was not surprising that Mi-yŏn's Mother wavered in her self-estimations. The perfect sort of female other for the Moviegoer, Mi-yŏn's Mother had been a model coworker in her husband's ambition—manlike, as was Big Mother. And in her husband, she found the perfect antidote to her effeminate and anachronistic father. She managed to escape the little world of her poor family, and even to outstrip the lives of her many relatives who in the short run had been able to preserve their childhood wealth. Indeed, thanks largely to her own efforts, today she and her family live better off than any of them (see chapter 8 on these disparities). But she wondered and worried about so many things. And so it had become harder and harder for her to bring herself to do what it takes to sustain her family's lifestyle and property. She even wondered about the ambition and industry that she had so painstakingly instilled in her children. She was sometimes aghast at the hard edges and the coolness she discerned in them; we can recall from chapter 4, for example, that she was surprised to find all of her children so interested in money. And in these reflections she thought back to her biological mother, a young woman who went unknowingly to "marry" a man with a barren legal wife, and tended lovingly to this man out of synch with the times, and lived in harmony with this legal wife. It was the harmony between her two mothers that Mi-yŏn's Mother continued to express to me as the most remarkable aspect of her past, though, interestingly, her brother considered their two mothers the most embarrassing feature of his past. Mi-yŏn's Mother also reflected back to her father's lack of ability, his generosity and longing, and to his hard life for having to leave behind his parents in the North, and the profound displacement that robbed him of his well-being. She felt deep remorse when she recalled the considerable scorn she had harbored for her father and biological mother while they were alive.

What, then, can we say about Mi-yŏn's Mother's gender subjectivity from these portraits of her mothers, father, and husband? As indicated in earlier chapters for other women, Mi-yŏn's Mother contemplated her life in dialogue with her understandings of gendered lack and excess. Because gender offers a flexible—though not indiscriminately so—sign system through which the workings of history are articulated, gendered subjectivities are constantly emergent and are thus narrated between excess and want, and via gendered others. Particularly apparent for Mi-yŏn's Mother is that male subjectivity, most centrally that of her father and husband, is narrated in relation to public or social narratives. In this way, gender subjectivities articulate with these gender sign systems as a language for talking about history and the nation. Indeed, Mi-yŏn's Mother's reflections on her father, mothers, and husband are constantly gendered and historicized. Moreover, because her evaluations of these figures have changed over the course of her life, we can observe significant shifts in the manner of her gendering and historicizing. Her father was quite ahistorical and effeminate early on though later she spoke of him as a particularly historical product and, if effeminate, a paragon of "traditional" and "communitarian" Korean virtues. We also heard how she articulated these traits through her father's purported *yangban* status. Similarly, while she celebrated Big Mother's masculine work on behalf of the family, she also disparaged aspects of this masculinized role in the broader course of Korean history. Parallel were Mi-yŏn's Mother's thoughts on her biological mother: in an earlier guise, she had lamented her limited female ways—inside the home, outside of the formal economy, and so forth—while later she appreciated precisely the refuge that this mother had fashioned of their humble home, and the feminine ways in which this mother had enabled Big Mother.

As suggested earlier in this chapter, between the lines of these contests over her parents and husband, we find gendered narratives of family—and, more broadly, social—reproduction in turbulent times. Mi-yŏn's Mother's narratives reveal that such calculations are always gendered, but not without reason, as they work in accordance with particular historical logics. Mi-yŏn's Mother's narration here does not reveal formulaic rules for the intersection of gender and history but rather, the ways in which gender and history are articulated.

Before closing this chapter, I turn briefly to the Moviegoer, whose gendered subjectivity, vis-à-vis her articulation of the historical and national subjectivity of her father and husband, was primarily as a negative space, of lacking, against gendered others. The Moviegoer's weak subjectivity was the product, she explained, of the effects of absent patriarchy on her abandoned mother. It was as if each parent suffered a loss of historical subjectivity, and in this she found the roots of a deep-seated feeling she had about herself—that she was somehow constrained, or frustrating for others to behold (*taptaphan saram*), both for having made little of herself and for feeling trapped for not having done so. While her husband stood for the vanguard of state-supported technological development, the Moviegoer lacked both the masculine qualities of a woman who achieves domestic mobility, like Mi-yŏn's Mother, and the feminine virtues of the *yangban* woman. She was not the attractive homemaker either, the leisure-class "modern" wife of the nuclear family—for those bourgeois trappings were strangers to her, and she was deeply skeptical of their familism. Despite her social reformist ideas she could not quite assert herself because her husband's unemployment and recent failure at even fossilized employment made her a protector of her husband's ego and well-being.

The Moviegoer once described to me the singularly "Korean" protagonist in *Buckwheat Season*, a film based on a colonial Korean short story of the same name. Written by Yi Hyo-sŏk in 1936, and often included in middle school or high school textbooks, the story depicts a bachelor itinerant peddler and is set in the colonial period. Little happens in the story other than the peddler's meeting with his son born out of wedlock, a son who does not know him. In the encounter, it is not openly registered that they are father and son; nor does the author detail the aftermath. Many South Koreans appreciate the profound drama that lies in this quiet and understated story. Knowing that I was interested in introducing South Korean films to an American audience, the Moviegoer opined that Americans would likely not understand the tragic appeal of this protagonist, because he is foremost a "man without subjectivity" (see Jager 1996a on the crisis of fatherhood and redemptive narratives of patriarchal succession). The accounts of both the Moviegoer and Mi-yŏn's Mother recall the play of masculinity as protagonist in the films about which this chapter began. The ambivalent portrayal of patriarchy there spoke also to the complexity of gender in turbulent times when social reproduction is makeshift and on the move.

We have seen that the displacement of men constitutes one important national and historical narrative in South Korea. As a narrative enacted through a more general gendered sign system about tradition and modernity, it continues to operate in South Korea through gendered attributions and subjectivities. Such narratives are at work, in often quite unmarked or even obfuscated ways, in the daily life of gender identities. This unmarked quality is important because the historical and nationalist narratives that have held sway in postcolonial South Korea are often heavy-handed in their determination of "proper" political domains and struggles such that many aspects of reality are undervalued for being outside of the properly political. Through attention to the complex ways in which historical and national narratives are gendered, we can appreciate the political character of women's gendered identities.

From these echoes of national narrative, I turn back, in chapter 8, to the minutiae of women's daily lives, specifically to the familial management of class differences and divides, through more details from Mi-yŏn's Mother's narratives and a reintroduction of Hye-min's Grandmother as well.

8

ALL IN THE FAMILY
Class Distances and Divides

My in-laws are something entirely different from my family.
They hailed from one of Korea's few early business cities, and
that's why my paternal uncle was against my marriage, saying
that all people from those places do is think about money . . .
My father made money, but it wasn't about 'this is mine, this
isn't yours' . . . My family wasn't interested in clothes and in
eating. But the only thing my in-laws cared about was food.
My mother-in-law had lived well as a child, but lost her father.
When my husband was studying abroad and we had nothing,
the only thing they could think about was that we would
come home and be rich and that then they could just sit back,
travel, and eat.

—Mrs. Pak

In this chapter we follow kinship lines in and out of the nuclear family: to
women's siblings, siblings-in-law, and cousins of various distances. Increasingly in anthropology, kinship is understood not as a static map of all
blood relations fanning out from "ego"—the center of the traditional kinship chart—but rather as a map, however lopsided and quixotic, that traces
the odd assembly of persons who matter (Carsten 2000; Stone 2000). The
kinship charts in this chapter, then, aim to trace the ties across which
things, ideas, and images are exchanged, and through which meaning is
made. The chapter focuses on the networks of Hye-min's Grandmother
and Mi-yŏn's Mother. As the two women with whom I talked most exten-
sively and with greatest pleasure, it is not surprising that the extent of their
enunciation of kinship networks stretched furthest.

I am interested in these kinship stories in four quite different senses, which should already be quite familiar to my readers. First, as stories that extend our understanding of the workings of education, symbolic, cultural, and economic capital in postwar South Korea, a matter explored most fully in discussion of the Laundress in chapter 5. Second, beyond the what-happened-to-whom-when, I am interested in what the women make of these networks, in the meaning-making of class differences and distances in the family. Third, I pay attention to the visceral expression and affect of this meaning-making: the feeling of encounters across these divides. Finally, I consider the workings of extended family meaning-making in concert with women's larger social visions, frustrations, or confusions; it is these crossroads at which I assert that in South Korea the culture of class and the politics of social justice begin in the family.

The accounts of class divides and class travel in this chapter are stories of the details of daily life: food, clothing, and manners, among others, loom large, as revealed so keenly in the comments of Mrs. Pak (see Nelson 2000, 71–84 for a wonderful discussion of women, food, and class). The stories of Hye-min's Grandmother and Mi-yŏn's Mother that follow are by no means alike even as they share idioms and concerns. Both cases render distinction, yet along different axes, and from quite different perspectives. Also, recalling chapter 6 on personality, the stories personalize to different degrees. For both women, it is primarily other women who inspire vivid stories of class distance and distinction. Also, for both—as for all the women in this book—these matters are not merely the stuff of commentary; to some extent they have drawn the lines of family ties and communication. All of the women told stories about the kinship lines along which resources had or had not been shared: about the uncles and cousins who should have helped this or that person more, or about the altruism of one or another relative that had really made a difference in someone's life. The norms that govern such distribution—the demands of largesse—are always complicated, because people's standing (the resources they really can muster) is never clear, nor is that of the people on the receiving end, and because of the endless social contests over how far and along which kinship lines largesse ought to extend (see Stack 1974). Of course, sharing of resources can follow social compunction and/or the heart; and the withholding of resources can speak to the breaking of social rules and/or to a dearth of heart. The tales are many, intense, and always vexed.

Hye-min's Grandmother: "Our" Women and "Their" Women

As the reader has heard, Hye-min's Grandmother had much to say about the women in "her family," foremost her sisters and Hye-min: that they were masculine, active, impatient, and so on. Again and again, Hye-min's Grandmother would tell me, "You can't ignore blood." But then she would sidestep with comments like this one: "But in the eyes of God, family background and the like shouldn't matter—really, we shouldn't even talk about that sort of thing at church." And then again, she would return to blood, "But, really, there's no way of getting around it!" Most of the relatives who danced across our conversations were women: women "like us" or "those" women of another sort. As this book has consistently stressed, distinction—class and otherwise—is inextricably gendered.

After several meetings, Hye-min's Grandmother presented me with a large photograph from her daughter's wedding. The photo was taken on the steps of her church—the very steps where Hye-min's Grandmother and I had often taken to meeting (convenient because I lived around the corner at the time). A standard family-wedding shot, some sixty relatives are lined up on the steps—the bride's relatives on one side and the groom's on the other. From that meeting on, this photo was a mainstay during our conversations, something to refer to when one or another relative came up in conversation. Beyond documenting the wedding, however, the photo tells another story. Annette Kuhn describes the photograph as "a prop, a prompt, a pre-text"; indeed, the memories evoked by photographs often have "little or nothing to do with what is actually in the picture" (1991, 18; see also Hirsch 1997).

At the time of the wedding, the photograph had been provided for free by the son (the same age as Hye-min's Grandmother) of her father's former farmhand (mŏsŭm). And therein lies a story: How was it that she had come to find herself on the receiving end of the charities of her family's former farmhand's son?—that "yin and yang had reversed themselves," as Hye-min's Grandmother put it. She recalled how when she was a child, her mother had given the now-photographer and his family leftover food and hand-me-down clothes and shoes. As the story goes, the photographer and one of his older brothers had made their way to Seoul and eventually helped to educate their siblings. The oldest brother joined the South Korean navy while the photographer began his career by doing odds and ends for a photo shop, where he also slept, under the porch at the entrance. More remarkable was the coincidence that Hye-min's Grandmother's hole-in-the-wall shop, her nadir, had been directly across the street from the prosperous photo shop of the former farmhand's son. All those farmhand's children, Hye-min's Grandmother explained, were smart and hardworking, and "even" the two daughters finished their high school equivalencies while working at factories. The navy brother, as it turned out, ended up marrying the daughter of a *chaebŏl* (conglomerate) owner.

Hye-min's Grandmother reconnected with the former farmhand's family not because their shops were a stone's throw away but because she ran into the photographer at church. He had asked her where she was living, and she told him that she had become "a beggar," meaning she was poor. Telling me the story, she twice dramatized—with big gestures, as she was prone to do—the photographer's shock, how he had jumped back aghast. After that the photographer's father, by then a widower, came to her shop: "He walked in the store and took my hand; clutching my hand solemnly he said," addressing her by a familiar form of her name. "'Your father has come.'" Her own father had died by then. "He cried. You see, he was the same age as my father, and had also been widowed early."

Every time Hye-min's Grandmother mentioned the photographer in conversation, and she did so quite often, it was to assert, usually quite optimistically, that the diligent are rewarded and that upward mobility is in the offing for the virtuous and the intelligent. Once, this remark heralded talk of the farmhand's son: "*Sangnom, yangban*—all of that is nothing today. Poor people can move up if they live diligently." Or, on another occasion: "There isn't much difference between the rich and the poor (*pinbu ch'ai*) today." Then citing as an example Chong Chu-yŏng, South Korea's most famous capitalist, chairman of the Hyundai Group, who died in 2001, she said, "In junior high school he peddled rice, but he worked really hard. Today anyone can become rich if they work really hard." But statements like these often followed and preceded others of a very different variety. Hye-min's Grandmother's thoughts on these matters are hard to pin down, as are those of most of the women in this book. Just before her proclamation that there were no more formal status distinctions in South Korea, she had asserted that the bottom line was education: "People who are educated live well. Having a good head is the most important thing now." And immediately preceding her thoughts on Chong Chu-yŏng, she had claimed, "Today owning land amounts to nothing unless a person has educated her children." Furthermore, her optimism was muted because she also professed that it was impossible for the children of farmers to live well unless they leave the countryside, that Seoul was overcrowded and it would be best if farming offered a viable livelihood and way of life, and that the children of those who a generation ago did not know to sell their land had been permanently set back.

If her optimism was intermittently marred, however, she also celebrated those who over the years have known what to do—like her father, who knew to sell the family's land and educate his children. Hye-min's Grandmother was forever saying how grateful she was to her parents for their hard physical labor, and for selling the land to educate their children. All of Hye-min's Grandmother's talk trod a fine line: between the sense that the deserving get rewarded and the notion that circumstances can be stacked against a person. Such was the fine line, the tension, which we explored in chapter 6 in the discussion of personality.

To return to the photograph, keeping its pretext in mind, Hye-min's Grandmother called upon it most often to show me the country-bumpkin look of one or another woman. She once described the image of her only brother's wife this way: "You see that one peeking out behind that ugly pink *hanbok* (Korean garment)? Do you see what I mean?" In a crowd of sixty, any single person is barely a thumbnail in the page-sized print, but for Hye-min's Grandmother those thumbnails spoke volumes. If a comment like this one sounds mean-spirited, the reader should know that Hye-min's Grandmother's lighthearted manner somehow mollified otherwise quite judgmental remarks.

That marriage sometimes weds family cultures worlds apart is widely appreciated (J. Bruner 1994). But this commonsensical understanding does not make it any easier for a woman to manage marriage and in-laws of an entirely other sort from her own family culture. Of the women's lives in this book, Hye-min's Grandmother's case is not extreme, but the differences were still significant. Her family was considerably more materially prosperous than that of her husband, which was "not really *yangban* but one of the village's two or three landlords." Consistent with Hye-min's Grandmother's thoughts on education to this day, she explained that she married him "for his intelligence." She grinned and then said, "I bargained well, didn't I—just look at my children: they are all smart." Her father-in-law had been a low-level civil servant, and the family had been of "good standing, better than my own." But with seven children, they had been poor. Also consistent with her thoughts on the countryside—how it so often held people back—was Hye-min's Grandmother's determination to marry away from farming, no matter how grand was the landlord whose son might have proposed. That her husband's father was a civil servant appealed to her; just as her father had known to sell the land, she knew to leave the countryside behind. She described that she and her husband were given nothing from her husband's family: "I married the poorest of the poor—they sent those kids off with nary a spoon." It was the proceeds from her own father's sale of his land, and the food her family sent, that settled and fed them in Seoul, as well as allowed them to host all of her siblings as they each migrated to Seoul. It was because her husband was kind, she explained, that she had been able to tend to her own siblings. Although we will see that Hye-min's Grandmother was quite disparaging of some members of her husband's family, she nonetheless praised her father-in-law and her husband, who was a gentleman with scholarly status not necessarily commensurate with economic standing "a *sŏnbi*, and as such gentle *(sunhada)* just like his father."

The lives of Hye-min's Grandmother's husband's siblings, three brothers and three sisters, have been quite various (see figure 1). Hye-min's Grandmother's husband himself had been a teacher before he tried his hand and failed miserably at business. He died just as his family was finally recovering economically. The eldest brother (A) was a carpenter: "He was poor—everyone was poor—they had two daughters and two sons but they couldn't educate any of them." The eldest sister (B) ended up in a regional city: her late husband had done well in a company—"although he was forever on the road"—and she ran a ten-room boardinghouse in a Japanese-style house. She had the means and desire to educate her children, but things did not turn out as she planned, because she was widowed early and the children did not have the acumen for studying. The second brother (C) became a salesman and educated five daughters through high school and sent their only son to college; his children have all remained in the provinces (i.e., not in Seoul). The second sister (D) "made it" only to elementary school and married a policeman who would later move to Seoul and become a minister; after some hard times, today they "live well" and own a home. D's daughters also live well, and her sons have managed to get educated by becoming ministers—an education, Hye-min's Grandmother noted, considerably cheaper than the regular route. The sister (E) immediately preceding Hye-min's Grandmother's husband has stayed in the countryside, in a village near their birthplace; a widow now, and the mother of four children, she farms their large holdings entirely by machine. Hye-min's Grandmother's husband's youngest brother (G), the family's youngest son and child, passed away early; his widow lives in subsidized housing and works as a janitor.

Hye-min's Grandmother most often contrasted two of her husband's elder sisters: the second (D), who had struggled hard in Seoul, and the third

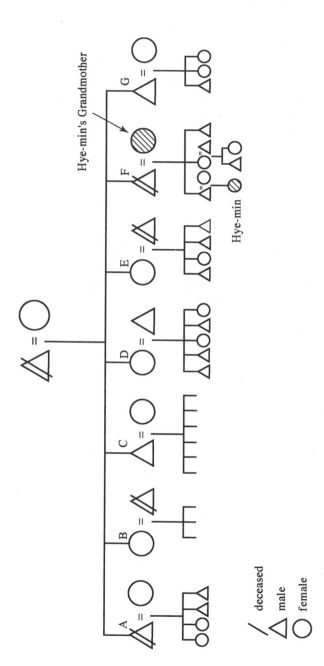

Figure 1. Hye-min's Grandmother's siblings-in-law, A–G, were often mentioned by Hye-min's Grandmother when talking about her life, particularly about differences between rural and urban kin.

(E), who stayed in the countryside. D was somehow missing from the wedding photo, but Hye-min's Grandmother pointed out E to note that she was fat and country-bumpkin-like. E was, Hye-min's Grandmother described, "nothing but a farm laborer." She had ended up staying in the countryside, Hye-min's Grandmother calculated, because she was not blessed with in-laws who could take over the farm, allowing her and her husband to go to Seoul. Hye-min's Grandmother explained that even though E had lots of land, it did not matter: "Even if farmers are rich, at the end of the day there is nothing left so they can't educate their children." E's children did not make it beyond high school: the eldest graduated from high school and now farms; the second is the wife of a rural pastor; the third is a junior high school graduate who works in Seoul; and the fourth is a high school graduate who has been struggling in Seoul. Hye-min's Grandmother summarized the story of those children this way: "E is a countryside-rich (*sigol puja*). They eat well. It wasn't that she didn't want to educate her children, but that the kids couldn't get in to college. The only thing those kids did was work on the farm, run errands for the farm, and drink *makkŏlli* (unrefined rice liquor, standard fare in Korean rural life). It wasn't that they couldn't have sold the land to send those kids to college . . ."

Hye-min's Grandmother was matter-of-fact in her contrast of D and E; she spoke of liking D better. "D's better. She's smarter . . . She's been hungry, and she has been able to educate her children . . . She is like my [late] husband: she was the top student in her class (*panjang*) and she had ambition (*yoksim*) for her children's education." D married a policeman, and although Hye-min's Grandmother did not think much of that "low-level" occupation (which recalls the Education Mother on her sister's marriage to a policeman), she conceded that it was much better than marrying a farmer as E had done: "At least a policeman is somewhat educated." But Hye-min's Grandmother's telling of D's more praiseworthy story ended neither at intelligence nor at ambition. It was also that D's religious conviction and prayers were rewarded: "She prayed under God, and at church to the ministers. The ministers were impressed by her diligence and by her pathetic circumstances. Because they saw that mother struggling, they tended carefully to [the religious education] of those children." In this way Hye-min's Grandmother meant to explain how it was that those sons had been able to become ministers. Hye-min's Grandmother was also matter-of-fact about the reality of poor sons choosing the ministry: "D's children figured out that if they became ministers they could help people and that when people are grateful for 'this,' they give money, and when they are grateful for 'that,' they give money. And when the deacons and deaconesses are thankful, they give money; and when the elders are thankful, they give money. So lots of money comes in. And when people are sick, they bring money . . ." Lest the reader understand this point cynically, Hye-min's Grandmother did not, I think, understand it as such; I do not believe she meant to question the sincerity of D's minister sons.

It was E who Hye-min's Grandmother had described as docile (sunhada), the kind of woman who waits for the persimmon to fall (chapter 3): "You don't talk; you just bear with things; you are kind and you don't make anything of yourself." D, who had, in contrast, managed to make ministers of her sons, had the same impatient and aggressive (kŭphan) personality of the women in Hye-min's Grandmother's own natal family: the personality that snatches the persimmon from the tree. "In this day and age," Hye-min's Grandmother explained, land alone will not suffice—a person has to be on the ball and impatient with things in order to succeed: "Otherwise, it is just a matter of today becoming tomorrow, and tomorrow becoming the next day and so on." Hye-min's Grandmother went on in that conversation to contrast her mother- and father-in-law with her own parents—as if to explain how E came to be so sunhada. Her own parents, who had known to sell the land in order to educate their children, were both impatient and ambitious (kŭphada), but her father-in-law was a sŏnbi.

The second sister (D), impatient and ambitious like Hye-min's Grandmother herself, was the one who picked out Hye-min's Grandmother to marry her ten-year-younger brother, Hye-min's Grandmother's late husband (F). D had married into Hye-min's Grandmother's village and spotted Hye-min's Grandmother at church. Hye-min's Grandmother offered interesting comparisons between the course of D's family and her own family in Seoul. Both families hit very difficult times in Seoul, but Hye-min's Grandmother and her husband had enough cash (from her family) to start a small shop; D and her husband, on the other hand, had absolutely nothing, so they peddled wares on the street. D's husband had taken an important turn in Seoul: after years of philandering when he was a policeman in the countryside, he had become a faithful husband, but nonetheless the family suffered terribly. Hye-min's Grandmother also noted that she and her husband did better educating their children, pointing out that having a shop, even a pitiful one, cannot be compared with having to work on the streets: "At least we had four walls and a place to sit down."

Consistent in this contrast that Hye-min's Grandmother drew between her two sisters-in-law (D and E) was her conviction about the countryside:

namely that at all costs—and she thought of D as having paid them—one must leave. Although E had "stayed behind" in large part because there had been no in-laws to farm, Hye-min's Grandmother went to great lengths to make sense of it all in terms of the two sisters' divergent personalities. Even though D's children had not fared as well as Hye-min's Grandmother's children, which Hye-min's Grandmother understood in the context of her own natal family's material advantage, she was convinced that D and her husband's toil bore fruit in their two minister sons and one daughter who had managed to marry up. She described that, above all, it was D's confidence in Seoul (and her faith) that accounted for the greater success of her children:

> Had D stayed in the countryside, things would not have turned out so
> well. You know what they say, "Send your son to Seoul and your horse
> to Cheju Island." Children need to go to big places: in Seoul there is so
> much to hear and to learn. In the countryside all you find are grannies.
> To turn your fate, a person needs to struggle in Seoul. And D's husband
> couldn't fool around with women in Seoul the way he had in the coun-
> tryside. D and her husband just prayed and prayed, hoping that those
> boys would become ministers. Poor people think to become ministers
> because you can do it without money. After all, Jesus was poor. If you
> go to divinity school, no one discriminates (ttajida) as to whether you
> went to college. As long as you believe and repent, anyone can become
> a minister. Furthermore, admission is easy, and the fees are cheap.

In addition to talking about her husband's sisters D and E, Hye-min's Grandmother spoke most often about the wife of her husband's late youngest brother (G), who had died on his job as a projectionist at a movie theater from gas poisoning. This widow, a janitor who was just one year younger than Hye-min's Grandmother, raised a son and two daughters alone. She managed to educate her son through college, and her daughters through high school, and Hye-min's Grandmother and her husband contributed small sums toward the son's school fees. Hye-min's Grandmother noted that although G's widow was smart, her life had been the most pathetic of all. That the widow's daughters could not go to college was not because of any lack of intelligence or ability but simply because they did not have enough money; here she drew, implicitly, a contrast with the children of her third sister-in-law (E) in the countryside—children who had the requisite funds but were lacking in drive. The widow, a farmer's daughter from

Hye-min's grandfather's (F) home village was a Catholic by birth and had remained very devout. Once, although she had just been speaking kindly of G's widow's plight, Hye-min's Grandmother paused to remark that uneducated people "are irksome (taptaphada) . . . Imagine, they can't even make out a single English letter." But, without missing a beat, she continued that the education levels of husbands and wives should be the same; she then again mentioned that the widow's daughters and son had all managed to marry college graduates. In this way, in keeping with discussions in chapter 6 on the discourse on personality, Hye-min's Grandmother's evaluation of the widow was not fixed.

On another occasion, Hye-min's Grandmother spoke about G's widow somewhat differently—with considerable sympathy. That day, she had just been speaking about the extent to which in South Korean recent history, status had been entirely determined by wealth: "If you become poor, you become a sangnom (derogatory for commoner); with money you are yangban." Furthermore, Hye-min's Grandmother went on, "Without money you can't be a part of the social world, without it your spirit (ki) dies . . . you end up having to live off of others (ŏdŏ mŏk'ko salge toenda), and you can't purchase anything so your heart (maŭm) dies." It was there that Hye-min's Grandmother brought up G's widow, precisely because hers is the case of a woman whose spirit (ki) has died—"She doesn't even want any of us to visit her." What followed, however, were Hye-min's Grandmother's quite critical assessments of G's widow's personal (and personality) failings.

> I don't know why her life hasn't gone better . . . If her religious life had been stronger, I don't think things would have turned out this way. Her heart (maŭm) is lacking. She is anxious (kŭnsim handa) all the time. You know how Korean women can be, moaning on and on: "I'm such a pitiable (pulssanghan) woman . . . I'm so distraught (soksanghada) . . . how long (ŏnje kkaji) will I have to go on like this?" If her religious conviction was stronger she would be able to overcome these feelings. And all of this weakens her constitution—because all she does is worry. Worrying leads nowhere. All that "woe is me . . ." (sinse t'aryŏng, the narrative convention of the telling of hard lives), what is the use of it, the point? Koreans have been like that forever, "Ahhh, why me? Why must I live like this? How long will this suffering go on?" But it's at that very moment when a person thinks to groan like that, that she should do something. If the only thing a woman does is bewail her lot, who is there to provide money for food? She had better get out there and work, what-

ever it takes, a street cart . . . A woman must throw away her pride . . . so she becomes a maid or pushes a cart, so what?

It was at this point in her soliloquy that Hye-min's Grandmother made her strongest criticism of G's widow: that she is prideful.

All the rest of us have suffered and prospered. All of my kids have done well, and all of them are smart. Now it is only her, and her legs hurt, so she bemoans her plight. She is an introvert (naesŏngjŏk) and she isn't active (hwalbalhada). She isn't like me. All that she can think of is her own embarrassment (ch'angp'i).

When I asked what G's widow had to be embarrassed about, Hye-min's Grandmother answered that it was because of her difficult relations with her (only) son and daughter-in-law, who had refused to live with and care for her. Changing her tone once again, Hye-min's Grandmother then registered how pathetic her situation was: "She will have to be a janitor until she dies . . . My husband used to cry just thinking about G's widow."

Clearly, Hye-min's Grandmother had conflicting ideas about G's widow. She respected that she went to some lengths to educate her children, but she was also certain that she could have gone further. At points she was empathetic, knowing how hard it can be to be poor, and appreciating the paucity of resources in G's in-law's family. But Hye-min's Grandmother reserved her harshest criticism for G's widow's personal style and wished that she would be more like Hye-min's Grandmother and Hye-min's Grandmother's sisters rather than like those other [South Korean] women who sit around bemoaning their fates.

Hye-min's Grandmother's thoughts on these three women (D, E, and G's widow) were complex. Woven throughout was an intricate fabric of identification and "dis-identification." Personality-wise, her kindred spirit was the second sister, (D). Having struggled economically in Seoul, she identified with G's widow, for they had suffered together. She distinguished herself confidently from the third sister (E), who did not manage to leave the countryside, and from G's widow's seemingly weak spirit. Intermittently, she considered a number of structural constraints: that E had received no help from her in-laws; that Hye-min's Grandmother had enjoyed considerably more parental material support than any of the other women; that it was impossible for rural children to compete in the educational marketplace; and that South Korean society did not abide those without money.

Alongside these structural considerations, however, Hye-min's Grandmother was also at home in quite a different moral discursive universe, in which personal traits can and do prevail: intelligence (or the fruits of education), vigor, and so on (echoing discussions in chapter 6).

From even this very small vantage point—from Hye-min's Grandmother's views on three of the women in her husband's family—we are privy to fascinating musings on South Korean social life and justice. At her most generous, the world commands its fates unfairly: those left behind in the countryside suffer; those without the good fortune to become educated are destined to fall forever further behind; and those without money are judged unkindly. But, she was also quick to blame more basic human composition: intelligence, personality, and the like. And finally there was the matter of religion: her conviction that faith itself will act. Here again, via religion, the personal appears displaced. But this too is complex, for religious conviction itself bespeaks personal traits, such as discipline and devotion. In the case of her own business success, she credited her and her husband's own business acumen alongside their having always closed the shop on Sunday to attend church; she was, however, not shy to note that the act of closing the shop itself had garnered faithful customers. Hye-min's Grandmother made it clear that, even though she was a small shopkeeper, people could pick her out for being different: "No one could believe that a woman like me—such a mŏtchaeng'i (elegant person)—was having to do this sort of work."

Mi-yŏn's Mother: Of Rich Relatives and Reversals

Mi-yŏn's Mother's South Korean story cannot be told without the stories of those relatives left behind in North Korea, and of those who left South Korea for the United States (see figure 2). At the heart of her story (as we began to see in chapter 7) were reversals: that her own birth family was never able to regain its status with the move to the south; that the branches of her family who had sustained their wealth in the south eventually lost it; and that she became perhaps the most prosperous of all her first and second cousins. Also central to her story was her visceral experience of class difference within her extended family because in her youth she traveled to and from, and also resided with, second cousins whose material circumstances were worlds above her own. As her stories in this chapter will reveal, those childhood class travels have been a critical template for her throughout her life: they nurtured her childhood ambition, just as they have also engendered her doubts about that very sort of ambition (see chapters 7 and 9).

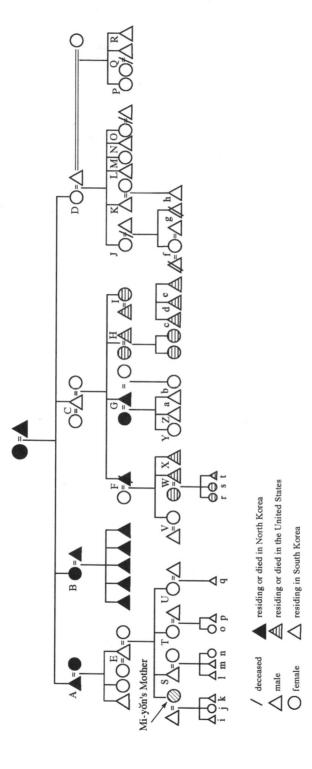

Figure 2. Mi-yŏn's Mother's Kin, A–t, around whom Mi-yŏn's Mother narrated much of her life and circumstances.

Mi-yŏn's Mother has reflected more, and further, on the issues this book considers than any of the other women featured, and perhaps this is because she and her imagination have ventured further. Her early years of travel across familial class divides are, I think, critical to those reflections.

Here I focus on Mi-yŏn's Mother's relations with, and meditations on, two families, charted in figure 2: that of her paternal great-uncle (C) and paternal great-aunt (D) (that is, the families of her grandfather's (A) only younger brother (C) and youngest sister (D)), whose offspring in Mi-yŏn's Mother's generation would be called, by the popular terms of U.S. kinship, second cousins. Mi-yŏn's Mother's nuclear family moved to Inch'ŏn, a city near Seoul, where they struggled economically because her father—never really acquiescing to the north-south division—was unable to hold a job. Having also come south, the families of this great aunt and uncle (C and D) lived in close proximity to one another in a then very prosperous neighborhood in Seoul, Hyoja-dong. It was, Mi-yŏn's Mother described, serendipity that while those families held onto southern land they had owned while still in the north, Mi-yŏn's family had earlier sold theirs. In our conversations, Mi-yŏn's Mother most often referred to those relatives (including thirteen "aunts" and "uncles"; and the relatives of her father's generation, second cousins once-removed by U.S. kinship terms; and fourteen second cousins in her own generation) with the name of the neighborhood: "Hyoja-dong." It was, after all, in their lavish homes in that upscale neighborhood that she had come to know them.

The divergence between these branches of the family had a deep history that extended to her childhood days in the north. For Mi-yŏn's Mother, though, the remarkable difference was that in the north, family wealth had been shared, but in the south, the divides became palpable in vast differences in the material well-being of the now residentially separated branches of the family. Some of the romantic reflection on northern days was no doubt childhood nostalgia. Pak Wan-so, South Korea's preeminent novelist on middle-class women, has one of her characters in *The Naked Tree* complain about people's romantic memories of "the north":

He was from the north, he lived a good life there. Of course, it couldn't have been like this. It was good then. How many times had I endured rambling talk of that kind? The monotonous words my mother chanted, the bragging of the painters babbling with spit foaming at the corners of their mouths, the empty words of longing people uttered, whether they were cleaning women or day laborers. Of course, it wasn't like this back then. It was good then. I didn't have the patience to hear them out because I thought delusions about the past were more miserable, in worse taste, than delusions about the future (1995, 11–12).

Mi-yŏn's Mother's paternal grandfather (A) had been the son of a "mere farmer" who, as the eldest son, had studied a bit at a Confucian academy (sŏdang). His younger brother (C), however, had managed to make a great deal of money, and with that, the whole family had prospered. On the matter of shared wealth, Mi-yŏn's Mother said, "Those were the days of the extended family (taegajok). You didn't divide wealth." She explained that C's money went to everyone, A's wife helped to take care of all of C's kids, and whatever there was, it was distributed amongst everyone. One of the emigrated daughters (I) of Mi-yŏn's Mother's great uncle (C) (and her dear friend and confidante to this day) surprised her during one visit to South Korea when she asserted that her own father (C) had made his money by collaborating with the Japanese. I had offered that assertion years before public and popular South Korean discourse had really begun to come to terms with that history. Even when Mi-yŏn's Mother shared this with me in the mid-1990s, it was still not the easiest personal history to disclose.

In the earlier days of our meetings, I was confused as to how it was that Mi-yŏn's Mother's father (E) had not been helped in South Korea by his wealthy uncle (C) and aunt (D), especially in light of Mi-yŏn's Mother's description of the distributive norms of her family. In our eighth meeting I finally asked outright why they had not helped, to which she replied, "Nancy, you've hit on a really important point." When her family had first come to South Korea, her father had indeed worked at a new business of his rich uncle's (C), but things had not worked out: "My father really wasn't that interested in money and he and his uncle were really of two different minds. Furthermore, my father wasn't the sort to give in to people easily. And he wasn't the kind who went around lowering his head, saying 'yes, yes' to people [i.e., to his uncle]. He was pretty distant from society," by which she meant from practical matters. On another occasion, Mi-yŏn's Mother's younger brother (S) confirmed that C had not liked his father: "In a word, my father wasn't very capable." As for her paternal great-aunt's (D) wealth, Mi-yŏn's Mother explained that that was another matter, since it was the wealth of a different surname. Interestingly in South Korea it is really in the figure of Mi-yŏn's Mother that these three families—her own and those of her paternal aunt and uncle (C and D)—meet; her siblings lived out lives quite untouched by these familial extensions, and furthermore by memories of the north. It was in just this sense that she considered herself to be quite different from her younger siblings. Hers is an excellent example of the huge differences that but a year or two can make in a sibling cohort.

Mi-yŏn's Mother's Childhood Class-Travels

In carving out a myriad of generational divides in what is, objectively rendered, the span of but a generation or two, Mi-yŏn's Mother's life has happened at crossroads, and across family cultures otherwise quite opaque from one another. It is precisely this vantage point that has made her the keen observer she is. She is, in a sense, uncomfortable with any one or another common sense; she is profoundly and forever dislocated (S. Hall 1996a). Over the course of her entire life, Mi-yŏn's Mother has spent time with wealthy people, but for most of it she has felt herself to be an outsider looking in. It is not an exaggeration to suggest that much of her reflective life has been spent balancing precariously between her deep-felt identification and dis-identification with the rich: an ambivalent space indeed— one I elaborate on throughout chapter 9.

Mi-yŏn's Mother's class travels, as I have taken to calling them here, did not begin with her days at Hyoja-dong but with her "Big Mother." Big Mother peddled wares to keep the family afloat, and Mi-yŏn's Mother was the one who accompanied her—to the countryside, to the city, everywhere. She went with her, for example, to pear fields near the area that would later become the Kimp'o Airport, and she listened as Big Mother did the calculations of the price at which she would need to sell them in Inch'ŏn in order to make a profit. Because Big Mother was unschooled, she did all of the calculations aloud, and Mi-yŏn's Mother learned to figure out when they had done well enough to be able to bring home some of those delicious pears for the family to share—just the sort of calculations that her siblings never learned to do. Big Mother also made sure to send Mi-yŏn's Mother to visit the rich relatives from both sides of the family in Seoul. In later years, Big Mother began to actively tailor her sales to the Hyoja-dong relatives, offering them imported goods such as stoves and refrigerators. These are just the experiences that Mi-yŏn's Mother understood to have formed her so very differently from her younger siblings.

> My younger sisters don't have the same attachment to money that I do.
> That attachment runs deep in me. . . . They just adjust to their circum
> stances and live on. I take things on more aggressively. When I lived

with the Hyoja-dong aunt [J], I saw how she bartered to buy really nice things. To this day I know how to pick out the best and barter for it. My sisters don't know how to do it; they just buy things at the listed price, and what's more, they don't know how to pick out what's good to begin with.

Mi-yŏn's Mother pointed out another difference between her and her sisters: they are too young to remember the wealthy days in North Korea (Kaesŏng) that she does; "all they have ever known is poverty." It was always, she described, hard for her to admit to the humble status of her family—it was precisely her class travels that made it so. Once, at her post-high-school bank job—a job she considered so miraculous in hard economic times—she could not bring herself to admit her family's poverty to her mostly considerably more privileged fellow employees. Not knowing, people wondered about her modest clothing, and even teased her for wearing the same things all the time.

The most intense class travels of her childhood were afforded by her several years of residence with her paternal great aunt's (D) eldest daughter's family (J, f, and g). As a young child she had been accustomed to the hand-me-downs from the Hyoja-dong families: beautiful clothes, the best of the day—many of them handmade in Hong Kong. Between those clothes and the ones her family could afford, there was, she described, a "heaven-and-earth difference." *Han* (bitterness, resentment), as explained in chapter 6, was not one of the key words of the women in this book, in spite of a widespread common sense of its salience for women generally. The only time that Mi-yŏn's Mother used that word, which the Moviegoer used when referring to having to care for her senile mother, was to describe her feelings for having grown up dressed in hand-me-downs. She did extend that *han* to the fact that, having been raised on hand-me-downs, she never developed her own sense of taste for clothing. When Mi-yŏn's Mother left Inch'ŏn in order to attend a humanities high school, with the hope of going to college, she and a friend lived with J because J had been recently divorced from her husband and needed help with her two children, particularly with her infant son (g). Although Mi-yŏn's Mother explained that she did household labor there, and even that she slept with the maids, she never spoke of having been recruited there "as a maid." Furthermore, she never voiced any resentment at having perhaps been "sent" by her family to serve as a maid in her relatives' home. Although it seems clear that some sort of household service was implicated in her residing with rich kin (quite typical at that time), the exact nature of Mi-yŏn's Mother's particular arrangement with that household remains a bit unclear to me.

Mi-yŏn's Mother's description of those Hyoja-dong families was such that we can imagine her paternal great uncle (C) was at the helm: rice and other foodstuffs were dispersed from his household, and often the extended family gathered there for meals. This was, in fact, an extension of what she had described for Kaesŏng, namely that her paternal great uncle (C), as the successful one in the family, had provided for all of his siblings. She also described that J often ate at her parents' house (D), where like Mi-yŏn's Mother's own, was a house with two wives: D was the legal wife, but her husband had taken a "second, meaning a second wife, or concubine," and for some years they all lived together. C was the relative to whom Mi-yŏn's Mother attributed her aforementioned remarkable bank employment.

Over our conversations, Mi-yŏn's Mother had so much to say about what it felt like to live with—be beholden to, serving—rich relatives. Once she told me that because of those childhood experiences in Hyoja-dong, she thinks she knows what it is like to be a minority in the United States.

> I was constantly aware of their gaze (nunch'i rŭl chuŏtta). When they ate meat, I couldn't bring myself to join—somehow I couldn't move my chopsticks to the platter. That is why when I employed maids (singmo) in the 1970s I tried hard to make them part of the family. When I think about it, I had been really good at middle school in Inch'ŏn, but in Seoul I was so busy running errands and doing chores . . . Those kids did really well, what with all of their tutors, but my grades went down. I remember thinking to myself, "What am I living for? Even if I were to make it to college what would the point be? What I really need to do is feed my [natal] family." If I had stayed in Inch'ŏn, I could have become a teacher, but I hated my family.

Here, Mi-yŏn's Mother reflected on her destiny to have landed in Seoul, and to have met these particular circumstances; she in part blamed her keen sense of her nuclear family's relative poverty in larger familial circles for having driven her to Hyoja-dong. So much of daily life in Hyoja-dong served to remind her of the class distances she had traveled. She spoke often about their having fed chocolates to K's little boy (h): "I would think 'How nice it would be if I could live like that, eating chocolate.'" When Mi-yŏn's Mother periodically visited her own family in those Hyoja-dong days, how at ease she felt and how much (more) she was able to enjoy eating. She said that, to this day, her sisters still tease her about how much she ate on those visits home and how fat she had been.

Mi-yŏn's Mother remembered J's home and all its décor. Those memories point, I think, two ways: to her early-childhood residence in a large home in the north, and to her carefully decorated home today, a home she has stayed in even as so many of similar means have elected for lavish apartments. In her descriptions of the décor and of the advantages that were afforded those Hyoja-dong children, we can almost recognize one-for-one the things that Mi-yŏn's Mother worked so hard to provide her own children: tutors, piano lessons, and the services of maids among them. She described the Hyoja-dong house as a "Western-style house with a Japanese-style feeling," with a huge wardrobe (chang), "the sort one seldom saw in the 1940s and 1950s" (Mi-yŏn's Mother's bedroom today is lined with the most beautiful of wardrobes I have ever seen in South Korea); a telephone; plants; paintings; a refrigerator, and a record player. Furthermore, it was not just the things that made an impression, but "the way they did things, like the way they arranged flowers on the piano." She reflected, "When I think about it now, all of that broadened my world." Moreover, she thinks of it all as her "education."

Most revealing of her family's standing was that Mi-yŏn's Mother slept with the maids, who were mostly close to her own age. She said the maids kept quitting because J's personality was so difficult. Mi-yŏn's Mother, though, begged them not to leave, because every time one of them left, there would be more to do and Mi-yŏn's Mother could not study. A constant in her descriptions of the very rich, including her Hyoja-dong relatives, were their bad or twisted personalities—mostly, it seemed, for being very spoiled. She recalled those children having "all sorts of tutors," and there were two live-in country girls (maids, singmo) who changed the coal briquettes. Mi-yŏn's Mother went on to explain how all of this—houses with women-in-waiting—would later wane in South Korea, because the young maids had all gone to factories, and coal-heated homes were abandoned for apartments heated by boilers and serviced by hired day maids (p'ach'ulbu). Mi-yŏn's Mother vividly recalled the round-the-clock tutoring her second cousins received. She remembered one of those tutors in particular, a young man who her second-cousin O used to refer to as "mongrel" (ttongkae). Mi-yŏn's Mother once mused about how she herself might have married him and even that O—had she been less uppity—might have. She spoke dreamily. The sense was that both she and O might have fared better if they could have seen past his poverty and bad looks (O ended up divorced and alone).

> One of [O's] tutors was a guy from Seoul National University study-
> ing to be a doctor. He was small, dark, and ugly, and she called him
> *ttongkae* (mongrel). He really liked me and sort of followed me around;
> once, he even came to my work and we sort of went out on a date, to a
> park. [Here, she smiled.] What if I had married him? He was really
> poor. He is probably a really good doctor today; he wasn't interested
> in money—he said that he wanted to be like Albert Schweitzer . . .
> I remember that Schweitzer once said that the only thing that remains
> at the end of a life is one's body and service. Schweitzer gave up all of
> his wealth to do what he did. He [the tutor] was really poor and wore
> the same shabby clothes every day.

Both Mi-yŏn's Mother and O, each for their own reasons, could not have married the tutor: Mi-yŏn's Mother because she was hell-bent on escaping poverty; O because she was spoiled and snobbish. In the years after O's early, failed marriage, Mi-yŏn's Mother tried to arrange marriages for her several times, but O disliked all the men, finding them unsubstantial *(sisihada)*.

Revealingly, Mi-yŏn's Mother had initially mentioned apartments that day because she had been talking about her paternal great-aunt's eldest son (K), the younger brother of the woman she stayed with in Hyoja-dong (J), marveling that he too—even with all that inheritance (material and other-wise)—had ended up in an apartment "not even in Seoul." Similarly the lady of the house (J) where Mi-yŏn's Mother had passed her high school days had managed to go through all of her money, and presently lives in a mod-est apartment. And her ill boy (g) died early. Today, Mi-yŏn's Mother helps J occasionally.

The Fate of the Hyoja-dong Relatives

The social stories of all of the Hyoja-dong siblings (J–R) of her father's generation were constants in Mi-yŏn's Mother's talk—mostly because things had not gone very well for them. None of them live today as well as she does, neither materially nor in terms of the successes of their children. She spoke most about the youngest daughter (O)—the one who had called her tu-tor "mongrel," "failed at marriage" early on, remained childless, has never worked, and has lived only on family money. All this in spite of the fact that

O "grew up just having lots of fun." O's marriage failed her because the husband in question had married her for her money. And thereafter, O was "too snobbish and picky" to find another man. Mi-yŏn's Mother spoke at great length about the extent to which O had been coddled as a child in every way.

One of O's older sisters, the second daughter (M), married a capitalist and lives well today. The children (P, Q, and R) of D's "second" were each given several houses apiece, but all of them have ended up living by chŏnse, in rent like arrangements, as well. For the life of her, Mi-yŏn's Mother could not figure out how this came to pass. Mi-yŏn's Mother remained close to D's "second," who today, in her eighties, has no place to live because her son (R) is propertyless. The "second," Mi-yŏn's Mother told me, was such a beautiful woman, "and those three children were so handsome. We all thought they would become great successes. The eldest (P) went to Ehwa Woman's University—at that time if you had money, you could go there—and those kids were not discriminated against as the children of a 'second.'"

The family of Mi-yŏn's Mother's paternal great-uncle (C) fared quite differently from that of his younger sister (D), in large part because many of the descendants have ended up in the United States. The person who came up most in our conversations was the youngest daughter (I) of that family, the one who surprised Mi-yŏn's Mother by calling her own father a collaborator—Mi-yŏn's Mother's almost agemate, whose hand-me-downs she wore as a girl. When I boarded in Mi-yŏn's Mother's home in the early 1980s, I met that youngest daughter's half–Korean American sons who spoke only English. They were visiting South Korea with their mother, and Mi-yŏn's Mother was glad I was there, to speak English with them. Just after graduating from a prestigious college, I had emigrated to the United States, marrying an American soldier she had met as his Korean-language tutor. Mi-yŏn's Mother thinks that I married an American both because her family's financial situation had worsened and because her father had taken a "second," so "she probably had a bad image of Korean men." To evidence just how rich that family had been in its prime, Mi-yŏn's Mother told me several times that the first son (F) had been sent from Kaesŏng to Seoul for yuhak (the word that today refers to "study abroad") for elementary school. The third son (H) was the first to follow his sister (I) abroad. F, the one who had studied "abroad" in Seoul "never learned how to do anything except on a very grand scale and eventually drank himself to death in his fifties." She remembered him from when she was young: he would flip through stacks and stacks of receipts, bragging to everyone about how rich he was.

Both F's sons (W and X) ended up in the United States. Y also emigrated as a pharmacist. W inherited all of his grandfather's property but lost everything and ended up managing a building owned by his aunt and uncle, I and her husband, in the United States; and X, "even after attending a good college in South Korea, ended up as a carpenter in the United States." The second son (G) of Mi-yŏn's Mother's paternal great-uncle (C) had been in the South Korean military, but before the Korean War had somehow returned to North Korea. They all figured that as the son of a rich man he was probably killed there. Both F and G had been Olympic-level equestrian riders in their youth and the family had harbored some hope that F might appear at the 1964 Olympics in Japan, but he did not. Mi-yŏn's Mother told me that I loves to write and has even thought to write about her family. Mi-yŏn's Mother's was convinced that for I such writing would serve as therapy for her longing for her lost brothers.

At various points in our conversations, Mi-yŏn's Mother spoke as if she felt she had been left behind in South Korea: "It was pathetic: people like me who stayed back." When she said that, she had just been musing on I's having left South Korea, perhaps because of all the American movies that I had watched as a college student. She remembered that I saw those movies three and four times each: "The longing for the United States those days was incredible. All the smart kids went to the United States." Once, she even declared that the "entire upper class" went to the United States. But the reality of the emigration of I and her siblings was, as it turned out, not so charmed at all—much more it had been the story of a family that was not able to hold its wealth and position in South Korea. When Mi-yŏn's Mother finally traveled to the United States for the first time, she saw that the only place where she could really find what she and her age cohort had dreamed of was on sets in the film studios in Hollywood. Irony aside, she would still exclaim about feeling "the greatness of America. American capitalism!" But she did go on to say that the reality of the United States was quite different from all of that, and furthermore, that by the 1980s the glamour of the United States had faded in the South Korean imagination. On one occasion Mi-yŏn's Mother had been talking about American goods and suddenly said, "Come to think about it, all the things we live with today, our so-called 'civilization' (munmyŏng), are the things we longed for in American movies!" She went on to say, "Part of me longed for America just so that I could eat chocolate all day long." Here we can recall the little Hyoja-dong boy who, to her surprise as a young girl, had been fed chocolate.

Once when Mi-yŏn's Mother and I were talking about Kaesŏng days, she lifted the glass plate on her vanity table to show me one of several photographs displayed there. Mi-yŏn's Mother appears in the middle of this faded photograph with two younger children in her lap and two somewhat older children flanking her shoulders. The older children are second cousins once removed (H and I). The younger children are her second cousin (Y), who also ended up leaving for the United States, and her own five-year-younger brother (S). I wrote in my field notes at the time, 1996, that I should include the photo in the book I would write, but the snapshot I took of the photograph is only visible enough to reconstruct in words here. Several things are interesting about this photograph. First, it demonstrates a point Mi-yŏn's Mother often made: that she grew up in a close-knit, widely extended family. Second, it underscores some of her points about class distances: while she and her brothers are wearing hand-knit sweaters, the others are wearing clothing purchased in a department store. This said, however, these class markings are not so obvious, because as Mi-yŏn's Mother had earlier stressed, her paternal grandmother was a woman of learning and leisure who stayed at home reading, sewing, and knitting—it was this grandmother who taught her daughter-in-law, Big Mother, how to read (who "broke her illiteracy" on classical women's stories, as Mi-yŏn's Mother once described). Finally, the picture took on significance for Mi-yŏn's Mother because with the exception of her and her brother, the others had all left for the United States. Indeed, immediately after she took out the photograph, she began talking at length about I. She pulled out a collection of U.S. newspaper articles about I, from several different years, including one from 1987; I was amazed that, almost a decade later, they were all neatly gathered at the front of Mi-yŏn's Mother's 1996 date book.

The Hyoja-dong relatives came up at almost every meeting we had, though Mi-yŏn's Mother more often reflected on the negative example they set, on what she had learned not to become. Once when she was talking about her paternal great-uncle's sons (F, G, and H), describing how snobbish they had been and how they had made their wives suffer by forcing them to live off of family wealth rather than their own earnings, she interjected that she had "learned so much from them." She had learned, she said, to hope "only to marry a sincere wage-earner from a background like my own." But because her husband has been unfaithful and more-often-than-not unkind, her many reflections on how it was that she came to marry him rang as ironical and sad. Such reflections for Mi-yŏn's Mother were necessarily vexed, for they ran alongside her own keen sense of all she had done to garner precisely the trappings of those Hyoja-dong lives. Above all she seemed to be juggling a number of complex life alternatives, each bidding for her attention, energy, and ethics—a tiring project, to say the least. These alternatives included: the kinship-based communalistic wealth of her northern childhood; the close-knit poverty of her postrefuge childhood in Inch'ŏn; the leisurely wealth of the Hyoja-dong relatives; the ranks of Seoul's nouveaux riches, and so on. Chapter 9 focuses on Mi-yŏn's Mother's management of these alternatives over time and over the course of her narratives.

The familial class relations of Hye-min's Grandmother and Mi-yŏn's Mother are quite different. The "other women" for Hye-min's Grandmother were primarily women across the divides of marriage, and of the city and countryside. Her primary others were country women who had failed to ride the times. For Mi-yŏn's Mother, the others have been rich and somewhat distant kin who nonetheless loomed very large in her life, her desires, and her life designs. Although the urban-rural divide did not operate for Mi-yŏn's Mother, the contrast of those who have and those who have not known deprivation was critical. While Hye-min's Grandmother's relationship to these other women was clear, in fact almost triumphant, Mi-yŏn's Mother's relationship was considerably more vexed because of her lifelong meditations on the meanings and ethics of the mobility desires that have so powerfully scripted her life. We saw that Hye-min's Grandmother often went quite far with personality, while Mi-yŏn's Mother stayed much closer to viewing personality as itself the product of privilege or deprivation: excess and want exerted a very heavy hand in her reading of the world. These narrative references recall discussions in chapter 6 of the play of personality in the rendering of lives and agency. Finally, pervading their respective management of class divides within their families were profound differences in their outlooks, from that of a contented and deeply religious widow in the case of Hye-min's Grandmother to Mi-yŏn's Mother's window of a woman in a troubled marriage, deeply concerned about the remaining years of her life. I think that Hye-min's Grandmother's case is somewhat exceptional. For most women of her generation, the day-to-day management of class distances and divides within the family is quite vexed and most often not conducive to smug senses of self, or clear, definitive senses of others.

We have seen that the casting, managing, and reeling in of the web of kinship ties is a narrative process in which people take stock variously of who they are and are not, and of how they do and do not want to live (see also Stack 1996). As we have seen for Hye-min's Grandmother and Mi-yŏn's Mother, class distances are not spoken of in the terms of social scientific categories but in the visceral terms of taste, priorities, values, gender, personality, and so on. In short, class is everywhere, but is often not spoken of as such (Ortner 1991). This chapter has shown that South Korea's postwar history has made strangers of many kin—that life's vicissitudes have flung them hither and thither in contemporary life and lifestyle. My hope is that these stories about the day-to-day management of kinship ties give us a feeling for the template from which people, and women in particular, render their sense about the larger world—the social world beyond kinship ties. Furthermore, I hope that this chapter has provided a feeling for the symbolic and cultural mills through which this rendering takes place for South Korean women of a particular generation and times, which I continue in chapter 9 through an extended discussion of Mi-yŏn's Mother.

9

WHEN IT'S ALL SAID AND DONE . . .

> It has always baffled me why those most interested in understanding
> and changing the barbaric domination that characterizes our moder-
> nity often—not always—withhold from the very people they are most
> concerned with the right to complex personhood . . . Complex person-
> hood means that all people . . . remember and forget, are beset by
> contradiction, and recognize and misrecognize themselves and others.
> Complex personhood means that people suffer graciously and selfishly
> too, get stuck in the symptoms of their troubles, and also transform
> themselves . . . Complex personhood means that the stories people tell
> about themselves, about their troubles, about their social worlds, and
> about their society's problems are entangled and weave between what
> is immediately available as a story and what their imaginations are
> reaching towards.
>
> —Avery F. Gordon, *Ghostly Matters*

This chapter focuses on Mi-yŏn's Mother, on the complicated fabric of her
reflections on life—her own, and the life project generally. This chapter's
title includes ellipses at the end because all talk is, as noted in earlier chapters, unfinished—the dialogue and reflection go on—and because the particular circumstances of these women's South Korean lives have made it so
difficult for anyone to speak definitively. Thus the ellipses follow "when it's
all said and done" to underscore how very hard it has been for many of the
women in this book to enjoy a seamless, easy relationship to their life
courses; their times and their circumstances have not lent themselves easily
to smug reflection.

Mi-yŏn's Mother has already figured in five of this book's chapters. In
chapter 2 I revealed a bit of our history together, of how I as a boarder in her

home came to know her. In chapter 3, the reader briefly met Mi-yŏn's Mother on yoksim (greed, ambition), highlighting her ambivalence on this construct; she regretted her own lack of yoksim for not having made her way to college, while she criticized the excessive yoksim of those who needlessly sent their children abroad for schooling. In chapter 4, in discussions of South Korea's contemporary educational gamble, I discussed her son, Mi-yŏn's brother, who in summer 2000 was enthusiastically pursuing the precarious cutting edge of South Korea's then new economy: venture capitalism. In chapter 7 I presented Mi-yŏn's Mother's birth family in considerable detail in order to consider the play of gender in the narration of the South Korean nation and history. And Mi-yŏn's Mother was featured in chapter 8 on account of her considerable class travels as a young person—namely, her early encounters with the much wealthier branch of her family.

This chapter builds on all that the reader has learned about Mi-yŏn's Mother, adding layers of information and reflection to discussions simplified in earlier chapters. My relationship with Mi-yŏn's Mother was, as I wrote in summer 2001, just three years shy of two decades including nearly twenty formal interviews from 1993 to 1996. The morass of detail that a relationship of this depth creates is such that there is little about her I can say simply. Noted in my earliest discussion of Mi-yŏn's Mother, in chapter 2, was my dismay at people's response to my earlier writings from this project that focused on her. Their responses revealed that my presentation had fallen far short of the nuance of her life, and I hoped this book would broaden her portrayal, leaving her less vulnerable to such misreading. This chapter presents my last chance to do so, although there is more to my decision to focus this book's final ethnographic chapter on Mi-yŏn's Mother than the longevity and intensity of our encounter, or my desire to defend her complexity to my reader.

This book's final ethnographic chapter features Mi-yŏn's Mother because of the way in which her personal narratives, her social mobility stories, speak to its themes. As I came to know these eight women, Mi-yŏn's Mother stood out for her struggling over how to evaluate her life. Quite simply, she is more vexed than the other women, and by "vexed" I mean tortured and confused. From year to year, meeting to meeting, conversation to conversation, and even sometimes sentence to sentence, Mi-yŏn's Mother wavered on both how she had and how she should or might have lived (see Kendall 1988 for consideration of competing versions in the narration of a South Korean shaman). Let me add that though vexed, Mi-yŏn's Mother is at once impressively insightful.

Asserting that social contests, historical and political, are sedimented in words and dialogues, I take the talk of Mi-yŏn's Mother to speak particularly eloquently for the sensibility and the structure of feeling of her times and generation. The contests her talk reveals are ones by no means unfamiliar to the other women here, though I do not mean to suggest that Mi-yŏn's Mother's narratives stand for her generation in any representative fashion. To the contrary, she lives a considerably more materially abundant life than the vast majority of the women of her generation and all of the other women who have figured in this book, except the Education Mother, and could even serve as a symbolic other to many of them. Mi-yŏn's Mother's self-professed economic and familial activities are furthermore precisely what lend her to be easily stereotyped, and yet it is apparent that all of the women in this book are keenly aware of the ways in which they can be seen as one type or another. Most important here is that "one type or another" refers not generally to one type of person, but specifically to one type of gendered person, one type of "woman." It has been this book's conviction that the struggles of the women here are always and inextricably gendered. In this chapter, the reader will see that most of Mi-yŏn's Mother's reflections settle, in the final analysis, on "being a man," "being a woman," and "the relations between men and women (namnyŏ kwankye)."

The struggles of Mi-yŏn's Mother revealed in this chapter are particular to her and her situation, but I am confident they speak to the structure of feeling during rapid social transformation. As the reader has seen, gender and class are critical to that transformation.

I began chapter 1 on social mobility stories, this book's textual and ethnographic pillar, as the narration of origins and destinations; from there, I furthermore asserted that class must not be wrested from origins and destinations as, among other things, narrative sites that entail the imaginary. Mi-yŏn's Mother's stories do just that: they look back and they look forward, and then they do so again, assessing what it all means "when it's all said and done." As Mi-yŏn's Mother said, "Being in my fifties, I now have fewer years left to live than the years I have lived already." The profound ambivalence of Mi-yŏn's Mother on these matters is best understood in the dialectic that constitutes persons, structures, and times, for it is not hers alone. It cannot be understood removed from South Korea's particular social and historical story. This said, however, the ambivalence is nonetheless hers and the reader meets it here in the particular feel of her discourse—a feel that I do not want to give away entirely to her generation or moment.

Organized thematically—people, activities, and decisions around which

Mi-yŏn's Mother's reflections were primarily centered—this chapter begins with her husband, Mi-yŏn's father, the ambivalent centerpiece of her adult life, the source of her greatest personal pain, the object of her greatest antipathy, and the other through whom she has most seriously and most variously contemplated her own ways of being and living. I turn then to Mi-yŏn's Mother's reflections on her economic activities, as household manager and the primary family moneymaker over the years, followed by her reflections on her education, particularly on her not having gone to college. Considered next are her copious reflections on the education of her two sons and of her daughter, Mi-yŏn (the middle child). Finally, I turn to Mi-yŏn's Mother on "her country," South Korea, and its future—"the direction we're heading," was how she most often put it to me, something that Mi-yŏn's Mother had been busily worrying about since the first days I knew her. Each of this chapter's subtitles ends with a comma followed by "herself" to indicate that, be it her husband, her economic activities, her education, her children's education, or her country, Mi-yŏn's Mother comes back, as I submit we all do in talk, to taking stock of herself in the picture.

Her Husband, Herself

> Tuhami did continue to speak the language of the "real" with but few lapses into what I took to be "the imaginary" . . . I did not then understand that the real was a metaphor for the true—and not identical with it. Tuhami had been speaking the truth from the very start, even in his interviews with Lhacen, but I had been listening only for the real, which I mistook for the true. The truth was for me the real masked by the metaphor. Such was my cultural bias.
> —Vincent Crapanzano, Tuhami

The reader encountered Mi-yŏn's father briefly in chapter 7, learning of his philandering, and of Mi-yŏn's Mother's ambivalent thoughts on his style: his remarkable abilities, zest for life, and perseverance, on the one hand; his selfishness and unkindness, on the other.

At some point in 1995–1996, the second major research period culminating in this book, Mi-yŏn's Mother began talking about her husband at much greater length and in considerably harsher tones. It was around the time of our eighth formal meeting that the nature and extent of her husband's philandering had become clear to Mi-yŏn's Mother; after that, she was quite forthright about those details, and through them reflected less sparingly on her husband. This is not, however, to say that she spoke only negatively of him. Indeed, perhaps ironically, she continued to admire the very health that could have sustained such philandering, and his vitality generally. In those months, I often received phone calls and even sudden visits from Mi-yŏn's Mother, during which she disclosed the latest details of his infidelity. The candor of our friendship was by then mutual, and I made disclosures of my own.

Throughout my 1990s time in South Korea, Mi-yŏn's Mother often reflected back upon the year her family spent in England, when her husband had been sent there as a branch manager for his corporation. The year abroad had made a very large impression, as it had offered another society, another way of living. The United States had long held sway in Mi-yŏn's Mother's imagination, and it is not surprising that this extended stay in the West engendered so much reflection. In this spirit I begin the discussion of her husband, from that venue. I am very fond of a photo from that year that she had placed under the glass top of her vanity table along with several other photos—one of which I described in chapter 8. Mi-yŏn's Mother, her daughter, and her husband are sitting on the lawn of what appears to be a college courtyard. They are all wearing jeans and T-shirts, she and her daughter, sneakers, and their heads are cocked upward, each looking up, a bit dreamy. When I first saw that photo it recalled something that she had said to me, during our fifth meeting:

> When I went to England I felt very grateful. I felt that my ancestors
> had done well by me—giving me the opportunity to go and see England.
> And I thought that if I had been able to go to England [after high
> school] I could have really done something there. When I practiced
> golf alone [in England], I thought about that again and again. I also
> used to think that way when I gazed up at the white glass at the University
> [where she took English classes]—that was all I could think about.

When I examined the photo, I imagined Mi-yŏn's Mother gazing up at the courtyard buildings, thinking about her might-have-been study abroad earlier in life. Immediately following the reflections quoted, Mi-yŏn's Mother spoke about her second cousin—(I) in chapter 8, one of her Hyoja-dong relatives—who had married an American and left for the United States shortly after college graduation. It was only once that Mi-yŏn's Mother told me that she had in fact wanted to study abroad in the United States but that there had been no one to support her.

It turned out that England was the backdrop for many of her reflections on her husband; it offered a different stage on which to see him, and in turn, in his reflection, herself. Many meetings after we spoke about her having looked up at that building in England and imagined other lives, she spoke of England and of her husband (our tenth meeting, in 1996). We had spent the better part of that evening together dining and attending an all-night prayer session at her youngest sister's evangelical church, to which this sister, after much cajoling, had convinced Mi-yŏn's Mother to attend. Mi-yŏn's Mother's health, mental and physical, was depleted, and she had then recently discovered her husband's infidelity. Her sister was sure that such a night would help Mi-yŏn's Mother, and furthermore she had hoped to make a religious woman of her. At that time, Mi-yŏn's Mother was nominally Catholic, having converted when she married her Catholic husband, but by then it was only her eldest son who sporadically attended church. In those days she had begun to think more and more fondly about her late father's Buddhist ideas and practices. Complicating her family's religious picture further, both of her mothers had late in their lives become devout Protestants (a not uncommon pattern). It would turn out that Mi-yŏn's Mother did not experience a religious conversion, but the evening had certainly been an experience (for me as well). Most important about the evening, perhaps, were its precipitating events: that she had finally revealed to her sisters the secrets of her marriage, secrets she had hidden for decades. Actually, by that time, even her children had learned about some of the most basic goings-on; certainly her deep depression of those days would have given something away.

The drive to the church that evening, in her car, required downtown driving at night in an unfamiliar and congested neighborhood. I was panicked because of her at once halting and treacherous driving, and selfishly I was thinking about my own personal safety in that megalopolis, which I knew ranked quite high worldwide for car-related death and injury. Meanwhile, Mi-yŏn's Mother was busily talking about her driving style and, by extension, about England, her husband, and her personal style beyond driving.

> My driving style is cautious. You can really see my personality in my
> driving style: I'm not aggressive, I can't make up my mind, and most
> of all I don't want to cause any trouble (p'ihae) to anyone else. I'm en-
> tirely different from my husband; he drives so quickly and skillfully.
> I used to think of my driving as so stupid (pabo katta), but when I went
> to England I came to think about it all differently because in England it
> was drivers like me, polite and cautious drivers, who were regarded
> more highly than brash and energetic drivers like my husband. In

general, manners are more respected there; I guess I should have been born an English person.

When asked, she agreed that her comments referred to much more than driving style—to an entire way of being. On another occasion she spoke about not having taken the driver's test in England, explaining that between the English-language street signs and the reversal of right and left (South Korean drivers sit on the left side of the car, English drivers on the right), she did not have the presence of mind to take the exam. Her husband, on the other hand, was the very first of all the South Koreans in their midst to pass the exam. She said that at the test he had been "calm and exacting, just as he needed to be." When Mi-yŏn's Mother mused that she should have been born an English person, she was imagining a society more conducive to her ways than to those of her husband.

Most of what Mi-yŏn's Mother had to say about her husband took stock of his enormous capabilities, while at once deriding his maniacal ambition and, above all, his extreme selfishness. On many occasions her evaluations wavered between these poles. In one breath, for example, she would speak of him both as a self-made man and as one who lives only for himself. She admired his calm—that no matter how large his burden or his workload, he never appeared overwhelmed or stressed—but she also often noted that he had enjoyed the luxury of being able to think of no one but himself. Mi-yŏn's Mother detailed his successes at work: "He is a model worker and everyone looks to him as an example of how to rise the ranks quickly: by forty he was a manager . . . then there was England, training in the United States, a Ph.D., a lectureship at a university, and now he is the head of [a national association]." Therein, however, was a story of total neglect of his family: "He didn't even treat his own children as well as boarders." Furthermore, she described him repeatedly as chillingly cold. Teary, she once spoke about why it was that Big Mother had needed to leave her and her husband's home: because in the years of her dementia, Mi-yŏn's father would not tolerate her knocking on their door several times a night. In the months we met before Big Mother passed away, in 1993, my conversations with Mi-yŏn's Mother were always punctuated by many phone calls from Big Mother. Mi-yŏn's Mother and her youngest son alternated answering them, and I would hear them say, "Don't worry, they [Mi-yŏn's Mother's brother and his wife] will be home soon." I remember being moved: it did not matter how many times she called, or within how few minutes of the last call, they always answered lovingly. We will see that Mi-yŏn's father had something to say about that love. Over the years of our meeting, Mi-yŏn's Mother chronicled the extreme costs of her husband's ways: costs mostly to others but to himself as well.

As in the case of thoughts on her driving, most often her reflections on her husband were coupled with self-reflection. Rejoinders like this one were common, "While I want to think quietly, my husband wants to do everything quickly." She had followed that comment immediately with: "I am worthless." While her husband could bear a heavy load without it seeming to take a toll on him, Mi-yŏn's Mother was convinced that stress had ruined her health; talk of her failed health and lack of physical vigor was constant during all of my meetings with her. Over the months that we had been meeting in 1995–1996 I had noticed the nervous way in which she had been stroking her neck—it was clear to me that there was a worry spot there. When I finally asked her about it—she had just mentioned needing to go to the doctors—she was flabbergasted that I had noticed, but it also seemed that she was relieved to talk about it.

Many of the traits through which Mi-yŏn's Mother drew a contrast between her husband and herself were gendered ones. She often, for example, noted that her husband's traits were ones well-suited to a man. In that regard, Mi-yŏn's Mother spoke about the ironic distribution of gendered traits among her children: her daughter, Mi-yŏn, being masculine exactly like her father, "more than Mi-yŏn could ever imagine"; her eldest son, much like herself; and her youngest son, a combination of the two. It was Mi-yŏn's "same personality that made her succeed, a personality that always bounces back." Mi-yŏn's Mother spoke of herself on that occasion, as "merely a spoiled girl from a rich family—not one to be able to rise up when the cards are down." Coming in our ninth meeting, this comment had surprised me for, until then, in spite of having detailed the ways in which she had been coddled as a child and even smothered with love, she had largely stressed her family's poverty during the Inch'ŏn years of her childhood. On another occasion, having just detailed the incredibly skillful way in which she had managed her investments in her children's education, Mi-yŏn's Mother shifted gears to praise her husband, "a man who turns everything to gold." But it was also just at that moment that she shed tears, bemoaning that she was "a woman who can't do anything alone," and that everything she had accomplished had all been on account of the help of Big Mother.

Mi-yŏn's Mother understood that some of her husband's traits, distinct from their gendered character, particularly his physical health and his profound coldness, were matters of familial culture. She described the "heaven-

and-earth difference" between her natal and marital families—which recalls the oft disjuncture across marital divides from chapter 8. Indeed, his mother was similarly a picture of health, and a woman who had caused Mi-yŏn's Mother considerable hardship in the early days of her marriage, such that she described having "closed her heart to her forever." In one of our discussions, Mi-yŏn's Mother began and, coming full circle, closed on her husband's and mother-in-law's inability to console the sick—their total lack of empathy. While her family had doted on sick people, coddling and cuddling them, his family knew nothing of physical vulnerability. When, in the earliest days of her marriage, she was really sick from the pregnancy with her first son, her husband only scolded her: "What is the matter with you!" Foremost among her accounts of the differences between her and her husband, and between their families, was the matter of community: hers was an upbringing through which she learned how to live for the collectivity, while her husband's had tutored him how to live only for himself. She often reflected that her largest mistake had been to assume that her husband lived, as she did, for their family. Learning over the years that he had squirreled away all of his earnings for himself, with no intent to donate them to the family coffers, she realized that she had been gravely mistaken. In moments of darker reflection, she said that it was her husband who taught her the loneliness of the human condition—"that in the final analysis we are alone." But her own upbringing had been so different: when Big Mother returned home from a day of work, she counted the earnings in front of the whole family, and they were understood to be collective funds. As such, her husband's approach to money struck Mi-yŏn's Mother as unthinkable, a violation of all that her own upbringing had taught her about money and family.

> My husband is the type who just thinks, "I have money—I can simply use my money to take care of things." But that sort of thinking is so inhuman (saram katchi anta). He thinks that it is sufficient to just send his mother money. My relationship with my mothers was like this [she pressed her hands together]. His mother thinks he is distant from her because of me, but in fact it is his personality—his American-style personality. He is really selfish.

As the reader has seen, even when deriding her husband, Mi-yŏn's Mother often spoke of her own weaknesses (although not necessarily moral ones) in contrast to him. There was, however, one occasion on which she noted that she had been somewhat of a match for her husband: talking about the hideous days of her early marriage, she said that she and her husband fought because "we both thought that we were great (challada)." I took this to mean that they had both considered themselves and their ways of being (family ways for her) superior.

When Mi-yŏn's Mother finally said outright (in our ninth meeting) that she "hated" her husband, it was for two reasons: because he likes pretty young women and makes big eyes at them, and because after ignoring his children throughout their childhood, he suddenly wanted to claim them in their adulthood, and with their adult successes, as his own. Her anger at his claiming their children is straightforward—how dare he, after all those years of doing and contributing nothing. The matter of his liking young and pretty women was one she had already long spoken of in terms of the qualities that he found lacking in her. Generalizing from her husband, Mi-yŏn's Mother several times spoke of men: "Men are robbers—they only like pretty women; I don't think highly of them!" She recalled with disdain how when she did on occasion get dressed up in England—donning finer clothes and makeup—the South Korean men in her midst were quick to ask her out for a meal, looking, she knew, for affairs. But her "basic composition" would never allow her to do such things. Indeed, Mi-yŏn's Mother did not dress in the stereotypical garb of a woman of her standing. She eschewed makeup and designer clothing, and stood out for having let her hair go gray, a decision inspired by her time abroad. Her husband, she said, "didn't want to see a woman's natural appearance—he wants a woman to be always laughing, pretty, and bright . . . He thought that he made a big mistake in choosing me: I was just home all the time and I didn't look pretty—so he really hated me." Once, though, she dressed herself up in the sapphires that Mi-yŏn had received from her in-laws prior to the marriage: "My whole life, I have never worn real jewelry, but when I went out in just plain slacks and a plaid shirt, and dressed it up in that jewelry, I could see that it was different—it really did do something for this gray hair and these wrinkles."

Of the "relations between men and women," Mi-yŏn's Mother condemned them: "They are hateful, horrible matters." She elaborated that, in the case of her husband, the relationship between men and women was only about "enjoy," she said in English. In our tenth meeting she reported her husband's goading her: "If you are so unsatisfied, go ahead and leave." He had charged that she was a woman who could not love and a woman incapable of letting herself get lost (ppajyŏdŭlji mothanda) in anything, not even love or religion. To those ugly comments he added that the only person she had ever loved or lost herself in was Big Mother. These were harsh criticisms, ones that she reflected upon the evening we attended the all-night prayer meeting together; they had touched a nerve, for she herself was baffled as to why she had been unable to immerse herself in some sort of religious practice. In the context of the widespread religious fervency of middle-class urban women in South Korea, it is not surprising that Mi-yŏn's Mother would have wondered about her own religious remove. Once Mi-yŏn's Mother called me late at night to talk about that, to ask me what I thought it was to immerse oneself in religion. Having never done so myself, I assured her that I was not the best consultant on the matter but proceeded (as I typically did) with some thoughts nonetheless.

Although Mi-yŏn's Mother never spoke of not being able to love, she often spoke of an inability to be feminine or charming to men. Her husband even went so far as to say to her once that he could not believe that he had been able to "stand her all those years." Interestingly, in these reflections on her own inability to pour on the charm for men (aekyo rŭl puriji mothanda), she joined the majority of the women in this book. She also spoke once—with remarkable candor—about her total bewilderment as to how women in marital situations akin to her own manage to sustain sexual relations with their husbands; she proceeded to tell me that she had even thought to consult a psychologist on the matter. It is not an exaggeration to say that the relations between men and women elided her generally. Once, when she had again mused on men as thieves, and the hardship of relations between men and women, she suggested that "80 to 90 percent of the women in South Korea have lived in this way—which explains why so many women have become such ardent Christians." Mi-yŏn often complained to her mother that the way her mother talked about men made it impossible for her to enjoy her own marriage life! As described briefly in chapter 7, Mi-yŏn chose a husband who was entirely unlike her own father. Mi-yŏn's Mother spoke to me at great length about a more desirable suitor Mi-yŏn had passed up. On one occasion, we spoke about Mi-yŏn's suitors over watermelon, and Mi-yŏn's Mother assigned pieces of watermelon to each of her daughter's suitors. The suitor in question, a lawyer, had been "number one in everything." Mi-yŏn's Mother admitted, "I fought so hard with her, but ultimately she was right." Although Mi-yŏn might have, in her mother's eyes, been like her father, she knew to not marry the likes of him.

Toward the end of our years of formal meetings, Mi-yŏn's Mother began to speak intermittently of her husband not only in terms of the harm he had caused others—foremost herself—but more broadly of his impoverishment as a person. In our earlier meetings she had occasionally spoken with understanding about his humble origins, about the pathology of his own background that might have driven his ambition (pathology that on occasion she recognized in herself as well): that his mother had been abandoned for another woman, and that he was from the discriminated-against Chŏlla provinces. But as time went on, it was more to his general human impoverishment that she spoke with some, albeit distant, sympathy: "When he finally has to step down from his position, he will be very sad, lonely, and pathetic. When it really comes down to it, no one really likes being with him —he frightens people." However, she wavered on these reflections as well, speculating, "It is probably tiring for people to be around him," then noting, "He is so good to those around him," at work. She was so surprised, in a similar vein, to discover that even her second cousin once removed in the United States, the well-educated and wealthy one who had married an American, had long felt uncomfortable with Mi-yŏn's Mother's husband.

She [the cousin] keeps inviting me to visit her [in the United States] and when I can't go, she asks whether it isn't because my husband won't allow me to go. When she and her husband came for a visit, my husband treated them like royalty: day and night he drove them all around. But the strange thing is that she said to me, "Why is it that the longer I have known him, the colder he becomes?" There is no getting around the fact that my husband has been very successful in the social world, but he has made some mistakes as well. Yes, he might have the warm heart that a man needs for playing with women, but why is it that so many people don't like him? He had taken her [the cousin] all around—to the best restaurants and concerts—and still that is what she had to say: how cold he was. Somehow she had figured out that he was cold. It is a matter of his character (in'gansŏng). In that sense he is a really unfortunate man. I feel exactly the same way about my mother-in-law: she is good to me, she gives me gifts and delicious things to eat, but none of it feels sincere (chinsim). I hate her. She isn't warm.

In the time that we were meeting, as aforementioned, Mi-yŏn's Mother had begun to confide in her sisters about her husband's extramarital relations. It was only then that she had begun to learn how very uncomfortable her sisters had long been with him—it was, in a sense, through their eyes that she had begun to admit to herself the true extent of her marital trials and to acknowledge that she had "lived a hard life."

It was three years into my formal research, in our tenth meeting, that she began our conversation with a radically altered version of how it was that she came to marry her husband. Until that time, she had always spoken of her marriage in terms of her husband's unflagging pursuit and his masculine style to match, a style that she stressed had made him attractive to her for so distinguishing him from her incapable (munŭnghan) father. As she said, "I married 180 degrees opposite from my father." However, when we spoke that day, she explained that once, during their courtship, she had been at his home when he left for the evening. By the time he returned, she had missed her bus home, and she ended up sleeping with him, then "ended up pregnant . . . It wasn't really that I wanted to marry him, but what could I do? I didn't know anything in those days." Here I should note that this story is typical on two counts: for claiming naiveté about sex and pregnancy; and because pregnant brides were quite common. She concluded the story that evening by proclaiming, "When it comes down to it, I really didn't expect much happiness out of life. I didn't have much hope." She furthermore reflected on not having gone after the much richer lawyer who had been pursuing her: "When I think back on it, what did I have to be proud of in those days? My family was poor and it wasn't particularly distinguished. My father didn't really do anything. There were two mothers in my home. I wasn't much of anything. I wasn't a particularly good student. And I didn't have much ambition or zeal for life (yoksim)." This account was interesting: it began on the particular circumstances of her pregnancy and ended on a quite different note—that she had been in no position to set her sights higher than the likes of her husband. Both of these points, in turn, differed from her by-then-longstanding account of her husband as the necessary and ideal antidote to her father. I take each version to be truthful for revealing truths of Mi-yŏn's Mother's reflective voice—truths of the narrative web through which she acts and reflects. As Vincent Crapanzano notes, we err when we look for the truth through narrow lenses (1980, 129–130).

Toward the end of our formal meetings, Mi-yŏn's Mother had begun to talk about divorce. At that time, she claimed the still-pending marriages of her sons precluded such action; today the youngest is still unmarried. In the years since then, she has more often spoken of financial concerns as precluding divorce—that none of their assets, though they are all mostly the fruits of her labor, are in her name. She mused on many occasions that she certainly would have put money away for herself had she really known what measure of man she had married. To make matters worse, Mi-yŏn's Mother was certain she would die first—that he would outlive her for being so healthy.

I think to myself that when I am done with all my work—raising, educating, and marrying my children—I will divorce him. It makes me crazy if I think about my dying: that he would use all that money on women—that he would never give any of it to the children.

Most often Mi-yŏn's father was not at home when we met, but on several evenings he was outside in the yard—visible through an enormous picture window that ran the entire length of the living room—practicing golf. There he was: proof of all that she described—working hard, honing a private skill, the picture of health.

Her Economic Activities, Herself

It is impossible to isolate Mi-yŏn's Mother's thoughts on her economic activities, her moneymaking, from those on her husband. Her reflections on her moneymaking for her family—through running boardinghouses, property management, and the buying and selling of apartments—are entirely tied up with her marital woes. As noted, all of the investment was registered in her husband's name, though he contributed nothing. There was, however, another and perhaps more important sense in which her husband was more directly implicated: as the instigator of the activity itself.

Over the course of our meetings, Mi-yŏn's Mother's oscillated between two quite divergent reflections on all of her (quite remarkable) economic activity. As the reader has learned in earlier chapters, Mi-yŏn's Mother spoke of her economic labor (nodong) in reference to her own childhood: to her early experience of plenty, to her nuclear family's material deprivation in the south, and to her experience of the wealth of her extended family in the south (see chapter 8). Thus she interpreted her material zeal as the result, in part, of twisted aspects of her own upbringing, most palpably, as learned in chapter 7, because of her keen sense of her father's economic inability. In this first sense, Mi-yŏn's Mother spoke of herself as embodying characteristics well-suited to moneymaking: material desire (yoksim) and the ability to work. It was in this vein that she said, "I guess the reason I flew to all those apartments south of the Han River [to trade in them] is because as a young woman everyone around me had lived so well and I wanted to live like them."

In a very different vein, however, Mi-yŏn's Mother claimed all of her economic work had been driven by her husband's ambition and desire. It was in that sense that she spoke at length about the extent to which she had been entirely unsuited to such pursuits, and, moreover, about the extreme personal costs of having sustained such activity. Although in this second voice, she attributed the engine of her economic activity to her husband, she was still entirely clear that the work had been her own, and resented any hint of his taking credit for her earnings. Mi-yŏn's Mother spoke tirelessly of the primary cost of her moneymaking—her physical health. With each new investment, each new economic worry, it was as if she had whittled away at a finite reserve. The idea that a person's health is a sort of zero-sum reservoir that can be spent early on in life is a prevailing one in South Korea. It is particularly pronounced in women's ideas about their health during pregnancy and immediately after birth. I have also encountered this notion in people's reflections on the costs of personal hardship during the Korean War. Although most often Mi-yŏn's Mother spoke about her health in terms of the toll of money matters, she once told me that in fact her health problems had begun when her family sought refuge during the Korean War—specifically that it was that because the countryside bathroom had been so much cruder than the one she had been accustomed to, she had repeatedly held off from using it for as long as possible.

On the matter of her economic activity, Mi-yŏn's Mother stressed that her health had been eaten away through such labor to indicate in part how profoundly unsuited she was to it.

> It was all so hard. I had no experience. I really hated it. He [her husband] told me to do it. I incurred so many debts and I was constantly panicked as to whether I would be able to repay them. He also told me to do the boardinghouse. I am the kind of person who has a really hard time making decisions. I even waver on what to buy at the grocery store. But I had no choice but to do it all. I really hate risks. So I became sick from all the worry. It was so hard. My body isn't strong: my heart flutters and pounds hard. I'm really not the sort of person to incur debts to others (sinse rŭl chiji mothanda)—I have my own pride (chajŏngsim). And I had to carry the entire burden (pudam) by myself. He left it all to me. He saw that I was kind (chakhada) [and would be obliging in pursuing his desires].

These sorts of reflections, however, did not stop Mi-yŏn's Mother from intermittently taking credit for her considerable skill in these matters, from noting, for example, that her early years of bank employment had served her well in that she was at ease in public offices, able to handle the bureau-cratic aspects of ownership and investment. Mi-yŏn's Mother even detailed making money with invisible money. She explained that she did all of her apartment purchasing in various people's names, and that she did it all by herself. (Purchasing in other people's names and hiding money in accounts under other people's names would later become illegal in South Korea.) She stressed, however, that she never engaged in money lending—clearly this marked the limits of acceptability for her. She also noted that it had been Big Mother who gave her the confidence to do it all, to make the purchases, take the risks, and so on. On yet another occasion, in 1995, Mi-yŏn's Mother put a quite different and gendered spin on having worked in the extra-income economy, suggesting that it had allowed her to retreat from the en-demic graft of the South Korean formal economy—that of regular jobs—and particularly that of the world of men. Her comments might ring oddly to many South Korean listeners who would perhaps cite the proverbial argu-ment between the pot and kettle.

> You know the story: that Christ told the people not to blame Mary Magdalene because hers were all of their sins. This is the same with Roh Tae Woo [South Korean President]: his crimes aren't his alone. Everyone in South Korea has lived that way. More than his crimes, I hate the people who are so quick to point their finger at him. The whole South Korean society works that way. From top to bottom, the whole country plays the same game. When I worked at the bank I saw how things were done—the bribes, the payments, and so on—and I decided then and there that I wouldn't live relying on that men's world, that I would earn money myself, my own way.

In these remarks, it is not clear that Mi-yŏn's Mother really meant to defend her economic activities according to some absolute standard. It seems to me, though, that she at least wanted to make it clear that her hard work had hardly been worse than business-as-usual in the men's working world where women have not really been welcome. These thoughts answered as well to the similar charges that her sisters made against her, and to the silent charges of so many, and of the media, of which she was no doubt aware—those charges that make her sort the other, as previously described. She seemed to be saying woe to the person who defends her virtue in a cor-rupt world.

Mi-yŏn's Mother's various reflections on her moneymaking are not necessarily so at odds with one another: one can be inclined toward activity for which one is deeply unsuited. I read the poles of her reflection in terms of deep-seated ambivalence about the moneymaking to which she devoted so many years of her life, and to which she is convinced she sacrificed her health and her youth. In her most pensive moments, and increasingly over the years, Mi-yŏn's Mother has been less concerned with the personal costs (or twisted origins) of her economic activity, and more interested in talking about the implications of a society driven by money—namely, the impoverishment of values.

> My thinking has really changed. My husband forgot my and my [eldest] son's birthdays, so he took us to a French restaurant in the Silla Hotel, which costs about a hundred dollars per person. The atmosphere was incredible: the music, the waiters all around you, potato soup, steak from France . . . But actually it made me feel sick. Who cares about how good things are? Even the waiters were high-class. Most of them had graduated from two-year colleges, and there were six of them surrounding us. But what does it show? That money can buy all that? It's all just money. People came with real musical instruments to sing happy birthday to me—that was the first time in my life. I encouraged my mother-in-law to come, but she had at first flatly refused. She eventually agreed begrudgingly and was wearing a sad face the whole way there, but my goodness, by the end of the evening, she was beaming ear-to-ear, so delighted with the whole thing—so was Mi-yŏn, for that matter. My mother-in-law was simply happy with the knowledge that such a restaurant exists and that she had eaten there. Yes, it really is a wonderful restaurant, but that isn't happiness. I don't feel good about it at all. It is better to eat humbly (sobak hage). My youngest son also enjoyed it. It was beautiful—the plates, the silverware, everything! It was really the atmosphere more than the food itself. My husband really likes that sort of style. He is extravagant.

I do not think that Mi-yŏn's Mother meant in any way, in offering such more-general comments on money, to exempt herself from its joys, or to deny that money had long motivated her. Rather, I take these sorts of comments to communicate her own ambivalence about her life. During another interview, Mi-yŏn's Mother said that people in South Korea "don't know to be afraid of money," and she went on to criticize all the moving that has taken place in South Korea for investment purposes only. Such a comment can ring a bit ironically, considering the many apartments she had bought and sold for investment purposes alone. Furthermore, when I met Mi-yŏn's Mother in 1983, after nine years of marriage, she had already moved residences five times, and was entirely tied up in economic activities (running a boardinghouse) and in economic investment. Mi-yŏn's Mother was frank about what she had done, admitting once: "It is getting harder and harder to make money in South Korea; things have become more like in the U.S.—you can't hide money anymore. It won't be easy for people to do what I have done." Mi-yŏn's Mother was thus well aware that much of her own activity spoke to precisely the values and practices that she had come to loathe. Once Mi-yŏn's Mother asked me what I thought happens to people after death. After a moment, I was relieved when she spoke: "A Buddhist friend of mine says that money has eyes, a mouth, a nose, and ears such that it always reveals itself after death," meaning that it reveals what a person has done while alive; it was then 1995, and she told me that President Roh's troubles—he was being tried for illicit financial activities—were a good example of just that, of money that talked.

To Mi-yŏn's Mother, having bought a house north of the Han River rather than an apartment south of it (those very apartments she had dizzily bought and sold) illustrated her priority in work over money in the following way: Although to the observer, Mi-yŏn's Mother's home may be, foremost, large, sumptuous, and carefully decorated, she stressed that the attention she lavished on this home (see chapter 2) was driven not by the interests of investment, but by the ethics of work and care. If wise investment had been her goal, she would have by now followed the vast majority of South Koreans of her means to cavernous apartments south of the river. Rather, she made the decision to buy this home in the name of stability (anjŏng) and with the understanding that domestic spaces should require labor. For Mi-yŏn's Mother, upper-class apartments were for those wealthy people who wanted nothing to do with caring for a home—who symbolically did not want to labor for the domestic but were, rather, only interested in leisure and play. "I hate the apartments in this country—we have taken all of the bad and none of the good from America; people decorate the insides of these apartments and beyond that there is no collective life: they live as strangers (namnam). There are many things I have to tend to in order to take care of this house, many details; most South Koreans, though, hate having to work—they hate that sort of labor." She stressed again and again that hers had been a decision to work on a home, to accept a home as something that required work rather than promise of profit: a lifestyle, not an investment. Implicit in her

statements was that she was not afraid of the upkeep of a home, even without maids. Indeed, over the decades I have now known her, in spite of her
considerable material ascendancy she has had less and less help at home, in
keeping with transformations in South Korea's wage structure. All of this
said, however, the reader might decide that Mi-yŏn's Mother's home was,
after all, foremost a powerful marker of class distinction.

The leisured rich—although not necessarily really wealthier than she was
—were an other for Mi-yŏn's Mother. She persistently defended her moneymaking to contrast herself with primary cohorts with whom she occasionally gathered: the mothers of Mi-yŏn's classmates at the prestigious girls'
arts high school; the wives of the other South Korean company managers
she had met in England; and the classmates from her own prestigious high
school (see Janelli and Yim n.d. on such organizations in relationship to
the social fabric of Seoul). She told me that she found it hard to gather with
these women (at typically regularized meetings—monthly, bimonthly, and
so on): "I couldn't help thinking that all those meetings are stealing time
away from my family, keeping me from doing things with my family." She
offered these comments in part to accept her husband's charge that she
could not plunge into things (ppajinda). Mi-yŏn's Mother considered her
humble childhood exceptional among all of those women, though it is unlikely the women's backgrounds in these groups were entirely uniform. She
often described those women as foremost wanting to be comfortable and
happy and largely living off of their fathers, and later, their husbands.

Contrasting these women's leisurely lives with hers of toil, she included
both her economic activities and her work on behalf of her children's education. Interestingly, she was entirely convinced that none of those other
rich women had even approached the extremes for their children that she
had for hers. In this sense she posed her (collectivistic) family labor against
their (selfish) personal leisure.

> The women from that high school [the one she attended] have just let
> their kids do whatever they wanted. They did not educate their children
> as well as I have. And none of them have made the money that I have.
> But who is to say? Look at my body [her weakness, etc.]—it is all be-
> cause of that. Sometimes I really regret all of it. I met one of my high
> school classmates in England and she said to me, "You should just live
> off of your husband's money! Why are you living like a superwoman
> that way?" That friend just lives happily, frolicking with her cat and
> dog, and eating delicious food. And she let her kids do whatever they

wanted for their education . . . She lives only for herself. She never gives anyone gifts. She never thinks of helping others. She chided me for even thinking about giving people presents.

Once, after a swim with Mi-yŏn's Mother at a private sports club (I recall being aghast at the exorbitant fee), she launched into a long discussion about the "lazy youth these days," bemoaning South Koreans nowadays simply refusing to work. She had gotten on the subject after overhearing some forty-something women at the sports club. She described "that type" of young woman swimming and golfing all day and sending all of her children to schools in the United States. ("Who knows who those kids even live with!") Mi-yŏn's Mother said, "As a woman, I hate to see other women playing like this—while men work"! Mi-yŏn's Mother and I went swimming together several times. (I also often swam with the Education Mother.) And as a long-term everyday swimmer, I was inadvertently engaged in one mark of class and gender privilege in South Korea, where my own then thirty-something health and strength were the object of curiosity, and even envy. After complaining about women at the sports club, Mi-yŏn's Mother turned to the quality of "maids these days." She then went on to "the entire next generation," explaining, "all people want to do nowadays is play and live well," thus repeating the refrain she often used in her descriptions of the "very rich" in order to distinguish herself from those who had never needed to work. We should perhaps listen in part to the run of such criticism as a comment on Mi-yŏn's Mother's more general malaise, one inextricable from the grist of her social critique.

In spite of the still-considerable material accoutrements in her midst, Mi-yŏn's Mother had become more and more interested in thinking about what it means to shed or to strip down. Questions about the nakedness of humanity compelled her. In such ruminations, however, she echoed the thoughts of a number of the other women in this book on the quality of human fiber as itself inextricable from family or class background. Later in this chapter we find this same tension in her thoughts about the ideal class or social structure for South Korea. Nonetheless, Mi-yŏn's Mother's thoughts revealed important meditations on material life, unbridled desire (*yokmang*), and personal adornment. Interestingly, when Mi-yŏn's Mother spoke to the bare bones of the human condition, she turned her reflections to the Korean War, a critical reference point for all of the women in this book, and a crucial marker of generation in South Korea generally; a commonsensical mark of difference is that drawn between those who know and those who do not know that war. Once Mi-yŏn's Mother spoke of the Korean War as her own preventive medicine (poyak) to mean that her experiences of refuge taught her life's bitterness—a lesson that young people need to learn. She had offered this to contrast herself with Mi-yŏn's enormously rich high school classmates, many of whom had already ended up "failing" at marriage—because, she surmised, they were spoiled. The ruminations below on the gist of humanity followed a discussion about her then still-yet-unmarried eldest son and his selection of a suitable wife.

> I've been thinking that when you take away all the outer layers (kkŏpchil)
> —education, family reputation (kamun), social standing, money, looks—
> what is left is sort of the pure person. It is that pure person that people
> should examine when they think to marry someone. I've been thinking
> back to six-two-five (yuk'i'o, the Korean War), when we all had nothing,
> absolutely nothing—when we were all stripped down to the essentials.
> But nonetheless everyone was able to make themselves from just that,
> from just their bodies, their lineage (ppyŏdae, literally bones). [I inter-
> rupted to ask what she meant by "ppyŏdae."] What I mean is whether
> or not they came from a good family (lineage, choŭn chiban) . . . I've also
> been thinking a lot about how women age in South Korea. When we are
> young we have those big eyes and such beautiful skin—young women
> are so gorgeous—but aging makes us into demons (imugi). Living in the
> midst of all that desire (yokmang), women come to look more and more
> like demons. To the extent that I possibly can, in the next years of my
> life I want to try to simplify my life and to look less demonlike—I plan
> to wear cotton and only on occasion silk.

That evening Mi-yŏn's Mother was indeed wearing a cotton T-shirt and chino pants, and no makeup. Despite the ironies in these comments—that the innermost essential, the bare bones of it all, is not a general human fiber, but, rather, the matter of a "good family"—we can nonetheless appreciate Mi-yŏn's Mother's spirit here, her deep-seated interest in stripping away at least some of the material world of desire. Interesting also (recalling the Laundress's comment in chapter 3 that a "woman's face after forty is the one she has made") is that when Mi-yŏn's Mother thought to speak about the barest human essentials, she turned immediately to women in particular. At its "most basic," humanity is gendered.

In Mi-yŏn's Mother's evocation here of the quality of a person's family or lineage, it is not so easy to know what she meant by "family": whether she meant to underscore social standing or status, or some sort of moral quality. My sense is that the two are inextricably intertwined for her. One point that was resoundingly clear throughout my conversations with Mi-yŏn's Mother was her belief in family collectivity, and less evenly, in collectivities generally. Here the reader can recall the contrasts she drew between her own and her husband's families, and in turn between herself and her husband. In this vein, however, there was a problem in her family history—one she knew only too well: namely that, for many years, Mi-yŏn's Mother had in fact had little to do with her two sisters. In our later meetings together, this was a sore point that she touched on often. As reviewed in chapter 7, ten and twelve years younger then Mi-yŏn's Mother, her sisters had been virtually raised in a different family culture, with no memory of life in the north or of the Korean War, and with little exposure to either the economic activities of Big Mother or the wealth of the Hyoja-dong relatives. Interestingly, though, in the same transcendent instant in which Mi-yŏn's Mother orally regretted this lapse of family solidarity on her part, she regretted most often having done little to secure more worldly (prosperous) futures (through better marriages) for her sisters.

As in my comments on the preceding example—in which Mi-yŏn's Mother evoked human essentials and family lineage in the same breath—I do not mean to take the simultaneous mention of family solidarity and of her sisters' material well-being as somehow incompatible. Rather, they are tied together by the warp and woof of Mi-yŏn's Mother's many ambivalent reflections on her life. The case of her sisters—her youngest sister had worked incredibly hard as a career banker, and her other sister as a school teacher—was important not only because their lives presented much humbler circumstances (in both cases in part because their husbands had failed miserably in business) but also because they had both been openly critical of Mi-yŏn's Mother's life for quite some time. Foremost, they had objected to the ways in which Mi-yŏn's Mother had made her money—as a number of the other women in this book would have objected. Theirs, then, had been a voice to which Mi-yŏn's Mother had needed to answer (to herself, if not to them directly). She had, at least in her accounts to me, answered in several ways. At times she charged that their lives had not actually been so different, in that they had all labored (as did Mi-yŏn, as a health professional). At other times, she asserted that her sisters had not woken up to the realities of being women in South Korea, realities that Mi-yŏn's Mother insisted had thwarted the development of their potential in their careers. Here she told me that over time they—particularly the youngest—had come to understand her points about persistent gender discrimination in South Korea. Furthermore, she explained, had she had a job outside the home, "I would not have been able to raise my children well. Women need to stay home, take their kids to lessons, and manage their studying—even if it is hard labor." But Mi-yŏn's Mother understands that her sisters also did what they did in response to the incapability (munŭng) of their father. Under the glass of her bedroom vanity table was another photo—one of Mi-yŏn's Mother, her two sisters, and her husband's sister; she once glanced at that photo and remarked, "It is only women here, all women whose husbands have not helped them."

At still other times, however, Mi-yŏn's Mother accepted her sisters' criticisms and admitted to appreciating their less materially motivated lives, their simpler goals. Such reflections did not, however, stop Mi-yŏn's Mother from regretting that she had not done more to secure more financially stable lives for them. As I have asserted throughout this book, beginning with the Education Mother's pocketbook story in chapter 1, disparities among siblings (perhaps particularly among sisters), and again among cousins and other consociates, always present rich food for thought. Mi-yŏn's Mother's thoughts about how she might have helped with her sisters' marriages are revealing:

My youngest sister was really pretty. When I think about it, on account of my husband's job, there were so many promising men around me. But things were really hard for me then, and those were also the days when my sister told me that she didn't want to live like me—running the boardinghouse and all that. Of course, I had chosen my own husband, so it wasn't really as if I could step in and insist on choosing my sisters' husbands. Actually I didn't get involved at all. I didn't even talk to them about it. But now that they don't live well, I really regret it. I really should have advised them. More than anything I feel bad about this because I could have so easily introduced them to my husband's junior colleagues at work, but the truth of the matter was that I was embarrassed by them: I thought that there was something insufficient (pujŏkhan myŏn) about them, so I didn't want to get involved in their marriages. It hurts me now to know that I thought that way. I could have found [my youngest sister] a good man and she wouldn't have had to struggle the way she has. When I think about it, it was all because fundamentally I didn't have confidence in myself. Also, there was another thing: she didn't think much of me—she thought of me as trifling (*sisihage*)—and I guess I must have figured that she probably knew what to do better than I would have.

These comments, like so many of Mi-yŏn's Mother's, are complex. She offered an unflattering admission: that it was because she was embarrassed by her sisters (and by extension her family background) that she had not introduced them to promising men. However, she spoke about her better-educated sisters' (they had both gone to college) disdain for the ways in which she had made money, to say that they had thought little of her and that she had not sported the necessary confidence to arrange marriages for them. Here again, her thoughts walk in opposite directions, residing together ambivalently.

Her Education, Herself

Moments before Mi-yŏn's Mother spoke about having looked up at the glass at the college in England and having ruminated on what her life might have been like had she studied abroad as a young woman, she had been saying that after Mi-yŏn's birth she really should have continued her studies "but, what with two small children and no washing machine . . ." She did not complete the thought.

As we have learned, for Mi-yŏn's Mother, the matter of not having gone on to college is a centerpiece of her life narration. Clear in chapters 4 and 5 is that the matter of education, its exclusions and its promises, is a critical feature of South Korea's post–Korean War story. As we saw in chapter 8, the matter of education for Mi-yŏn's Mother was intimately tied to her decision to leave her family in Inch'ŏn for college-bound studies in Seoul. And it was in Seoul that her life became so closely tied with the lives of her wealthy kin. Most often, and consistently throughout the earlier phase of this research, Mi-yŏn's Mother told the story that she yearned to leave her family both to get away from the father she loathed, and to set her sights higher than what had been planned for her (attendance at a normal high school that would have prepared her to become a teacher). She would come to regret that decision, venturing that she would have been better off becoming a high school teacher and avoiding the difficult years in the nest of rich relatives. She also mused once that she would have done better boarding in Seoul rather than living off the largesse of rich kin—an oppressive largesse, as it turned out. It was, ironically, the experience of living with rich relatives that had kept her from succeeding in school. Later, however, Mi-yŏn's Mother would tell this story differently on several counts. As for her departure to Seoul, she once surprised me by suggesting that, quite to the contrary, the motivation had not been hers at all.

> Oh but I could have never done that alone. I only went because it was my friend's mother's idea. I really was just a spoiled child. Everyone did everything for me. My problem was that I had no ability to rely on myself, no sense of independence (ŭijiryŏk).

As for not having gone to college, it is important to note that we were nearly a half year into our discussions before the fact that Mi-yŏn's Mother had not gone to college was ever on the table. I had figured it out—in spite of oblique references to college—in our third formal meeting. But early on, Mi-yŏn's Mother vaguely sustained an impression of having gone to college by stressing the excellence of her prestigious high school, a high school from which "any girl could have gone to college." She had also made the point that the girls who attended that high school had already met their challenge: namely the fabulously competitive entrance to the high school itself. It was only in a recent review of my field notes that I was reminded I had decided that in our fifth meeting I would refer in passing to the matter of her not having gone to college. And indeed, such a mention during that meeting made no particular waves. It was in our sixth meeting that Mi-yŏn's Mother then made explicit mention of not having gone to college; furthermore, it was then that she revealed she had never made it clear to her children that she had not attended college—perhaps "college" had long floated in her household, obliquely, in much the way it had in our first meetings. It is, however, unlikely that her children did not know, given the innumerable school forms that ask for parents' education level. I was shocked to recall why it was in 1993 that Mi-yŏn's Mother had purportedly decided to admit to me formally that she had not gone to college. She explained that she decided to tell me because of something quite personal I had told her.

In the months following her admission of not having attended college, Mi-yŏn's Mother had several things to say about the sequence of relevant events. First, she implied obliquely that her unthinkable and enviable bank employment had obviated college attendance. Second, and very differently, she spoke often of having passed up the opportunity to attend a newly founded university where a couple who had been renting a room in one of her Hyoja-dong's relative's home had become professors. She described that lost opportunity in two quite different ways. On the one hand, she attributed it to her personality, or style. She had been unable to brave the waves at work to make such an arrangement possible, thus asserting that she was lacking in the requisite ambition and strength. She described that she was fearful of the attention (*nunch'i*) that such negotiations would have called to herself. And in an entirely different vein, she blamed the missed chance on her own snobbishness. She stressed that she had flatly refused to believe in the worth of the new university and that she had been unable to bring herself to take the opportunity seriously. (By today there is considerable status accorded any university in Seoul.) Here, we can recall her fleeting admission that she had in fact considered herself, and her family background, superior to her husband.

> At that time, [the renters'] university was laughable. I could have gone there so easily, but all I could do was think that the school was so absurd. I thought that it was a place where only people with no ability gathered. I wasn't able to think ahead to where it would be ten or twenty years later. I was so stupid (*pabo katta*); I really should have gotten more advice from that couple. Now that I see my husband having a Ph.D., I really should have done that.

And in a much later interview, talking about the renter, who was a professor:

> All I could think was how ridiculous he was. He had even studied abroad in Japan, but I just kept thinking, "After all that, and this is all that he could become!" There he was: living in a small rented room. If only I could have known to go to him! But only teaching *there*—he seemed so pathetic, hopeless, and nervous. All I could think was, "What a waste!"

In these reflections we can recognize the contrast between Mi-yŏn's Mother's sense of herself as "the spoiled child" versus "the enterprising, deprived child" that we have met several times before.

By 1995 and into 1996 Mi-yŏn's Mother intermittently offered yet again differing explanations on both not having gone to college, and its significance. She described having settled for bank employment as revealing of her total lack of self-confidence and self-worth; earlier, however, she had described that same employment as "like plucking a star from heaven" and as the mark of her "true advantage" (for having procured the job thanks to family connections). In this different vein, she attributed her lackings both to her experiences in Hyoja-dong, having lived there as a poor cousin and a maid, and to a more general sense of her personal unimportance in the face of her nuclear family's poverty: "As an eldest daughter, I felt too apologetic (*mianhan kŏt*) to attend college. Also, I wasn't calculating enough to have gone." Similarly she recalled her difficulties in using the spending money for high school that Big Mother had given her: "I just couldn't use the money earned from her labor (*nodong*)—I couldn't bring myself to buy school stuff with it, especially not the delicious breads in the school cafeteria. Instead I bought clothes for my family." Again, from a slightly different perspective, she once blamed her great-uncle for getting her the job that prevented her from going to college. And yet again, she would also more matter-of-factly recall: "How stupid (*pabo katta*) I was to have gone to the movies on Sundays rather than study."

Later still in our encounters, she would refer most directly to the fact that her grades had fallen during high school such that I began to wonder whether or not she had in fact enjoyed the choice of going to college: "After all, it wasn't as if I had been studying under a mother's love or nourished by home cooking." Once, she did suggest quite explicitly that it had not been a matter of not having been able to attend college, but a matter of not having had the grades that would have allowed her to enter a respectable major (entrance requirements were differentiated by field of study, and majors were evaluated differentially at even the same college): "If I couldn't get into the medicine or pharmacy departments, it seemed better to get a job rather than to enter an arts-and-sciences department." That Mi-yŏn's Mother's grades would have fallen with her move to Seoul makes sense, both because Seoul schools would have been more competitive than those elsewhere and because of duties at her relatives' house.

Mi-yŏn's Mother's sense of the costs of not having attended college varied. Only one time, in our eighth meeting, she suggested that not having gone to college did have an impact on her marriage prospects, that she had enjoyed a wonderful reputation in Hyoja-dong, but men had lost interest when they discovered she had only graduated from high school. We have also listened to Mi-yŏn's Mother say that she wished she could have earned a Ph.D. as her husband had managed to. In the next section, on her children's schooling, we learn more of her thoughts on education. We also meet her sense that it is her lack of education which has tethered her to her marriage. Having learned in earlier chapters, through Mi-yŏn's Mother and a number of the other women featured, for South Korea education is what ensures a person will be treated "like a human being." In this vein, it is interesting that Mi-yŏn's Mother once told me she had never made it entirely clear to her husband that she had once enjoyed prospects to continue on to college. She had kept this from him, she told me, "so as to not hurt his confidence." At one point Big Mother—frustrated by the way in which Mi-yŏn's Mother was being treated by her husband and in-laws—decided she would speak about those earlier prospects to Mi-yŏn's Mother's sister-in-law (to bolster her regard), who in fact turned out to be really surprised. Mi-yŏn's Mother mused: "I really should have told people." She once noted that for all Big Mother had done for her, the one thing that she had not been able to do was guide her in her education.

Her Children's Education, Herself

We saw above that Mi-yŏn's Mother defended her educational and material zeal in the face of her others: women of the leisure classes who eschew labor and live only for themselves. Interestingly, then, in the same way that Mi-yŏn's Mother would be rendered other by many women in this book for what appears to be greedy, materialistic, and familistic ways, she too distinguished herself from the female other. As I have argued throughout this book, radical social transformation produces precisely such gendered others. If Mi-yŏn's Mother defended against these feminine others her zeal for educating her children, she was also ambivalent about the extent to which she had lived for and through her children's education.

Mi-yŏn's Mother was quite matter-of-fact on the origins of this zeal, both her own and more generally in South Korea. First, she easily assumed that women's own biographies were a part of the story. In 1993, when we were watching television, women with their heads held down flashed across the news hour; Mi-yŏn's Mother explained that they were being arraigned for some sort of social misdeed, usually related to bribery or illicit extra-wage income. She then remarked, "More mothers are arrested that way because mothers' love for their children is greater. They think, 'My children have to live better than I have.' " She was matter-of-fact about her efforts for her children having been to compensate (posang) for her own unanswered education dreams: "My own opportunity has passed, so I guess that is why I looked for compensation in my children. In our society there is a time (ttae) in which you have to do things, and after that it is too late—mine had already passed." She also spoke of her marital unhappiness as an important factor in her zeal: "Having given up on my own happiness, I decided to live for my children."

The second and, for Mi-yŏn's Mother, entirely obvious reason for mothers' work on behalf of their children's education was the simple understanding that "the only way to survive in this society is to study." Echoing many others, Mi-yŏn's Mother offered that the only way to be treated like a person in South Korea is to be educated. She craned her neck upward to signal literally that one has to be educated in South Korea to be looked up to.

Mi-yŏn

Beyond the understandings of mothers' general education dreams for their children, Mi-yŏn's Mother had some very specific thoughts about the education of daughters. For daughters it was not the workings of education deprivation generally that she spoke of, but rather the workings of gender discrimination that called for something distinct for daughters: a skill, a talent. It was in this context that Mi-yŏn's Mother became obsessed—as she would readily admit—with Mi-yŏn's musical education, specifically with that most fascinating of global bourgeois fetishes, the piano (we can recall the piano in *Romaensŭ Ppappa* noted in chapter 7; see also K. H. Kim n.d.; cf. Freire 1996, 22). But for Mi-yŏn's Mother the piano was more than that: it was a profoundly gendered symbol for a world in which it was so hard for a woman to have something of her own. Mi-yŏn's Mother's miserable marriage had convinced her that a woman needed something and that some sort of toil, even a profession, was not enough; she needed an artistic talent, such as music, because "there is no real way to live as a woman (*yŏja rosŏ sal kil i ŏpta*) . . . even if women go out into society there is no real way for them to make money . . . Women aren't free to live the way men do."

> As a woman you need a special skill or talent in order to be recognized. Our society is such that men's work is considered great and important (*taedanhage*) while women's work is but a matter of course (*tangyŏnhage*). It isn't that I think like that, but everyday a woman's work is the same, and if on only one day something isn't right—the rice is bad, let's say— the men protest . . .

There was still more to Mi-yŏn's Mother's heartfelt ideas about women, education, and the arts. In our ninth meeting, Mi-yŏn's Mother really surprised me: she arrived at my place, announcing that she had something really important to tell me. As those were the days of considerable sagas over her husband's infidelity, I figured that it was something about that. I did not push her for the secret, figuring sooner or later she would tell me. The surprise for me was that what she ended up telling me was actually something she had told me very early on in our meetings, actually with very little ado (see chapter 7, p. 204). Clearly, in the intervening years, the recollection had taken on new significance, and she had even made a secret of it.

> I have never told anyone this before. I was sitting with my husband on a bench in Tŏksugung—we weren't married yet. I told him that I didn't believe in gender discrimination (namnyŏch'abyŏl), but he said that women needed to act (or move, umjigyŏya handa) on behalf of men (namja rŭl ŭihayŏ). I had thought that we could have a discussion about these matters, but I gave up—we were never going to reach an agreement. After we got married I could feel with my skin the things that he had said that day . . . It wasn't that he was planning to divorce me or anything like that, but he wanted to discipline me, to mold me in his own image (chagi sik ŭro). So we fought all the time . . . He never even touched one diaper. I had such feelings against him (chŏhang'gam). The only thing I could think then was that women needed to be educated, that women were the ones who needed the good education. That was what I was lacking. I didn't know about this sort of gender discrimination, because in my house growing up we had all lived as equals. So that is why I was determined to teach Mi-yŏn to play the piano. [My eldest son] has some hard feelings about that—that he never got to learn to play an instrument; so these days he runs about dangling a violin . . . I thought about divorce a hundred times, but I couldn't do it . . .
> If I could have only had a room like this and enough to eat, I would have left.

As she said that, she looked around my tiny, so-called one-room system, a mini-studio apartment of sorts—which I was renting from her! These memories had become secrets for her perhaps because her pre-marriage conversation with her husband foretold her difficult marital life—that women should act only on behalf of men. In that brief exchange on a park bench were the seeds of her suffering to come—a suffering that propelled the life she would live on behalf of her children, and, in particular, the dreams that she would try to fulfill for her only daughter, Mi-yŏn. Once, Mi-yŏn's Mother was particularly frank about the ways in which Mi-yŏn herself had been the object of her husband's gender discrimination: "He hated her because she was a daughter. He could not bear her screaming, yelling that he could not sleep. So I brought her to my family—she was basically raised by my family."

The extremes to which Mi-yŏn's Mother went for Mi-yŏn's musical education, first the piano and later voice, constitute a drama of their own: she sent Mi-yŏn to piano lessons rather than nursery school, making it absolutely mandatory, "like going to school or to the hospital." Later on, hoping to send her to an arts middle-and-high school, she provided her no other after-school activities, only piano and voice. She even paid no heed to the fact that Mi-yŏn's general grades were middling—"I could never have imagined that she would end up becoming a health professional." In all of this she stretched the family budget to accommodate the very best for Mi-yŏn's music. As to how it is that Mi-yŏn eventually left music, I only heard the story once, and I am sure that I do not have the whole story. Mi-yŏn's musical studies had gone well, and she was slated to enter the music department of a top university. When it came to the day of the tryouts, Mi-yŏn's teacher, a woman who Mi-yŏn's Mother said had adored Mi-yŏn, instructed Mi-yŏn's Mother to bring a bribe for the examiners, and she even named the staggering amount. The story goes that Mi-yŏn's Mother had neither the wherewithal nor the will to follow through with the bribe (as anthropologist Jesook Song suggested to me, this account is unlikely given the extremes to which Mi-yŏn's Mother had already gone on behalf of Mi-yŏn's musical career). In a similar vein, Mi-yŏn's Mother also told me that Mi-yŏn, who had been present when the call arrived, had told her that she did not want to live that way. Mi-yŏn's Mother hoped that Mi-yŏn would try again a year later, but Mi-yŏn made a radical turn, deciding that she would instead apply to medical school, which required an additional year of training. Then, a year later, she did not get into a medical department, and entered a public administration program but a year after that entered the college-admission ring for a third time, in another health-related field, and passed. Mi-yŏn's Mother spelled out for me the enormous amount of money that it had taken for Mi-yŏn's change of direction: "I put ten times more into her than went into most kids."

Although Mi-yŏn did indeed become a health professional, Mi-yŏn's Mother has never stopped telling me about her musical talents and accomplishments. Mi-yŏn's Mother often lamented, "What a waste (ant'akkapta)!" But over the years, on many occasions, Mi-yŏn's Mother has described the continued life and importance of the musical skills that she so very carefully nurtured in Mi-yŏn. For example, Mi-yŏn's Mother's described how Mi-yŏn, having given two performances in her health professional school, was recognized foremost for her musical talent: "Her teachers even asked her, 'Why did someone like you come here?' " indicating her talent. For Mi-yŏn's Mother, the sense that music was, after all, what mattered most, affirmed her sense of things: that her daughter's health profession is labor and music is art. Mi-yŏn's Mother also attributed Mi-yŏn's many suitors to her musical talent. Once, though, she tweaked the attribution slightly differently: she suggested that perhaps Mi-yŏn was celebrated with so many good marriage introductions because she had introduced so many of her arts high school girlfriends to her male classmates who had wanted to marry musically accomplished women. Most remarkable to me were Mi-yŏn's Mother's thoughts on why Mi-yŏn had managed to win a prestigious internship in a health specialty, which today she practices in a lucrative private clinic in a regional city. Mi-yŏn's Mother described Mi-yŏn's internship as "no different than studying abroad"; she also noted that Mi-yŏn was the first woman to have this particular internship. She told me Mi-yŏn was surrounded by men with grades much higher than hers. [So I asked, "Well how was it then that she was accepted?"] She paused, then proceeded with a glimmer in her eye:

> One of the professors knew about her musical talent, that she could
> sing and play the piano. He must have thought that it was amazing
> for someone with all those talents to have made it so far [in a scientific
> field], and so he realized her considerable ability (nŭngryŏk). So I think
> that is how she was accepted.

One can understand the story of Mi-yŏn's Mother—on the piano and on the course of music in Mi-yŏn's career—variously. Some readers might insist that the story has absolutely nothing to do with gender discrimination, in spite of Mi-yŏn's Mother's own insistence. Such a reader would, I think, suggest instead that this is the naked story of a bourgeois woman: Mi-yŏn's Mother had, pure and simple, purchased for Mi-yŏn the upwardly mobile trappings of Western musical achievement, trappings that were the province of girls from fine families. I think, however, that such a reading would do Mi-yŏn's Mother, and Mi-yŏn, an injustice. I prefer instead to both appreciate the conservative gender-and-class coordinates of the piano for Mi-yŏn and her Mother *and* to listen to Mi-yŏn's Mother's story: one that speaks to the radical dislocations of the course of her life, creating her desires for

Mi-yŏn's musical achievement, dislocations that have also made for the structures of feeling at the heart of this book.

Mi-yŏn's Brothers

Mi-yŏn's brothers each had complex college-entrance sagas: sagas that featured Mi-yŏn's Mother prominently. Her eldest son had failed on the first go-around. In response Mi-yŏn's Mother made what she would later consider a mistake, by managing to get him into one of the best college-examination cram schools (hagwŏn), which turned out to be above his level. Eventually he got into a third-tier regional college, but upon graduation, he was unable to find work. Without telling anyone, he made his way to another college-entrance cram school, this time for medicine. At the time, Mi-yŏn's Mother was already in England with her husband, and when she came back, her son was nowhere to be found (these events recall the story of the Education Mother from chapter 4). She eventually found the cram school in question, only to learn that his grades had been poor and that he was no longer attending. Finally she found him in a "third-rate study hall—it wasn't even a cram school—living with a bunch of guys in a lousy room, eating lousy food, and surrounded by books, like someone who had never even been to college!"

Mi-yŏn's Mother made a decision about this son: "I needed to somehow get him set, to sow his future." Against his will, she insisted that he come to England, where she had decided she would personally manage his English-language education, as he had majored in English in college. They attended an English-language program together. Taking the placement exams with her son, she learned how little confidence he had: he, the college graduate of an English department, kept turning to her for answers to the questions. As it turns out, she was placed considerably higher than he was, but she asked them to send her to a lower-level classroom so as to not one-up her son. By then her husband had essentially given up on this son, imagining that he was destined for low-level employment at best. When the son returned to South Korea, his father arranged for a job for him through a hometown contact, an uneducated friend from his youth who had succeeded in business. As it turns out, though, behind their backs, the son had taken the employment exam for a prestigious bank: Mi-yŏn's Mother only learned all of this when she opened a letter for him and discovered that he had passed. Her husband, she described, "went crazy" with happiness and lamented that he had underestimated his son. Against his parents' insistence, the son refused to take time off to prepare for the oral exam because preparation in the past had only led to failure. He did, as it turned out, pass the oral exam and was hired. Again and again, Mi-yŏn's Mother insisted that he had passed the oral exam because of his honesty: foremost because he had made no bones about having been a poor student. She also attributed his turnaround in life to both the English skills that he had honed in England and to the personal confidence that he had developed there—both under her tutelage.

The youngest son—whom the reader met in some detail in chapter 4, and who is now caught up in South Korea's venture-capital sector—similarly failed the college-entrance exam of his choosing on the first round. That Mi-yŏn's Mother had not been in a state to take the driver's exam in England —in contrast to her husband's being the first to pass, as previously noted— was because she had been so upset about this son's failing his college-entrance exam. Her devastation here might have been exacerbated because of a sense that she should have been with him; mothers typically hover near when their children (particularly sons) are preparing for the college-entrance exams. On a second round of tests, he had been accepted by a much-lower-ranked school, which he attended for two days and decided he would wait and try again. In the meantime, he served his mandatory military duty, which proved an experience that had a decisive effect on his confidence. During his high school years, he had only considered his failings, keenly aware of those students who were outperforming him: "[In the military] though, I realized how well I had lived. The guy who slept to my right came from a poor family and had been unable to go to college so he worked in a low-level technical job. The guy on my left did some sort of sales with his brother right out of high school . . ." Eventually this youngest son would study for and succeed in entering a prestigious university for engineering, where he was awarded a full fellowship. Mi-yŏn's Mother laughed about her husband bragging to people about his youngest son studying "for free" on account of a fellowship he had won. She laughed because of how ignorant he was of the vast extent of her monetary investment in that son prior to that point.

The Meaning and Worth of Education

As we have gathered, and as with so many of the objects of her active mental life, Mi-yŏn's Mother is of several minds about education. As stressed in chapter 4, education calculations have necessarily been complex over transformations in South Korean education and occupational structure: the worth and promise of education capital has been in flux (here we can recall Mi-yŏn's Mother's regrets over not attending a college that at the time she considered unsubstantial but that today she considers worthy). On the one hand, Mi-yŏn's Mother had long spoken of education as the ultimate social salve in South Korea, according respect and garnering employment. On the other hand, in a gendered vein, we have seen that she found standard education capital somewhat suspect—preferring for Mi-yŏn the piano, and insisting that somehow, even in her health career, it was the piano that had afforded her opportunity. She also had serious misgivings about both the nature of South Korean education, and the zeal that is prerequisite to education success, a zeal that she knew only too well. She both celebrated that zeal—and her own efforts on behalf of her children—and wondered about the wisdom of it all. In chapter 4 we listened to Mi-yŏn's Mother's positive appraisal of the changed status hierarchy of post-IMF South Korea that allowed people to pursue their own interests—she had spoken of people returning to farming or opening restaurants—while at the same time she spoke of wanting her youngest son to stay close to traditional employment instead of chasing the venture economy. Mi-yŏn's Mother described that the problem of overly involved mothers was twofold: it made for ungrateful children, and it squandered women's energies, away from larger social problems. In the later years of our meetings, Mi-yŏn's Mother often spoke about the possibility of not passing on any of the family money to her own children and instead somehow contributing it to society.

Beyond the matter of women squirreling all of their energies away for their children, Mi-yŏn's Mother also expressed considerable ambivalence over the extent to which (South Korean) education is, after all, worthy of the social value it is accorded. Over the years she had come to think, as she once described, that people should rather live freely (chayuropta). She charged that "South Korean education is nothing but memorization," and she often waxed enthusiastically about the experiential education that she could gather was at the heart of anthropological field research. Again and again she told me how wonderful it was that I had (for my dissertation research) actually gone and lived in the countryside. Furthermore, she once insisted, "The more a person gets educated in South Korea, the worse: our education teaches people to live only for themselves, not for society." Taken together, these (self-)critiques are profound: the doting mother squanders her own energies away from the broader social good, just as her children learn how to live only for themselves. This said, however, these are widely shared—and often voiced—critiques in South Korea.

During conversations with Mi-yŏn's Mother in my most recent visits in 2000 and 2001, she told me that she had begun to have doubts about her children's lives: their driven day-to-day existences and their interest in money—an interest that baffles her, although perhaps not my reader by this point in her story. She tells her youngest son to "stop studying so hard—to be a regular guy, to be happy." Not surprisingly, these sorts of thoughts carry her back to her own childhood, and to transformations in her appraisal of her own upbringing.

> Now I can understand my father, who told me to be middling in school. These days, I too want the same for [my son]—to be middling. But I hated that my father didn't care about my studying, so I just left. That expression, "There is truth in being average (p'yŏngbŏmsok e chilli ga itta)," now I can see what it means. A spinster middle school teacher of mine taught me that expression, and at the time, I didn't know what it meant. But now I do. She was probably speaking as an unmarried woman [not being "average" herself]. I try and tell my kids things that will help them in their lives—we owe that to the people we love. When they don't listen I feel so frustrated.

In the days after Mi-yŏn's moving out, having married, Mi-yŏn's Mother read through all of Mi-yŏn's school notebooks. She cried over the idealism she found there. Mi-yŏn had written, "I want to work on behalf of pitiable people." Mi-yŏn's Mother thought to herself, "Ah, so Mi-yŏn had those sorts of ideas then." She seemed to be musing that the long haul of Mi-yŏn's education—of her own extraordinary toil and monetary investment—was over now, and she wondered about its meaning. No doubt these reflections are more prosaic than they might seem, in that they are the thoughts of a woman who has already managed to successfully educate her children. Such ruminations are harder to come by from those in the middle of educating their children.

Although Mi-yŏn's Mother might have advocated being middling in school, or even that education should not be so important to a person's social standing and respect, she believed deeply that passion for education makes for the greatest contentment in life: passion in the sense of a calling, that one follows a vocation that is somehow unfettered by the material world. There is no question that one of the reasons Mi-yŏn's Mother was in many senses an ideal anthropological interlocutor is because of her own profound respect for the life of the mind. Particularly fascinating is that she was in part reconciled to her own lack of education because her better-educated consociates—all of those rich women in the various social circles described—were in fact not so very different from her: they too had not lived according to their education. And as for women who worked, like her sisters, they too had labored as she had. At her healthiest moments, Mi-yŏn's Mother contrasted herself with those women, priding herself for having worked, unlike the leisured rich, and for having labored at home to manage her children's futures. She had this to say about the wealthy wives of high-level corporate officers who had been in England with her:

All of those women are highly educated—one of them even graduated from the Seoul National University department of law. They can really stand for South Korea's pretty and stylish women. But they are all exactly the same as I am. The key question is whether a person can *pursue* what they have majored in for the entire course of their lives. I really think that the happiest people on earth are those that can continue to do something with their major until they die—maybe write some reports or a book . . . In that way you can return to society what you have been given. In contemporary society, it is not ambition or desire (*yoksim*), power (*kwŏlryŏk*), or money that is really the ideal.

When I suggested to Mi-yŏn's Mother that her vision did not necessarily require education attainment, she was quick to disagree: "One really needs to have some academic experience in order to be able to find an interest like that. And you really need an education if you are going to make that interest connect to your life."

Mi-yŏn's Mother had grown ambivalent about her own children's education—unsure of the fruits of all their zeal, and of hers behind theirs. But we also know that none of these reservations stopped her from wishing that she herself might have earned a Ph.D. or from musing that the truest joy in life was the passion of the mind that she understood as part and parcel of schooling.

Mi-yŏn's Mother: Her Country, Herself

I turn now to Mi-yŏn's Mother's more overtly political thoughts: overt in the sense that they index the public world. The reader may observe that these build easily on her thinking closer to home. This convergence should not surprise: a central tenet of this book has been that people's social (justice) calculations begin at home, in and along the lines and times of families.

Throughout this book, I have stressed the public nature of women's narratives, however private they may have seemed. I have argued that their narratives speak to, and are intersected by, public narratives and ideologies, much as I have argued for the public nature of women's work in the making of class. This said, it is also the case that many of these women had their own very clear voice on unquestionably public concerns: from elections to education policies, housing to agriculture, and national unification to land policies. Here we can recall, for example, the Janitor speaking about education (chapter 4), or the Moviegoer on apartment costs and social services (chapter 6). Mi-yŏn's Mother, for her part, was an oft-commentator on the more political goings-on in her midst. And more generally, she often spoke from her own life to the fate of the nation—worried about the course of her national times. Indeed, every time we met was an occasion for Mi-yŏn's Mother to first and last confirm with me her keen sense that South Korea was up to no good, somehow headed in the wrong direction, and that South Koreans had lost their moral fiber. She even spoke of the demise of South Koreans' national character.

Many of Mi-yŏn's Mother's more overtly political thoughts drew upon observations close to home: a premise of this book is that class, for example, is developed and learned *at* home and, as we saw in chapter 8, across the lines of the extended family. Certainly, as we have already seen, she drew upon her considerable education and economic experience in crafting her sense of the social world. Foremost, perhaps, she drew upon her observations of her husband and his work. Quite simply, she understood that his career spoke to the making of the contemporary leadership class (*chido-jakŭp*). That is, she understood that it is the selfish and the immoral who have been rewarded, an understanding shared by many of the women included in this book. Broader still than the question of who occupies leadership positions in the government or corporate sector were her comments on the social structure itself. Mi-yŏn's Mother's portrait of the social world was a topsy-turvy one, as she felt that all the wrong people had risen to the top to become the wealthy and the powerful. Her own vision, though, had a strange but not illogical bedfellow: her considerable belief in open mobility, particularly through education. So, then, for Mi-yŏn's Mother, the paths to wealth and to positions of leadership were not necessarily closed (she and her husband are both cases in point: he for leadership and she for wealth), but the problem was rather the ethics of who makes it. Mi-yŏn's Mother had imagined that it was the most ethically suspect, the likes of her husband, who had risen. She never tired of detailing how effectively her husband managed to use other people, herself included. Exemplary for her was the setup that he had finessed when he had been stationed in the provinces for two years. She described his driver-maid husband-and-wife team: how well they served him and how well he handled them. When her brother, by contrast, was stationed in the provinces, he lived in tiny quarters with no help. When I suggested that this might have been due to company differences or to their relative standing in their respective companies, she insisted, rather, that it spoke to her husband's decision to use money for himself, and to his effective management of people.

In some vague sense, it seemed that Mi-yŏn's Mother harbored a romantic vision of a yesteryear in which a deserving, moral, and educated class of people (men?) was in charge. In that spirit, she wondered aloud whether democracy itself was inherently so good. She spoke about the necessary pyramid structure of society that in South Korea was instead collapsing to the middle, and she even mused about the strengths of communism (in North Korea).

> In the past there were *yangban* (hereditary elite), *sŏnbi* (scholars/gentle-
> men), and *sangnom* (derogatory term for commoners). The *yangban*
> and *sŏnbi* didn't have anything to do with work or money, so the
> people below them did all of that. But now that we are a democracy
> and supposedly everyone is equal, everything has become topsy-turvy.
> Everything is all messed up. We've taken this democratization stuff
> in the wrong direction. We've learned all the wrong things.

To say that things had become topsy-turvy, Mi-yŏn's Mother placed one hand on top of the other and then quickly reversed her hands. She struggled to imagine which societal form would promote the most ethical order, in which deserving and (properly) educated people lead society. Most of her laments in our meetings over the years had been to say that the wrong people and the wrong social vision were leading the day. That her husband's case was emblematic of South Korean society was something her sisters had never tired of telling her: that he was exactly the sort of South Korean to make it to the top. In thinking about things gone awry, the pyramid tipped or collapsed, Mi-yŏn's Mother also took hints from her childhood, imagining, for example, that those kind-hearted tutors at her rich relatives' houses (see chapter 8) had perhaps not fared so well in contemporary South Korea. It was not entirely clear, though, whether she counted her own wealthy and quite educated childhood kin as among those who would have ideally held their positions at the top of the pyramid (which, as we learned, they did not).

> These days, people have no fear of money, and you can no longer be-
> come rich just from hard work and a good salary. People don't want to
> get rich by working, but by real estate. And then others are jealous of
> them, so nobody is happy. People who used to be nothing are getting
> fat. The smart people need to be rich, but that doesn't happen. We need
> to create a new class of people who will work hard for the country.

Mi-yŏn's Mother had appreciated that in England, a nobility of sorts had seemed to have held their sway without, she gathered, any necessary interest in money. In South Korea, by contrast, she asserted that it was money that had become king. Here, we can recall Mi-yŏn's Mother's aforementioned meditations on the essence of humanity—or the bones of it all—which also wavered between a radical equality and a measurement of a man or a woman by class and family background. I am struck that in Mi-yŏn's Mother's view that the world was off-kilter, she longed both for a world in which the likes of those Hyoja-dong tutors could succeed and for a world that would have somehow saved better social positions for those from "fine" families. It is impossible to grasp the ambivalence or confusion of these reflections—or even seemingly incompatible ideological positions—without appreciating the ways in which they have been peopled by her: by the cast of characters in her immediate vicinity and the life courses they have taken. As I have stressed repeatedly, this is the landscape or relief against which the women here figured their political visions.

Mi-yŏn's Mother's political ideas were part and parcel of her sense of the West—primarily the United States—and of North Korea. She thought of the West as the source of corrupting influences—her romance with England aside. "So," she said, "educated people today know about Hemingway and Shakespeare, but we managed to live in the past without knowing all of that." In comments about North Korea, she praised communism, suggesting that "perhaps it is better—after all in a democracy who is to say that the majority is smarter?" There is no question that, having come south herself, Mi-yŏn's Mother could imagine herself elsewhere. Once she mused that had her family not come south, "I would have been North Korean today; I'd be poor." She paused, though, to say, "then again, I've known poverty here." She went on to add, though, that in spite of communism's great ideals, "in fact, people need competition" and that "furthermore, in the North it is only the elite who live well." Mi-yŏn's Mother was nonetheless steadfast in her praise for North Korea's "pure water," namely that they had not imbibed Western ways. In the case of South Korea, she foremost blamed the West for the culture of marital infidelity (hardly a historically substantiated claim), which she knew well through her husband. These somewhat disparate thoughts are thus the building blocks of a cultural geography through which Mi-yŏn's Mother perceived the world.

Mi-yŏn's Mother joined several of the other women (foremost the Moviegoer) in a vague hankering to do something for the world. In recent years, as she came to terms with the reality of her husband, she thought about taking her time and money to do something for society. As to what that might be, she was not sure—"something for the unemployed, perhaps?" She had also begun to think about directing her eldest son, in some ways the least settled in his career path, toward some sort of a social-service career: "Maybe he should stop—stop taking those tests one after another to move up a grade in the bank—and instead learn something that he can use for society. I mean, we have so many social problems—maybe he would be wiser to learn about one of those at this point." It was after her speech to this effect that she spoke about our human responsibility to set those we love on course; she assured me that she would, if she ever thought she needed to, do the same for me.

In the next and concluding chapter I reflect upon the women in this book in the light of South Korea's compressed modernity.

10

CONCLUSION
Living Through
Compressed Modernity

> Things have changed so quickly in South Korea and we have
> become rich so fast that people don't know what to do. Even
> at my level, which, of course, isn't the highest level at all—
> we're just average—when I think about it, I really don't know
> how I should live. Should I just focus on my own family?
> Or should I do something for society? Nothing is clear.
> —Mi-yŏn's Mother (November 2, 1995)

This conclusion will, I hope, answer the simplest and hardest question of all: What have this book's social mobility stories and analyses taught us about the South Korean experience of modernity? It also addresses how this book contributes more specifically to our understanding of women and class in contemporary South Korea. After braving these queries, I return to Mi-yŏn's Mother, to her thoughts on the written word, in a coda.

Compressed Modernity

If there is any consensus among scholars about South Korea's experience of modernity, it is about its compressed pace. Sociologist Hagen Koo writes of South Korea's modernization as "one of the swiftest and most *compressed* processes of proletarianization the world has seen" (2001, 24, emphasis added). Similarly, South Korean sociologist Kyung-Sup Chang describes it as the "most drastic and *compressed* process of national development in human history" (1999, 51, emphasis added). Finally, South Korean anthropologist and feminist activist Cho Hae-joang describes South Korea's "*compressed* rush to growth" (2000, 65, emphasis added). My point here is not to proclaim South Korea's modern development *the* most compressed, but to assert the robust consensus that indeed something very dramatic happened in South Korea.

If there is a consensus about the fact of compression, there is, as can be expected, less agreement as to what this compression has meant for the more than 47 million people who live in South Korea and again for the many South Koreans who have emigrated. For starters, much social-science literature on South Korea has not even posed such a question, instead celebrating the country's successful development. There are, however, many scholars who critique the vast celebratory literature on South Korea's compressed development or modernity by focusing on the darker side of the picture: the human costs and discontents of development (see, for example, Abelmann 1996; Cumings 1997; S. K. Kim 1997; Koo 2001; Lie 1998). It is in this vein that preeminent American historian of the Koreas Bruce Cumings remarked: "I still do not understand why the immense sacrifice that the Korean people made to drag their country kicking and screaming into the late-twentieth-century rat race should merit such uncritical, well-nigh hysterical enthusiasm from academics who presumably are not paid for their views" (1997, 384). This critical literature, although rich and varied in its own right, has been best at capturing economic and political costs (from poverty to labor exploitation) and at documenting the many popular political and economic struggles of the postliberation decades.

The women the reader has met here, however, are not the obvious subjects of the literature that challenges development. They neither stand for South Korea's most economically or politically dispossessed, nor are they activists or even affiliated with any activist organization. On both of these counts, however, they join the vast majority of South Koreans: neither exceptionally poor nor particularly politically active (see S. Moon 2002).

This book, then, contributes differently to the understanding of South Korea's compressed modernity. It contributes by paying attention foremost to the experience of compressed modernity in terms of a structure of feeling (R. Williams 1973) or taste (Bakhtin 1981), as described in chapter 1. I have asserted that the social mobility stories of this book capture the sensibility of an era and a generation of women who have lived their lives through this compressed modernity. What, then, is that taste, feeling, or sensibility? The answer, not surprisingly: the melodrama of mobility. Melodrama was discussed in chapter 1 to suggest that its mode reveals the feeling of living through recent South Korean history. Melodrama works for places and times like postcolonial South Korea because it poses questions that make sense, because it preserves the tension and ambivalence of daily life, and because it opens conversation. To recall, it helps people to wonder: Could it really have been like that? Is this-or-that her fault or the fault of her place and times? Are private worlds ever really so private? Who is to say who is a good or bad person? What is the right way to live? And so on. Compressed modernity has, I submit, engendered precisely these sorts of questions.

In her article titled provocatively " 'You are entrapped in an imaginary well': the formation of subjectivity within compressed development—a feminist critique of modernity and Korean culture," Cho Hae-joang suggests that South Korea's compressed development and its attendant "busy lifestyle" have diminished people's "capacity for thinking" or "self-reflection." She goes on: "The busier people are, the more convenient it is to think in terms of *dichotomies.* Men and women, adults and children, our people and your people . . . those who took piano lessons as a child and those who did not" (2000, 55, emphasis added). Needless to say, these are dramatic assertions. Cho is a cultural and social critic in and of South Korea whom I have long admired; I take her assertions seriously. But I beg to differ. Throughout this book I have argued that the women featured here are speaking in *anything but* dichotomies. Do I mean, then, to say that in South Korea there are no—or have never been—"speakers of dichotomy"? No. Certainly there is considerable rhetoric, both personal and political, that fixes the world in just such a way, but this by no means prevails in these women's talk about the world.

With this assertion in mind, let me quickly review. In chapter 1, the idea of melodrama was introduced through one woman's story to say that in every element of her telling, the Education Mother resisted easy classification or conclusion. Introductions in chapter 2 to the women in this book, demonstrate how difficult it is to place them in any fixed class position or space. Chapter 3 asserts that words are sites of powerful contests and that their meanings are hard to pin down; as such, I offered that women were using these words to contest any simple understanding or fixing of their worlds, and in some cases to powerfully critique those worlds. Chapter 4 maintains that discussions with these women were hardly conclusive about education and what it takes to succeed at it, what it promises those who do succeed, or how it should ideally be configured. Chapter 5 made the point that statistical realities of mobility in South Korea and subjective perceptions of the opportunity for mobility are inextricable so as to confuse any easy or dichotomous thinking. Chapter 6 extended my first chapter's claims about melodrama: that the personal and the social (or the domestic and the political) are enmeshed and no clear dichotomies are to be found there either. Likewise in chapter 7, prevailing social discourses on men are shown to disallow facile dichotomous gender thinking or attribution. Women's talk about their kin in chapter 8 stressed the ambivalent world of class distinction within the family. And finally, chapter 9 showed the rather constant disruption or even betrayal of Mi-yŏn's Mother's stories. Thus, I have argued not only for the disruption of dichotomies in a theoretical vein but asserted that such is the work and effect of these women's talk and meaning-making.

Having defended that these women do not speak in dichotomies, do I mean then to assert this with wild enthusiasm or optimism? Not necessarily. For one thing, I am no believer in the personal comfort of deep-seated ambivalence; I think that the experience of compressed modernity has been difficult for many people. For another, I do not take complexity or ambivalence to be necessarily politically progressive or productive. The reader will have no doubt noted many conservative thoughts that run through these women's talk, from critiques of working mothers to criticisms of women not submissive to their husbands and of divorce. But, contra Cho's assertions above, I think that the women in this book have an enormous "capacity for self-reflection."

Speaking to an important paradox, the women in this book reveal that their lives have seen both so much change and so much constancy. In discussing the 1990s in chapter 1, I underscored the repeated political disappointments over the course of South Korea's modernity: that so often the promise of real or radical reform has been dashed. On the one hand, these women have had to adjust to many changed aspects of daily life—from its material to its ethical aspects. On the other hand, there are some political and economic aspects of South Korea that have remained much the same. This paradox does not make for easy sorting of the world, and it is in this context that words, stories, and lives have stubbornly resisted uniform meaning which, as suggested in chapter 1, makes for the sort of theorizers that we find in these women (Gwaltney 1980; Lemert 1993).

Class has been at the heart of this paradox—for the melodrama of mobility aside, much remains unchanged. Despite some robust ideologies that assert to the contrary, such as the celebration of unbridled mobility or the assertion of a meritocracy, much of the character of social stratification has held constant. On the matter of mobility, I am perhaps more conservative than many observers of South Korea who put great emphasis on South Korea's post–Korean War level playing field both because of the Korean War and land reform (Cumings 1997, 270, 301; Lie 1998, 7–14, 52). While there is no question that many have found themselves in new situations, as argued in chapter 5, there has been in fact much less relative mobility. That is, the inequality of people's comparative chances of mobility has changed very little, different from structural changes of the labor market in which, for example, more people come to occupy nonmanual positions. What all of this means, simply, is that the women in this book are right to intermittently feel that not much in the way of their circumstances or chances in relation to those of other people has changed.

Class identifications have, in this paradoxical context, been just as hard to pin down. Origins and destinations—critical to class identifications—have hardly stood still for the women in this book. In chapter 1, I turned to theorists of class who refuse hard-and-fast distinction between objectivism and subjectivism. The reader can recall Bourdieu's idea that the subjective is always already part of the objective: that alongside the structural factors— labor markets, incomes—are the subjective evaluations and identifications such that human lives, identities, and relations can never derive from "objective" structures, and class is made and always in flux (Katznelson 1986; E. P. Thompson 1968). To these understandings, I also introduced several thinkers on human development to appreciate that these subjective processes happen in the context of, and over the course of, the familial, intergenerational nexus (see, for example, Bertaux 1981; Steedman 1986). Class identities, then, are inextricable from what happens to people in families and to the manner in which they recall and reconstruct their childhoods. With enormous flux of both structural features, such as the shape of the labor market or the GNP per capita, and subjective features, including the simultaneous confidence in open mobility and sense of inequality of opportunity, or the coexistence of belief in political and economic reform and disappointment when these reforms seem to change so little, many people's class identifications have been in flux. The reader has seen such shifting identifications in the course of even single conversations, like that of the Janitor describing her sons' education in chapter 4, or over the course of conversations: the Laundress on her own achievements, in chapter 5; Hyemin's Grandmother on her rural sisters-in-law, in chapter 8; or Mi-yŏn's Mother on her own social location, in chapters 8 and 9.

In spite of my commitment to a perspective on class as made and in flux, at many points in this book, I have seemed to unquestioningly employ the language of class, for example "middle" or "working class"; alas, it is a language difficult to avoid (for a sustained ethnographic study that is more careful in this vein, see Hartigan 1999). Of course, South Koreans employ a language of class themselves, as do most of the world's people. Indeed, the idiom of class has its own social life, one that often preexists any one or another analyst's hand at things (Urciuoli 1993). Although I think that I have at many points fallen prey to language that renders class too simply, statically, and uniformly, I nonetheless am hopeful that the lives and narratives of the women who have figured here are poignant reminders that class is made of relations and identifications spun of human thread and that talk itself can be taken as one such critical strand. Here the reader can recall discussions in the introduction that challenge conventional ways in which social groups are understood. There I argued for an appreciation of narrative's central role in the making of networks and groups (Kelleher 2000, 2003; Somers 1994; H. C. White 1992).

Certainly, for South Korea these sorts of ambivalent and shifting identifications have mattered for thinking about groups, group identifications, and the engine of social change. For even only the last fifteen years, class or political identifications have been unstable. Notable in this regard, for example, have been the seemingly rapid retreat of white-collar sympathy in the interests of labor after 1987; mid-1990s class solidarity around white-collar unionizing (e.g., of teachers); workers' identifications with the middle class into the 1990s resulting in the wane of union activity; or, again, the enormous challenges posed to middle-class identities with the IMF Crisis, in which many people's economic circumstances and horizons were suddenly and drastically transformed (Koo 1999, 2001). It is clear that at various points in South Korea's recent past, working-class, middle-class, and shared middle-working-class identifications (or consciousness) have mattered enormously. These identifications have been critical to groundswells of human energy that have called for and achieved progressive change, be it in April 1960 against the Rhee Regime; in May 1980 against Chun Doo Hwan's military takeover; in June 1987, calling for democracy; or later that 1987 summer, calling for labor reform; or in January 1997, for labor reform again.

The paradox I have been describing—the simultaneous sense of constancy and constant change—must also be understood in terms of South Korea's ambivalent relationships to the West. This ambivalence is further complicated because of the particular relationship of the South Korean elite to the West. On the one hand, elites have been handmaidens in the project of Western modernity. On the other hand, South Korean state nationalism has at many points circled the Korean cultural wagons, proclaiming the superiority of things Korean. How, then, have nonelite South Koreans posed themselves vis-à-vis the West? Critical here is the absence of a bourgeois hegemony: unlike the West, "South Korea's civil society arose not under the leadership of the bourgeoisie, but in opposition to it" (Koo 1999, 58; see also Eckert 1993). Across the narratives in this book we find both considerable disdain for the "elite" and aspirations for the trappings of the materially privileged. Here the reader will also recall many of the women's ambivalence about Western social and cultural norms and practices (e.g., Mi-yŏn's Mother on her husband's "American-style personality," or "Americans who only care about the insides of their apartments"; the Janitor's proclamations about a college education not mattering in the West; or the Education Mother's comments on the differences of a woman getting educated in the United States). K. S. Chang summarizes the ambivalence about the West this way:

> After all, the Westernization paradigm was historically oppressive to grassroots Koreans: the Japanese and the American colonial governments coercively transplanted it without much consultation with Koreans and, subsequently, the South Korean ruling elite ordered them to accept all the social, political and economic conditions for it . . . Neither their implicit consensus on growing out of the not-so-glorious past nor their actual pursuit of Western systems led to a national consensus on, or valuing of, Westernization (1999, 50).

At the heart of this ambivalence about the West (and the elite) have been women and the family. The cultural nationalism I have just described, as the reader might recall from chapter 7, is often virulently conservative— particularly concerning women and the family. In this regard, the reader may recall many of the women extolling the virtues of women at home and singularly devoted to their children and husbands—against a vague sense of Western ways or values. The Confucian revivalism, both preceding and heightened into the IMF Crisis—among other things, decrying "family breakdown" (J. Song 2002) and championing the somewhat mythical extended Korean family (K. S. Chang 1997)—has relied on a chauvinistic, essentialist portrayal of Koreanness (H. J. Cho 1998a, 2001; Robinson 1991). I am grateful to a number of Koreanists who have been wonderfully attentive to the ways in which "Confucianism" and "the family" (as two key tenets of social and cultural conservatism) have been carefully and repeatedly rein-vented. These observers warn us to be careful not to assume that such dis-courses refer to real social practices either in the past or the present (see in particular K. S. Chang 1997; Janelli and Yim 1993, chapter 1; and Kendall 1996, chapter 3). Here I would have to agree with Cho, about dichotomous thinking, in that the women in this book do intermittently employ these sorts of essential cultural narratives or distinctions. But I would stress that they do so intermittently, unevenly and—most importantly—critically. Just as readers might bristle at a "traditional" or neo-traditional moment in one or another woman's conversation, the talk shifts. I hope that I have suffi-ciently underscored these sorts of shifts across the landscape of the talk of the women in this book.

For Whom Do They Stand?

Having considered the sources of these women's capacity for self-reflec-tion, the reader still wonders about these women's representativeness. How representative, for example, are their complex class identifications, their ambivalent evocation of the West, or their engagement with conservative gender discourses? Do I take this capacity to simply speak to the shared ex-perience of compressed modernity of their generation? Or is this capacity, this experience, somehow uniquely gendered? As I asserted in this book's opening pages, ethnography is always vexed on the matter of representa-tiveness. Put simply, for whom and for what can the women featured here speak or stand? Alternatively, we may pose the question this way: Why is it that these women of this generation have sensed and spoken about the world in these particular ways? Here I leave the province of my fieldwork and can only speak with considerable caution.

I do think that the sensibilities portrayed in this book are gendered. Gender matters everywhere, and it certainly has for women of this genera-tion, whose social roles and horizons have been sizeably scripted and con-strained for being women. So too does their generation matter because they have lived through the experiences of colonialism, a major war, national di-vision, the mobilization of the population in the name of development and anticommunism and so on; and because they are keenly aware of the para-dox on which I began this chapter.

If I have hemmed these women narrowly, let me now proceed otherwise. Perhaps larger than the question of these women's representativeness is that of their contribution. I have suggested that for their critical role as talkers and caretakers in and about family and social life, the women of this generation have made a particular contribution to the sensibilities—class among them—of their place and times. These women have had an important hand in the narrative constitution of social life. Namely, in their narration of how they have understood their own lives and the lives near to theirs, both along and beyond the lines of kinship, they have made critical contributions to shaping the very ways in which South Koreans understand themselves. My hunch, however, is that twenties-something South Korean young men and women—let alone teenagers—would likely find many of the struggles of the women in this book quite remote from their own lives. Nonetheless, this is not to say that the contours, idioms, and feel of these women's struggles would be entirely unfamiliar to young South Koreans. As I have repeatedly asserted, sea changes do not take place in such a tidy fashion: they tack this way and that, leaving all of us a bit betwixt and between. It is in this sense that I am not willing to limit the words, stories, and sensibilities of the women of the generation featured here to an isolated generational moment. And, it is in this sense that, at my bolder moments, I am prone to assert that these women, and others like them, have literally fashioned the prevailing sensibilities of contemporary South Korea. But as I wrote in this book's opening pages, it is the bravado of a sentence like the one I just wrote that tempts me to retreat into precisely the generational and historical specificity of the women in this book.

What I imagine, then, is young people's likely ambivalent response. I could not agree more with H. J. Cho's understanding that the experience of compressed modernity puts a particular strain between the generations (2002). For my part, I remain most at home with South Koreans of the generation that figures in this book and with that of their children (thirty- and forty-something)—children who lived through the 1980s as young adults (and are my own contemporaries). As for those who came of age in the 1990s—the South Korean contemporaries of my students at the University of Illinois at Urbana-Champaign, some of them recent immigrants from South Korea—I am a bit at sea. Having watched some of the films that this generation has made blockbusters of, leaves me only more perplexed. At first glance it seems that these films have been cut from a whole other cloth. But this exceeds a discussion of South Korea because my late-teen and twenty-something non-Korean students are also entirely at home with these films. But then, just as I have settled into declarations of generational difference today, some of these films digress or flash back to reveal structures of feeling that would find easy company in this book (e.g., Chuyuso sŭpkyŏk *sagŏn* [Attack at the gas station] 1999, directed by Kim Sang-jin). Does this surprise me? No. South Korea remains the hurried outcome of compressed modernity. It also remains a divided nation and one struggling with considerable political, economic, and cultural sea changes. I do not underscore these features of South Korea to suggest its uniqueness in the world of nations or the singularity of its people. Quite to the contrary, the ambivalence I portray here is, I think, the modern rule, not exception. The "complex personhood" described by Gordon in her quote beginning chapter 9 is by no means South Koreans' alone (1997, 4).

No doubt South Korea will continue to change. No doubt some South Koreans will continue to sense that less has really changed than some will have asserted. No doubt many South Koreans will continue to see their interests and identifications anew. And certainly, in the midst of all this, there is no doubt that talk will continue to both reflect and make the day, in the sense in which Bakhtin wrote (1981). If South Korea's experience of modernity has been compressed—as indeed it has—and in turn, entirely enmeshed in global processes, it is nonetheless a modernity fashioned locally and particularly (Koo 1999, 63–64). To that locality and particularity, this book has offered the talk and stories of a generation of South Korean women. This book opened with a gorgeous passage from Zora Neale Hurston's *Their Eyes Were Watching God*, a passage about a woman, Janie, who had "tried to show her shine" against all odds, against having had the horizon—"the biggest thing God ever made"—choked about her ([1937] 1990, 85–86). I continue to marvel at how the women in this book have been able to shine—to take back the horizon.

CODA

> Memory . . . is no longer the narrative of external adventures
> stretching along episodic time. It is itself the spiral movement
> that, through anecdotes and episodes, brings us back to the almost
> motionless constellation of potentialities that the narrative retrieves.
> The end of the story is what equates the present with the past, the
> actual with the potential. The hero is who he was.
>
> —Paul Ricoeur, On Narrative

From their very start to their final finish, all books are a collection of words—a prosaic thought indeed. This one has also paid attention to the work of words themselves. As I have written earlier, all of the women in this book considered their lives worthy of the written word. We could ask of them, "Worthy in what sense?" Although I do not presume that all of their answers would be the same, I think there would be common themes: among them their lives having been hard and their having been witness to earth-shattering transformations in the world about them. I return to words I borrowed from John Langston Gwaltney in chapter 1 to suggest that their lives have made theorists of them: "principled survival in a familial and communal context . . . is a preeminently analytical process" (1980, xxx). All of the women here are trying to, in the words of Laurel Kendall, a long-term anthropological observer of South Korea, "get a grip" on the vertigo of South Korean (post)modernity (2002, 3).

When it's all said and done, it has been the premise of this book that these women's words can help us to get a grip on that vertigo, to theorize and begin to comprehend it. It is in the service of that goal that I have used their words and stories. I left much of Mi-yŏn's Mother's words and stories for this book's final ethnographic chapter because, as I wrote in chapter 9, her reflective voice goes so very far for my aims in this work. Eloquent on so many matters, Mi-yŏn's Mother not surprisingly had also thought deeply about the written word. In 1993 toward the end of my 1992–1993 field research, Mi-yŏn's Mother spoke about the falsity of writing, a falsity that she described had kept her from writing—in spite of a deep desire to do so:

> My Big Mother also wrote letters. And she was good at that too. I want to write letters but I have a problem with them. When I think about the vast distance between the reality of my married life and the love letters that my husband wrote me, I can't help but mistrust the written word. I would also like to keep a diary, but in the early years of my marriage I looked at my husband's diary and found nothing there but criticisms of my laziness and other negative traits. That made me crazy and it made me hate the written word. I hate writing because of its falsity.

In 1995 Mi-yŏn's Mother spoke again about writing, this time saying that she would love to write down her thoughts but that she did not have a talent (*chaeju*) for writing. Within moments, however, leaving the matter of her talent behind, she spoke again about her husband:

> My husband really ruined the idea of leaving things in writing for me because in the early days of our marriage he would write down all of his frustrations with me and leave them lying around for me to see. My blood boiled at the things he had written. I felt that I never wanted to leave anything in this world on paper. But in the last few years, I have wanted to write things down.

Mi-yŏn's mother once told me about some of the things that she had started to jot down after she dropped her husband off at the train station—at the time he was commuting to a branch office in a regional city. She had, however, been so unsatisfied with what she had written that she ended up tearing it up. She told me about three of the thoughts she had wanted to put down on paper that day.

> One was about a feeling that came to me when I was driving. I suddenly realized the grace (*ŭnch'ong*) of God: that the same sunlight shines down on the beggar, the man in jail, the president, on everyone, just that same—that is the grace of God.

Another was about our need to return to nature.

And another was that God links people's pasts, presents, and futures. But, all of us, we get so caught up in the present.

It is not Mi-yŏn's Mother's seemingly sudden evocation of God that interests me here. Her stories have revealed a life of so much activity and work: a life lived very much in the present and deeply engaged in the social work of class and difference, in the discernment of infinitesimal social differences. I have taken Mi-yŏn's Mother and the other women in this book to speak for the structure of feeling of lives lived in the vortex of transformation, to speak for the melodrama of mobility. These thoughts that Mi-yŏn's Mother wanted to write down (and did) are transcendent. These are thoughts that step back to take stock of it all—self-reflective thoughts; and they are thoughts that unbridle themselves from the immediacy of the moment—from that "present" that she spoke of, and of which Ricouer wrote (1981, 182). In meeting Mi-yŏn's Mother and all of the women in this book, and in hearing quite a bit of their discerning and discriminating talk, I hope that the reader has also come to appreciate that transcendence is no stranger to the structure of feeling of contemporary South Korea.

Mi-yŏn's Mother's thoughts on writing give me pause, for I have just left so many women's words—and *so many of hers*—on paper. With Mikhail Bakhtin, whose thoughts on words I discussed in the introduction, Mi-yŏn's Mother appreciated the extent to which words are loaded, shot through with all that is the social world. Mine are not meant to offer the final word. If they have been of service to the project of getting a feeling for a place, time, and generation, I am satisfied.

REFERENCES

Abbott, Pamela, and Roger Sapsford. 1987. *Women and Social Class.* New York: Tavistock Publications.

Abelmann, Nancy. 1996. *Echoes of the Past, Epics of Dissent: A South Korean Social Movement.* Berkeley: University of California Press.

———. 1997a. Narrating Selfhood and Personality in South Korea: Women and Social Mobility. *American Ethnologist* 24 (4): 784–812.

———. 1997b. Women's Class Mobility and Identities in South Korea: A Gendered, Transgenerational, Narrative Approach. *The Journal of Asian Studies* 56 (2): 398–420.

———. 2002. Women, Mobility, and Desire: Narrating Class and Gender in South Korea. In *Under Construction: The Gendering of Modernity, Class, and Consumption in the Republic of Korea,* ed. L. Kendall, 25–53. Honolulu: University of Hawai'i Press.

Abelmann, Nancy, and John Lie. 1995. *Blue Dreams: Korean Americans and the Los Angeles Riots.* Cambridge: Harvard University Press.

Abu-Lughod, Lila. 1993. *Writing Women's Worlds: Bedouin Stories.* Berkeley: University of California Press.

———. 1995. The Objects of Soap Opera: Egyptian Television and the Cultural Politics of Modernity. In *Worlds Apart: Modernity Through the Prison of the Local,* ed. D. Miller. London: Routledge.

———. 1997. The Interpretation of Culture(s) After Television. *Representations* 59: 109–134.

———. 2000. Modern Subjects: Egyptian Melodrama and Postcolonial Difference. In *Questions of Modernity,* ed. T. Mitchell, 87–114. Minneapolis: University of Minnesota Press.

Abu-Lughod, Lila, and Catherine A. Lutz. 1990. Introduction: Emotion, Discourse, and the Politics of Everyday Life. In *Language and the Politics of Emotion,* ed. C. A. Lutz and L. Abu-Lughod, 1–23. New York: Cambridge University Press.

Allen, Robert. 1995. *To be Continued . . . Soap Operas Around the World.* New York: Routledge.

Amsden, Alice. 1989. *Asia's New Giant: South Korea and Late Industrialization*. New York: Oxford University Press.

An, Jinsoo. 1998. Anxiety and Laughter in Korean Comedy Films. In *Post-Colonial Classics of Korean Cinema*, ed. C. Choi, 31–38. Irvine: Korean Film Festival Committee at the University of California, Irvine.

———. n.d. Screening the Redemption: Christianity in Korean Melodrama. In *Gender, Genre, and National Cinema: South Korean Golden Age Melodrama*, ed. K. McHugh and N. Abelmann. Forthcoming.

Ang, Ien. [1982] 1985. *Watching Dallas*. London: Metheun.

Ang, Ien, and Jon Stratton. 1995. The End of Civilization as We Knew It: Chances and the Postrealist Soap Opera. In *To be Continued . . . Soap Operas Around the World*, ed. R. Allen, 122–144. New York: Routledge.

Appadurai, Arjun. 1991. Global Ethnoscapes: Notes for a Transnational Anthropology. In *Recapturing Anthropology*, ed. R. G. Fox, 191–210. Santa Fe: School of American Research Press.

Armstrong, Nancy. 1987. *Desire and Domestic Fiction: A Political History of the Novel*. New York: Oxford University Press.

Bakhtin, Mikhail. 1981. *The Dialogic Imagination: Four Essays*. Trans. C. Emerson and M. Holquist. Austin: University of Texas Press.

Battaglia, Debbora. 1995. Problematizing the Self. In *Rhetorics of Self-Making*, ed. D. Battaglia, 1–15. Berkeley: University of California Press.

Bertaux, Daniel. 1981. Introduction. In *Biography and Society: The Life History Approach in Social Sciences*, ed. D. Bertaux, 1–15. Beverly Hills, Calif.: Sage Publications.

———. 1994. The Anthroponomic Revolution: First Sketch of a Worldwide Process. *Annals: International Institute of Sociology* 4:177–192.

———. 1995. Social Genealogies Commented On and Compared: An Instrument for Observing Social Mobility Processes in the "Longue Durée." *Current Sociology* 43:69–88.

Bertaux, Daniel, and Paul Thompson. 1993. Introduction. In *International Yearbook of Oral History and Life Stories*. Vol. 2 of *Between Generations: Family Models, Myths, and Memories*, ed. D. Bertaux and P. Thompson, 1–12. Oxford: Oxford University Press.

———. 1997. Introduction. In *Pathways to Social Class: A Qualitative Approach to Social Mobility*, ed. D. Bertaux and P. Thompson, 1–31. Oxford: Clarendon Press.

Bertaux-Wiame, Isabelle, and Paul Thompson. 1997. The Familial Meaning of Housing in Social Rootedness and Mobility: Britain and France. In *Pathways to Social Class*, ed. D. Bertaux and P. Thompson, 124–182. Oxford: Clarendon Press.

Bhabha, Homi. 1994. Between Identities (Interviewed by Paul Thompson). In *Migration and Identity*. International Yearbook of Oral History and Life Stories, vol. 3, ed. R. Benmayor and A. Skotnes, 184–199. New York: Oxford University Press.

Bourdieu, Pierre. 1985. The Social Space and the Genesis of Groups. *Theory and Society* 14 (6): 723–744.

———. 1987. What Makes a Social Class? On the Theoretical and Practical Existence of Groups. *Berkeley Journal of Sociology* 32:1–17.

———. 1990. Social Space and Symbolic Power. In *In Other Words: Essays Towards a Reflective Sociology*. Stanford: University of Stanford Press.

Brandt, Vincent. 1980. Some Factors Associated with Social Mobility Among Migrant Squatters in Korea. In Papers of the First International Conference on Korean Studies, pp. 1207–1226. Sŏngnam, Korea: The Academy of Korean Studies.

———. [1971] 1990. *A Korean Village: Between Farm and Sea*. Prospect Heights, Ill.: Waveland Press, Inc.

Briggs, Charles L. 1986. *Learning How to Ask: A Sociolinguistic Appraisal of the Role of the Interview in Social Science Research*. Cambridge: Cambridge University Press.

Brooks, Peter. [1976] 1995. *The Melodramatic Imagination: Balzac, Henry James, Melodrama, and the Mode of Excess*. New Haven, Conn.: Yale University Press.

Bruner, Edward. 1986. Experience and Its Expressions. In *The Anthropology of Experience*, ed. V. W. Turner and E. M. Bruner, 3–30. Urbana: University of Illinois Press.

Bruner, Jerome. 1986. *Actual Minds, Possible Worlds*. Cambridge: Harvard University Press.

———. 1994. The "Remembered" Self. In *The Remembering Self: Construction and Accuracy in the Self-Narrative*, ed. U. Neisser and R. Fivush, 41–54. New York: Cambridge University Press.

Carsten, Janet. 2000. *Cultures of Relatedness: New Approaches to the Study of Kinship*. New York: Cambridge University Press.

Chang, Kyung-Sup. 1997. The Neo-Confucian Right and Family Politics in South Korea: The Nuclear Family as an Ideological Construct. *Economy and Society* 26 (1): 22–42.

———. 1999. Compressed Modernity and its Discontents: South Korean Society in Transition. *Economy and Society* 28 (1): 30–55.

Chang, Yunshik. 1991. The Personalist Ethic and the Market in Korea. *Comparative Studies in Society and History* 33:106–129.

Cho, Eunsun. n.d. The Stray Bullet and the Crisis of Korean Masculinity. In *Gender, Genre, and National Cinema: South Korean Golden Age Melodrama*, ed. K. McHugh and N. Abelmann. Forthcoming.

Cho Hae-joang. 1988. *Han'guk ŭi yŏsŏng kwa namsŏng* (Korean men and women). Seoul: Munhak kwa Chisŏng.

———. 1995. Children in the Examination War in South Korea: A Cultural Analysis. In *Children and the Politics of Culture*, ed. Sharon Stephens, 141–168. Princeton: Princeton University Press.

———. 1998a. Constructing and Deconstructing "Koreanness." In *Making Majorities: Constituting the Nation in Japan, Korea, China, Malaysia, Fiji, Turkey, and the United States*, ed. D. C. Gladney, 73–91. Stanford: Stanford University Press.

———. 1998b. Male Dominance and Mother Power: The Two Sides of Confucian Patriarchy in Korea. In *Confucianism and the Family*, ed. W. H. Slote and G. A. DeVos, 187–207. New York: State University of New York Press.

———. 2000. "You are entrapped in an imaginary well": the formation of subjectivity within compressed development—a feminist critique of modernity and Korean culture. Trans. M. Shin. *Inter-Asia Cultural Studies* 1 (1): 49–69.

———. 2001. Sopyonje: Its Cultural and Historical Meaning. In *Im Kwon-Taek: The Making of a Korean National Cinema*, ed. D. E. James and K. H. Kim, 134–156. Detroit, Mich.: Wayne State University Press.

———. 2002. Living with Conflicting Subjectivities: Mother, Motherly Wife, and Sexy Woman in the Transition from Colonial-Modern to Post-Modern Korea. In *Under Construction: The Gendering of Modernity, Class, and Consumption in the Republic of Korea*, ed. L. Kendall, pp. 164–194. Honolulu: Hawai'i University Press.

Cho, Hee-yeon. 2000. The Structure of South Korean Developmental Regime and Its Transformation—Statist Mobilization and Authoritarian Integration in the Anticommunist Regimentation. *Inter-Asia Cultural Studies* 1 (3): 408–426.

Cho, Ŭn. 1990. "Han'guk sahoe esŏ ŭi sŏng kwa kyegŭp: sŏng punjŏljŏk kyegŭp kujo wa kyegŭp punsŏk e taehan siron" (Gender and class in Korean society: a thesis on gender-stratified class structure and class analysis). In *Han'guk sahoe ŭi pip'anjŏk insik* (A critical reflection on Korean society), ed. Han'guk Sahoehakhoe, 257–298. Seoul: Nanam.

Choi, Chungmoo, ed. 1997. Special Issue: The Comfort Women. *Positions: East Asia Cultures Critique* 5(1).

———. 1998. The Magic and Violence of Modernization in Post-Colonial Korea. In *Post-Colonial Classics of Korean Cinema*, ed. C. Choi, 5–12. Irvine: Korean Film Festival Committee at the University of California, Irvine.

Choi, Jang Jip. 1993. Political Cleavages in South Korea. In *State and Society in Contemporary Korea*, H. Koo, 13–50. Ithaca: Cornell University Press.

Choi, Jung-Ah. 2002. Classed Schooling, Classless Identity: Schooling Experiences of Returning Dropouts in South Korea. Ph.D. diss., University of Illinois at Urbana-Champaign.

Chŏn, Kwang-hŭi, and T'ae-hwan Kwŏn. 1991. In'gu idong kwa sahoe idong (Population mobility and social mobility). In *Sahoe kyech'ŭng: Iron kwa silche* (Social stratification: theory and reality), ed. S. N. U. S. Yŏn'guhoe, 531–549. Seoul: Tasan Publishers.

Chung, Hye Seung. n.d. Toward a Strategic South Korean Cinephilia: A Transnational Détournement of Hollywood Melodrama. In *Gender, Genre, and National Cinema: South Korean Golden Age Melodrama*, ed. K. McHugh and N. Abelmann. Forthcoming.

Cisneros, Sandra. [1981] 1991. *The House on Mango Street*. New York: Vintage Books.

Clifford, James. 1986. Introduction: Partial Truths. In *Writing Culture: The Poetics and Politics of Ethnography*, ed. J. Clifford and G. E. Marcus, 1–26. Berkeley: University of California Press.

Cotton, James, and Kim Hyung-a van Leest. 1996. The New Rich and the New Middle Class in South Korea: The Rise and Fall of the Golf Republic. In *The New Rich in Asia: Mobile Phones, McDonalds and Middle-Class Revolution*, ed. R. Robinson and D. S. G. Goodman, 185–203. New York: Routledge.

Crapanzano, Vincent. 1980. *Tuhami: Portrait of a Moroccan*. Chicago: University of Chicago Press.

———. 1992. *Hermes' Dilemma and Hamlet's Desire: On the Epistemology of Interpretation*. Cambridge: Harvard University Press.

Crompton, Rosemary. 1993. *Class and Stratification: An Introduction to Current Debates*. Cambridge, Mass.: Polity Press.

Cumings, Bruce. 1981. *The Origins of the Korean War: Liberation and the Emergence of Separate Regimes*. Princeton: Princeton University Press.

———. 1997. *Korea's Place in the Sun: A Modern History*. New York: W. W. Norton and Company.

———. 2002. Colonial Formations and Deformations: Korea, Taiwan, and Vietnam. In *Parallax Visions: Making Sense of American–East Asian Relations at the End of the Century*, ed. B. Cumings, 69–94. Durham, N.C.: Duke University Press.

Deuchler, Martina. 1977. The Tradition: Women During the Yi Dynasty. In *Virtues in Conflict: Tradition and the Korean Woman Today*, ed. S. Mattielli, 1–48. Seoul: Royal Branch of the Asiatic Society.

Dissanayake, Wimal. 1993. Introduction. In *Melodrama and Asian Cinema*, ed. W. Dissanayake, 1–9. New York: Cambridge University Press.

Dorfman, Ariel. 1991. Someone Writes to the Future: Meditations on Hope and Violence in García Márquez. In *Some Write to the Future: Essays on Contemporary Latin American Fiction*, ed. A. Dorfman, 201–222. Durham, N.C.: Duke University Press.

Eckert, Carter. 1993. The South Korean Bourgeoisie: A Class in Search of Hegemony. In *State and Society in Contemporary Korea*, ed. H. Koo, 95–130. Ithaca: Cornell University Press.

Elder, Glen H. Jr. 1974. *Children of the Great Depression: Social Change in Life Experiences*. Chicago: University of Chicago Press.

Elsaesser, Thomas. [1972] 1987. Tales of Sound and Fury: Observations on the Family Melodrama. In *Home is Where the Heart Is: Studies in Melodrama and the Woman's Film*, ed. C. Gledhill, 43–69. London: British Film Institute.

Em, Henry. 1993. Overcoming Korea's Division: Narrative Strategies in Recent South Korean Historiography. *Positions: East Asia Cultures Critique* 1 (2): 450–485.

———. 1995. Yi Sang's "Wings" Read as an Anti-colonial Allegory. *Muae* 1:105–111.

Fabian, Johannes. 1983. *Time and the Other: How Anthropology Makes Its Object*. New York: Columbia University Press.

Featherman, David L., F. Lancaster Jones, and Robert M. Hauser. 1975. Assumptions of Social Mobility Research in the U.S.: The Case of Occupational Status. *Social Science Research* 4:329–360.

Flanagan, Owen, and Amélie Oksenberg Rorty. 1990. Introduction. In *Identity, Character, and Morality: Essays in Moral Psychology*, ed. O. Flanagan and A. O. Rorty, 1–15. Cambridge: MIT Press.

Foucault, Michel. 1972. *The Archaeology of Knowledge*. New York: Harper and Row.

Freire, Paulo. 1996. *Letters to Cristina: Reflections on My Life and Work*. New York: Routledge.

Frye, Northrop. 1964. The Motive for Metaphor. In *The Educated Imagination*. Bloomington: Indiana University Press.

Giddens, Anthony. 1973. *The Class Structure of the Advanced Societies*. London: Hutchinson University Library.

Ginsburg, Faye D. 1989. *Contested Lives: The Abortion Debate in an American Community*. Berkeley: University of California Press.

Glaser, Barney G., and Anselm L. Strauss. 1971. *Status Passage*. Chicago: Aldine Atherton.

Gledhill, Christine. 1987. The Melodramatic Field: An Investigation. In *Home Is Where the Heart Is: Studies in Melodrama and the Woman's Film*, ed. C. Gledhill, 5–39. London: British Film Institute.

Goldthorpe, John H. 1983. Women and Class Analysis: In Defense of the Conventional View. *Sociology* 17 (4): 465–488.

Goldthorpe, John H., with Catriona Llewellyn and Clive Payne. 1980. *Social Mobility and Class Structure in Modern Britain*. Oxford: Clarendon Press.

Good, Mary-Jo DelVecchio, and Byron Good. 1988. Ritual, the State, and the Transformation of Emotional Discourse in Iranian Society. *Culture, Medicine and Psychiatry* 12:43–63.

Gordon, Avery F. 1997. *Ghostly Matters: Haunting and the Sociological Imagination*. Minneapolis: University of Minnesota Press.

Grinker, Richard Roy. 1998. *Korea and Its Futures: Unification and the Unfinished War*. New York: St. Martin's Press.

Gwaltney, John Langston. 1980. *Drylongso: A Self-Portrait of Black America*. New York: Random House.

Haboush, JaHyun Kim. 1991. The Confucianization of Korean Society. In *The East Asian Region: Confucian Heritage and Its Modern Adaptation*, ed. G. Rozman, 84–110. Princeton: Princeton University Press.

Halbwachs, Maurice. 1950. *The Collective Memory*. New York: Harper and Row.

Hall, Catherine. 1992. *White, Male, and Middle Class: Explorations in Feminism and History*. New York: Routledge.

Hall, Stuart. 1996a. Minimal Selves. In *Black British Cultural Studies: A Reader*, ed.

J. Houston, A. Baker, Manthia Diawara, and Ruth H. Liwdeburg, 114–119. Chicago: University of Chicago Press.

———. 1996b. The Question of Cultural Identity. In *Modernity*, ed. D. H. Stuart Hall, Don Hubert, and Kenneth Thompson, 596–611. Cambridge, Mass.: Blackwell Publishers.

Han, Do-Hyun. 1993. Capitalist Landownership and State Policy in 1989–1990 in South Korea. *Korea Journal of Population and Development* 22 (2): 155–166.

Han'gŭl Hakhoe. 1992. *Uri mal k'ŭn sajŏn*. Seoul: Ŏmungak.

Hartigan, John Jr. 1999. *Racial Situations: Class Predicaments of Whiteness in Detroit*. Princeton: Princeton University Press.

Hirsch, Marianne. 1997. *Family Frames: Photography, Narrative, and Postmemory*. Cambridge: Harvard University Press.

Hong, Doo-Seung. 1999. Review of *In Pursuit of Status: The Making of South Korea's "New" Urban Middle Class*, by Denise Potrzeba Lett. *Contemporary Sociology* 28 (6): 677–678.

Hong, Doo-seung, and Hagen Koo. 1993. *Sahoe kyech'ŭng * kyegŭp non* (Social stratification * class theory). Seoul: Tasan Publishers.

Hurston, Zora Neale. [1937] 1990. *Their Eyes Were Watching God*. New York: Harper & Row.

Jager, Sheila Miyoshi. 1996a. A Vision for the Future; or, Making Family History in Contemporary South Korea. *Positions: East Asia Cultures Critique* 4 (1): 31–58.

———. 1996b. Women, Resistance and the Divided Nation: The Romantic Rhetoric of Korean Reunification. *Journal of Asian Studies* 55 (1): 3–21.

———. 2003. *Narratives of Nation-Building in Korea: A Genealogy of Patriotism*. Armonk, N.Y.: M. E. Sharpe.

Janelli, Dawnhee Yim. 1982. Faith, Fortune-telling, and Social Failure. In *Religions in Korea: Beliefs and Cultural Values*, ed. E. H. Phillips and E. Y. Yu, 59–69. Los Angeles: Center for Korean-American and Korean Studies (California State University, Los Angeles).

Janelli, Roger L., and Dawnhee Yim. n.d. South Korea's Great Transformation. In *The Cambridge History of Korea*. Vol. 4, *Modern Korea*, ed. B. Cumings. Cambridge: Cambridge University Press.

———. 1993. *Making Capitalism*. Stanford: Stanford University Press.

Jeong, Insook, and Michael J. Armer. 1994. State, Class, and Expansion of Education in South Korea: A General Model. *Comparative Education Review* 38 (4): 531–545.

Jung, Yong Duck, and Gilbert B. Siegal. 1985. Testing Perceptions of Distributive Justice in Korea. In *Administrative Dynamics and Development: The Korean Experience*, ed. B. W. Kim, J. David S. Bell, and C. B. Lee, 380–404. Seoul: Kyobo Publishing Co.

Kang, Hŭi-ch'ŏl. 2000. Hŏnpŏp chaep'anso kwawoe kŭmji ippŏp uihŏn kyŏljŏng (chaep'an'gwan 9 myŏng chung 6 myŏng) (The Supreme Court rules that the regulation against home tutoring is unconstitutional [upheld by 6 of 9 judges]). Internet Han'gyŏrye 21. April 27.

Kaplan, Ann E. 1993. Melodrama / Subjectivity / Ideology: Western Melodrama Theories and Their Relevance to Recent Chinese Cinema. In *Melodrama and Asian Cinema*, ed. W. Dissanayake, 9–28. New York: Cambridge University Press.

Katznelson, Ira. 1986. *Working-Class Formation: Nineteenth Century Patterns in Western Europe and the United States.* Princeton: Princeton University Press.

Kelleher, William F. Jr. 2000. Making Home in the Irish/British Borderlands: The Global and the Local in a Conflicted Social Space. *Identities* 7 (2): 139–172.

———. 2003. *Telling Identities: The Work of Memory in Northern Ireland.* Ann Arbor: University of Michigan Press.

Kendall, Laurel. 1985. *Shamans, Housewives, and Other Restless Spirits: Women in Korean Ritual Life.* Honolulu: University of Hawai'i Press.

———. 1988. *The Life and Hard Times of a Korean Shaman: Of Tales and the Telling of Tales.* Honolulu: University of Hawai'i Press.

———. 1996. *Getting Married in Korea: Of Gender, Morality, and Modernity.* Berkeley: University of California Press.

———. 2002. Introduction. In *Under Construction: The Gendering of Modernity, Class, and Consumption in the Republic of Korea*, ed. L. Kendall, 1–24. Honolulu: University of Hawai'i Press.

Kerckhoff, Alan C. 1989. On the Social Psychology of Social Mobility Processes. *Social Forces* 68 (1): 17–25.

Kim, Byoung-Kwan. 1993. Structural Changes and Continuity: Industrialization and Patterns of Career Occupational Mobility in Korea, 1954–1983. Ph.D. diss., Harvard University.

Kim, Byung-Kook. 2000. The Politics of Crisis and a Crisis of Politics: The Presidency of Kim Dae-Jung. In *Korea Briefing 1997–1999: Challenges and Change at the Turn of the Century*, ed. K. Oh, 35–74. Armonk, N.Y.: M. E. Sharpe, Inc.

Kim, Chong-un. 1983. Introduction. In *Postwar Korean Short Stories: An Anthology*, ed. C. U. Kim, vii–xxxviii. Honolulu: University Press of Hawai'i.

Kim, Choong Soon. 1988. *Faithful Endurance: An Ethnography of Korean Family Dispersal.* Tucson: Arizona University Press.

Kim, Dae-Il, and Robert H. Topel. 1995. Labor Market and Economic Growth: Lessons from Korea's Industrialization, 1970–1990. In *Differences and Changes in Wage Structures*, ed. R. B. Freeman and L. F. Katz, 227–264. Chicago: University of Chicago Press.

Kim, Eun Mee. 1997. *Big Business, Strong State: Collusion and Conflict in South Korean Development, 1960–1990.* New York: State University of New York Press.

Kim, Hyun Mee. 1995. Labor, Politics, and Women's Subject in Contemporary Korea. Ph.D. diss., University of Washington.

Kim, Kyung Hyun. 2002. Korean Cinema and Im Kwon-Taek: An Overview. In *Im*

Kwon-Taek: The Making of a Korean National Cinema, ed. D. E. James and K. H. Kim, 19–46. Detroit, Mich.: Wayne State University Press.

———. n.d. Lethal Work: Domestic Space and Gender Troubles in The Happy End and The Housemaid. In *Gender, Genre, and National Cinema: South Korean Golden Age Melodrama*, ed. K. McHugh and N. Abelmann. Forthcoming.

Kim, Mi-suk. 1993. Adŭl kwa ttal—chiban esŏ tŏ ttŭgŏun kŭ tŭrama (Son and daughter—more controversial drama at home). *Saemi kip'ŭn mul* (march): 146–151.

Kim, Myung-hye. 1992. Late Industrialization and Women's Work in Urban South Korea: An Ethnographic Study of Upper-Middle-Class Families. *City & Society* 6 (2): 156–173.

———. 1993. Transformation of Family Ideology in Upper-Middle-Class Families in Urban South Korea. *Ethnology* 32 (1): 69–85.

———. 1995. Gender, Class, and Family in Late-Industrializing South Korea. *Asian Journal of Women's Studies* 1:58–86.

Kim, Nan-jin. 1996. Kkum ŭl mandŭnŭn p'andora ŭi sangja (The dream-making Pandora's box). *Cine* 21 (19 March).

Kim, Seung Kyung. 1997. *Class Struggle or Family Struggle? Lives of Women Factory Workers in South Korea*. New York: Cambridge University Press.

Kim, Sin-bok. 1983. Recent Development of Higher Education in Korea: Quantity, Quality and Equality. *Korea Journal* 23 (10): 20–30.

Kim, Soyoung. 1998. Questions of Woman's Film: The Maid, Madame Freedom, and Women. In *Post-Colonial Classics of Korean Cinema*, ed. C. Choi, 13–21. Irvine: Korean Film Festival Committee at the University of California, Irvine.

Kim, Sŭngok. [1965] 1990. Seoul: Winter 1964. In *Modern Korean Literature*, ed. P. H. Lee, 216–232. Honolulu: University of Hawai'i Press.

Kim-Gibson, Dai Sil. 1999. *Silence Broken: Korean Comfort Women*. Parkersburg, Iowa: Mid-Prairie Books.

Kohn, Melvin L. 1989. Social Structure and Personality: A Quintessentially Sociological Approach to Social Psychology. *Social Forces* 68 (1): 26–33.

Kondo, Dorinne. 1990. *Crafting Selves: Power, Gender, and Discourse of Identity in a Japanese Workplace*. Chicago: University of Chicago Press.

Koo, Hagen. 1984. The Political Economy of Income Distribution in South Korea: The Impact of the State's Industrialization Policies. *World Development* 12 (10): 1029–1037.

———. 1987. The Emerging Class Order and Social Conflict in South Korea. *Pacific Focus* 2 (2): 95–117.

———. 1999. Modernity in South Korea: An Alternative Narrative. *Thesis Eleven* 57:53–64.

———. 2001. *Korean Workers: The Culture and Politics of Class Formation*. Ithaca: Cornell University Press.

Koo, Hagen, and Doo-Seung Hong. 1980. Class and Income Inequality in Korea. *American Sociological Review* 45:610–626.

Korea National Statistical Office. 1995. Population and Household Census Report.

Kuhn, Annette. 1991. Remembrance. In *Family Snaps: The Meanings of Domestic Photography*, ed. J. Spence and P. Holland, 17–25. London: Virago Press.

Kurz, Karen, and Walter Müller. 1987. Class Mobility in the Industrial World. *Annual Review of Sociology* 13:417–442.

Kwon, Huck-ju. 1999. The Welfare State in Korea: The Politics of Legitimation. Oxford: St. Antony Press.

Kwon, Insook. 2000. Militarism in My Heart: Women's Militarized Consciousness and Culture in South Korea. Ph.D. diss., Clark University, Worcester, Mass.

Lareau, Annette. 1989. *Home Advantage*. London: Falmer Press.

Lee, Keehyeung. 2001. Towards a Cultural History in the Korean Present: Locating the Cultural Politics of the Everyday. Ph.D. diss., University of Illinois.

Lee, June J. H. 2002. Discourses of Illness, Meanings of Modernity: A Gendered Construction of Sŏnginbyŏng. In *Under Construction: The Gendering of Modernity, Class, and Consumption in the Republic of Korea*, ed. L. Kendall, 55–78. Honolulu: University of Hawai'i Press.

Lee, Man-gap. 1980. Out-migration of the Rural Population and Rural Development. In *Papers of the First International Conference on Korean Studies*, p. 1245. Sŏngnam, Korea: The Academy of Korean Studies.

Lee, Soo-Jung. 2000. Displacement in/of a Nation. Talk given at American Anthropological Association Meetings in San Francisco, 15–19 November.

Lee, Young-il. 1988. *The History of Korean Cinema: Main Currents of Korean Cinema*. Trans. Richard Lynn Greever. Seoul: Motion Picture Promotion Corporation.

Lemert, Charles. 1993. Social Theory: Its Uses and Pleasures. In *Social Theory: The Multicultural and Classic Readings*, ed. C. Lemert, 1–3. Boulder, Colo.: Westview Press.

Lent, John A. 1990. *The Asian Film Industry*. Austin: University of Texas Press.

Lett, Denise Potrzeba. 1998. *In Pursuit of Status: The Making of South Korea's "New" Urban Middle Class*. Cambridge: Harvard University Asia Center.

Levi, Primo. 1995. *Moments of Reprieve*. New York: Penguin Books.

Lewis, Linda S. 2002. *Laying Claim to the Memory of May: A Look Back at the 1980 Kwangju Massacre*. Honolulu: University of Hawai'i Press and Center for Korean Studies, University of Hawai'i.

Lewis-Fernández, and Arthur Kleinman. 1994. Culture, Personality, and Psychopathology. *Journal of Abnormal Psychology* 103 (1): 67–71.

Lie, John. 1998. *Han Unbound: The Political Economy of South Korea*. Stanford: Stanford University Press.

Lipset, Seymour Martin, and Hans L. Zetterberg. 1959. Social Mobility in Industrial Societies. In *Social Mobility in Industrial Society*, ed. S. M. Lipset and R. Bendix, 11–75. Berkeley: University of California Press.

Ma, Ning. 1993. Symbolic Representation and Symbolic Violence: Chinese Family Melodrama of the Early 1980s. In *Melodrama and Asian Cinema*, ed. W. Dissanayake, 29–58. New York: Cambridge University Press.

MacCabe, Colin. 1976. Theory and Film: Principles of Realism and Pleasure. *Screen* 17 (3): 9–11.

Mann, Michael. 1986. The Origin of Social Power. Vol. 1 of *A History of Power from the Beginning to* A.D. *1760*. Cambridge: Cambridge University Press.

Martin, J., and C. Roberts. 1984. Women and Employment: A Lifetime Perspective. London: HMSO.

Mauss, Marcel. [1938] 1985. A Category of the Human Mind: The Notion of Person; the Notion of Self. In *The Category of the Person: Anthropology, Philosophy, and History*, ed. M. Carrither, S. Collins, and S. Lukes, 1–25. New York: Cambridge University Press.

Maxwell, William. 1980. *So Long, See You Tomorrow*. New York: Vintage International.

McHugh, Kathleen Anne. 1999. *American Domesticity: From How-to Manual to Hollywood Melodrama*. New York: Oxford University Press.

———. 2001. South Korean Film Melodrama and the Question of National Cinema. *Quarterly Review of Film and Video* 18 (1): 1–14.

———. n.d. South Korean Film Melodrama and the Question of National Cinema. In *Gender, Genre, and National Cinema: South Korean Golden Age Melodrama*, ed. K. McHugh and N. Abelmann. Forthcoming.

McHugh, Kathleen, and Nancy Abelmann, eds. n.d. *Gender, Genre, and National Cinema: South Korean Golden Age Melodrama*. Forthcoming.

Moon, Okpyo. 1990. Urban Middle Class Wives in Contemporary Korea: Their Roles, Responsibilties and Dilemma. *Korea Journal* 30:30–43.

Moon, Seungsook. 1998. Gender, Militarization, and Universal Male Conscription in South Korea. In *The Women and War Reader*, ed. L. A. Lorentzen and J. Turpin, 90–100. New York: New York University Press.

———. 2002. Carving Out Space: Civil Society and the Women's Movement in South Korea. *Journal of Asian Studies* 61 (2): 473–500.

Moore, Henrietta L. 1999. Whatever Happened to Women and Men? Gender and other Crises in Anthropology. In *Anthropological Theory Today*, ed. H. Moore, 151–171. Cambridge, UK: Polity Press.

Mulvey, Laura. 1989. Melodrama Inside and Outside the Home. In *Visual and Other Pleasures*, ed. L. Mulvey, 63–77. Bloomington: Indiana University Press.

Mun, So-jŏng. 1995. Kajok saenghwal ŭi pyŏnhwa wa yŏsŏng ŭi sŏngjang (Changes in family life and the growth of women). In *Han'guk sahoesa ŭi ihae* (Understanding Korean social history), ed. Y. Shin, M. Park, and P. Kim, 453–485. Seoul: Munhak kwa Chisŏngsa.

Na, Do-hyang (Na, To-hyang). [1927] 1974. Dumb Samyong. Trans. K. R. Song and E. Albone. *The Korea Times* (Sunday) 5 May.

Nam Ch'un-ho. 1988. Inongmin ŭi chigŏp idongsa rŭl t'onghaesŏ pon han'guk sahoe ŭi kyegŭp kujo pyŏnhwa (Changes in the Korean class structure as seen through the history of rural migrants' occupational mobility). In *Hyŏndae Han'guk chabonjuŭi wa kyegŭp munje* (The problem of capitalism and class in contemporary Korea), ed. Han'guk Sahoe Yŏn'guhoe, 84–119. Seoul: Han'-guk Sahoe Yŏn'guhoe.

Nelson, Laura. 2000. *Measured Excess: Status, Gender, and Consumer Nationalism in South Korea*. New York: Columbia University Press.

Newman, Katherine S. 1993. *Declining Fortunes: The Withering of the American Dream*. New York: Basic Books.

O'Nell, Theresa DeLeane. 1996. *Disciplined Hearts: History, Identity, and Depression in an American Indian Community*. Berkeley: University of California Press.

Ochberg, Richard L. 1994. Life Stories and Storied Lives. In *The Narrative Study of Lives*. Vol. 2, ed. A. Lieblish and R. Josselson, 113–144. Exploring Identity and Gender. London and New Delhi: Sage Publications.

Ogle, George E. 1990. *South Korea's Dissent within the Economic Miracle*. London: Zed Press.

Oh, Byung-Hun. 1975. Students and Politics. In *Korean Politics in Transition*, ed. E. R. Wright, 111–152. Seattle: University of Washington Press.

Ong, Aihwa. 1990. State versus Islam: Malay Families, Women's Bodies, and the Body Politic in Malaysia. *American Ethnologist* 17:258–276.

Ortner, Sherry B. 1991. Reading America: Preliminary Notes on Class and Culture. In *Recapturing Anthropology*, ed. R. G. Fox, 163–189. Santa Fe, N.Mex.: School of American Research Press.

———. 1996. Making Gender. In *Making Gender: The Politics and Erotics of Culture*. Boston: Beacon Press.

Paek, Uk-in. 1993. Taejung ŭi sam kwa Han'guk sahoe pyŏnhwa ŭi yoch'e (The life of the masses and transformations of Korean society). In *Han'guk minju-juŭi ŭi hyŏnjaejŏk kwaje: Chedo, kaehyŏk mit sahoe undong* (The current process of Korean democracy: system, reform, and social movements), ed. Haksui Tanch'e Hyŏpŭihoe, 212–239. Seoul: Ch'angjak kwa Pip'yŏngsa.

Pak, Kyŏng-suk. 1993. Han'guk yŏsŏng ŭi kyoyuk sujunbyŏl kyŏrhon yuhyŏng ŭi pyŏnhwa (Changes in the tendency of women's marriage by education level). Masters thesis, Seoul National University.

Pak, Suk-cha. 1991. Kyegŭp yŏn'gu ŭi punsŏk tanwi: kihon yŏsŏng ŭi kyegŭpchŏk chiwi (The units of class analysis: the class position of married women). In *Sahoe kyech'ŭng: Iron kwa silche* (Social stratification: theory and reality), ed. S. N. U. S. Yŏn'guhoe, 383–400. Seoul: Tasan Publishers.

Pak Wan-so. 1995. *The Naked Tree*. Trans. Y. N. Yu. Ithaca, N.Y.: East Asia Program, Cornell University.

Papaneck, Hanna. 1989. Family Status-Production Work: Women's Contribution to Social Mobility and Class Differentiation. In *Gender and the Household Domain: Social and Cultural Dimensions*, ed. M. Krishnaraj and K. Chanana, 97–116. London: Sage Publications.

Park, Mee-Hae, and Doo-Seung Hong. 1994. Kyech'ŭng insik e issŏsŏ ŭi yŏsŏng ŭi kiyŏ (Women's contribution to a family's social status). *Han'guk Sahoehak* (Korean Sociology) 28:101–120.

Park, Myoung-Kyu. 1995. Han'guk sahoe pyŏndong ŭi ch'use wa hyŏndae Han'guk sahoe (The trends of Korean social change and contemporary Korean society). In *Han'guk sahoesa ŭi ihae* (Understanding Korean social history), ed. Y. Shin, M. Park, and P. Kim, 523–549. Seoul: Munhak kwa Chisŏngsa.

Park, So Jin. 2001. Women's Management of Their Children's Participation in the South Korean Private Educational Market: Classed and Gendered Work in the Context of Neoliberal Education Reform. Paper. University of Illinois.

Peacock, James L., and Dorothy C. Holland. 1993. The Narrated Self: Life Stories in Process. *Ethos* 21 (4): 367–383.

Pile, Steve, and Nigel Thrift. 1995. Introduction. In *Mapping the Subject: Geographies of Cultural Transformation*, ed. S. Pile and N. Thrift, 1–12. New York: Routledge.

Plath, David. 1980. *Long Engagements: Maturity in Modern Japan*. Stanford: Stanford University Press.

Rapp, Rayna. 1982. Family and Class in Contemporary America: Notes Toward an Understanding of Ideology. In *Rethinking the Family: Some Feminist Questions*, ed. B. Thorne and M. Yalom, 49–70. New York: Longman.

Reay, Diane. 1998. *Class Work: Mothers' Involvement in their Children's Primary Schooling*. Bristol, Penn.: University College London Press.

Ricoeur, Paul. 1981. Narrative Time. In *On Narrative*, ed. W. J. T. Mitchell, 165–186. Chicago: University of Chicago Press.

Robinson, Michael. 1984. National Identity and the Thought of Sin Ch'ae-ho: *Sadaejuŭi* and *Chuch'e* in History and Politics. *Journal of Korean Studies* 5:121–142.

———. 1991. Perceptions of Confucianism in Twentieth-Century Korea. In *The East Asia Region: Confucian Heritage and Its Modern Adaptation*, ed. G. Rozman. Princeton: Princeton University Press.

Rofel, Lisa. 1994. Liberation Nostalgia and a Yearning for Modernity. In *Engendering China: Women, Culture, and the State*. Harvard Contemporary China, vol. 10, ed. C. K. Gilmartin, G. Hershatter, and T. White, 226–249. Cambridge: Harvard University Press.

———. 1999. *Other Modernities: Gendered Yearnings in China After Socialism*. Berkeley: University of California Press.

Rorty, Amélie Oksenberg. 1976. A Literary Postscript: Characters, Persons, Selves, Individuals. In *The Identities of Persons*, ed. A. O. Rorty, 301–323. Berkeley: University of California Press.

Rosaldo, Michelle Z. 1984. Toward an Anthropology of Self and Feeling. In *Culture Theory: Essays on Mind, Self, and Emotion*, ed. R. A. Levine and R. A. Shweder, 137–157. Cambridge: Cambridge University Press.

Rosaldo, Renato. 1980. *Ilongot Headhunting 1883–1974*. Stanford: Stanford University Press.

Rothman, William. 1993. Overview: What Is American Film Study All About. In *Melodrama and Asian Cinema*, ed. W. Dissanayake, 254–278. New York: Cambridge University Press.

Sartre, Jean-Paul. [1964] 1981. *The Words: The Autobiography of Jean-Paul Sartre*. New York: Vintage Books.

Schiffrin, Deborah. 1996. Narrative as Self-Portrait: Sociolinguistic Constructions of Identity. *Language in Society* 25:167–203.

Schmid, Andre. 1997. Rediscovering Manchuria: Sin Ch'aeho and the Politics of Territorial History in Korea. *Journal of Asian History* 56 (1): 26–46.

———. 2002. *Korea between Empires: 1895–1919*. New York: Columbia University Press.

Schwartz, Theodore. 1992. Anthropology and Psychology. In *New Directions in Psychological Anthropology*, ed. T. Schwartz, G. M. White, and C. A. Lutz, 324–349. New York: Cambridge University Press.

Scott, Joan. 1988. Gender: A Useful Category of Historical Analysis. In *Gender and the Politics of History*, ed. J. Scott, 28–50. New York: Columbia University Press.

———. 1992. Experience. In *Feminists Theorize the Political*, ed. J. Butler and J. W. Scott, 22–40. New York: Routledge.

Seth, Michael. 2000. "Examination Mania": South Korea's Entrance Exam System. *Acta Koreana* 3:35–55.

Sennett, Richard, and Jonathan Cobb. 1973. *The Hidden Injuries of Class*. New York: Random House.

Sewell, William H. Jr. 1985. *Structure and Mobility: The Men and Women of Marseilles, 1820–1870*. New York: Cambridge University Press.

Shweder, Richard A. 1990. Cultural Psychology—What is it? In *Cultural Psychology: Essays on Comparative Human Development*, ed. J. W. Stigler, R. A. Shweder, and G. Herdt, 1–43. New York: Cambridge University Press.

Smith-Rosenberg, Carol. 1986. Writing History: Language, Class, and Gender. In *Feminist Studies/Critical Studies*, ed. T. de Lauretis. Bloomington: Indiana University Press.

Soh, Chunghee Sarah. 2000. From Imperial Gifts to Sex Slaves. *Social Science Japan Journal* 3 (1): 1–33.

Sŏl, Tong-hun. 1994. Han'guk nodongjadŭl ŭi sedaegan sahoe idong 1987–1989 nyŏn, samujik kwa saengsanjik ŭi namnyŏ nodongja rŭl chungsim ŭro (Intergenerational social mobility of Korean laborers, 1987–1989, with a focus on male and female office and production workers). In *Kyegŭp kwa han'guk sahoe* (Class and korean society), ed. Han'guk Sahoe Yŏn'guhoe, 237–278. Seoul: Hanul.

Somers, Margart R. 1994. The Narrative Constitution of Identity: A Relational and Network Approach. *Theory and Society* 23 (5): 605–649.

Song, Bok. 1985. Kyegŭp kaldŭng kwa kyegŭp kujo (Class conflict and class structure). In *Han'huk sahoe wa kaldŭng ŭi yŏn'gu* (Research on Korean society and conflict), ed. H. S. Hakhoe, 101–126. Seoul: Hyŏndae Sahoe Yŏn'guso.

Song, Jesook. 2002. Transgressing Gendered Welfare? The East Asian Economic Crisis in South Korea, 1997–2001. Paper presented at Sociocultural Anthropology Workshop, 7 February, at University of Illinois at Urbana-Champaign.

Sørenson, Annemette. 1994. Women, Family and Class. *Annual Review of Sociology* 20:27–47.

Spence, Jo. 1991. Shame-work: Thoughts on Family Snaps and Fractured Identity. In *Family Snaps: The Meanings of Domestic Photography*, ed. J. Spence and P. Holland, 228–236. London: Virago.

Stack, Carol B. 1974. *All Our Kin: Strategies for Survival in a Black Community.* New York: Harper and Row.

———. 1996. *Call to Home: African Americans Reclaim the Rural South.* New York: Basic Books.

Stack, Carol B., and Linda M. Burton. 1993. Kinscripts. *Journal of Comparative Family Studies* 24 (2): 157–170.

Steedman, Carolyn. 1986. *Landscape for a Good Woman.* London: Virago.

Stone, Linda. 2000. *Kinship and Gender: An Introduction.* Boulder, Colo.: Westview Press.

Taylor, Charles. 1985. The Person. In *The Category of the Person: Anthropology, Philosophy, and History*, ed. S. C. Michael Carrither and Steven Lukes, 257–281. New York: Cambridge University Press.

———. 1989. *Sources of the Self.* Cambridge: Harvard University Press.

Thomas, James Philip. 1993. Contested from Within and Without: Squatters, the State, the *Minjung* Movement, and the Limits of Resistance in a Seoul Shanty Town. Ph.D. diss., University of Rochester, New York.

Thompson. E. P. 1968. *The Making of the English Working Class.* London: Penguin.

Thompson, Paul. 1981. Life Histories and the Analysis of Social Change. In *Biography and Society: The Life History Approach in the Social Sciences*, ed. D. Bertaux, 29–45. Beverly Hills, Calif.: Sage Publications.

———. 1993. Family Myth, Models, and Denials in the Shaping of Individual Life Paths. In *International Yearbook of Oral History and Life Stories.* Vol. 2, *Between Generations: Family Models, Myths, and Memories*, ed. D. Bertaux and P. Thompson, 13–38. Oxford: Oxford University Press.

———. 1997. Women, Men, and Transgenerational Family Influences in Social Mobility. In *Pathways to Social Class*, ed. D. Bertaux and P. Thompson, 32–61. Oxford: Clarendon Press.

Tierney, William G. 1998. Life History's History: Subjects Foretold. *Qualitative Inquiry* 4 (1): 49–70.

Tilly, Charles. 1984. *Big Structures, Large Processes, Huge Comparisons.* New York: Russel Sage Foundation.

Toren, Christina. 1996. For the Motion (2) (1989 Debate: the Concept of Society Is Thoroughly Obsolete: part 1). In *Key Debates in Anthropology*, ed. T. Ingold, 72–76. New York: Routledge.

Turim, Maureen. 1993. Psyches, Ideologies, and Melodrama: The United States and Japan. In *Melodrama and Asian Cinema*, ed. W. Dissanayake, 155–178. New York: Cambridge University Press.

Turner, Ralph H. 1988. Personality in Society: Social Psychology's Contribution to Sociology. *Social Psychology Quarterly* 51 (1): 1–10.

Urciuoli, Bonnie. 1993. Representing Class: Who Decides? *Anthropological Quarterly* 66 (4): 203–210.

Wacquant, Loïc J. D. 1991. Making Class: The Middle Class(es) in Social Theory and Social Structure. In *Bringing Class Back In*, ed. S. G. McNall, R. F. Levine, and R. Fantasia, 39–64. Boulder, Colo.: Westview Press.

Wagner, Edward W. 1974. The Ladder of Success in Yi Dynasty Korea. *Occasional Papers on Korea* 1:1–8.

Walby, Sylvia. 1986. Gender, Class, and Stratification: Towards a New Approach. In *Gender and Stratification*, ed. R. Crompton and M. Mann, 23–39. Cambridge, UK: Polity Press.

Watt, Ian. 1957. *The Rise of the Novel: Studies in Defoe, Richardson and Fielding*. Berkeley: University of California Press.

Weber, Steven. 2000. The Virtual, the Real, and the Not-Yet-Imagined: Meaning, Identity and Community in a Networked World. Paper read at Jewish Public Forum Seminar, 6 June, National Jewish Center for Learning, New York City.

Weiner, Margaret. 1999. "Pay No Attention to the Man Behind the Curtain": Irreverent Notes on Gender and Ethnography. *Anthropology and Humanism* 24 (2): 95–108.

Welch, Nancy. 1996. The Road from Prosperity. *The Three Penny Review* 64 (winter): 14–16.

White, Geoffrey M. 1992. Ethnopsychology. In *New Directions in Psychological Anthropology*, ed. T. Schwartz, G. M. White, and C. A. Lutz, 21–46. New York: Cambridge University Press.

White, Harrison C. 1992. *Identity and Control: A Structural Theory of Social Action*. Princeton: Princeton University Press.

Williams, Linda. 1998. Melodrama Revised. In *Refiguring American Film Genres: History and Theory*, ed. N. Browne, 42–88. Berkeley, Los Angeles, and London: University of California Press.

Williams, Raymond. 1973. *The Country and the City*. New York: Oxford University Press.

———. 1976. *Keywords: A Vocabulary of Culture and Society*. New York: Oxford University Press.

Woo, Jung-en. 1991. *Race to the Swift: State and Finance in Korean Industrialization*. New York: Columbia University Press.

Woolf, Virginia. [1929] 1981. *A Room of One's Own*. New York: Harcourt Brace Jovanovich.

Yi, Ch'ang-gon. 2000. Pinpukyŏkch'a (The widening gap between the rich and the poor). *Han'gyŏre* 21, no. 550 (18 October).

Yi, Eunhee Kim. 1993. From Gentry to the Middle Class: The Transformation of Family, Community, and Gender in Korea. Ph.D. diss., University of Chicago.

Yoon, In-jin. 1997. *On My Own: Korean Business and Race Relations in America.* Chicago: University of Chicago Press.

Yoshimoto, Mitsuhiro. 1993. Melodrama, Postmodernism, and Japanese Cinema. In *Melodrama and Asian Cinema,* ed. W. Dissanayake, 101–126. New York: Cambridge University Press.

You, Pal-Moo. 1981. Sedaegan ŭi sahoe idong kwa kyoyuk kihoe pulp'yŏngdŭng (Intergenerational social mobility and the inequality of educational opportunity). Master's thesis, Seoul National University.

INDEX

References to figures are in **boldface** type

Abu-Lughod, Lila, 22, 169
activism. *See* political activism
Adŭl kwa ttal (A son and a daughter), 40,
    101–110, 113
age: middle-aged/elderly, 3, 37–38, 158–159,
    180; women, 3, 158–159, 260, 289. *See also*
    generations; life cycle
agency, 135, 165–168, 174, 185–186, 203. *See
    also* individual; personality; selfhood
agricultural labor, 37, 134, 138. *See also* farmers
ambivalences, 28, 32, 132, 133, 283–287, 290;
    Education Mother's, 113; key words, 61–62;
    Laundress's, 161; male gaze, 74, 201;
    Mi-yŏn's Mother's, 31, 130, 203, 230,
    241–243, 256–257, 261, 263, 274, 276, 279;
    patriarchy in film, 213; young people's
    responses, 289
Ang, Ien, 25
Appadurai, Arjun, 16
architecture: collapses, 6, 7; rural, 42–43. *See
    also* housing
arts, Mi-yŏn's Mother and, 47, 268–271
authoritarianism, 7, 139. *See also* military rule;
    repression

Bakhtin, Mikhail, 76, 290; heteroglossia,
    13, 59–60, 62, 98,164; socio-ideological
    systems, 12–13, 31, 60, 71, 133; words/
    language, 12–13, 14, 23, 59–60, 62, 70,
    98, 293
Battaglia, Debbora, 166–167, 185
Bertaux, Daniel, 15–16, 20
Big Mother (Mi-yŏn's Mother's), 48, 206–209,

230, 246–250, 255; labor, 206, 208, 230,
    266; literacy, 237; masculine traits, 206–210,
    212; and Mi-yŏn's Mother's in-laws, 267
boardinghouse, Mi-yŏn's Mother, 47, 48, 206,
    210, 240–241, 254, 257
Bourdieu, Pierre, 18–19, 132, 285
bribery, 67, 155, 255, 267, 270
Brooks, Peter, 23, 25–27
Bruner, Jerome, 28
Buckwheat Season, 212–213
business. *See* capitalism; income; labor; small
    business

capital: class, 52–53, 151–152; cultural, 82,
    152; different types, 19, 119, 146; education,
    81, 114, 136, 140, 141, 142, 273–274; sym-
    bolic, 146. *See also* capitalism; resource
    networks
capitalism, 134; American, 236; Chong Chu-
    yŏng, 207, 217; crony, 126; Education
    Mother on, 110; IMF Crisis and, 7; melo-
    drama and, 23; morality, 174; state-led
    chaebŏl, 126; venture, 101, 126, 129–130, 241,
    273. *See also* investment
capitalist class, 143
Catholics, 57, 152, 245. *See also* Christianity
ch'akhada: Hye-min's Grandmother and, 82,
    84; Laundress, 63–69; Moviegoer, 69,
    70–71, 73, 78
challada: Laundress and, 66; Mi-yŏn's Mother
    and husband, 249; Moviegoer and, 71–74,
    77, 78, 165, 170, 174; Twins' Mother,
    78–79, 80, 81

ch'amta: Hye-min's Grandmother and, 82, 84; Janitor and, 85, 86; Laundress, 83; Moviegoer, 74, 76–77, 78, 83, 172; Moviegoer's husband, 172

Chang, Kyung-Sup, 7, 281, 287

Chang Myŏn, 5, 190–191

characters, 167–168; good/evil, 26, 29; melodrama, 23, 25, 26, 28, 29; Mi-yŏn's Mother's, 279; Moviegoer's stories/soap operas, 174, 181–183; and persons, 167–168. See also personality

child care: and divorce, 161; Hye-min's Grandmother, 39; Laundress's grandchildren, 149, 156, 160; by mother's mother or mother-in-law, 76, 149, 156; Moviegoer's grandchildren, 178; women's education and, 107. See also child rearing

child rearing: Laundress's marriage and, 66–67, 72–73, 150, 152; Mi-yŏn's Mother, 262; Mi-yŏn's Mother's kin, 233–235; Moviegoer, 72–73, 76, 178; of munŭnghan men, 88, 102–103; personality made in, 87–88. See also child care; education

Cho, Hae-joang, 11, 209, 281–282, 283–284, 288, 289

Christianity, 37–38, 57; Catholics, 57, 152, 245; Hye-min's Grandmother, 39, 54–55, 57, 89–90, 92, 221–222, 226; Laundress, 57, 63, 152; Mi-yŏn's Mother, 57, 245, 250; Moviegoer, 57, 170–171, 175; Mrs. Pak, 57, 96; persons, 168; soap opera, 181, 184; village, 43

Chun Doo Hwan, 5, 6, 7, 126, 127, 286

civil service work, 103, 109, 124–125, 176, 178, 218–219

class, 2, 8, 17–20, 29, 284–286; anxiety and realignment (1990s), 7, 100; author-women meetings inflected by, 34, 52, 57; capitalist, 143; class work, 100–131, 132, 149; complexity, 28, 57, 125, 132, 162; Education Mother's identity, 9, 17, 55; Education Mother's reading of, 28; Education Mother's son's education and, 110–111; family and, 19–22, 31, 81, 135, 145–147, 215, 230–239, 277, 285; and gender, 81, 132, 145–149; Hye-min's Grandmother identity, 54–55, 92; Janitor identity, 53–54, 116–117, 118, 125; language of, 285–286; Laundress identity, 54, 135, 150, 151–152,

162; leadership, 277; and limited mobility, 140; maps, 52–58; Mi-yŏn's Mother identity, 55; Mi-yŏn's Mother's kin travels, 226–228, 230–239, 263–266; Moviegoer identity, 46, 55, 70, 170; and narrative, 18, 19, 20, 81; Mrs. Pak identity, 55, 56–57; post-Korean War period, 19–20, 134, 135, 141–144, 285; reproduction of, 3, 100, 111, 145–149, 203; and social transformation, 10–11, 19–20, 28, 242, 284–285; in transgenerational perspective, 20, 135; Twins' Mother identity, 55–56; women's importance, 21, 22, 33, 34, 52–58, 135, 145–149, 161–162; words and, 13, 57–58, 61–62, 68–69, 92, 97–98. See also elites; labor; social mobility; tradition

class capital, 52–53, 151–152

class consciousness, 19, 142–143, 286

clothes: hanbok, 93, 218; insurance saleswoman, 75; Mi-yŏn's Mother, 231, 237, 249, 260; Moviegoer, 75

Cold War period, 109, 110, 125, 139

collapses, 278; architectural, 6, 7; economic, 6, 7, 142–143. See also International Monetary Fund (IMF) Crisis

college education. See higher education

colonialism, 31; in film, 197–198, 212–213; gender sign systems, 201; Japanese (1910–1945), 5, 138, 141, 143, 150, 179, 287; Liberation (1945), 5, 6, 114, 139–140, 141; male displacement, 188, 202; Mi-yŏn's Mother and, 278, 279–280; U.S., 139, 287. See also imperialism

communism: anticommunism, 5, 125

Confucianism, 126; academy, 29; and capitalism, 67; and family, 154, 287–288; film, 192; gendered, 201–202; revival, 287; sŏnbi, 168, 173, 174, 175, 204, 222, 278; Twins' Mother's family, 56, 79; widow's chastity, 154. See also yangban

countryside, 34–46; education, 34–45, 54, 118, 120, 223–226; Hye-min's Grandmother and, 219–226; Janitor leaving, 117–118; Moviegoer's husband returning to, 176–177; rural/urban divide, 43, 53–54, 220, 238. See also farmers; villages

Crapanzano, Vincent, 17, 61, 243, 252

crimes, financial, 7, 67, 155, 255–257, 267, 270

cultural capital, 82, 152
Cumings, Bruce, 282

democracy, 5, 144, 190–191, 286; cold-war,
139; elections, 4, 5, 6–7; European social,
126; labor reforms, 68, 286; Mi-yŏn's
Mother and, 278, 279
depression, 210, 245
development: class, 19; compressed, 281–288;
developmentalist view, 21, 136–140, 162,
164; economic, 5, 6, 10, 21, 120, 134,
136–140, 143–144; selfhood, 21, 75, 82–83.
See also modernity
dialogic nature: of melodrama, 23–24, 29; of
words/talk/narratives, 11, 12, 17, 61, 62, 76
discrimination, gender: education, 102–104,
107–108, 120, 122, 150–151, 268–272;
Mi-yŏn's Mother and, 204–205, 261–262,
268–272; by mother-in-law, 205. See also
feminism; patriarchy
displacement: male, 31, 187–213; Mi-yŏn's
Mother, 55, 230, 271–272. See also
emigration
divided families, North-South Korea, 10, 48,
106, 109–110, 139
divorce, 161, 252–253, 269
Dorfman, Ariel, 25

eating, Mi-yŏn's Mother, 232–233, 236, 256
economics: bribery, 67, 155, 255, 267, 270;
collapse, 6, 7, 142–143; costs of modernization, 282; development, 5, 6, 10, 21, 120,
134, 136–140, 143–144; education emigration, 72–73; Education Mother, 50, 103,
106; Education Mother's brothers, 98,
108–109; formal economy, 50, 53, 66–67,
145, 148, 255; inflationary, 143; informal
economy, 66–67, 134, 148; Janitor, 50, 54,
114; Laundress, 50, 53, 66–67, 68, 136;
ministers, 221–222; Mi-yŏn's Mother, 50,
210–211, 226, 230–231, 243, 248, 253–263;
Mi-yŏn's Mother's father, 203–204, 229;
Moviegoer, 50, 56, 70, 172–174; Mrs. Pak,
50, 214; Park regime, 191; restructuring, 31;
Rhee regime, 190; usury, 49, 91; women
not bettering family, 56–57, 166, 172–174,
177, 180; women prototypes, 49, 50, 66–67.
See also capitalism; class; farmers; income;
investment; labor; poverty; resource net-

works; small business; social transformation; wealth
education, 30, 100–133, 164; after-school,
127, 155; class and, 52–53, 110–112; college
entrance exams, 45, 111–112, 122, 155, 192;
countryside, 34–45, 54, 118, 120, 223–226;
Education Mother, 55, 103, 113; Education
Mother's brother, 109, 113; Education
Mother's mother and, 106, 109, 113; Education Mother's son, 8, 30, 98, 100, 101,
110–113; emigration, 40–41, 45, 50–51, 56,
72–73, 96–97, 128, 129, 241; extracurricular, 127, 159, 268–271; gender discrimination over, 102–104, 107–108, 120, 122,
150–151, 268–272; high school entrance
exams, 264; husbands'/brothers' levels,
147; Hye-min's Grandmother, 53, 82;
Hye-min's Grandmother's children, 222;
Hye-min's Grandmother's kin, 221,
223–226; after IMF Crisis, 30, 100, 114,
126–127, 130–131, 159; Janitor, 53, 125;
Janitor's family, 30, 54, 100, 114–126; labor
and, 114, 120–122, 124, 128–130, 136, 138,
141–142, 147–148, 154–155; Laundress, 53,
147, 150–151; Laundress's brothers, 136,
142, 150–151; Laundress's children, 54, 67,
136, 142, 149–150, 151, 153, 155, 157, 159,
164; Laundress's father, 135, 150, 151;
Mi-yŏn's Mother, 53, 55, 93–94, 151, 231,
232, 233, 243, 263–267, 273–274; Mi-yŏn's
Mother on meaning and worth of, 273–276,
277; Mi-yŏn's Mother's children, 94, 100,
128–131, 210, 241, 243, 247, 258, 267–276;
Mi-yŏn's Mother's kin, 233–234, 235;
Moviegoer, 53; Moviegoer's children, 55,
171; Moviegoer's husband, 170, 176; music,
268–272; and occupational status, 114,
120–122, 124, 130; Mrs. Pak, 53, 57, 95;
privatized, 126, 127; questioned value of,
274, 275–276; Rhee regime, 190; tutoring,
233–234; Twins' Mother and family, 53, 56,
79–81; women, 106, 107, 113, 122–123, 142,
268–269; women prototypes, 49; women's
before marriage, 147–148. See also higher
education
education capital, 81, 114, 136, 140, 141, 142,
273–274
Education Mother, 8, 46–47, 50, 52, 133;
brothers, 88, 97–98, 101, 102–103, 106,

(Education Mother, *continued*)
108–109, 111, 113; class identity, 9, 17, 55; daughter, 46, 49–50, 51; economics, 50, 103, 106; education of son, 8, 30, 98, 100, 101, 110–113; education of women, 106, 107, 113; father, 10, 106, 109–110, 113; housewife, 53; key words, 97–98; Korean War, 109–110, 139; marriage, 29, 57, 106, 108, 110; mother, 10, 27–29, 88, 98, 102, 105–106, 108–111, 113; sister's pocketbook, 8–17, 27–30, 50, 65, 88, 101–108; travel abroad, 9, 51

Ehwa University, 181, 182, 235

elites: ambivalence toward, 286–287. *See also* middle class; upper class; *yangban*

Elsaesser, Thomas, 23, 25, 26

emigration: education outside Korea, 40–41, 45, 50–51, 56, 72–73, 96–97, 128, 129, 241; employment outside Korea, 51, 55, 136, 149–150, 155–156, 170, 195, 197; from villages, 117–118, 140, 150, 156, 218–219. *See also* displacement; United States; urbanization

England: Mi-yŏn's Mother, 51, 244–246, 272, 273, 276, 279

Enlightenment Period, Korean, 173

equality: of opportunity, 136–145. *See also* gender; inequality; social justice

ethics. *See* morality/ethics

ethnography, 17, 32, 33–34, 61, 288

family, 2, 214–239; abroad, 50–51, 94, 97, 149–150, 155, 157, 195, 226, 235–237; *chokpo*, 79, 114; and class, 19–22, 31, 81, 135, 145–149, 215, 230–239, 277, 285; class work, 100–131, 132, 149; Confucianism and, 154, 287–288; context of personal narrative, 11, 19–20; divided families, 10, 48, 106, 109–110, 139; Education Mother, 8–17, 27–30, 49–50, 97–98, 100, 101–113; extended, 31, 150–154, 214–239, 277; Hye-min's Grandmother, 40–41, 51, 82, 89, 92–93, 214, 215, 216–226; Janitor's, 42, 44, 86, 114–126; joint classification, 145–146; local systems, 15–16; married women's natal, 146–147, 151–154, 161–162; Mi-yŏn's Mother, 50, 51, 94, 214, 260–261; mobility studies of households, 145–149; morality, 21; social reproduction, 3, 92, 145–149; surname associations, 114; in transgenerational perspective, 20, 135, 162; two heads,

158; wedding photo, 216–217, 218; women determining course of, 21, 157–158, 174; women not bettering economics of, 56–57, 166, 172–174, 177, 180. *See also* child care; child rearing; fathers; kinship networks; marriage; men

farmers, 34–43, 120–121, 130; characters, 168; farmers' movement, 34–36, 42–45; Hyemin's Grandmother and, 217–221; land reform, 138, 139–140, 285. *See also* agricultural labor; countryside

fathers, 190; *Adŭl kwa ttal* (A son and a daughter), 108; displacement, 203–213; Education Mother's, 10, 106, 109–110, 113; and husbands' class positions, 147; Hye-min's Grandmother and, 216, 217, 218–219; Janitor's, 115; Laundress's, 135, 136, 140, 150, 151; Mi-yŏn's Mother's, 87, 203–206, 210, 211, 228, 229, 243, 252, 275; Moviegoer's, 172, 173, 204; Twins,' 56, 79, 80–81. *See also* patriarchy; patrilineal kinship

feminine traits, 202–203; displacement, 189; Education Mother and, 29, 65; men's, 189, 204, 205, 210, 211–212; Mi-yŏn's Mother and, 250; national, 31, 201, 202; "other" women, 66, 83, 91–92, 185, 216–226, 238, 249, 258–259, 267, 275–276; virtues, 84, 202, 212; women's, 62–69, 83–85, 93, 189, 209, 210, 212

feminism, 21, 104–105, 161, 171. *See also* discrimination, gender

films, 22–23, 24, 31; *Buckwheat Season*, 212–213; compressed modernity and, 289–290; Golden Cinema Age (1950s–1960s), 23, 31, 189, 191–201; male subjectivity, 189, 191–201; Moviegoer and, 44, 70, 74, 77, 170, 173, 175; *Pak Sŏbang* (Neighbor Pak), 56, 189, 193–197, 200–201; patriarchy, 31, 108, 191–197, 200–201, 213; *Pŏng'ŏri Samnyong'i* (Deaf-mute Samnyong'i), 189, 197–201; *Romaensŭ Ppappa* (Romance papa), 189, 191–193, 200–201, 204; Western, 26, 170, 236

Frye, Northrop, 16

gender, 2, 20–22, 31, 133, 216, 242, 288; *Adŭl kwa ttal* (A son and a daughter), 101–110; class and, 81, 132, 145–149; displacement, 31, 187–213; feminism, 21, 104–105, 161,

171; generosity, 88–98; greed, 67, 88–98; key words and, 61–62, 68–69, 82–98; melodrama and, 26; narrating, 203–213; nation, 201–203; Mrs. Pak's family's views, 57; piano as symbol, 268–272; sign systems, 22, 201–203, 211; social mobility studies, 145–149; and social transformation, 201, 242, 267, 288; subjectivity, 21–22, 31, 187–213; in transgenerational perspective, 134–136, 162. *See also* discrimination, gender; feminine traits; marriage; masculine traits; men; patriarchy; patrilineal kinship; women

generations, 2–3, 20, 288–290; class development, 19; Education Mother's stories, 101; Mi-yŏn's Mother's kin, 230; mobility, 146–147; refusal of daughters, 209; subjectivity, 285; transgenerational perspective, 20, 134–136, 149–163; women's education before marriage, 147–148. *See also* age; family; modernity; social transformation; tradition

Gledhill, Christine, 25, 26

Golden Cinema Age (1950s–1960s), 23, 31, 189, 191–201

Gordon, Avery F., 240, 290

grassroots movements, 6, 287; farmers, 34–36, 42–45. *See also* political activism

Hall, Stuart, 16–17

han, 171, 231–232

Hanbo financial scandal, 7

hanbok, 93, 218

health: cerebral palsy, 35; clubs, 9, 259; depression, 210, 245; Mi-yŏn's career, 270–271, 274; Mi-yŏn's Mother's, 210, 245, 247, 254; Mi-yŏn's Mother's husband, 209–210, 243–244, 247–248, 252–253; Mi-yŏn's Mother's son, 130; Moviegoer's mother, 76, 171; stress, 79, 80–81, 247

higher education: cram schools, 272; Ehwa University, 181, 182, 235; entrance exams, 45, 111–112, 122, 155, 192, 272–273; films on, 196–197; Janitor's stories, 114–124; Mi-yŏn's Mother, 263–267, 273–274; rapid expansion (1980s), 3, 143; Seoul National University, 79, 80, 118, 183, 184, 276; South Korean attendance, 116; student uprisings, 5, 68, 178, 190–191; value decline, 121–122, 123, 142, 143, 154–155

Hollywood, films, 26, 236

Hong, Doo-Seung, 134

housewives, 149; Education Mother, 53; Laundress on work of, 160–161; Moviegoer, 72, 75, 173, 212; Mrs. Pak, 53; Twins' Mother, 53; types, 49, 72, 75, 208. *See also* child care

housing: *chŏnse* system (one-room-system apartment building), 47, 53, 156, 235, 269; Education Mother, 50; farm, 35; high class apartments, 52, 53, 117, 257; home ownership, 53, 55, 109, 118, 119, 153, 156, 160, 170; Hye-min's Grandmother, 54; Janitor, 44, 53, 116–117, 119; Laundress, 156; Mi-yŏn's Mother, 47, 48, 203, 206, 257–258; Mi-yŏn's Mother's boardinghouse, 47, 48, 206, 210, 240–241, 254, 257; Mi-yŏn's Mother's kin, 228, 233, 234, 235; Moviegoer, 55, 170, 179; shantytown, 53, 116–117; Twins' Mother, 55–56; village, 41–43. *See also* real estate investment

husbands: brothers/fathers and, 147; gender and production biases toward, 145–146; Hye-min's Grandmother's, 31, 218–219, 222; Janitor's, 86–87, 117–118; Laundress's, 63, 135, 152, 153–154, 157, 158, 162; Mi-yŏn's, 209, 250; Mi-yŏn's Mother's, 48, 93, 209–210, 237, 243–254, 265, 266–270, 272–273, 277–278, 280, 292; Moviegoer's, 55, 70, 74–78, 165, 166, 170, 172–180, 212; Moviegoer's mother's, 172; Twins' Mother's, 56, 79–81; wives' employment discordant with that of, 148; women nurturing egos of, 66, 91, 157. *See also* marriage

Hye-min, 39–40, 51

Hye-min's Grandmother, 34, 39–41, 45–47; Christianity, 39, 54–55, 57, 89–90, 92, 221–222, 226; class identity, 54–55, 92; daughter's wedding, 216; economics, 50, 217, 222; education, 53, 82; education of women, 106; family, 40–41, 51, 82, 89, 92–93, 214, 215, 216–226; in formal economy, 53; key words, 82–85, 89–93, 222; kinship networks, 31, 214, 215, 216–226; **220**, 238–239; marriage, 57, 218–219; and "other" women, 91–92, 216–226, 238; small business, 54–55, 82, 222, 226

Hyoja-dong, Mi-yŏn's Mother kin, 228, 230–238, 244, 264–266

ideology. See *sasang* (ideology)

imagination: narrative engaging, 11, 242; networks, 46; real and imaginary, 11, 16, 17, 25, 243; social, 2, 16–17, 100; sociological, 15, 16

IMF Crisis. See International Monetary Fund (IMF) Crisis (1997–2001)

imperialism: and melodrama, 24; U.S. political and cultural, 139. See also colonialism

Inch'ŏn, Mi-yŏn's Mother, 228, 231, 232, 238, 263

income: egalitarian distribution, 141; Janitor, 54, 86; Laundress's, 135; Laundress's children, 54; reduction percentages, 126; women non-wage, 50, 66–67, 146, 148–149, 255

individual, 12, 13, 164; psychology, 26; social mobility, 135, 138, 144–145; social paired with personal, 14, 165. See also agency; characters; personality; selfhood

industrial labor, 55, 104, 118, 137, 138, 140, 141, 153, 177

inequality, 14–15, 143–145; Education Mother and, 13; Janitor and, 41, 116–117; Laundress and, 158; Moviegoer and, 55, 179–180; unchanged, 285. See also discrimination, gender; equality; social justice

inheritance law, 154

insurance saleswomen, 75, 165

International Monetary Fund (IMF) Crisis (1997–2001), 4, 6, 30; bailout, 4, 126; Confucianism and, 287; and education, 30, 100, 114, 126–127, 130–131, 159; and employment, 30, 45, 130, 148, 159; middle class, 286; and real estate, 47; and state-corporate collusion, 7, 126; status hierarchy changed after, 274

investment: extracurricular education, 127; married women's, 146; Moviegoer on, 71; stock market, 9, 126, 130; venture capitalism, 101, 126, 129–130, 241, 273. See also real estate investment

Janelli, Dawnhee Yim, 169

Janitor, 41–44, 45–46; class identity, 53–54, 116–117, 118, 125; daughter in Japan, 51, 120, 122; economics, 50, 54, 114; education, 53, 125; education of family, 30, 54, 100, 114–126; education of women, 122; housing, 53, 116–117, 119; key words, 85–89; labor, 41, 44, 53, 116, 119; wages, 54, 86

Japan: ammonia plant, 177; collaborators, 176, 179, 229, 235; colonial rule (1910–1945), 5, 138, 141, 143, 150, 179, 287; Janitor's daughter, 51, 120, 122; Moviegoer's kin, 176; normalization treaty, 190

justice. See social justice

Kang, Mr., 34, 36–39, 44, 45–46, 57, 149

Kang Tae-jin, 193

Kashi namu kkot (The thorny branch flower), 166, 180–186

Kendall, Laurel, 67, 147, 168, 291

key words, 2, 22, 30, 59–99, 164; class and, 57–58, 61–62, 68–69, 92, 97–98; complexity, 30, 57–58; conflicted, 14–15, 61–62, 65, 164, 283–284; Education Mother, 97–98; gender and, 61–62, 68–69, 82–98; *han* not included, 171, 231; Hye-min's Grandmother, 82–85, 89–93, 222; Janitor, 85–89; Laundress, 63–69, 91; Mi-yŏn's Mother, 93–95; Moviegoer, 69–78, 165; Mrs. Pak, 95–98; Twins' Mother, 78–81

Key Words (R. Williams), 60, 61, 62

ki: Education Mother and, 98, 101, 106, 109, 111; Hye-min's Grandmother and, 224; Mi-yŏn's Mother, 204–205

Kim, Byoung-Kwan, 138–139, 141

Kim Dae Jung, 4, 7, 101, 126, 160

Kim Mi-suk, 107–108

Kim, Myung-hye, 146, 149

Kim Yŏng-mo, 134

Kim Young Sam, 4, 6, 7, 67

kinship networks: characters, 168; day-to-day management of, 31, 214–239; defined, 214; Hye-min's Grandmother, 31, 214, 215, 216–226, **220**, 238–239; Janitor's wealthy, 117–118; Mi-yŏn's Mother, 31, 214, 215, 226–239, **227**, 244, 263–266; village-Seoul, 42, 43, 117–118, 119, 219. See also family; patrilineal kinship

kkaeda, 64–65, 67

Koo, Hagen, 141, 143, 281

Koreanness, 202, 205, 212, 287–288. See also tradition

Korean peninsula: divided families, 10, 48, 106, 109–110, 139; North-South unification, 160; partition (1945–1948), 5, 10. See also colonialism; Korean War; North Korea

Korean War, 31, 138–139; Education Mother's stories, 109–110, 139; Hye-min's Grandmother, 39; Janitor's education, 125; male displacement, 187, 188; Mi-yŏn's Mother, 205, 254, 259–260.

Kuhn, Annette, 216

kŭphada: Hye-min's Grandmother and, 83–84, 89, 222; Janitor, 85, 86

Kwangju Uprising (May 1980), 5, 126

labor, 286; abroad, 51, 55, 136, 149–150, 155–156, 170, 195, 197; activism, 5, 44, 45, 68; agricultural, 37, 134, 138; bribes for, 155; civil service, 103, 109, 124–125, 176, 178, 218–219; clerical, 134; development and, 120, 136–140; education and, 114, 120–122, 124, 128–130, 136, 138, 141–142, 147–148, 154–155; employment exam, 272–273; formal economy, 50, 53, 66–67, 145, 148, 255; gains, 6–7; and gender in social mobility studies, 145; Hye-min's Grandmother and, 54–55, 82, 218–219; industrial, 55, 104, 118, 137, 138, 140, 141, 153, 177; informal economy, 66–67, 134, 148; insurance saleswomen, 75, 165; Janitor, 41, 44, 53, 116, 119; Janitor's children, 123–124; Laundress, 38–39, 53, 63, 69, 135, 146, 149, 153, 155; law (1997), 7; male displacement, 192–193; manual, 7, 134, 141; married women's, 146, 147; Mi-yŏn's brothers, 128–130, 272–273; Mi-yŏn's Mother, 53, 93–94, 203, 206, 230, 231–232, 253, 254–255, 257–259, 264–266, 276; Mi-yŏn's Mother's father, 205, 228; Mi-yŏn's Mother's husband, 246; Mi-yŏn's Mother's mothers, 206, 208, 230, 266; motherhood vs. career, 178; Moviegoer, 53, 55, 173; Moviegoer's husband, 55, 74, 170, 175–180; necessity of women's, 160; occupational status, 114, 120–122, 124, 130; Mrs. Pak and, 95–96; Park regime and, 191; for personal fulfillment, 158; post-Korean War, 134, 136–138, 141; reforms, 68, 286; urban, 134, 137, 138; U.S. military employment, 51, 154; white-collar, 134, 138, 155, 286; women's before marriage, 148, 153; young women's, 156–157. See also housewives; income; small business

land ownership: Hye-min's Grandmother and, 218, 222; Janitor's family, 42, 117, 119; Mi-yŏn's Mother's kin, 228, 236; yangban, 56. See also real estate investment

land reform, 138, 139–140, 285; farmers' movement, 34–36, 42–45

language: Chinese characters, 115; of class, 285–286; college exams in, 155, 272; of day, 12–15, 59–60; England, 272; English/Korean, 63–64, 188; private/public narrative, 11, 12, 21–22, 31, 187–213, 276–280; subjectivity, 188; translations, 63–64, 69. See also talk; words

Laundress, 30, 34, 38–39, 45–46, 53, 132–133, 141; children, 51, 54, 66–67, 72–73, 132–133, 136, 149–159; Christian, 57, 63; class identity, 54, 135, 150, 151–152, 162; class resources, 146, 153; economics, 50, 53, 66–67, 68, 136; education, 53, 147, 150–151; education of brothers, 136, 142, 150–151; education of sons, 54, 67, 136, 142, 149–150, 151, 153, 155, 157, 164; education of women, 106; family abroad, 51, 136, 149–150, 155, 157; father, 135, 136, 140, 150, 151; key words, 63–69, 91; labor, 38–39, 53, 63, 69, 135, 146, 149, 153, 155; marriage, 57, 63, 64–68, 72–73, 132, 142, 150, 152, 158; 1990s, 149–158; newspaper reading, 53, 151; and "other" women, 66, 91–92; summer (2000), 158–163; transgenerational perspective, 135–136, 149–163

Lemert, Charles, 15

Lett, Denise Potrzeba, 144

Liberation (1945), 5, 6, 114, 139–140, 141

life cycle, 3, 6, 20, 158–159. See also age

life histories, 2, 15–17, 20

love: marriage, 57, 63; Mi-yŏn's Mother, 204, 205, 210, 246–247, 249–250

Lutz, Catherine, 169

maids, Mi-yŏn's Mother and, 231–234, 258, 259

marriage: abusive, 57, 63, 64–68; arranged, 63, 117; class identities of women before, 147–148, 150; difficult, 55, 57; divorce, 161, 252–253, 269; Education Mother, 29, 57, 106, 108, 110; Education Mother's daughter, 46, 50; Education Mother's sister, 10; Hye-min's Grandmother, 57, 218–219; Hye-min's Grandmother's daughter's wedding, 216; Janitor, 117–118; Mr. Kang, 37; labor after, 146, 147; Laundress, 57, 63, 64–68, 72–73, 132, 142, 150, 152, 158; love, 57, 63; in melodramas, 172; Mi-yŏn, 250, 271;

(marriage, *continued*)
Mi-yŏn's brothers, 272–273; Mi-yŏn's
Mother, 55, 57, 204–205, 237, 249–253,
266–270; mobility through, 104–105, 142;
Moviegoer, 55, 57, 70, 74–78, 165, 166, 170,
172–180; "old Miss"/"old Mr.," 37; pregnant brides, 252. *See also* husbands; widows
Marxism, 17–18, 134–135. *See also* communism
masculine traits: displacement, 31, 187–213;
men's, 88, 189, 204, 209, 247, 252; *munŭnghan*, 88, 204; national, 31, 201, 202;
women's, 9, 29, 39–40, 82, 89, 189, 202,
203, 206–210, 212, 247
melodrama, 2, 8, 22–27, 168, 282–283; cross-
cultural, 24–25; defined, 23; Education
Mother's sister's pocketbook, 9, 10–11,
27–29; excess, 23, 25, 27, 107–108, 181;
moments, 27, 28, 196–197; open/closed,
26–27, 185; plot, 23; primary focus, 25–26;
sensibility, 23–25, 100, 165, 282–283; of social transformation, 22–24, 27, 31, 56, 143,
189–201; *See also* films; novels; television
soap operas
men, 20–22; authority, 31, 194, 195; capitalism, 67; displacement, 31, 187–213; feminine traits, 189, 204, 205, 210, 211–212;
household heads, 160–161; masculine traits,
88, 189, 204, 209, 247, 252; mobility studies, 145, 149; *munŭnghan*, 86–88, 102–103,
204, 205, 252, 262; subjectivity/national
narratives, 31, 187–213; tenant farmers'
movement, 34, 42; and women's class contributions to household, 146–147. *See also*
fathers; gender; husbands; men; patriarchy;
patrilineal kinship
middle-aged, 3, 37–38, 158–159, 180
middle class, 52, 134, 286, 287; after-school
programs, 155; downward mobility, 7, 54,
126, 143; Education Mother, 9, 17, 50, 52,
111; films, 191–193; Hye-min's Grandmother, 54, 92; Janitor and, 53, 117, 118,
124; Laundress's brothers, 153; Laundress's sons, 157; Mi-yŏn's Mother, 50, 52,
271–272; Moviegoer and, 70, 170, 180, 212;
novels, 228–229; religious fervency, 250;
Twins' Mother, 52, 56; "unemployed"
"housewives," 149; *yangban* equated with,
144

Middle East, job emigration, 55, 155–156, 170
military duty, mandatory, 273
military employment, U.S., 51, 154
military rule: Chun Doo Hwan, 127, 286; Park
Chung Hee, 5, 191; U.S.-centered, 139
Mi-yŏn: education, 94, 243, 268–272, 274,
275; gendered traits, 247; marriage, 209,
250, 271; school notebooks, 275
Mi-yŏn's Mother, 31, 46–50, 52, 240–281,
291–292; Christianity, 57, 245, 250; class
identity, 55; class-travels to kin, 226–228,
230–239, 263–266; displacement, 55, 230,
271–272; economics, 50, 210–211, 226,
230–231, 243, 248; education, 53, 55,
93–94, 151, 231, 232, 233, 243, 263–267,
273–274; education of children, 94, 100,
128–131, 210, 241, 243, 247, 267–276;
family abroad, 51, 94, 97, 226, 235–237;
father, 87, 203–206, 210, 211, 228, 229,
243, 252, 275; gendered subjectivity, 31,
187, 203–213; husband, 48, 93, 209–210,
237, 243–254, 265, 266–270, 272–273,
277–278, 280, 292; key words, 93–95; kinship networks, 31, 214, 215, 226–239, **227**,
244, 263–266; Korean War, 139; labor, 53,
93–94, 203, 206, 230, 231–232, 253, 254–
255, 257–259, 264–266, 276; marriage, 55,
57, 204–205, 237, 249–253, 266–270;
mothers, 48, 205–212, 230, 237, 246–250,
255, 266, 267; "other" women, 258–259,
267, 275–276; politics, 276–280; sisters,
261–263; sons' education, 100, 128–131,
241, 243, 272–273, 275; travel abroad, 51,
236, 244; vexed, 237–238, 241; writing,
292–293
mobility. *See* social mobility
modernity, 127, 281–292; compressed, 31–32,
281–288, 289–290; gendered, 22, 201;
Mi-yŏn's Mother and, 205; nation, 201;
and personhood, 240; social relations, 138,
139–140; theory, 137; threshold to, 139;
Western selfhood, 166; women as products
of, 55. *See also* development; technologies
mŏngch'ŏnghada, 87; Hye-min's Grandmother
and, 84; Moviegoer, 69, 71–73, 74, 78, 165,
174; Twins' Mother, 79
monnada, 63–69, 71, 79, 87
morality/ethics: family, 21; Hye-min's Grandmother, 83, 226; Laundress, 65–66, 68;

melodrama, 26–27, 29; Mi-yŏn's Mother, 277–278; Moviegoer, 71–73, 174, 179; persons, 168. See also Confucianism; virtues

mothers-in-law: child care by, 76, 149, 156; gender discrimination by, 205; Mi-yŏn's Mother's, 248, 251, 256; Mrs. Pak's, 214

Moviegoer, 30–31, 44–46; Christianity, 57, 170–171; class identity, 46, 55, 70, 170; daughter's activism, 44–45, 46, 70, 75, 171, 178, 179; economics, 50, 56, 70, 172–174; education, 53; family abroad, 51, 55, 170, 178; father, 172, 173, 204; gendered subjectivity, 212–213; key words, 69–78, 165; labor, 53, 55, 173; lending money to sisters, 70–71, 78; marriage, 55, 57, 70, 74–78, 165, 166, 170, 172–180; mother, 76, 171, 172–173, 181–182, 231; and "other" women, 91–92, 185; personality, 165–166, 170–186; self-consciousness, 70, 74, 77, 165; television soap operas, 44, 166, 174, 180–186

movies. See films

munŭnghada, men, 86–88, 102–103, 204, 205, 252, 262

music, Mi-yŏn's Mother and, 48, 268–272

Na To-hyang, 197–200

The Naked Tree (Pak Wan-so), 228–229

Nam Chi-yŏn, 180–181, 184–185

narrative, 2, 11, 14–15, 21–22, 133, 286; class and, 18, 19, 20, 81; family context, 11, 19–20; fictions and, 133; gender, 203–213; and identification, 16–17; imagination through, 11, 242; kinship, 238–239; national, 31, 187–213; ontological, 13, 19; personality, 166, 169; private, 11, 21–22, 276–277; public, 11, 21–22, 31, 187–213, 276–280; representational, 13, 19; social groups, 11, 18, 286. See also melodrama

nationalism, South Korean, 126, 287

national narratives: male displacement, 31, 187–213. See also public narrative

neoliberal reforms, 126–127

networks, 18, 46, 52–58, 286. See also kinship networks; resource networks; social networks

New Zealand, Laundress's son, 51, 149–150, 155

North Korea: communism, 278, 279–280; divided families, 10, 48, 106, 109–110, 139;

ideology of state autonomy, 188; Janitor's education, 125; Mi-yŏn's Mother's family, 48, 203, 205, 226–231, 236; Mi-yŏn's Mother's sense of, 279–280; North-South unification, 160; nostalgia of, 228–230; partition (1945–1948), 5, 10

nostalgia, 205; film, 197; of north, 228–230; soap opera, 101–102

novels: melodramatic, 24; Moviegoer and, 44; nostalgia of north, 228–229

Ortner, Sherry, 20, 21

pabo katta, 87; Hye-min's Grandmother and, 84, 85; Mi-yŏn's Mother, 245, 265, 266; Moviegoer, 69–78, 174, 178

Mrs. Pak, 50–52; Christianity, 57, 96; class identity, 55, 56–57; daily life, 215; economics, 50, 214; education, 53, 57, 95; education abroad for children, 50–51, 97; education of women, 106; housewife, 53; in-laws, 214; key words, 95–98; marriage, 57; travel abroad, 51

Pak Jin-suk, 102–108

Pak Sŏbang (Neighbor Pak), 56, 189, 193–197, 200–201

Papaneck, Hanna, 149

Park Chung Hee, 5, 6, 126, 189, 191

patriarchy, 162; character, 168; Education Mother and, 28–29; in films, 31, 108, 191–197, 200–201, 213; gender sign systems, 201–203; Laundress and, 150–151, 154, 157, 158; male subjectivity, 188–197, 200–202; Mi-yŏn's Mother and, 204, 205, 206, 207; Moviegoer and, 174, 212; reproduction of, 157, 202; soap opera, 104, 107–108, 181; women's resources, 146, 148. See also discrimination, gender

patrilineal kinship: Education Mother and, 9; film, 192; gender discrimination, 205; Janitor's, 119; Laundress's, 136, 154; male subjectivity, 188, 192; Moviegoer's, 173, 176; Twins' Mother, 80; and women's contribution to class identity, 21, 146, 149

pep'ulda, 89–92

personality, 22, 30–31, 164–186; Adŭl kwa ttal (A son and a daughter), 103–104; child rearing making, 87–88; Education Mother's, 106; Education Mother's mother's, 10, 27;

(personality, *continued*)

Education Mother's sister's, 9–10, 27, 29, 30, 65, 101, 103; favored/exemplary, 170; Hye-min's Grandmother and, 84, 222–226, 238; Laundress's basic, 65, 68; Laundress's husband, 152; melodrama, 26; Mi-yŏn's Mother and, 233, 238, 247, 265; Moviegoer, 165–166, 170–186. *See also* characters; feminine traits; individual; key words; masculine traits

personhood: complex, 240, 290. *See also* selfhood

persons: characters and, 167–168. *See also* individual

photographs, 216; Hye-min's Grandmother's, 216–217, 218; Mi-yŏn's Mother's, 237, 244

piano, Mi-yŏn's Mother and, 268–272, 274

political activism, 5–6, 282; civil unrest/student protest, 5, 68, 126, 144, 178, 190–191; farmers' movement, 34–36, 42–45; labor, 5, 44, 45, 68; Moviegoer's daughter, 44–45, 46, 70, 75, 171, 178, 179; 3-8-6 generation, 45

politics: costs of modernization, 282; Laundress on, 160; Mi-yŏn's Mother, 48, 276–280; political patronage, 7, 126, 144. *See also* authoritarianism; colonialism; political activism; presidents; repression; social justice; social/political reform; social transformation

Pŏng'ŏri Samnyong'i (Deaf-mute Samnyong'i), 189, 197–201

poverty, 282; approbation of, 144; education and, 155; Hye-min's Grandmother and, 54, 83, 217, 218–219, 224; income reduction percentages, 126; Janitor and, 53; Laundress and, 68, 154, 155, 156; Mi-yŏn's Mother, 230–234, 238, 247, 266, 279; Moviegoer's childhood, 173; rich-poor gap, 126, 143, 159; shantytown, 116–117; village, 42; war memory, 139

presidents: Chang Myŏn, 5, 190–191; Chun Doo Hwan, 5, 6, 7, 126, 127, 286; Kim Dae Jung, 4, 7, 101, 126, 160; Kim Young Sam, 4, 6, 7, 67; Park Chung Hee, 5, 6, 126, 189, 191; Roh Tae Woo, 5, 6, 67, 255, 257; Syngman Rhee, 5, 6, 190, 286

private narrative, 11, 12, 21–22, 276–277

public narrative, 11, 21–22, 31, 187–213, 276–280. *See also* politics

real: imaginary and, 11, 16, 17, 25, 243; individual not center of, 12; and "others," 49; social mobility, 137, 142–144. *See also* truth

real estate investment, 156; Education Mother, 9, 50, 103; Education Mother's mother, 106; home ownership, 53, 55, 109, 118, 119, 153, 156, 160, 170; Mi-yŏn's Mother, 47–48, 50, 52, 210, 247, 253–257, 269; women prototypes, 49, 50, 67, 71. *See also* housing; land ownership

reform. *See* social/political reform

religion: Buddhism, 245, 257; Unification Church, 43. *See also* Christianity

representativeness, women's, 49, 288–290

repression: state, 5, 190, 191. *See also* authoritarianism

reproduction: class, 3, 100, 111, 145–149, 203; of patriarchy, 157, 202; social, 3, 92, 145–149

resource networks: class, 56, 143; kinship, 56, 215, 229; Laundress's, 153–154, 162; in transgenerational perspective, 135, 162; women's contribution to household, 146, 153. *See also* capital; economics

Rhee, Syngman, 5, 6, 190, 286

Ricoeur, Paul, 291, 293

Roh Tae Woo, 5, 6, 67, 255, 257

Romaensŭ Ppappa (Romance papa), 189, 191–193, 200–201, 204

Rorty, Amélie Oksenberg, 167, 168, 185

Saem i kip'ŭn mul, 107–108

Sampung Department Store, 6, 7

sangnom, 114–115, 125, 152, 179, 278

Sartre, Jean-Paul, 164, 168

sasang (ideology): *chuch'e* (state autonomy), 188; Education Mother's father's, 110, 113

Scott, Joan, 167

self-consciousness: Laundress, 151; Moviegoer's, 70, 74, 77, 165; women's, 70

self-employment. *See* small business

selfhood, 11, 166–170; and class, 19; development, 21, 75, 82–83; epistemologies, 166–167, 185–186; imagination and, 16–17; melodrama and, 26; Moviegoer, 174. *See also* agency; individual; personality; self-consciousness; self-reflection; subjectivity

self-reflection, 283, 284, 288, 293. *See also* selfhood

Seoul, 33–40; Education Mother's mother's property, 106; Hye-min's Grandmother, 217–218, 219, 222–223; Hyoja-dong kin of Mi-yŏn's Mother, 228, 230–238, 244, 264–266; Janitor, 43–44, 117–119; Laundress family, 140, 150, 156; Mi-yŏn's Mother, 47, 204, 205, 228, 230–238, 263–266; Moviegoer's husband, 176; village ties, 42, 43, 117–118, 119, 219

Seoul National University, 79, 80, 118, 183, 184, 276

sewing, Laundress, 39, 63, 149, 153

sex: comfort women, 188; Mi-yŏn's Mother and, 250, 252; widows' socially enforced celibacy, 27, 154

sexism. See discrimination, gender

shantytown, 53, 116–117

Sin Sang-ok, 191, 197

small business, 134; Hye-min's Grandmother, 54–55, 82, 222, 226; Laundress, 38–39, 153, 155; Laundress's son, 51, 149–150; Moviegoer's sister, 51

Sŏ Kwan-mo, 134

soap operas. See television soap operas

social change. See social transformation

social imagination, 2, 16–17, 100

socialism, 110, 139

social justice, 28, 116, 144, 186; for diligent, 55, 71, 179, 217; Education Mother's sister, 9–11; Hye-min's Grandmother on, 217–218; after IMF Crisis, 126; and kinship networks, 31, 215, 276; Mi-yŏn's Mother and, 259–260, 279, 280; for moral, 174, 179; Moviegoer and, 55, 71, 174, 179–180, 185; neoliberal reforms and, 127. See also inequality; morality/ethics; social/political reform

social mobility, 2, 15–16, 20, 30, 132–163; centrality of narrative and gender to, 133; class work for, 100; downward, 7, 10, 28, 54, 126–127, 143; individual, 135, 138, 144–145; through marriage, 104–105, 142; melodrama of, 282–283; open, 138–143, 157, 277; real, 137, 142–144; recent history of South Korean, 136–145; relative, 137, 285; sociological attention to, 134–135; structural, 137–138; upward, 138, 142, 197, 217, 271; women in the picture, 145–149, 174. See also class; social mobility stories

social mobility stories, 2, 3–4, 11, 15–16, 242;

destinations, 2, 3, 242; facts/fictions, 30, 132–163; familial context, 8–17, 19–20, 101–113; gendered subjectivity, 31, 187, 203–213; origins, 2, 3, 242; personality, 164–186; transgenerational perspective, 135–136, 149–163. See also education; Education Mother; Hye-min's Grandmother; Janitor; key words; Laundress; melodrama; Mi-yŏn's Mother; Moviegoer; Mrs. Pak; social mobility; Twins' Mother

social networks, 13–14, 146–147, 149. See also kinship networks

social/political reform, 5, 6, 7; education, 127; gender sign systems, 201; labor, 68, 286; land, 138, 139–140, 285; neoliberal, 126–127; promise unfulfilled, 5, 284. See also democracy; political activism; social justice

social relations, 18, 19, 22, 29; "modern," 138, 139–140. See also class; gender

social reproduction, of families, 3, 92, 145–149

social transformation, 3–7, 16, 134, 286–287; class and, 10–11, 19–20, 28, 242, 284–285; countryside, 36; education and, 129–131; and equality/inequality of opportunity, 136–145; films and, 22–23, 31, 189, 198, 200–201; gender and, 21–22, 201, 242, 267, 288; Laundress on (Summer 2000), 158–163; male displacement, 31, 188, 189, 198, 200–201; melodrama of, 22–24, 27, 31, 56, 143, 189–201; Mi-yŏn's Mother and, 258; and others, 267; structure of feeling, 14, 137, 140, 242, 282–283, 289–290, 293; women's economic and social roles, 21, 164; words/stories and, 13, 14, 60, 98–99, 133. See also collapses; democracy; development; Korean War; modernity; social mobility; social/political reform

sociological imagination, 15, 16

sociology, South Korean, 134–135

Somers, Margaret R., 13–14, 18, 19

sŏnbi, 168, 173, 174, 175, 204, 222, 278

Sŏngsu Grand Bridge, 6, 7

status, 144; abolishment of, 139, 141; displacement and, 189; education and occupational, 114, 120–122, 124, 130; family production of, 149; Hye-min's Grandmother on, 224. See also capital; class; gender; social mobility; tradition

Steedman, Carolyn, 13–16, 19, 20, 87

stock market, 9, 126, 130. *See also* venture capitalism

stress: Mi-yŏn's Mother, 247; Twins' Mother, 79, 80–81

structuralism, 18, 169

structural mobility, 137–138

structure of feeling, 14, 137, 140, 242, 282–283, 289–290, 293

student uprisings, 5, 68, 178, 190–191

subjectivity: within compressed development, 283; gendered, 21–22, 31, 187–213; Korean meaning, 188; Laundress on mobility, 162; Mi-yŏn's Mother and, 31, 187, 203–213; "modern," 166; Moviegoer, 212–213. *See also* selfhood

sunhan, 82, 84, 85, 222

sunjong ham, 84, 85, 96

taedanhada: Laundress (*taedanhada*), 66, 67, 68, 69; Moviegoer and, 178

talk, 2, 8, 11, 286, 290; Christianity, 38; dialogic, 11, 61; research, 34; unfinished, 240; women's, 1, 4, 12–13, 30. *See also* key words; social mobility stories

taptaphada: Hye-min's Grandmother and, 41, 82, 224; Janitor, 85; Moviegoer, 77, 78, 82, 85, 174, 212; Twins' Mother, 81, 82

technologies: ammonia plant, 177; new, 60–61, 126, 128–129

television soap operas, 22, 23, 24; *Adŭl kwa ttal* (A son and a daughter), 40, 101–110, 113; Education Mother and, 101, 102, 103, 105–106, 113; Hye-min's Grandmother and, 40; *Kashi namu kkot* (The thorny branch flower), 166, 180–186; Laundress and, 38; Moviegoer and, 44, 166, 174, 180–186; non-Western, 24–25, 27; *taptaphada*, 77; Western, 24–25, 26–27

Thompson, Paul, 15–16, 20, 135

Toren, Christina, 14, 18

tradition: Koreanness, 202, 205, 212, 287–288; *sangnom*, 114–115, 125, 152, 179, 278; women, 168, 173–174, 182, 202. *See also* Confucianism; *yangban*

transportation: countryside, 38; Mi-yŏn's Mother's driving, 245–246, 273; Seoul, 33, 38; traffic accident rate, 6

truth, 31, 243, 252. *See also* real

ttajida, 83, 85–86

Twins' Mother, 50, 52; class identity, 55–56; difficult marriage, 57; economics, 50; education, 53, 56, 79–81; housewife, 53; husband, 56, 79–81; key words, 78–81; and "other" women, 92

Unification Church, 43

United States: colonialism, 139, 287; education emigration, 40–41, 45, 51, 72, 128, 129; employment emigration, 136, 155; Hye-min's Grandmother's family, 40–41, 51; Janitor and, 123; Janitor's brother, 51; Laundress on, 160, 161; military employment, 51, 154; Mi-yŏn's Mother and, 51, 128, 129, 226, 235–237, 244, 251, 257; and Rhee regime, 190

upper class, 143; apartments, 52, 53, 117, 257; emigration to U.S., 236; Mi-yŏn's Mother and, 47, 49; Twins' Mother, 56; women's contributions to status as, 146, 148–149. *See also* wealth

urbanization: Hye-min's Grandmother, 219; labor, 134, 137, 138; Laundress's family, 150; Mi-yŏn's Mother, 228; Moviegoer's husband, 176; rural/urban divide, 43, 53–54, **220**, 238. *See also* Seoul

usury, 49, 91

venture capitalism, 101, 126, 129–130, 241, 273

villages: emigration from, 117–118, 140, 150, 156, 218–219; Janitor, 41–43, 114, 117–119, 150; land reform, 138, 139–140, 285; reconstructed, 42–43; Seoul ties, 42, 43, 117–118, 119, 219; shantytown, 53, 116–117. *See also* countryside; farmers

virtues: feminine, 84, 202, 212; household status and women's, 146; Laundress and, 65–67, 69, 154; Moviegoer, 78; traditional, 212. *See also* diligent; morality/ethics

wealth: Janitor's kin, 117–118; leisured rich, 258–259, 267, 275–276; Mi-yŏn's Mother's kin, 226–229, 230–238, 263–266; rich-poor gap, 126, 143, 159. *See also* upper class

Weberian theory, 17–18, 134

West: ambivalence toward, 286–287; films of, 26, 170, 236; individual, 12; in Korean

films, 193–197; melodrama, 24–25, 26–27;
Mi-yŏn's Mother's sense of, 279–280;
"modern" selfhood, 166. *See also* England;
United States
White, Geoffrey M., 169
White, Harrison, 14
widows: Education Mother's mother, 27;
Hye-min's Grandmother and family, 39, 57,
84; Janitor, 44, 57; socially enforced celibacy, 27, 154
Williams, Linda, 27
Williams, Raymond, 14, 59, 60, 61, 62, 99
women, 2, 8, 20–22, 33–58; age, 3, 158–159,
260, 289; author meeting, 33–52, 57; class
importance, 21, 22, 33, 34, 52–58, 135,
145–149, 161–162; comfort, 188; contributions, 21, 146–149, 288–289; and domestic
melodrama, 26; education of, 106, 107, 113,
122–123, 142, 268–269; family course determined by, 157–158, 174; feminine traits,
62–69, 83–85, 93, 189, 209, 210, 212; identities made by stories, 14; ignored by mobility understandings, 30; Laundress on roles
of, 158; life cycle stages, 3, 6, 158–159;
masculine traits, 9, 29, 39–40, 82, 89, 189,
202, 203, 206–210, 212, 247; "nonworking," 146; "other," 49, 66, 83, 91–92, 185,
216–226, 238, 249, 258–259, 267, 275–276;
"our" and "their," 216–226; plausible,
180–185; pseudonyms, 8; representativeness, 49, 288–290; self-consciousness, 70;
in social mobility picture, 145–149; subjectivity, 22, 188, 189; talk, 1, 4, 12–13, 30;

theorists, 15, 291; traditional, 168, 173–174,
182, 202; types, 15, 49, 50, 66–67, 72, 75,
208, 242; unmarried, 145, 275; young working, 156–157. *See also* gender; marriage
words, 291, 293; accent of, 13, 23, 62; dialogic nature of, 12, 61, 62, 76; heteroglot,
13, 59–60, 62, 98, 164; inequality in, 13,
14–15; Laundress, 39, 63–69; productive,
13–14; taste, 13, 23, 282; translations,
63–64, 69. *See also* key words; narrative;
writing
work: class, 100–131, 132. *See also* labor
writing, 17, 34, 292–293

yamjŏnhada, Hye-min's Grandmother and, 85
yangban, 278; Education Mother's mother
and, 10, 28, 98, 102, 105, 106; in film, 197–
198, 201; gendered, 201–202; Janitor and,
114–116, 117–118, 125; Laundress kin, 136,
150, 151; middle class equated with, 144;
Mi-yŏn's Mother's father, 203–204, 205–
206, 212; Moviegoer and, 172–173, 174, 179;
munŭnghan and, 87, 88; Twins' Mother's
family, 56, 79. *See also* Confucianism
yoksim, 88–98; Education Mother and, 97–98,
111; good/bad, 90, 92; Hye-min's Grandmother and, 89, 90, 91, 92; Laundress and,
91, 152; Mi-yŏn's Mother and, 93–95, 207,
241, 252, 253, 276; Moviegoer lacking, 172,
175, 179; Moviegoer's husband, 172; Mrs.
Pak and, 95–98; soap opera writer's,
184–185; Twins' Mother, 80. *See also challan*
yŏlsimhi salda, 90, 91

ABOUT THE AUTHOR

Nancy Abelmann received her B.A. in East Asian studies from Harvard University and her doctorate in social anthropology from the University of California, Berkeley. She has published books on social movements in contemporary Korea (*Echoes of the Past, Epics of Dissent: A South Korean Social Movement*, University of California Press, 1996) and on Korean America (*Blue Dreams: Korean Americans and the Los Angeles Riots*, with John Lie, Harvard University Press, 1995). She is coeditor, with Kathleen McHugh, of *Gender, Genre, and National Cinema: South Korean Golden Age Melodrama*, forthcoming. Currently she is completing a transnational ethnography of the educational trajectories of Korean American public-college students as they articulate with the educational histories of their émigré parents. Abelmann is an associate professor of anthropology, East Asian languages and cultures, and women's studies at the University of Illinois at Urbana-Champaign, and a teaching faculty member of Asian American studies.

Production Notes for Abelmann/*The Melodrama of Mobility*

Cover design by Chris Crochetière.

Text design and composition by B. Williams & Associates in QuarkXPress using Quadraat and Quadraat Sans.

Printing and binding by The Maple-Vail Book Manufacturing Group.

Printed on 60 lb. Sebago Eggshell, 420 ppi.